P9-AQC-593

Sandra K. Roe, MS
Editor

The Audiovisual Cataloging Current

The Audiovisual Cataloging Current has been co-published simultaneously as *Cataloging & Classification Quarterly*, Volume 31, Numbers 2 and 3/4 2001.

Pre-publication REVIEWS, COMMENTARIES, EVALUATIONS . . .

"No source I have ever read has put it all together the way this book does. Written by experts in their various areas, there is insight, history, problem solving, the day-to-day work world, and the most current practice. Nancy Olson's cutting-edge chapter 'Cataloging Remote Electronic Resources' is of particular value."

Richard L. Harwood, MLS
Cataloging Coordinator
Collection Management Department
Libraries Division
Broward County Board
of County Commissioners
Lauderdale Lakes
Florida

More pre-publication
REVIEWS, COMMENTARIES, EVALUATIONS . . .

"UNIQUE AND IMPRESSIVE. A necessary purchase for new and experienced AV catalogers. Not only does this book have the most up-to-date information on several aspects of cataloging audiovisual formats, it provides a thorough history of AV cataloging."

Sue Neumeister, MLS
Former OLAC President; Head
Bibliographic Control/Receipts
State University at Buffalo
New York

"ALL THE GREAT WRITERS, TEACHERS, AND LECTURERS ARE HERE: Olson, Sandberg-Fox, Intner, Weihs, and Yee. This eclectic collection is sure to find a permanent place on many catalogers' bookshelves. . . . SOMETHING FOR EVERYONE. . . . Explicit cataloging guidelines and AACR2R interpretations galore."

Verna Urbanski, MA, MLS
Chief Media Cataloger
University of North Florida
Jacksonville

The Haworth Information Press
An Imprint of
The Haworth Press, Inc.

The Audiovisual Cataloging Current

The Audiovisual Cataloging Current has been co-published simultaneously as *Cataloging & Classification Quarterly*, Volume 31, Numbers 2 and 3/4 2001.

The *Cataloging & Classification Quarterly*™ Monographic "Separates"

Below is a list of "separates," which in serials librarianship means a special issue simultaneously published as a special journal issue or double-issue *and* as a "separate" hardbound monograph. (This is a format which we also call a "DocuSerial.")

"Separates" are published because specialized libraries or professionals may wish to purchase a specific thematic issue by itself in a format which can be separately cataloged and shelved, as opposed to purchasing the journal on an on-going basis. Faculty members may also more easily consider a "separate" for classroom adoption.

"Separates" are carefully classified separately with the major book jobbers so that the journal tie-in can be noted on new book order slips to avoid duplicate purchasing.

You may wish to visit Haworth's Website at . . .

http://www.HaworthPress.com

. . . to search our online catalog for complete tables of contents of these separates and related publications.

You may also call 1-800-HAWORTH (outside US/Canada: 607-722-5857), or Fax 1-800-895-0582 (outside US/Canada: 607-771-0012), or e-mail at:

getinfo@haworthpressinc.com

The Audiovisual Cataloging Current, edited by Sandra K. Roe, MS (Vol. 31, No. 2/3/4, 2001). *All the great writers, teachers, and lecturers are here: Olson, Fox, Intner, Weihs, Weitz, and Yee. This eclectic collection is sure to find a permanent place on many catalogers' bookshelves. . . . Something for everyone. . . . Explicit cataloging guidelines and AACR2R interpretations galore." (Verna Urbanski, MA, MLS, Chief Media Cataloger, University of North Florida, Jacksonville)*

Managing Cataloging and the Organization of Information: Philosophies, Practices and Challenges at the Onset of the 21st Century, edited by Ruth C. Carter, PhD, MS, MA (Vol. 30, No. 1/2/3, 2000). *"A fascinating series of practical, forthright accounts of national, academic, and special library cataloging operations in action. . . . Yields an abundance of practical solutions for shared problems, now and for the future. Highly recommended." (Laura Jizba, Head Cataloger, Portland State University Library, Oregon)*

The LCSH Century: One Hundred Years with the Library of Congress Subject Headings System, edited by Alva T. Stone, MLS (Vol. 29, No. 1/2, 2000). *Traces the 100-year history of the Library of Congress Subject Headings, from its beginning with the implementation of a dictionary catalog in 1898 to the present day, exploring the most significant changes in LCSH policies and practices, including a summary of other contributions celebrating the centennial of the world's most popular library subject heading language.*

Maps and Related Cartographic Materials: Cataloging, Classification, and Bibliographic Control, edited by Paige G. Andrew, MLS, and Mary Lynette Larsgaard, BA, MA (Vol. 27, No. 1/2/3/4, 1999). *Discover how to catalog the major formats of cartographic materials, including sheet maps, early and contemporary atlases, remote-sensed images (i.e., aerial photographs and satellite images), globes, geologic sections, digital material, and items on CD-ROM.*

Portraits in Cataloging and Classification: Theorists, Educators, and Practitioners of the Late Twentieth Century, edited by Carolynne Myall, MS, CAS, and Ruth C. Carter, PhD (Vol. 25, No. 2/3/4, 1998). *"This delightful tome introduces us to a side of our profession that we rarely see: the human beings behind the philosophy, rules, and interpretations that have guided our professional lives over the past half century. No collection on cataloging would be complete without a copy of this work." (Walter M. High, PhD, Automation Librarian, North Carolina Supreme Court Library; Assistant Law Librarian for Technical Services, North Carolina University, Chapel Hill)*

Cataloging and Classification: Trends, Transformations, Teaching, and Training, edited by James R. Shearer, MA, ALA, and Alan R. Thomas, MA, FLA (Vol. 24, No. 1/2, 1997). *"Offers a comprehensive retrospective and innovative projection for the future." (The Catholic Library Association)*

Electronic Resources: Selection and Bibliographic Control, edited by Ling-yuh W. (Miko) Pattie, MSLS, and Bonnie Jean Cox, MSLS (Vol. 22, No. 3/4, 1996). *"Recommended for any reader who is searching for a thorough, well-rounded, inclusive compendium on the subject." (The Journal of Academic Librarianship)*

Cataloging and Classification Standards and Rules, edited by John J. Reimer, MLS (Vol. 21, No. 3/4, 1996). *"Includes chapters by a number of experts on many of our best loved library standards. . . . Recommended to those who want to understand the history and development of our library standards and to understand the issues at play in the development of new standards." (LASIE)*

Classification: Options and Opportunities, edited by Alan R. Thomas, MA, FLA (Vol. 19, No. 3/4, 1995). *"There is much new and valuable insight to be found in all the chapters. . . . Timely in refreshing our confidence in the value of well-designed and applied classification in providing the best of service to the end-users." (Catalogue and Index)*

Cataloging Government Publications Online, edited by Carolyn C. Sherayko, MLS (Vol. 18, No. 3/4, 1994). *"Presents a wealth of detailed information in a clear and digestible form, and reveals many of the practicalities involved in getting government publications collections onto online cataloging systems." (The Law Librarian)*

Cooperative Cataloging: Past, Present and Future, edited by Barry B. Baker, MLS (Vol. 17, No. 3/4, 1994). *"The value of this collection lies in its historical perspective and analysis of past and present approaches to shared cataloging. . . . Recommended to library schools and large general collections needing materials on the history of library and information science." (Library Journal)*

Languages of the World: Cataloging Issues and Problems, edited by Martin D. Joachim (Vol. 17, No. 1/2, 1994). *"An excellent introduction to the problems libraries must face when cataloging materials not written in English. . . . should be read by every cataloger having to work with international materials, and it is recommended for all library schools. Nicely indexed." (Academic Library Book Review)*

Retrospective Conversion Now in Paperback: History, Approaches, Considerations, edited by Brian Schottlaender, MLS (Vol. 14, No. 3/4, 1992). *"Fascinating insight into the ways and means of converting and updating manual catalogs to machine-readable format." (Library Association Record)*

Enhancing Access to Information: Designing Catalogs for the 21st Century, edited by David A. Tyckoson (Vol. 13, No. 3/4, 1992). *"Its down-to-earth, nontechnical orientation should appeal to practitioners including administrators and public service librarians." (Library Resources & Technical Services)*

Describing Archival Materials: The Use of the MARC AMC Format, edited by Richard P. Smiraglia, MLS (Vol. 11, No. 3/4, 1991). *"A valuable introduction to the use of the MARC AMC format and the principles of archival cataloging itself." (Library Resources & Technical Services)*

Subject Control in Online Catalogs, edited by Robert P. Holley, PhD, MLS (Vol. 10, No. 1/2, 1990). *"The authors demonstrate the reasons underlying some of the problems and how solutions may be sought. . . . Also included are some fine research studies where the researchers have sought to test the interaction of users with the catalogue, as well as looking at use by library practitioners." (Library Association Record)*

Library of Congress Subject Headings: Philosophy, Practice, and Prospects, by William E. Studwell, MSLS (Supp. #2, 1990). *"Plays an important role in any debate on subject cataloging and succeeds in focusing the reader on the possibilities and problems of using Library of Congress Subject Headings and of subject cataloging in the future." (Australian Academic & Research Libraries)*

Authority Control in the Online Environment: Considerations and Practices, edited by Barbara B. Tillett, PhD (Vol. 9, No. 3, 1989). *"Marks an excellent addition to the field. . . . [It] is intended, as stated in the introduction, to 'offer background and inspiration for future thinking.' In achieving this goal, it has certainly succeeded." (Information Technology & Libraries)*

National and International Bibliographic Databases: Trends and Prospects, edited by Michael Carpenter, PhD, MBA, MLS (Vol. 8, No. 3/4, 1988). *"A fascinating work, containing much of concern both to the general cataloger and to the language or area specialist as well. It is also highly recommended reading for all those interested in bibliographic databases, their development, or their history." (Library Resources & Technical Services)*

Cataloging Sound Recordings: A Manual with Examples, by Deanne Holzberlein, PhD, MLS (Supp. #1, 1988). *"A valuable, easy to read working tool which should be part of the standard equipment of all catalogers who handle sound recordings." (ALR)*

Education and Training for Catalogers and Classifiers, edited by Ruth C. Carter, PhD (Vol. 7, No. 4, 1987). *"Recommended for all students and members of the profession who possess an interest in cataloging." (RQ-Reference and Adult Services Division)*

The United States Newspaper Program: Cataloging Aspects, edited by Ruth C. Carter, PhD (Vol. 6, No. 4, 1986). *"Required reading for all who use newspapers for research (historians and librarians in particular), newspaper cataloguers, administrators of newspaper collections, and–most important–those who control the preservation pursestrings." (Australian Academic & Research Libraries)*

Computer Software Cataloging: Techniques and Examples, edited by Deanne Holzberlein, PhD, MLS (Vol. 6, No. 2, 1986). *"Detailed explanations of each of the essential fields in a cataloging record. Will help any librarian who is grappling with the complicated responsibility of cataloging computer software." (Public Libraries)*

AACR2 and Serials: The American View, edited by Neal L. Edgar (Vol. 3, No. 2/3, 1983). *"This book will help any librarian or serials user concerned with the pitfalls and accomplishments of modern serials cataloging." (American Reference Books Annual)*

The Future of the Union Catalogue: Proceedings of the International Symposium on the Future of the Union Catalogue, edited by C. Donald Cook (Vol. 2, No. 1/2, 1982). *Experts explore the current concepts and future prospects of the union catalogue.*

The Audiovisual Cataloging Current

Sandra K. Roe, MS
Editor

The Audiovisual Cataloging Current has been co-published simultaneously as *Cataloging & Classification Quarterly*, Volume 31, Numbers 2 and 3/4 2001.

The Haworth Information Press
An Imprint of
The Haworth Press, Inc.
New York • London • Oxford

Published by

The Haworth Information Press®, 10 Alice Street, Binghamton, NY 13904-1580 USA

The Haworth Information Press® is an imprint of The Haworth Press, Inc., 10 Alice Street, Binghamton, NY 13904-1580 USA.

The Audiovisual Cataloging Current has been co-published simultaneously as *Cataloging & Classification Quarterly*™, Volume 31, Numbers 2 and 3/4 2001.

© 2001 by The Haworth Press, Inc. All rights reserved. No part of this work may be reproduced or utilized in any form or by any means, electronic or mechanical, including photocopying, microfilm and recording, or by any information storage and retrieval system, without permission in writing from the publisher. Printed in the United States of America.

The development, preparation, and publication of this work has been undertaken with great care. However, the publisher, employees, editors, and agents of The Haworth Press and all imprints of The Haworth Press, Inc., including The Haworth Medical Press® and Pharmaceutical Products Press®, are not responsible for any errors contained herein or for consequences that may ensue from use of materials or information contained in this work. Opinions expressed by the author(s) are not necessarily those of The Haworth Press, Inc.

Cover design by Thomas J. Mayshock Jr.

Library of Congress Cataloging-in-Publication Data

The audiovisual cataloging current / Sandra K. Roe, editor.
p. cm.
Co-published simultaneously as Cataloging & classification quarterly, v. 31, nos. 2 and 3/4, 2001.
Includes bibliographical references and index.
ISBN 0-7890-1403-3 (alk. paper) – ISBN 0-7890-1404-1 (pbk. : alk. paper)
1. Cataloging of audio-visual materials. 2. Subject headings–Audio-visual materials. 3. Audio-visual library service. I. Title: Audio-visual cataloging current. II. Roe, Sandra K. III. Cataloging & classification quarterly.

Z695.66 .A93 2001
025.3′47–dc21 2001039986

For Nancy B. Olson

∞ ALL HAWORTH INFORMATION PRESS BOOKS AND JOURNALS ARE PRINTED ON CERTIFIED ACID-FREE PAPER

Indexing, Abstracting & Website/Internet Coverage

This section provides you with a list of major indexing & abstracting services. That is to say, each service began covering this periodical during the year noted in the right column. Most Websites which are listed below have indicated that they will either post, disseminate, compile, archive, cite or alert their own Website users with research-based content from this work. (This list is as current as the copyright date of this publication.)

Abstracting, Website/Indexing Coverage	Year When Coverage Began
• *BUBL Information Service: An Internet-based Information Service for the UK higher education community <URL:http://bubl.ac.uk/>*	**1994**
• *CNPIEC Reference Guide: Chinese National Directory of Foreign Periodicals*	**1995**
• *Computing Reviews*	**1994**
• *Current Awareness Abstracts of Library & Information Management Literature, ASLIB (UK)*	**1997**
• *Current Cites [Digital Libraries] [Electronic Publishing] [Multimedia & Hypermedia] [Networks & Networking] [General]*	**2000**
• *FINDEX <www.publist.com>*	**1999**
• *FRANCIS. INIST/CNRS <www.inist.fr>*	**1999**
• *IBZ International Bibliography of Periodical Literature*	**1995**
• *Index Guide to College Journals (core list compiled by integrating 48 indexes frequently used to support undergraduate programs in small to medium sized libraries*	**1999**
• *Index to Periodical Articles Related to Law*	**1989**

(continued)

- *Information Science Abstracts <www.infotoday.com>* **1992**
- *Informed Librarian, The <http://www.infosourcespub.com>* **1993**
- *INSPEC <www.iee.org.uk/publish/>* **1983**
- *Journal of Academic Librarianship: Guide to Professional Literature, The* **1997**
- *Konyvtari Figyelo (Library Review)* **1995**
- *Library & Information Science Abstracts (LISA)* **1989**
- *Library & Information Science Annual (LISCA) <www.lu.com/arba>* **1998**
- *Library Literature & Information Science* **1989**
- *PASCAL <http://www.inist.fr>* **1999**
- *Periodica Islamica* **1994**
- *Referativnyi Zhurnal (Abstracts Journal of the All-Russian Institute of Scientific and Technical Information–in Russian)* **1992**

Special Bibliographic Notes related to special journal issues (separates) and indexing/abstracting:

- indexing/abstracting services in this list will also cover material in any "separate" that is co-published simultaneously with Haworth's special thematic journal issue or DocuSerial. Indexing/abstracting usually covers material at the article/chapter level.
- monographic co-editions are intended for either non-subscribers or libraries which intend to purchase a second copy for their circulating collections.
- monographic co-editions are reported to all jobbers/wholesalers/approval plans. The source journal is listed as the "series" to assist the prevention of duplicate purchasing in the same manner utilized for books-in-series.
- to facilitate user/access services all indexing/abstracting services are encouraged to utilize the co-indexing entry note indicated at the bottom of the first page of each article/chapter/contribution.
- this is intended to assist a library user of any reference tool (whether print, electronic, online, or CD-ROM) to locate the monographic version if the library has purchased this version but not a subscription to the source journal.
- individual articles/chapters in any Haworth publication are also available through the Haworth Document Delivery Service (HDDS).

The Audiovisual Cataloging Current

CONTENTS

ABOUT THE EDITOR

Sandra (Sandy) K. Roe, MS, earned her master's degree in Library and Information Science from the University of Illinois at Urbana-Champaign (UIUC). She is the Cataloging Unit Coordinator and Nonprint Cataloger at Minnesota State University, Mankato. Her current committee work includes the ALA/ALCTS/CCS/SAC Subcommittee on Metadata and Subject Analysis, the Working Group on Transfer of Bibliographic Records for Cataloging Purposes for the MINITEX/LDS Joint Standards Review Task Force, and the Database Quality Management Task Force for the MnSCU/PALS Cataloging Users Group. Ms. Roe is also News Editor for *Cataloging & Classification Quarterly* and has done book indexing for the Publications Office of the Graduate School of Library & Information Science at UIUC. From 1997-1999 she was Technical Services Librarian at Dakota State University in Madison, SD.

Preface

Generally, audiovisual materials are defined as being "not print." They are materials that convey their information in some way other than text on a printed page. They have also been called "nonbook," "nonprint," and "special formats" and sometimes require equipment to use. Audiovisual materials include sound recordings, film and video, graphic materials, electronic resources, three-dimensional objects, maps, and microforms. Some audiovisual formats, like film loops, have become obsolete; others are new and still proving their marketability, like DVDs; yet others are not one distinct format like those listed above, but some combination of two or more.

Though the term "audiovisual" is often associated with school libraries and can conjure up memories of filmstrips and AV equipment deliveries to classrooms, many audiovisual formats have become ubiquitous. In its latest description of what a librarian does, the Labor Department's *Occupational Outlook Quarterly* says that librarians are "just as likely to organize websites and CDs as books and magazines."[1] Of the thirteen chapters devoted to de-

[Haworth co-indexing entry note]: "Preface." Roe, Sandra K. Co-published simultaneously in *Cataloging & Classification Quarterly* (The Haworth Information Press, an imprint of The Haworth Press, Inc.) Vol. 31, No. 2, 2001, pp. xv-xvii; and: *The Audiovisual Cataloging Current* (ed: Sandra K. Roe) The Haworth Information Press, an imprint of The Haworth Press, Inc., 2001, pp. xv-xvii. Single or multiple copies of this article are available for a fee from The Haworth Document Delivery Service [1-800-342-9678, 9:00 a.m. - 5:00 p.m. (EST). E-mail address: getinfo@haworthpressinc.com].

© 2001 by The Haworth Press, Inc. All rights reserved.

scription in the *Anglo-American Cataloguing Rules, 2nd ed. 1998 rev.*, Part I, seven concern audiovisual materials. There are so many audiovisual formats, in fact, that not all have been included in this work. Maps, printed music, graphic materials, and microforms have been excluded.[2,3]

The purpose in titling this collection *The Audiovisual Cataloging Current* is to emphasize that these papers present an up-to-date discussion on many aspects of cataloging audiovisual formats and that they reflect on the historical and ongoing development and commitment to audiovisual cataloging within cataloging's broader history.

The first section, Cataloging Audiovisual Formats, contains seven articles based on individual formats. Included are articles on the cataloging of sounding recordings (music and non-music), video recordings (including DVDs), electronic resources (local and remote), three-dimensional objects, and kits. The History of Audiovisual Cataloging section depicts the development of nonbook cataloging practices and codes as being both the work of dedicated individuals as well as the work of associations determined to work together. Three articles speak to Subject Access Issues in the third section. Still images, audiovisual training materials, and moving images are addressed, respectively. In each case, traditional vocabularies used to describe books were found to be less than sufficient, and new subject vocabularies more appropriate to the format are described or suggested. These efforts both influence and are influenced by other developments such as electronic thesauri, taxonomies, online catalog displays, and website design. The final section, AV and AV User Groups by Library Type, contains four articles that discuss what users of school, public, academic, and special libraries need from their audiovisual material collections and catalogers.

In addition to the authors and editor, this publication is the result of the efforts of many individuals who freely lent their expertise as article referees or helped in some other way to shape the content. As is so often the case with nonbook materials, this editor certainly sees this work as one of mixed responsibility. I extend my heart-felt thanks to each of the following: Shelley Bader, Mark Bowman, Janis F. Brown, Ruth Carter, Pauline Atherton Cochrane, Jackie Dooley, John W. Edwards, Joanna Fountain, Betsy Friesen, Karen Granger, Janice Hardy, Samantha Hastings, Kathryn Henderson, Janet Swan Hill, Cathy Kolbinger, Kitty Kringen, Logan Ludwig, Bob Mead-Donaldson, David Miller, Alice Mitchell, Cindy Richardson, Thom Saudargas, Wendy Sistrunk, Sue Stancu, Gary Strawn, Brian Taves, Verna Urbanski, Jean Weihs, Blanche Woolls, Tom Yee, Brad Young, and Jen Young. Thanks also to Barbara Tillett and the Joint Steering Committee for Revision of

AACR who graciously allowed three authors access to the as yet unpublished Chapter 9 "Electronic Resources" in order that these articles might reflect the most current information possible.

Sandra K. Roe
Mankato, MN
December 22, 2000

NOTES

1. Olivia Crosby, "Information Experts in the Information Age," *Occupational Outlook Quarterly* (Winter 2000-01): 3. Available online at URL: *http://www.bls.gov/opub/ooq/2000/Winter/art01.pdf.*

2. For coverage of cartographic topics, see Paige G. Andrew and Mary Lynette Larsgaard (eds.), *Maps and related cartographic materials: cataloging, classification, and bibliographic control* (Binghamton, N.Y.: The Haworth Information Press, 1999). Also published as *Cataloging & Classification Quarterly*, 27 no. 1-4 (1999).

3. Although this work does not contain an article about the descriptive cataloging of graphic materials, see Alexander and Meehleib's article for a discussion on subject indexing of visual materials.

Illustrations by Diana K. Black.

Cataloging Popular Music Recordings

Terry Simpkins

SUMMARY. This paper provides an overview of the cataloging process for popular music sound recordings, from the initial description of the item to the final assignment of subject headings and name and/or title access points. While isolated aspects of the process have been covered in general elsewhere, little has been written describing the entire process especially as applied to popular music recording cataloging specifically. The paper also briefly discusses useful reference sources for popular music cataloging and problems of indexing and keyword searching as they relate to popular music recordings. *[Article copies available for a fee from The Haworth Document Delivery Service: 1-800-342-9678. E-mail address: <getinfo@haworthpressinc.com> Website: <http://www.HaworthPress.com> © 2001 by The Haworth Press, Inc. All rights reserved.]*

KEYWORDS. Sound recordings, popular music, cataloging, keyword searching, subject cataloging, descriptive cataloging, music cataloging, compact discs, jazz

Terry Simpkins is Music Cataloger and Music Archives Librarian at Middlebury College, Middlebury, VT 05753. He holds a BS in Writing and Science from MIT, an MM in Organ Performance from Westminster Choir College, and an MLS from the University of Illinois.

The author would like to thank his colleagues at Middlebury College, Jerry McBride and Richard Jenkins, for their assistance in the preparation of this paper.

[Haworth co-indexing entry note]: "Cataloging Popular Music Recordings." Simpkins, Terry. Co-published simultaneously in *Cataloging & Classification Quarterly* (The Haworth Information Press, an imprint of The Haworth Press, Inc.) Vol. 31, No. 2, 2001, pp. 1-35; and: *The Audiovisual Cataloging Current* (ed: Sandra K. Roe) The Haworth Information Press, an imprint of The Haworth Press, Inc., 2001, pp. 1-35. Single or multiple copies of this article are available for a fee from The Haworth Document Delivery Service [1-800-342-9678, 9:00 a.m. - 5:00 p.m. (EST). E-mail address: getinfo@haworthpressinc.com].

© 2001 by The Haworth Press, Inc. All rights reserved.

INTRODUCTION

Cataloging recordings of popular music[1] presents challenges to both experienced music catalogers and novices alike. While many aspects of cataloging popular music recordings are identical to cataloging recordings of Western art music,[2] certain problems seem to arise more frequently with popular music material. The dizzying speed with which the music industry releases new recordings, the lag time between new styles of music and the creation of Library of Congress (LC) subject headings to cover them, the frequent mixture of format types–is it a sound recording or a computer program?–and the global "cross-pollination" of music styles are just a few of the problems popular music catalogers encounter every day. This article aims to examine these problems and offer practical strategies for coping with them. In order to present this information in as orderly a fashion as possible, this discussion mirrors the arrangement of topics in *Anglo-American Cataloging Rules, 2nd edition, 1998 revision* (AACR2).[3] It begins with an overview of the descriptive cataloging process and then examines issues related to the formulation of main and added entries. The article closes with a discussion of subject cataloging issues.

Like every other type of cataloging, cataloging popular music recordings requires a few essential tools. These include AACR2, *Library of Congress Rule Interpretations* (LCRI),[4] LC *Music Cataloging Decisions* (MCD),[5] *Library of Congress Subject Headings* (LCSH),[6] and documentation explaining the MARC bibliographic format (MARC21) such as *MARC 21 Format for Bibliographic Data*[7] or OCLC's *Bibliographic Formats and Standards.*[8] Jay Weitz's *Music Coding and Tagging* is also useful for cataloging music materials using the MARC format, although it is now seriously outdated.[9]

The cataloging process usually begins with a technical reading of the item aimed at determining the chief source of information according to AACR2 rules 6.0B1. It moves through the transcription and descriptive processes, and then shifts to the assignment of access points and subject headings. Some libraries then classify their recordings using the LC classification schedules or some other scheme, but most libraries dispense with this in favor of simply assigning the item an accession number; this paper does not discuss classification issues relating to sound recordings.

PROBLEMS OF DESCRIPTION

Richard Smiraglia has covered the descriptive portion of sound recording cataloging in detail.[10] His books cannot be recommended highly enough to all music catalogers, regardless of one's level of experience, for an overview of this portion of the cataloging process. Suzanne Mudge and D. J. Hoek have also written a useful article aimed specifically at describing jazz, blues, and popular 78-rpm records.[11] I will concentrate here on points of particular relevance to popular music catalogers working with contemporary recording formats.

Title

According to AACR2 6.0B1, the chief source of information for a sound recording is usually the item itself (the disc, cassette, LP, etc.) and any attached label(s). This raises two potential difficulties. For older formats such as cassettes, LPs, or 45-rpm singles where there are labels on both sides of the disc or cassette, both labels are considered to be part of the chief source. If the item lacks a collective title, rule 6.1G1 provides two methods for describing the item: as a single unit (i.e., transcribing data from both labels) or by making a separate bibliographic description for each separately titled work on the recording. The former approach is the one currently used by the Library of Congress (LCRI 6.1G1). The latter approach was standard practice prior to the adoption of AACR2; if this method is used, rule 6.1G4 provides guidance for formulating the physical description area and for the creation of "With" notes.

Another problem is that many recording companies treat the disc label as more of a decorative area than an informational one. In this situation, 6.0B1 instructs us to take information from the accompanying textual material, the container, or other sources, in that order. A complementary rule, 6.7B3, tells us to indicate the source of the title proper in a note if it comes from somewhere other than the chief source. Compact discs and cassettes can cause confusion here due to the presence of a plastic container through which the accompanying insert is visible. If the title is taken from the front of this insert (visible through the closed container), MCD 6.0B1 tells us to treat this as if it were part of the container, and we should formulate our note accordingly (Figure 1).

FIGURE 1. Bibliographic record for compact disc with no information on the label. Note: the bibliographic records shown in this and the following examples are incomplete; only the portions relevant to the topic under discussion and the MARC21 fields 100, 245, 260, and 300 are shown.

100 0# $a Prince. $4 prf
245 10 $a Prince and The New Power Generation $h [sound recording].
260 ## $a Burbank, CA : $b Paisley Park, $c p1992.
300 ## $a 1 sound disc : $b digital ; $c 4 3/4 in.
500 ## $a Title from container.

General Material Designation (GMD)

The general material designation (GMD) normally presents few problems. Although rule 6.1C1 presents this as an optional addition to the title area, most libraries follow the related LCRI and routinely include the GMD "sound recording." The GMD (MARC21 245 $h) immediately follows the title proper (MARC21 245 $a and, if present, $n and $p). This means that, for an item lacking a collective title, the GMD follows the first title, excluding subtitles, other title information, etc. The GMD should always be enclosed in square brackets.[12]

Statement of Responsibility

The statement of responsibility area is covered by AACR2 rule 6.1F1. Here for the first time in AACR2 chapter 6 we encounter the division between popular and art music. Rule 6.1F1 states:

> If the participation of the person(s) or body (bodies) named in a statement found in the chief source of information goes beyond that of performance, execution, or interpretation of a work (as is commonly the case with "popular," rock, and jazz music), give such a statement as a statement of responsibility. If, however, the participation is confined to performance, execution, or interpretation (as is commonly the case with "serious" or classical music and recorded speech), give the statement in the note area.[13]

In other words, performers of popular music are presumed to bear more intellectual responsibility for their works than performers of art music. (As we will see, this difference in treatment is also apparent in LCRI

21.7B, which instructs catalogers not to provide name-title analytics for the contents of popular music sound recordings.) If, then, the performer's name is present in the chief source of information, generally transcribe it in the statement of responsibility area (MARC21 245 $c). If the name appears as part of the title, rule 1.1F13 instructs us to transcribe it in the statement of responsibility area only if it is required for clarity *or* if the name also appears separately in the chief source of information (Figure 2).

Rule 6.1F1 also allows catalogers to include in the statement of responsibility producers who have some form of artistic or intellectual responsibility for a recording, so long as they are named prominently in the item (i.e., in the chief source). Although producers often do have considerable artistic responsibility for popular recordings, they are rarely named prominently in the item and rarely transcribed in the statement of responsibility area.

Publication Information

The most problematic aspects of the publication area for popular music recordings are determining the name of the publisher and the date of publication. According to AACR2 rule 6.4D2, if there is both a publisher's name and a trade name on a recording, the trade name should be used in the publisher's name area (MARC21 260 $b). Smiraglia makes the useful observation that the trade name usually appears in conjunction with the manufacturer's number,[14] and, according to rule 6.0B2, this information can be taken from virtually anywhere on the entire item. In practical terms, this means to record the name of the record label on the item (i.e., the name that users would most likely be familiar with), not the name of the parent company (which is often found in the fine print on the bottom of the container verso). For example, if the name "Columbia/Legacy" appears on the label and container spine

FIGURE 2. Performer's name appearing in the chief source of information both as part of the title and separately, as a statement of responsibility. Both occurrences are transcribed in the 245 field.

100 1# $a Lam, Sandy, $d 1966- $4 prf
245 10 $a Clang rose $h [sound recording] : $b the brand new Sandy Lam / $c Sandy Lam.
260 ## $a Japan : $b Rock Records, $c p1999.
300 ## $a 1 sound disc : $b digital, stereo. ; $c 4 3/4 in.

while "Sony Music Entertainment"–the parent company–appears in fine print on the CD container, then "Columbia/Legacy" would be transcribed as the publisher name. Finally, LCRI 6.4D1 also tells us to apply the optional provision in AACR2 rule 6.4D1 and to include the name of the distributor, if one is present, in the publication area.

Assigning a publication date can be tricky because of the frequency with which popular music is repackaged and recycled. For example, a work may be plucked from its original source (whether an album, single, or unreleased alternate take gathering dust somewhere inside a record company's archives) and then repackaged as part of a "greatest hits" compilation. The repackaged compilation itself may then be reissued every few years as recording technology advances, or as a performer's commercial value waxes and wanes. It is entirely possible, therefore, for an item to bear several dates; unfortunately, these often do not reflect the publication date of the current incarnation, but rather the publication date of the original (or an intermediate) issue.

The Ⓟ symbol has been used since 1971 to refer to the copyright date of recorded sound.[15] In situations where there is only one Ⓟ date applying to the whole item, that date should be used as the copyright date (MARC21 260 $c) if it seems likely to apply to the item in hand; LCRI 1.4F5 instructs us to transcribe the Ⓟ symbol as "p" in the date area. If, however, there is no Ⓟ date, or multiple Ⓟ dates, none of which cover the entire item, or if the one Ⓟ date present is clearly not the publication date of the item in hand (e.g., a single date of "1973" on a compact disc), the cataloger must infer a date of publication. In the latter instance, LCRI 1.4F5 tells us to apply the optional AACR2 rule 1.4F5 and transcribe the Ⓟ date following the inferred date of publication (Figure 7). The publication date can sometimes be inferred from the latest Ⓟ date on the item, or from an outside source such as the *All-Music Guide*.[16] Sometimes a copyright (©) date referring to newly authored booklet notes can provide a clue as to the publication date. On older recordings (pre-1971), a © date can usually be assumed to be the publication date. In any event, an inferred date should always be placed in square brackets to indicate that it was supplied by the cataloger (Figure 3).

Physical Description

The physical description area (MARC21 300 $a, $b, $c, and $e) is usually straightforward for catalogers. AACR2 6.5A-E clearly explains the terminology to use and the order in which the information should

FIGURE 3. Compact disc with multiple copyright dates. The selections originally appeared on albums released between 1973-1979. This compilation originally appeared as an LP in 1979, and was subsequently reissued on CD in 1986.

110 2# $a Electric Light Orchestra. $4 prf
245 10 $a ELO's greatest hits $h [sound recording] / $c Electric Light Orchestra.
246 3# $a Electric Light Orchestra's greatest hits
246 3# $a Greatest hits
260 ## $a Los Angeles : $b Jet Records, $c **[1986]**
300 ## $a 1 sound disc : $b digital ; $c 4 3/4 in.

Dates on label: ℗ 1973, 1974, 1975, 1976, 1977, 1979
Dates on container and booklet: © 1979, 1986/℗ 1973, 1974, 1975, 1976, 1977, 1979

appear, and provides excellent examples of the most common recording formats. There are, however, two potentially confusing issues to note. Rule 6.5B2 instructs us to record the playing time of the recording in parentheses after the extent of the item (MARC21 300 $a). The related LCRI gives instructions on estimating the duration if the only ones given are those of the recording's parts. However, this LCRI itself is modified by MCD 6.5B2, which instructs catalogers to give the total duration of a recording only when the recording contains one work. This means that, since most popular music recordings include more than one work, libraries following Library of Congress practice will only rarely include the duration of the recording in the physical description area.

The other difficulty stems from AACR2 rule 6.5C7, which instructs catalogers to record the number of sound channels (using the abbreviations "stereo.," "mono.," or "quad.") (MARC21 300 $b) when this information is readily available. The MCD for this rule tells us to not record any term at all if the information is not explicitly stated on the item. The indication does not necessarily have to be on the disc label, however. Jazz compact disc reissues frequently include the term "stereo." in a reproduction of the cover art from the original LP,[17] and, assuming that there is no reason to suspect that the information is inaccurate, this should be noted in the physical description area. In MARC records, if a term such as "stereo." or "mono." is included in the physical description area, the relevant code should also be included in the Physical Description fixed field (MARC21 007/04–Configuration of Playback Channels). Similarly, this field should be coded as "unknown" (MARC21 007/04 code u) if the item does *not* indicate the type of sound.[18]

One final point that deserves mention is that information pertaining to materials accompanying a sound recording can be included either in this area (MARC21 300 $e) or in the note area (discussed below). As rule 1.5E1 implies, and MCD 1.5E1 makes explicit, these options are mutually exclusive–if the information is provided here do not make a note and vice versa. Experience has shown that information relating to the presence of accompanying liner notes is usually given in the note area. This area allows considerably more detail to be included in the bibliographic record than does the physical description area.

Notes

Notes for sound recordings (MARC21 5XX) are usually quite extensive. They provide a way for catalogers to include information not otherwise present in the bibliographic record. Traditionally, this area is thought of as primarily descriptive; as Smiraglia writes, "[n]otes are made to allow users to make relevance judgments when looking at descriptions in a catalog."[19] However, with the widespread use of computerized library catalogs, keyword searching has become both commonplace[20] and, at least for musical materials, effective.[21] Leazer found that keyword searches are especially useful for retrieving musical works on recordings that lack name-title or title added entries–such as is the case with recordings that contain a large number of works–or when the desired title is distinctive rather than generic.[22] Both conditions apply to most popular music recordings. The notes area, then, has assumed a new role in addition to its original, primarily descriptive one, namely as a rich source of uncontrolled access points. It is a role that has evolved from, as Cutter described it, simply "assist[ing] in the choice" of an item[23] to "[enabling] a person to find [an item] of which the author, the title, [or] the subject is known."[24] It is important, therefore, that notes for popular music recordings be both succinct yet specific and informative. One especially useful aid to formulating concise, helpful notes is Ralph Hartsock's *Notes for Music Catalogers,*[25] which provides examples of nearly every type of note a music cataloger will need to make.

The order of notes in the bibliographic record is *not* random; it is carefully prescribed in the rules set forth under AACR2 6.7B. Some notes are relatively straightforward, such as notes relating to the availability of other formats (AACR2 rule 6.7B16). Others can pose more difficulties; these are the ones on which I would like to concentrate here.

The first note in the bibliographic record is the publisher's number note, covered by AACR2 rule 6.7B19 (MARC21 028 $a and $b provide additional access to the publisher's number and name, respectively).[26] Often, there are varying publisher's numbers on the disc label, spine, and/or container; MCD 6.7B19 instructs catalogers to record *only* the form on the recording itself (Figures 4 and 8). Not every number that appears on a recording is bibliographically significant. For example, "DIDX" numbers frequently appear on compact discs issued by New World Records, Blue Note Records, and other labels. However, these numbers are not assigned by the record label, but are merely lot numbers assigned by the manufacturer of the compact disc–in this case, Sony Disc Manufacturing–for quality control purposes.[27] It is extremely unlikely that any user would be aware of these numbers, much less search the catalog for them, and their presence merely clutters up the bibliographic record.

The next note relates to the artistic form and/or medium of performance, constructed according to AACR2 rule 6.7B1.[28] Bearing in mind the dual function of notes in the catalog record discussed above, this note is especially important when cataloging popular music recordings. LC subject headings do not always describe popular music genres in the same way aficionados of those genres do.[29] However, in the artistic form note catalogers can use uncontrolled genre terms to assist users looking for specific musical styles. Terms such as "ambient music" or "cool jazz" may carry a great deal of meaning for connoisseurs of those styles, but neither of these are established LC subject headings.[30] Such notes should be formulated concisely, yet include as many useful keyword terms as necessary (Figures 5 and 6).

An alternative to using the form/genre note this way is to include index terms in a locally defined subject field in the MARC record such as

FIGURE 4. Compact disc with multiple manufacturer's numbers. The container spine number is not transcribed according to MCB 6.7B19.

028 00 $a 60726-2 $b Elektra
100 1# $a Bragg, Billy. $4 prf
245 10 $a Back to basics $h [sound recording] / $c Billy Bragg.
260 ## $a New York, N.Y. : $b Elektra, $c p1987.
300 ## $a 1 sound disc : $b digital ; $c 4 3/4 in.
500 ## $a Elektra: 60726-2.

On disc: 60726-2
On container spine: 9 60726-2

FIGURE 5. Statement of medium note utilizing uncontrolled genre terms that may be useful for keyword searching.

```
110 2# $a Sounds from the Ground (Musical group) $4 prf
245 10 $a Kin $h [sound recording] / $c Sounds from the Ground.
260 ## $a Sedona, Ariz. : $b Waveform, $c p1996.
300 ## $a 1 sound disc : $b digital ; $c 4 3/4 in.
500 ## $a Electronic ambient techno music.
```

MARC21 field 653 (Index Term-Uncontrolled) or, for OCLC users, field 690 (Local Subject Added Entry-Topical Term). Including these fields in the local catalog's subject index and using them consistently may in fact provide users with better subject access than simply using a note field included in the general keyword index; the drawback to this method is that the library must then develop and maintain its own local subject thesaurus. However, for institutions that collect heavily in specific areas that are poorly covered by LCSH, this may be the best option.[31]

One major problem in cataloging unfamiliar music is determining just what, exactly, the genre is. Obviously, the first place to look is the item itself. Do the program notes provide any useful information? Are there any short style or genre terms printed on the back upper corner of the container? Clues like these can provide starting points for further investigation. If the cataloger is already familiar with popular music styles, and has access to playback equipment, there's no substitute for listening to portions of the recording. Frequently, though, the cataloger is forced to turn to outside sources for assistance.

Though a comprehensive list of reference sources is beyond the scope of this article, there are some basic resources with which popular music catalogers should be familiar.[32] One general resource, available both in print and online versions, is the *All Music Guide*. Though it includes reviews and descriptions of recordings of all kinds of music, it is perhaps more useful for its descriptions of various popular music styles and its lists of representative artists working in those areas, including contemporary genres such as rap and house music.[33] The *Oxford Companion to Popular Music*[34] and *The Penguin Encyclopedia of Popular Music*[35] are both thorough, single-volume reference sources, while *The Encyclopedia of Popular Music*[36] is an authoritative multi-volume work. For mainstream rock music, *The New Rolling Stone Encyclopedia of Rock & Roll*[37] is a good place to start. More obscure bands, including many from outside the United States, are well served by *The Trouser Press Guide to '90s Rock,*[38] a blunt, but knowledgeable, resource. The *Rock Encyclopedia*[39] covers bands and musicians from the ever-popular '60s rock era. For jazz, there is the familiar *New Grove Dictionary of Jazz.*[40] I also like the *Penguin Guide to Jazz*[41] for its inclusion of recording data and performers alongside the reviews. Country music is well served by *The Encyclopedia of Country Music*[42] and *Country Music: The Encyclopedia.*[43] Finally, for the inexhaustible body of non-Western music somewhat bizarrely known as "world music," *World Music: The Rough Guide*[44] provides a concise overview of a wide array of music from around the globe. Though obviously neither as comprehensive nor as scholarly as *The Garland Encyclopedia of World Music,*[45] its compact size makes it well suited for a cataloger's reference shelf. Not to be overlooked too is the venerable *New Grove,*[46] which provides extensive commentary on the music of many different regions of the world, even if these articles are not specifically geared toward popular music.

Following the language note (MARC21 546 $a), if any, AACR2 rules 6.7B3-6.7B5 provide instructions for making notes related to the source of the title proper, any variant titles found on the item, and parallel titles. As with any sound recording, popular music recordings may feature variant titles on the insert or on the front, back, or spine of the container. Generally these variants are also traced using MARC21 field 246 $a (Varying Form of Title) (Figures 3, 8 and 18). Portions of titles can also be traced if deemed useful, as is often the case with "greatest hits" compilations (Figure 3).

Rule 6.7B6 provides instructions for creating statement of responsibility notes. As mentioned above, statements of responsibility for popular music recordings generally focus on performers rather than composers. However, if a popular music recording consists of songs by one or two principal composers (as in the case when a single band member is the primary songwriter), a simple note can be constructed or, in many cases, quoted right from the item or accompanying material. In the latter case it would be transcribed with quotation marks, followed by an indication of the source of the information (Figure 6).

Popular music recordings also usually include a statement of responsibility note for the performers (MARC21 511 $a). These notes are especially useful for facilitating keyword searches for specific groups or individuals when tracing them as added entries is, for whatever reason, impractical. There may simply be, for example, too many performers on a recording to justify the time and expense of doing authority work for

FIGURE 6. Statement of medium note for keyword searching and statement of responsibility note indicating composer credit.

100 1# $a Carmody, Kev. $4 prf
245 10 $a Eulogy (for a black person) $h [sound recording] / $c Kev Carmody.
260 ## $a Australia : $b Festival Records, $c p1991.
300 ## $a 1 sound disc : $b digital ; $c 4 3/4 in.
500 ## $a Protest songs and popular music from Australia.
500 ## $a "All songs composed and arranged by Kev Carmody"--Insert.

each individual heading, yet each performer can at least be included in the performer note as an alternative means of access. Another common situation occurs when musical groups have significant turnover among band members. In these cases, detailed performer notes are often the only way for users to easily find recordings of specific individual musicians. A note that includes the band members' names in parentheses following the group name can again provide keyword access for the individual musicians (Figure 7). Just how extensively a cataloger should research a group's history is, of course, impossible to generalize. It all depends on the cataloger, the institution, the particular recording, and the resources at hand. However, if the information is available in the notes to the item in hand, there is little reason to omit it from the bibliographic record.

If a recording features numerous performers, as in the case with "samplers" and other anthologies, AACR2 rule 6.7B6 includes a provision for incorporating this information into the contents note (MARC21 505). This has the advantage of making the bibliographic record somewhat clearer for the user by visually linking the performers together with the selections on which they appear (Figures 11 and 12).

Rule 6.7B7 provides instructions for creating edition and history notes. The two most common types of edition and history notes for popular music are those pertaining to reissues (MARC21 500 $a) and those pertaining to recording data (MARC21 518 $a; formatted recording date and location information is included in MARC21 033). Both of these notes provide important discographical information. Whenever possible, reissue notes include information about the original issue's label and manufacturer's number, title, and year of release. These notes are particularly valuable when made in conjunction with an added entry for the original album title (MARC21 740 $a), but even the notes alone will provide some access via keyword searching (Figure 8).[47] Again, how extensively a cataloger researches the discographical history of a particular recording or the details of a particular recording session will differ according to the individual cataloger and institutional policies, but if the information can be readily obtained it should ideally be included in the bibliographic record.

The most common physical description notes for popular music sound recordings, AACR2 rule 6.7B10, are those pertaining to the presence of multiple containers and, for compact discs, a simple "Compact disc" note. (Physical description notes concerning the type of recording method used (analog or digital) are no longer made as per MCD 6.7B10.) A note describing the presence of multiple containers is included when the number of containers and the number of discs differ (except in the common situation of multiple discs in one container), e.g., "Six discs in 3 containers." The "Compact disc" note should be coded as a general note (MARC21 500 $a), not as a system requirements note (MARC21 538 $a), since it refers to the physical description of the item in hand, not to the resources required to play it. This note is, once again, useful for keyword searching. Although most online catalogs allow users to limit searches by the broad category of "sound recording," it is less common to be able to directly limit a search to a specific *type* of sound recording, e.g., CD, LP, or cassette.[48] With many systems, the only way to search for a specific format is via a keyword search. Since the word "compact," unlike "cassette," for example, does not appear in the physical description area, a separate note is crucial for this type of keyword search to succeed. It also makes the format explicitly clear to the user in plain English, something that the description "1 sound disc: digital; 4 3/4 in." does not.

Increasingly, audio compact discs are being combined with computer programs and marketed under such terms as "Enhanced CD" or

FIGURE 7. Detailed performer note listing band members' names within a performing group.

100 1# $a Dylan, Bob, $d 1941- $4 cmp $4 prf
245 14 $a The basement tapes $h [sound recording] / $c Bob Dylan & The Band.
260 ## $a New York, N.Y. : $b Columbia, $c **[198-?], p1975**.
300 ## $a 2 sound discs : $b digital ; $c 4 3/4 in.
511 0# $a Bob Dylan, vocals, piano, acoustic guitar ; The Band (Robbie Robertson, guitar, drums, vocals ; Richard Manuel, piano, drums, harmonica, vocals ; Rick Danko, electric bass, mandolin, vocals ; Garth Hudson, organ, clavinette, accordion, tenor sax, piano ; Levon Helm, drums, mandolin, electric bass, vocals).

FIGURE 8. Notes and added entries relating to previous releases of the same recording. Notice the added title entries (MARC21 740 $a) for the original album issues included in this box set; notice also the MARC21 028 $b fields for the original issue numbers and labels (i.e., Capitol, not Mosaic; the Mosaic numbers are from the reissue).

028 00 $a MD4-168 $b Mosaic
028 00 $a MD6-168 $b Mosaic
028 00 $a 72438-19192-2-4 $b Mosaic
028 00 $a T-692 $b Capitol
028 00 $a T-721 $b Capitol
028 00 $a T-820 $b Capitol
028 00 $a T-933 $b Capitol
028 00 $a ST-933 $b Capitol
028 00 $a T-1143 $b Capitol
028 00 $a ST-1143 $b Capitol
028 00 $a T-1095 $b Capitol
100 1# $a Teagarden, Jack, $d 1905-1964. $4 prf
245 14 $a The complete Capitol fifties Jack Teagarden sessions $h [sound recording].
246 3# $a Complete Capitol '50s Jack Teagarden sessions
260 ## $a Stamford, Conn. : $b Mosaic, $c p1996.
300 ## $a 4 sound discs : $b digital, mono., stereo. ; $c 4 3/4 in.
500 ## $a Mosaic: MD4-168 (box and disc 1); MD6-168 (discs 2-4); additional no. on discs: 72438-19192-2-4.
500 ## $a Previously released on Capitol as T-692 (Coast concert); T-721 (This is Teagarden); T-820 (Swing low, sweet spiritual); T-933/ST-933 (Jazz ultimate); T-1143/ST-1143 (Shades of night); and T-1095 (Big T's Dixieland Band).
518 ## $a Recorded at Capitol Studios, Los Angeles, Oct. 18, 1955-Jan. 11, 1957 (Coast concert, This is Teagarden, Swing low, sweet spiritual); Riverside Plaza Hotel, New York City, Sept. 16, 1957 (Jazz ultimate); Capitol Studios, New York City, Feb. 10-12, 1958 (Shades of night); and Universal Studios, Chicago, Apr. 14-15, 1958 (Big T's Dixieland Band).
740 02 $a Coast concert.
740 02 $a This is Teagarden.
740 02 $a Swing low, sweet spiritual.
740 02 $a Jazz ultimate.
740 02 $a Shades of night.
740 02 $a Big T's Dixieland Band.

On container spines: 168 (not transcribed according to MCD 6.7B19).

"CD+." This type of material presents a number of challenges to the cataloger, not least of which is whether to catalog it as a sound recording or a computer file. Most commonly, these items are treated as sound recordings, with information relating to the software aspect of the item entered into the bibliographic record as well. This means, at a minimum, providing a true system requirements note explaining the equipment necessary to access the software portion of the disc; this note is constructed according to AACR2 rule 9.7B1. The MARC21 006 fixed field (Additional Material Characteristics) should also be included in the record; frequently the term "Enhanced CD," or whatever term appears on the item, is given as a quoted note as well (Figure 9). In online catalogs that are able to exploit the 006 field, users may then retrieve these items whether they limit their searches by the sound recordings format or by the computer files format. Not all online catalogs are able to take advantage of the MARC21 006 field in this way, unfortunately, which means that users of those catalogs who want to limit their searches by format must guess correctly which is the primary one or else the record will not be retrieved.

Sometimes enhanced CDs present additional unexpected challenges to overcome, such as solving Italian cryptograms in order to determine the password necessary to access the software (Figure 10). In this example, a search of discussion groups on the WWW provided the official password as well as an alternative.[49]

Most popular music recordings include inserts that can provide personnel details, program notes, recording information, and/or lyrics. As mentioned above, this information can be included either in the physical description area or in an accompanying material note (AACR2 6.7B11). Notes should be made only when the accompanying material is somehow significant; MCD 6.7B11, though rather confusedly worded, states that the mere fact of being physically separable from the

FIGURE 9. Notes for an enhanced CD. The 006/00 position is coded "m" for computer file; 006/09 is coded "i" for interactive multimedia. In this example, the phrase "Enhanced CD" appears on the chief source of information; therefore, it is not necessary to include the source of the phrase in the note.

006/00 = m 006/09 = i
110 2# $a Neri per caso (Musical group) $4 prf
245 10 $a Neri per caso $h [sound recording].
260 ## $a Italy : $b EMI, $c p1997.
300 ## $a 1 sound disc : $b digital ; $c 4 3/4 in.
500 ## $a Compact disc.
500 ## $a "Enhanced CD."
538 ## $a System requirements for enhanced CD: Macintosh or Windows compatible (system 7.55 or Windows 95 recommended); at least 4 MB RAM; Quicktime; monitor capable of displaying 640x480 screen resolution; 2X speed or faster Multisession enabled CD-ROM drive.

FIGURE 10. Enhanced CD requiring password for access. Here, a "Restrictions on Access" note (USMARC 506 $a) is used to provide information on the passwords needed to access the CD-ROM software, and a general note is also provided describing the alphabet sequences on the label.

006/00 = m 006/09 = i
100 1# $a Baglioni, Claudio. $4 prf
245 10 $a Viaggiatore sulla coda del tempo $h [sound recording] / $c Claudio Baglioni.
260 ## $a [Italy] : $b Columbia, $c p1999.
300 ## $a 1 sound disc : $b digital ; $c 4 3/4 in.
500 ## $a Label contains two alphabet sequences used to decode password for multimedia access.
506 ## $a Use ACIDULO or INGLOBAI as password to access multimedia portion of CD.
538 ## $a System requirements: PC or Macintosh.

main item does not by itself make the accompanying material important. Smiraglia offers useful guidelines for determining significance, advising catalogers to make a note only when the accompanying material is "substantial" or when it "provides information that is unique, such as a discography or historical or biographical information that cannot be found in standard reference sources."[50] The language of the note is, of course, left to the discretion of the cataloger, but it is usually worded something like "Program notes and lyrics in Spanish with English translations (25 p.: ill.) inserted in container." If the insert includes colored illustrations, as is frequently the case with popular recordings, the note can be modified to include the standard abbreviations "col. ill." or "ill. (some col.)." As in the physical description area, the pagination of the insert should be bracketed if it is supplied by the cataloger.

Contents notes are covered by AACR2 rule 6.7B18. Most popular music recordings are anthologies, and since LCRI 21.7B instructs catalogers not to make analytical added entries for "pop, folk, ethnic, or jazz" music, contents notes often provide the sole means of access to individual works contained on popular music recordings. Therefore, it is essential that these notes be formulated as completely as possible. For popular music, the form of the note is usually straightforward. An MCD from August 2000 for rule 6.7B18 provides instructions for constructing more complicated types of contents notes, including those for multipart sets. The durations of the individual works should be included in the contents note when they are known. LCRI 6.7B18 and 6.7B10 provide instructions for those cases where only the durations for the individual parts of a work are known; this occurs infrequently with popular music. Composers are often omitted from popular music contents notes, in keeping with the de-emphasis of the composer in popular music cataloging, but if the information is present and significant, such as is often the case with jazz recordings of "standards," it can be helpful to include this information as well. As mentioned above, complex performer information is also sometimes better suited for inclusion in the contents note rather than in a separate performer note (Figure 11).

MARC21 allows contents notes to be tagged either as a "basic" note (Figure 11) or as an "enhanced" note (Figure 12); the form of the note is indicated by a 2nd indicator of 0 in the MARC21 505 tag. Although the

FIGURE 11. Basic contents note with multiple performers and composers.

245 00 $a Celtic music today $h [sound recording].
260 ## $a Danbury, CT : $b Green Linnet, $c p1997.
300 ## $a 1 sound disc : $b digital ; $c 4 3/4 in.
505 0# $a Broken wings / Dougie MacLean (Cherish the Ladies) (5:16) -- John's got school tomorrow / Simon Thoumire ; The Northsea Chinaman / Jim Sutherland ; The bus spotter's reel / Simon Thoumire (Simon Thoumire Three) (3:54) -- Dbulamban (Altan) (3:42) -- The morning star ; The Caoilte Mountains (Martin Hayes) (3:17) -- Beam me up / Rare Air (Rare Air) (4:05) -- Alasdair mhic cholla ghasda (Capercaillie) (2:29).

FIGURE 12. Enhanced contents note with multiple performers and composers. Adjacent statements of responsibility (such as the Rare Air selection) are entered in the same subfield $r. However, adjacent titles (such as The morning star and The Caoilte Mountains) are entered in separate subfield $t.

245 00 $a Celtic music today $h [sound recording].
260 ## $a Danbury, CT : $b Green Linnet, $c p1997.
300 ## $a 1 sound disc : $b digital ; $c 4 3/4 in.
505 00 $t Broken wings / $r Dougie MacLean $r (Cherish the Ladies) $g (5:16) -- $t John's got school tomorrow / $r Simon Thoumire ; $t The Northsea Chinaman / $r Jim Sutherland ; $t The bus spotter's reel / $r Simon Thoumire (Simon Thoumire Three) $g (3:54) -- $t Dbulamban $r (Altan) $g (3:42) -- $t The morning star ; $t The Caoilte Mountains $r (Martin Hayes) $g (3:17) -- $t Beam me up / $r Rare Air (Rare Air) $g (4:05) -- $t Alasdair mhic cholla ghasda $r (Capercaillie) $g (2:29).

MARC tagging of the enhanced note is somewhat more complex, the form of note remains the same. There are advantages and disadvantages to the use of enhanced notes. The main advantage is that it can allow every title on every recording anthology to be incorporated into the catalog's title keyword index (not just the general keyword index), and performers and composers can likewise be included in the catalog's author/name keyword index. (This assumes, of course, that these indexes exist and are profiled to include the appropriate 505 subfields.) The primary disadvantage is that, unless a library performs substantial retrospective enhancement of their database, the presence of a mixed database (i.e., with some contents notes in enhanced form and some in basic form) can be misleading for users. Most users will not realize that, if only a portion of the database contains the enhanced notes, a truly thorough search will involve querying both the general keyword index and the title or author keyword index (if indeed they know to make the distinction between the different types of keyword indexes at all). And if both indexes need to be searched anyway for a fair proportion of queries, it is reasonable to question the efficiency of including the enhanced notes at all. However, if retrospective conversion of pre-existing basic contents notes were undertaken–at least for anthologies–then the use of enhanced notes could be a powerful access tool indeed.

ACCESS POINTS

As we have seen, AACR2 chapter 6 provides detailed instruction on how to describe sound recordings. It does not, however, provide guidance on constructing access points in order to retrieve these descriptions from the catalog. For rules concerning name and title access, we must turn to chapters in Part 2 of AACR2, the most relevant portions being chapters 21-22 and 24-25. Subject access is not covered by AACR2 at all; for that, one must turn to whichever subject thesaurus is being applied for rules on how to construct the headings. Since many libraries use LCSH for musical works, this is the example I will discuss below.

Main Entry

The rules for determining main entry are found under AACR2 21.23. Rule 21.23A pertains to recordings of one work (or portions thereof). Recordings of this type occur infrequently in popular music, but when they do, the main entry will normally be the composer (MARC21 100).

This is one of the few occasions when cataloging popular music recordings that the composer is given preference to the performer (rule 21.23B, below, provides another example of this) (Figure 13). Rule 21.23B applies to anthologies of works written by one composer (or composers working as a team). Here, again, the recording is entered under the name of the composer (Figure 14). Occasionally, as in this example, recordings of this type require a collective uniform title; these will be discussed in detail below.

Rule 21.23C is commonly applicable to popular music recordings because these recordings are usually anthologies containing works by

FIGURE 13. Jazz recording containing one work. The main entry is under the composer Charles Mingus as instructed by AACR2 21.23A. Gunther Schuller receives an added entry as editor and as the person responsible for completing the work.

100 1# $a Mingus, Charles, $d 1922- $4 cmp
245 10 $a Epitaph $h [sound recording] / $c Charles Mingus.
260 ## $a New York, NY : $b Columbia, $c p1990.
300 ## $a 2 sound discs : $b digital ; $c 4 3/4 in.
500 ## $a Extended jazz composition; edited and in part completed by Gunther Schuller.
511 0# $a Various soloists, acc. by large jazz ensemble ; Gunther Schuller, conductor.

FIGURE 14. Jazz recording of songs by one composer. The main entry is under Cole Porter as composer of the songs. Ella Fitzgerald and Buddy Bregman are given added entries as principal performers. The uniform title does *not* include the addition "arr." because these songs are still performed here as vocal works; see AACR2 25.35C2.

100 1# $a Porter, Cole, $d 1891-1964. $4 cmp
240 10 $a Songs. $k Selections
245 10 $a Ella Fitzgerald sings the Cole Porter song book $h [sound recording].
260 ## $a New York, N.Y. : $b Verve Records, $c p1993.
300 ## $a 2 sound discs : $b digital ; $c 4 3/4 in.
511 0# $a Ella Fitzgerald, singer ; arrangements and orchestra conducted by Buddy Bregman.
700 1# $a Fitzgerald, Ella. $4 prf
700 1# $a Bregman, Buddy. $4 cnd

multiple composers. Here we return to the idea of the performer as having preeminence over the composer in popular music. Main entry in this case is the "principal performer." LCRI 21.23C provides specific guidelines for determining exactly who the "principal performer" is. First, the principal performer *must* appear on the chief source of information. If there is only one performer on the chief source of information, that performer is the principal performer. If there are two or more, the principal performers are those given prominence by virtue of typography or layout. However, if all of the performers are listed using the same typography in the chief source, do not assume that those at the beginning of the list are more prominent than those at the end simply by virtue of their placement; they might all be considered "principal." If there are two or three principal performers, AACR2 21.23C instructs us to choose the first named as the main entry and include subsequent performers as added entries. If there are more than three principal performers, we no longer have to worry about it and simply choose the title of the recording as main entry. This occurs frequently with sampler discs, recordings of live music festivals such as Woodstock, or recordings based on television programs such as Austin City Limits, all of which usually feature a variety of performers.

There is one trap to avoid when determining the number of principal performers. Popular music recordings often include performers whose names seem like one corporate entity, e.g., Buddy Holly and the Crickets or Banjo Dan and the Mid-Nite Plowboys. However, for cataloging purposes, each of these examples actually consists of two names. MCD 21.23C, referring to MCD 24.1A, provides guidance for personal names appearing with the name of a group. This type of name is treated as two separate performers, one a personal name and one a corporate body. To use the first example, if these were the only names on the chief source of information, the heading for Buddy Holly, being listed first, would be chosen as the main entry (*not* Buddy Holly and the Crickets), while the heading for the Crickets would be an added entry.

Uniform Titles

Uniform titles and name-title analytical entries are rather uncommon in popular music cataloging. Even when a popular recording consists exclusively of songs written by one composer/performer, the uniform title is usually omitted from the bibliographic record (Figure 15).

The main exception to this practice occurs when a performer or group of performers records works by a different composer, e.g., Ella Fitzgerald singing songs by Cole Porter or Gil Evans playing the music of Jimi Hendrix. In this case, the main entry is for the composer of the works under AACR2 21.23B and an appropriate uniform title is formulated (usually "Songs. Selections," with "arr." added if necessary) (Figures 14 and 16).

MCD 25.34C provides additional instructions for formulating uniform titles for recordings of songs by composers such as George Gershwin and Cole Porter. These composers wrote songs sometimes as part of theatrical productions and sometimes as independent works. When both types of songs are found on a recording, the MCD instructs us to choose "Songs. Selections" (with or without "arr.," as appropriate) as the uniform title (i.e., not a broader heading such as "Selections,"

FIGURE 15. Collection of popular songs by one compser, but no uniform title.

100 1# $a Harvey, Polly Jean. $4 prf $4 cmp
245 10 $a Is this desire? $h [sound recording] / $c P J Harvey.
260 ## $a New York : $b Island Records, $c c1998.
300 ## $a 1 sound disc : $b digital ; $c 4 3/4 in.
500 ## $a "All songs written by Polly Jean Harvey"--Insert.

FIGURE 16. Collection of popular songs by one composer, with uniform title. The main entry is under Jimi Hendrix as composer. Gil Evans and the Gil Evans Orchestra receive added entries as principal performers and/or arranger. Notice that the uniform title includes the qualifier "arr.," not because these works were originally written for a rock group and are performed here by a jazz big band, but because they were originally vocal works now performed as instrumental selections (AACR2 25.35C2).

100 1# $aHendrix, Jimi. $4 prf
240 10 $a Songs. $k Selections; $o arr.
245 14 $a The Gil Evans Orchestra plays the music of Jimi Hendrix $h [sound recording].
260 ## $a New York, N.Y. : $b Bluebird, $c p1988.
300 ## $a 1 sound disc : $b digital, stereo. ; $c 4 3/4 in.
500 ## $a Big band arrangements of rock songs.
511 0# $a Gil Evans, keyboards, conductor, and arranger ; Gil Evans Orchestra.
700 1# $a Evans, Gil, $d 1912- $4 arr $4 cnd $4 prf
710 2# $a Gil Evans Orchestra. $4 prf

"Vocal music. Selections," etc.). However, if there is evidence that *all* the songs in the collection are from larger works of a single type (such as musicals), then the uniform title would consist of the name of the type followed by "Selections."

One final note about popular music uniform titles. When they do occur, uniform titles for popular music are formulated just as any other music uniform title with one exception: the use of the addition for arrangements ("arr.") (MARC21 240/700 $o). Since popular music cataloging is "performer-driven," different versions of popular musical works are not considered to be arrangements unless they are *radically* different, not just variations in style; such variations are basically what AACR2 considers popular music to be all about.[51] This is made explicit in AACR2 25.35C2. The idea of an "arrangement" in popular music is limited to an instrumental work that is performed as a vocal piece, or *vice versa*. Therefore, a (hypothetical) recording of Johnny Rotten singing songs by Lennon and McCartney would *not* consist of arrangements, at least from a cataloger's perspective.

Added Entries

Access to popular recordings is usually enhanced through the inclusion of added entries for manufacturer's numbers, performers' names, variant titles, and, occasionally, titles of the individual works or albums.[52] AACR2 rules 21.29-21.30 (and the related LCRIs and MCDs) govern the formation of added entries. Rule 21.29C is especially important, as it allows catalogers to make added entries for names (personal or corporate) or titles if catalog users might suppose that the item would be found under that heading or title. In other words, if someone might reasonably search for an item under a particular name or title, include it as an added entry even if there is no other specific justification for doing so. The point here is to try to anticipate how users might explore the library catalog.

For popular music recordings, the most obvious added entries to make are for performers. This is specifically sanctioned by LCRI 21.29D, which instructs us to make added entries for all performers named on a recording, including corporate bodies, except those who appear on only a small number of works or receive a main entry heading as principal performer. Another exception is made for situations where a performer functions entirely or primarily as a member of a corporate body that is represented by a main or added entry. In this case, we do not make a second entry for the personal name of the performer. For example, if Robbie Robertson appears on a recording solely as a member of the group The Band, we would include an entry for the group name, but not for Robertson as an individual. (This again underscores the importance of making detailed performer notes.) Even if the corporate body is *not* formally named, section 3 of LCRI 21.29D instructs that we should not create added entries for individual performers within that body in cases where, if the corporate body *were* named, we would create an added entry for that body instead. In other words, if the individual performer functions as a member of a corporate body that would normally receive its own added entry, do not make an entry for the individual even in those cases where the corporate body does not receive an entry because it lacks a formal name. Catalogers should remember, however, that they are free to create added entries for virtually any performer if it is supposed that users might search for the item under that performer's name.

This exception for individual performers functioning within corporate bodies does not apply, however, to jazz recordings. Jazz recordings commonly feature *ad hoc* groups that have as much to do with the exigencies of the record label as with the wishes of the session leader. Frequently these groups do not have a collective name, but here catalogers *should* make added entries for each individual performer (unless, of course, the individual appears on only a few selections or receives a main entry heading), even if one performer is given greater prominence than the others (Figure 17).

FIGURE 17. Jazz recording made by an unnamed corporate body. This is an example of the exception for jazz recordings in LCRI 21.29D, section 3. Entries are made for each individual performer even though (a) one (Bobby Hutcherson) is given greater prominence than the others and (b) they function as members of an unnamed corporate body which, if it had a name (such as "The Bobby Hutcherson Quintet") would itself receive an added entry.

100 1# $a Hutcherson, Bobby. $4 prf
245 10 $a Stick-up $h [sound recording] / $c Bobby Hutcherson.
260 ## $a Beverly Hills, Calif. : $b Blue Note, $c [1997], p1969.
300 ## $a 1 sound disc : $b digital ; $c 4 3/4 in.
511 0# $a Bobby Hutcherson, vibraphone ; Joe Henderson, tenor saxophone ; McCoy Tyner, piano ; Herbie Lewis, double bass ; Billy Higgins, drums.
700 1# $a Henderson, Joe, $d 1937- $4 prf
700 1# $a Tyner, McCoy. $4 prf
700 1# $a Lewis, Herbie. $4 prf
700 1# $a Higgins, Billy. $4 prf

Though detailed comments about actually formulating name headings are beyond the scope of this paper, I would like to offer some brief thoughts on the topic. Because catalogers of all types of material routinely deal with names that have not yet been added to the National Authority File (NAF), it is necessary to have a basic understanding of how headings are formulated. Detailed instructions for formulating personal and corporate names are found in AACR2 chapters 22 and 24 (and the corresponding LCRIs), respectively. For both types of name, the starting point is the form found on the item in hand. For personal names, if a birth date is readily ascertainable, and especially if one is found on the item, LCRI 22.17 instructs us to include it in the heading. This may save a bit of clean-up work if and when the authoritative form of the name is finally established, especially if it is established based on the same item. The most common corporate headings in popular music cataloging involve the names of performing groups. These headings frequently will have the qualifier "(Musical group)" added to the name. However, if the name contains a word such as "Band" or "Group" that conveys the idea of a corporate body, or if it contains a collective noun or a number (e.g., the Ben Folds Five), do not add the qualifier. If the name is ambiguous, the qualifier should be added. In all cases, the qualifier is added to convey the idea of *corporateness,* not musicality.

Though, as stated above, name-title analytics are not usually made for popular music recordings, title access can and should be enhanced in other ways. AACR2 rule 21.30J covers the creation of added entries for significant variants of the title proper. The corresponding LCRI is lengthy and discusses several of the most common types of variants that may occur. The LCRI is directed primarily towards printed materials, but MCD 21.30J nevertheless instructs us to turn to this LCRI for guidance with recordings as well. Of particular interest to catalogers of popular music is the section of the LCRI that suggests that added title entries should be made "more or less automatically" for cover titles (and presumably, by extension to sound recordings, container titles) and parallel titles (MARC21 246 $a). Added entries should also be made for other titles that users might reasonably assume to be the main title of the item. The Beatles' eponymous 1968 recording provides us with a well-known example; the title proper is simply *The Beatles* but the album is widely referred to as *The White Album.*[53] This latter title should be included in the catalog record if for no other reason than its sheer ubiquity in popular culture (Figure 18).

This example also illustrates the two most common MARC21 tags for title added entries for popular music.[54] For items with a collective ti-

FIGURE 18. Example of two types of title added entries: one in the 246 relating to the entire album, the others in the 740s for analytical title added entries.

110 2# $a Beatles. $4 prf
245 14 $a The Beatles $h [sound recording].
246 3# $a White album
260 ## $a Hollywood, Calif. : $b [Apple Records] : $b Mfd. by Capitol Records, Inc., $c [1995]
300 ## $a 2 sound discs : $b analog, 33 1/3 rpm, stereo. ; $c 12 in.
500 ## $a Also known as: The white album.
505 ## $a Back in the U.S.S.R. -- Dear Prudence -- Glass onion -- Ob-la-di, ob-la-da -- Wind honey pie -- The continuing story of Bungalow Bill -- While my guitar gently weeps -- Happiness is a warm gun -- Martha my dear -- I'm so tired -- Black bird -- Piggies -- Rocky Raccoon -- Don't pass me by -- Why don't we do it in the road? -- I will -- Julia -- Birthday -- Yer blues -- Mother Nature's son -- Everybody's got something to hide except me and my monkey -- Sexy Sadie -- Helter skelter -- Long, long, long -- Revolution 1 -- Honey pie -- Savoy truffle -- Cry baby cry -- Revolution 9 -- Good night.
740 02 $a Back in the U.S.S.R.
740 02 $a Dear Prudence.
740 02 $a Glass onion.

[Remaining title added entries omitted]

tle, MARC21 246 is used for titles associated with the whole item "whether or not the title is on the item,"[55] as in the Beatles example. However, for items without a collective title, tag 246 is used for titles related to the title proper, usually the first work named in the chief source of information. The former case is the one most commonly encountered in popular music cataloging, although catalogers working with cassettes and 45 rpm singles will sometimes encounter the latter. MARC21 740, on the other hand, is used as an uncontrolled access point only for "independent works contained within the item and for titles of related items."[56]

Added entries for works "contained within the item" are covered by AACR2 21.30M. Two methods for providing access to works contained within anthologies have already been discussed: through keyword searching used in conjunction with detailed contents notes (either basic or enhanced) or through enhanced contents notes that are included in the catalog's author and title indexes. Uncontrolled analytical title added entries provide a third method. Individual libraries need to determine which method best suits their needs, or which method suits their needs in specific instances. For example, one library might choose to routinely add enhanced contents notes to anthologies. A second library with different needs might use basic contents notes exclusively. Still another institution might decide to use uncontrolled analytics when there are less than a specified number of works on the recording, say 10 or 15, and rely on basic or enhanced contents when there are more than that. In any case, it is important that the cataloger has some understanding of both the local user needs and the catalog's indexing structure in order to make informed decisions about which fields to rely on for access.

Added entries for related works are allowed under AACR2 21.30G. It is extremely useful to users if catalogers include title added entries for recordings containing complete (or substantially complete) reissues of titles previously released under different names (Figures 8 and 19).

This allows users searching for the original issue to locate the reissue easily–and, perhaps, serendipitously–even if it has been reissued under a different title. Though this type of entry can certainly improve access to reissued works, it is always important to use judgement when assigning title added entries. For example, if added entries were made for every album title represented on a sampler or "greatest hits" recording, users searching under the name of the original album title would also (or instead) retrieve the sampler, even though the latter might contain only one or a few selections from the original.

Subject Access

Subject cataloging can be difficult even under the best of circumstances, when the thesaurus of choice closely mirrors the structure and

FIGURE 19. Title added entries for a reissue. In this instance, further research on OCLC turned up cataloging for the original issue under a different title than that stated in the liner notes; both titles are therefore traced as added entries.

100 1# $a Broonzy, Big Bill, $d 1893-1958. $4 prf
245 10 $a Trouble in mind $h [sound recording] / $c Big Bill Broonzy.
260 ## $a Washington, DC : $b Smithsonian Folkways Recordings, $c p2000.
300 ## $a 1 sound disc : $b digital ; $c 4 3/4 in.
500 ## $a Previously released recordings; "[m]ost of the material comes from a New York session ... released as [Big] Bill Broonzy sings country blues (Folkways 31005) [1957]"--Insert, p. 3.
740 02 $a Bill Broonzy sings country blues.
740 02 $a Big Bill Broonzy sings country blues.

terminology of the discipline being described. Under less than ideal circumstances–such as attempting to apply LCSH with its bias towards Western art music to popular music from around the world–the task can be exceedingly frustrating.[57] Library users looking for popular music are probably best served by combining a controlled subject terminology such as LCSH with some form of alternative indexing or keywords. The indexing/keywords aspect has been discussed in some detail above. This section will deal with providing subject access through LCSH.

An excellent starting point for understanding the principles behind music subject analysis is J. Bradford Young's introduction to the 2nd ed. of *Music Subject Headings*.[58] Young provides an overview of constructing headings for all types of music materials, including popular music materials, and discusses essential topics such as chronological subdivisions and access to non-Western materials. Another indispensable resource is *Subject Cataloging Manual: Subject Headings*[59] (SCM:SH) which compiles what were originally internal LC memoranda on the creation and use of LC subject headings for the benefit of the wider cataloging community.[60] The relevant instruction sheets from SCM:SH are also reproduced in *Music Subject Headings*;[61] catalogers will want to pay particular attention to H 1916.5, which deals specifically with jazz and popular music, and H 1917, which covers ethnic music and music with a national emphasis.

For most major American forms of popular music such as rock, jazz, blues, country, etc., LCSH works fairly well.[62] All catalogers with even a passing acquaintance with popular music cataloging are familiar with such headings as "Rock music," "Blues (Music)," "Country music," etc. These major headings–along with the catch-all "Popular music" and the headings "Popular instrumental music," "Jazz" and "Bluegrass music"–can also be subdivided by certain time periods. These subdivisions, however, are each individually established under the main heading and are not directly interchangeable. For example, a jazz recording from the mid-1920s would receive the heading "Jazz–1921-1930" but a blues recording from the same era would receive "Blues (Music)–To 1931," the subdivisions generally reflecting the historical development of each style. SCM:SH H 1916.5 provides guidance on the use of these headings, and instructs us to choose the period subdivision on the basis of when the music was popular or, if that is unknown, the date of recording. The instruction sheet further limits us to two period subdivisions; if more are needed to describe the item, they should be omitted.

In many cases headings other than the broad terms described above will fit the item more precisely. A jazz recording may more specifically be described as "Bop (Music)," "Dixieland music," or "Big band music." Country music might actually be "Bluegrass music" or "Honky-tonk music." Rock music encompasses a whole slew of related terms, including "Heavy metal (Music)," the now quaintly anachronistic "Grunge music," "Punk rock music," and many others. Frequently, searching LCSH or the online subject authority file for terms that exhibit a narrower relationship to one of the major headings will turn up a heading more appropriate for the item in hand.

Popular music headings do not routinely emphasize specific instrumentation the way art music headings do. However, there are exceptions. The Library of Congress has established headings that incorporate the medium of performance for certain genres commonly associated with specific instruments. These headings are not governed by the rules for pattern headings or free-floating subdivisions, and must be specifically authorized by LCSH. Examples include headings such as "Guitar music (Slack key)" and "Piano music (Blues)." Recordings of non-Western music that highlight particular instruments also occasionally receive headings of the type "[Instrument] music" in order to emphasize this aspect.

For jazz, SCM:SH H 1916.5 provides rather detailed instructions for bringing out the medium of performance. Recordings of solo instruments such as Sonny Rollins' *The Solo Album*[63] are assigned headings that reflect the medium of performance, in this case "Saxophone music (Jazz)." Section 1a. also instructs us, unfortunately, to assign the same type of heading to a recording of a "featured instrument" within an ensemble, e.g., a recording of a quintet led by a saxophonist and Sonny Rollins' solo jazz saxophone recording would both receive the same subject heading. However, according to section 1b. of the same instruction sheet, a recording of a solo instrument "accompanied" by a jazz ensemble requires a heading of the type "Trumpet with jazz ensemble."[64] A fuller discussion of the term "Jazz ensembles" is found in SCM:SH H 1917.5, section 3b.(7). This term is never used by itself ("Jazz" is used instead). The singular form is used only to designate a group of two or more solo instruments accompanied by a different ensemble (e.g., "Jazz ensemble with band") or to designate an accompanying group (e.g., "Guitar and piano with jazz ensemble"). Finally, vocal jazz music requires the heading "Jazz vocals."

Non-Western music poses considerable difficulties for most subject catalogers to describe accurately and consistently and, therefore, for users to find easily. Kaufman's report discusses some of the difficulties in applying LCSH to non-Western music, such as the scattering of music from one place throughout the subject file and the timeliness of LC headings, although LCSH has been improved considerably for non-Western music since 1983 when Kaufman's book was written. Kaufman also provides a list of LCSH subject headings classified by geographic area that might be helpful as a starting point for assigning headings to non-Western music;[65] however, this list, too, is now dated and should be used with caution.

Catalogers working with non-Western materials should certainly familiarize themselves with SCM:SH H 1917. This instruction sheet provides an overview of various approaches to take in order to bring out major aspects of this music. In general, one should consider providing access for the ethnic group from which the music derives; the individual religious groups responsible, if any; the genre, type or style of music; the language, for headings such as "Songs, Lingala;" additional headings for musical instruments, if necessary; and other headings such as topical headings, special types of dance music, or headings for featured instruments. For non-Western popular music, the most common access points from the list above are probably those for genre and language.

For catalogers unfamiliar with this type of music, the challenges concerning language and genre are manifold. Simply determining the language of a recording can sometimes be virtually impossible given the scanty and unreliable program notes that frequently accompany these recordings. Deborah Pierce in her essay makes the eminently sensible suggestion of getting to know local experts with special language expertise.[66] Failing this, however, the *Ethnologue*[67] can be useful for at least narrowing down the list of possibilities for a given country.

Another problem is that headings for specific genres, as noted above, are frequently lacking from LCSH, although new headings can always be proposed through LC's Subject Authority Cooperative Program (SACO).[68] However, before immediately resigning oneself to a general heading such as "Popular music–Algeria," catalogers should check to see if an established narrower term–in this case "Rai (Music)"–is more appropriate. It may still be desirable to include the broader heading in the record in order to use a chronological subdivision.

The LCSH heading "World music" should be used with care. The scope note for this subject heading specifically limits it to music that combines traditional rhythms from around the world with elements of jazz and rock. Thus, the term should only be applied to hybrid forms of music that deliberately mix disparate styles; it should not be applied to non-Western popular music styles indiscriminately the way it is frequently used by record labels and music retailers.

Finally, there are a few headings appropriate for certain popular music recordings regardless of genre or country of origin. The heading "Live sound recordings" pertains to recordings of events performed in front of an audience and recorded as they occur. "Demo recordings" is a heading used for sample recordings usually made by unsigned bands or artists and sent to record labels in hopes of landing a recording contract. The heading "Picture discs (Sound recordings)" can be used for recordings, usually LPs, with colorful artwork printed directly on the plastic recording surface. Lastly, the heading "Alternate takes (Sound recordings)" is used for those recordings–usually jazz, blues or rock–that feature multiple versions of individual songs that usually are not issued at the time of a recording's first release but only included in later reissues.

CONCLUSION

This paper has attempted to provide an overview of the cataloging process for popular music sound recordings, from the initial description of the item to the final assignment of subject headings and name and/or title access points. While isolated aspects of the process have been admirably covered in general elsewhere, little has been written describing the entire process applied specifically to popular music sound recording cataloging. Hopefully, I have been able to cover some of the most common problem situations catalogers might encounter when working with this material, and have provided a few suggestions for sources to turn to when further assistance is needed in this complicated, occasionally frustrating, but always rewarding task.

NOTES

1. For the purposes of this paper, "popular music" is broadly defined as including rock, country, rap, jazz, blues, etc., and also similar or related styles from parts of the world outside the United States. I do not include "folk" or traditional music in this discussion; this type of music presents another set of problems for the music cataloger, including but certainly not limited to its own problems of definition.

2. Cognizant of the fact that most short, convenient terms for distinguishing the notated music of the Western music canon ("classical," "art," "serious," etc.) from the generally non-notated, more commercially-oriented music designed for widespread dissemination and consumption ("pop," "commercial," etc.) are fraught with peril and bias, I also realize that I have to call them *something*. Therefore I will stick to the terms "art music" and "popular music," respectively, with the full knowledge that "art music" can be popular and "popular music" can be artistic.

3. Michael Gorman and Paul W. Winkler, eds., *Anglo-American Cataloguing Rules,* 2nd ed., 1998 revision (Chicago: American Library Association, 1998). Also available in: *Cataloger's Desktop* (Washington, D.C.: Library of Congress, Cataloging Distribution Service, 1994-). Quarterly CD-ROM.

4. *Library of Congress Rule Interpretations*, 2nd ed. 2 vol. (Washington, D.C.: Library of Congress, Cataloging Distribution Service, 1989-). Also published in: *Cataloging Service Bulletin* (Washington, D.C.: Library of Congress, 1978-). Quarterly. Also available in: *Cataloger's Desktop* (Washington, D.C.: Library of Congress, Cataloging Distribution Service, 1994-). Quarterly CD-ROM.

5. Betsy Gamble, ed., *Music Cataloging Decisions: As Issued by the Music Section, Special Materials Cataloging Division, Library of Congress in the Music Cataloging Bulletin through December 1991* (Canton, Mass.: Music Library Association, 1992). Also published in: *Music Cataloging Bulletin* (Ann Arbor, Mich.: Music Library Association, 1970-). Monthly. Also available in: *Cataloger's Desktop* (Washington, D.C.: Cataloging Distribution Service, 1994-). Quarterly CD-ROM.

6. Library of Congress, *Library of Congress Subject Headings* (Washington, D.C.: Library of Congress, 1975-). Annual. Kept current by: Library of Congress, *L.C. Subject Headings Weekly Lists* (Washington, D.C.: Cataloging Distribution Service, 1984-1994). Weekly lists since 1997 available online at URL: *http://lcweb.loc.gov/catdir/cpso/cpso.html#subjects.*

7. Library of Congress, *MARC 21 Format for Bibliographic Data: Including Guidelines for Content Designation,* 1999 ed., 2 vol. (Washington, D.C.: Library of Congress, 1999). The *MARC 21 Concise Format for Bibliographic Data* is also available online at URL: *http://lcweb.loc.gov/marc/bibliographic/ecbdhome.html.*

8. OCLC Online Computer Library Center, *Bibliographic Formats and Standards,* 2nd ed. (Dublin, OH: OCLC Online Computer Library Center, 1996). Also available online at URL: *http://www.oclc.org/oclc/bib/about.htm.*

9. Jay Weitz, *Music Coding and Tagging: MARC Content Designation for Scores and Sound Recordings,* 1st ed. (Lake Crystal, Minn.: Soldier Creek Press, 1990). A new edition is in preparation: Jay Weitz, *Music Coding and Tagging: MARC 21 Content Designation for Scores and Sound Recordings,* 2nd ed. (Belle Plaine, Minn.: Soldier Creek Press, 2001).

10. Most recently in Richard Smiraglia, *Describing Music Materials: A Manual for Descriptive Cataloging of Printed and Recorded Music, Music Videos, and Archival Music Collections,* 3rd ed., rev. and enl. (Lake Crystal, Minn.: Soldier Creek Press, 1997), 43-80.

11. Suzanne Mudge and D.J. Hoek, "Describing Jazz, Blues, and Popular 78 RPM Sound Recordings: Suggestions and Guidelines," *Cataloging & Classification Quarterly,* 29, no. 3 (2000): 21-48. This article also includes a useful bibliography for dating early jazz, blues, and popular music recordings.

12. *MARC 21*, 245/p. 4. Prior to 1993, catalogers using OCLC were allowed to omit the brackets from the GMD–they would be supplied automatically when cards were printed. This is no longer the case; see *Bibliographic Formats and Standards,* 2:23.

13. *AACR2,* 165.

14. Smiraglia, *Describing Music Materials,* 47-48.

15. Smiraglia, *Describing Music Materials,* 48.

16. Michael Erlewine et al., eds. *All Music Guide: The Experts' Guide to the Best Recordings from Thousands of Artists in all Types of Music,* 3rd ed. (San Francisco,

CA: Miller Freeman, 1997). Also available online at URL: *http://www.allmusic.com/index.html.*

17. One record label that does this routinely is Blue Note Records.

18. *Bibliographic Formats and Standards*, 0:32; the Library of Congress follows a slightly different policy, coding all new sound recordings as "stereo." (MARC21 007/04 code s) unless it is known to be otherwise, even if the term "stereo." is not included in the physical description area (electronic communication from Jay Weitz, June 15, 2000).

19. Smiraglia, *Describing Music Materials,* 51.

20. Charles R. Hildreth, "The Use and Understanding of Keyword Searching in a University Online Catalog," *Information Technology and Libraries* 16, no. 2 (June 1997): 52-62; and not just among library users, but among library staff as well, see Terry Ballard, "Comparative Searching Styles of Patrons and Staff," *Library Resources & Technical Services* 38, no. 3 (July 1994): 293-305.

21. Gregory H. Leazer, "The Effectiveness of Keyword Searching in the Retrieval of Musical Works on Sound Recordings," *Cataloging & Classification Quarterly* 15, no. 3 (1992): 15-55; Joy Tillotson, "Is Keyword Searching the Answer?" *College & Research Libraries* 56, no. 3 (May 1995): 199-206, also finds keyword searching in a general context reasonably effective; however, for competing views, see Hildreth, "Use and Understanding of Keyword Searching" and also Jonathan C. Marner, "Measuring the Success of Keyword Search Strategy in an Online Catalog," *Technical Services Quarterly* 11, no. 2 (1993): 1-11.

22. Leazer, "Effectiveness of Keyword Searching," 32.

23. Charles A. Cutter, "Rules for a Dictionary Catalog," in *Readings in Library Cataloguing,* ed. R. K. Olding (London: Crosby Lockwood & Son, 1966), 37.

24. Ibid.

25. Ralph Hartsock, *Notes for Music Catalogers: Examples Illustrating AACR2 in the Online Bibliographic Record* (Lake Crystal, Minn.: Soldier Creek Press, 1994), 165-351.

26. AACR2 6.7B19 treats this note as one of the last ones to appear in the catalog record; however, LCRI 6.7B19 instructs catalogers to make this note the first one.

27. Monica Shovlin, Director of Marketing for Sony Disc Manufacturing in the United States, telephone communication with author, Aug. 8, 2000.

28. The form or genre can also be included in the bibliographic record in coded form in the "Comp" fixed field (MARC21 008/18-19), if necessary in conjunction with the MARC21 047 $a field. The set of defined codes is limited, however, so the cataloger must often choose a code for a broader genre than that used in either the artistic form note or the subject heading(s). For example, the code for "Popular music" (pp) would probably be used for reggae, although the code for "Other forms not found on this list" (zz) is another possibility.

29. Compare, for example, the list of popular music styles collected by The ARChive of Contemporary Music found on their website at URL: *http://www.inch.com/~arcmusic/list.html*, with those found in the LCSH; my unscientific sampling of 100 ACM terms found only 24 matches in LCSH as either established headings or searchable cross-references.

30. The drawback of course is that a successful keyword search for "cool jazz" will *not* retrieve those records for which the genre term in the note area is "West Coast jazz"! As ever in cataloging, consistency is the user's friend.

31. For one example of the use of local subject access via the OCLC 690 field, and for a discussion of local name and subject access in general, see Mark McKnight, "Cataloging Local Popular Sound Recordings," *LLA Bulletin* 51 (1988): 71-75.

32. For an excellent, detailed bibliography of reference material for popular music resources, see Music Library Association, Bibliographic Control Committee, Working Group on Popular Music Sources, *Sources for Authority Work in Cataloging Popular Music,* 199-?, <*http://www.music.indiana.edu/tech_s/mla/wgpms/wgpms.htm*> (Nov. 10, 2000).

33. Specialized sources of information about contemporary styles such as rap, house, jungle, etc., include Sean Bidder, *House: The Rough Guide* (London: Rough Guides, 1999); Peter Shapiro, *Drum 'n' Bass: The Rough Guide* (London: Rough Guides, 1999); and Tim Barr, *Techno: The Rough Guide* (London: Rough Guides, 1999). A brief but useful online resource is: Bill Werde, "Talking Music: Sounds from the Dance Floor," *New York Times on the Web,* Mar. 13, 2000 <*http://www.nytimes.com/library/music/031300dj-intro.html*> (Nov. 14, 2000); this article provides an overview of 5 main types of dance music with sound clips and small discography for each.

34. Peter Gammond, *The Oxford Companion to Popular Music* (Oxford; New York: Oxford University Press, 1991).

35. Donald Clarke, ed., *The Penguin Encyclopedia of Popular Music,* 2nd ed. (London; New York: Penguin Books, 1998).

36. Colin Larkin, ed., *The Encyclopedia of Popular Music,* 3rd ed., 8 vol. (New York: Muze UK, 1998).

37. Patricia Romanowski and Holly George-Warren, eds., *The New Rolling Stone Encyclopedia of Rock & Roll* (New York: Fireside, 1995).

38. Ira A. Robbins, ed., *The Trouser Press Guide to '90s Rock: The All-New Fifth Edition of The Trouser Press Record Guide* (New York: Simon & Schuster, 1997). To be used in conjunction with the 4th ed.: Ira A. Robbins, ed., *The Trouser Press Record Guide,* 4th ed. (New York: Collier Books, 1991).

39. Lilian Roxon, *Rock Encyclopedia* (New York: Grosset & Dunlap, 1969); Jon Pareles, ed., *The Rolling Stone Encyclopedia of Rock & Roll,* 1st ed. (New York: Rolling Stone Press/Summit Books, 1983) is also useful for rock bands of yore.

40. Barry Kernfeld, ed., *New Grove Dictionary of Jazz* (London; New York: Grove's Dictionaries of Music, 1988).

41. Richard Cook and Brian Morton, *The Penguin Guide to Jazz on Compact Disc,* 4th ed., completely rev. and updated (London; New York: Penguin Books, 1998).

42. Paul Kingsbury et al., eds., *The Encyclopedia of Country Music: The Ultimate Guide to the Music* (New York: Oxford University Press, 1998).

43. Irwin Stambler and Grelun Landon, *Country Music: The Encyclopedia* (New York: St. Martin's Press, 1997).

44. Simon Broughton, Mark Ellingham, and Richard Trillo, eds. *World Music: The Rough Guide,* 2 vol. (London: Rough Guides, 1999-2000). Vol. 1 covers Africa, Europe, and the Middle East; vol. 2, available October 2000, covers Latin America, Caribbean, India, Asia and the Pacific.

45. Bruno Nettle and Ruth M. Stone, eds. *The Garland Encyclopedia of World Music,* 10 vol. expected (New York: Garland Publishing, 1998-). Vols. 3, 6-7, 10 forthcoming.

46. Stanley Sadie, ed. *The New Grove Dictionary of Music and Musicians,* 20 vol. (Washington, D.C.: Grove's Dictionaries of Music, 1980); also noteworthy is "Appen-

dix A: Index of Terms Used in Articles on Non-Western Music, Folk Music and Kindred Topics," in *New Grove,* vol. 20, 733-819. The 2nd ed. of *New Grove* is scheduled for publication in January 2001.

47. Mosaic Records, for example, a mail-order company specializing in reissues of jazz recordings, frequently includes several complete albums in one reissued set. The title of the reissue, however, is never the same as any of titles of the original albums and thus the original titles are impossible to retrieve in the catalog unless explicitly traced in the bibliographic record. Mosaic is particularly helpful in that they provide extensive session and discographical details for all of their releases.

48. Limiting in an online catalog is usually accomplished using the bibliographic record Type code (MARC21 Leader/06) rather than the more specific Physical Description fixed field (MARC21 007, especially MARC21 007/01 (specific material designation) and 007/03 ([playing] speed)); see *MARC 21* for details.

49. Deja.com, available at URL: *http://www.deja.com/usenet*, is a powerful resource for searching and explaining Usenet discussion groups on the WWW.

50. Smiraglia, *Describing Music Materials,* 56.

51. For example, AACR2 rule 21.23D1 defines popular, jazz, and rock music as music in which the role of the performer goes "*beyond* that of performance, execution, or interpretation" (emphasis added). This seems to imply that popular, rock, jazz, etc. performers are expected to alter the music substantially and inject more of their own personality and style into the performance than are performers of art music.

52. See Weitz, *Music Coding and Tagging,* 69-83 for a thorough discussion of input conventions regarding the 028 field and manufacturer's numbers.

53. The Beatles, *The Beatles,* Apple Records SWBO 101; remarkably, an Aug. 30, 2000 search for this title in the online *All-Music Guide* turned up five other albums with this title, but *not* the Beatles' recording. The album was listed under its true title with the common title following in brackets. Further proof that the world needs catalogers now more than ever.

54. Other relevant tags are MARC21 730 $a and 700 $t; the former is used if the added title is a uniform title; the latter, if the title is part of a name/title added entry.

55. *MARC 21*, 246/1.

56. *Bibliographic Formats and Standards*, 7:17; *MARC 21,* 740/1 puts it in more precise, if somewhat less intelligible, form: "This field is used for added entries for uncontrolled related titles and uncontrolled analytical titles."

57. See Harriette Hemmasi and J. Bradford Young, "LCSH for Music: Historical and Empirical Perspectives," *Cataloging & Classification Quarterly* 29, no. 1/2 (2000): 135-158 for historical context.

58. J. Bradford Young, "Introduction to the Structure and Use of Library of Congress Subject Headings for Music and Material About Music," in *Music Subject Headings: Compiled from Library of Congress Subject Headings,* compiled by Harriette Hemmasi, 2nd ed. (Lake Crystal, Minn.: Soldier Creek Press, 1998), 1-28.

59. Library of Congress, *Subject Cataloging Manual: Subject Headings,* 5th ed. (Washington, D.C.: Library of Congress, 1996). Also available in: *Cataloger's Desktop* (Washington, D.C.: Cataloging Distribution Service, 1994-). Quarterly CD-ROM.

60. Young, "Introduction," 2.

61. Harriette Hemmasi, comp., *Music Subject Headings: Compiled from Library of Congress Subject Headings,* 2nd ed. (Lake Crystal, Minn.: Soldier Creek Press, 1998), 30-69.

62. Although, unfortunately, the application of the term "music" is inconsistent in popular music subject headings; some headings include the term as part of the heading directly ("Popular music"), others include it in parentheses ("Blues (Music)") or even omit it altogether ("Jazz").

63. Sonny Rollins, *The Solo Album,* Fantasy OJCD-956-2.

64. It should be noted that there is considerable confusion in the OCLC database concerning the use of these two forms of headings. They seem to be used almost interchangeably, and this is clearly not the intent of the SCM:SH instruction sheet. Headings of the sort "[Instrument] with jazz ensemble" are perhaps more applicable to Western art music than to jazz (for example, Claude Bolling's suites or some works by Gunther Schuller), since it implies a more discrete division between the soloist and the accompanying ensemble than is rarely found in true jazz groups. (One could argue, however, that recordings such as those made by Miles Davis with Gil Evans fit the category of "solo instrument accompanied by jazz ensemble" and should be assigned headings of the type "Trumpet with jazz ensemble" rather than "Trumpet music (Jazz).") The problem lies in making the distinction between a "featured instrument" in an ensemble and a soloist "accompanied" by an ensemble. The assignment of headings would be much clearer for catalogers and patrons alike if headings of the type "[Instrument] music (Jazz)" were reserved for solo jazz music while headings such as "[Instrument] music with jazz ensemble" were reserved for music in which the main instrument was *either* featured or accompanied.

65. Judith Kaufman, *Library of Congress Subject Headings for Recordings of Western Non-Classical Music* (Philadelphia: Music Library Association, 1983), 40-46.

66. Deborah L. Pierce, "What Do You Do When Hotchiku Music Arrives in the Library?: Providing Access to World Music Materials," in *World Music in Libraries,* ed. Carl Rahkonen (Canton, Mass.: Music Library Association, 1994), 44.

67. Barbara F. Grimes, ed., *Ethnologue: Languages of the World,* 13th ed. (Dallas, Tex.: Summer Institute of Linguistics, 1996). Also available online at URL: *http://www.sil.org/ethnologue/.* The 14th ed. is scheduled for publication in September 2000.

68. See the SACO WWW home page at *http://lcweb.loc.gov/catdir/pcc/saco.html* for details on submitting subject heading proposals to LC.

Cataloging Non-Music Sound Recordings

Robert B. Freeborn

SUMMARY. Non-music sound recordings are a unique and often overlooked format with special characteristics that need to be considered in terms of bibliographic control and access. This article is intended to aid those catalogers who don't normally handle such formats by providing both a list of recommended tools and practical advice on all areas of the bibliographic record. *[Article copies available for a fee from The Haworth Document Delivery Service: 1-800-342-9678. E-mail address: <getinfo@haworthpressinc.com> Website: <http://www.HaworthPress.com> © 2001 by The Haworth Press, Inc. All rights reserved.]*

KEYWORDS. Non-music sound recordings, audiobooks, cataloging

When librarians talk about cataloging sound recordings, they are usually referring only to those materials featuring musical content. While this is completely understandable it is also most unfortunate, as there is a wealth of audio materials in our collections that contain little,

---

Robert B. Freeborn is Music/AV Cataloger and Military Studies Selector for The Pennsylvania State University Libraries. He earned a Bachelor of Arts in Music from Washburn University of Topeka, KS, a Master of Music in History and Literature from Kansas State University, and a Master of Library Science from Emporia State University (E-mail: rbf@psulias.psu.edu).

[Haworth co-indexing entry note]: "Cataloging Non-Music Sound Recordings." Freeborn, Robert B. Co-published simultaneously in *Cataloging & Classification Quarterly* (The Haworth Information Press, an imprint of The Haworth Press, Inc.) Vol. 31, No. 2, 2001, pp. 37-51; and: *The Audiovisual Cataloging Current* (ed: Sandra K. Roe) The Haworth Information Press, an imprint of The Haworth Press, Inc., 2001, pp. 37-51. Single or multiple copies of this article are available for a fee from The Haworth Document Delivery Service [1-800-342-9678, 9:00 a.m. - 5:00 p.m. (EST). E-mail address: getinfo@haworthpressinc.com].

© 2001 by The Haworth Press, Inc. All rights reserved.

if any, music. Novels, poems, theater productions, training materials, lectures, and interviews are just some of the non-music examples that have found their way to records, cassettes, and compact discs. In fact the first words recorded by Thomas Edison onto his phonograph were from the nursery rhyme "Mary Had a Little Lamb."[1]

If one's library contains a large centralized technical services department, then it is quite likely that the special formats cataloger will handle all non-music sound recordings. However, if each subject library at one's institution contains its own technical services department, or if one's library has a limited technical services department, then it is very likely that these materials will end up in the hands of a cataloger who hasn't been trained to handle them. The purpose of this article is to present both an overview of the cataloging process for non-music sound recordings, and to lend practical assistance to those unfamiliar with these materials. It will start with a list of recommended cataloging tools, and continue with a field-by-field examination of the MARC21 bibliographic record and their corresponding *Anglo-American Cataloguing Rules, 2nd edition, 1998 revision* (AACR2) Chapter 6 areas.[2] Examples of MARC21 records for non-music sound recordings are appended.

TOOLS OF THE TRADE[3]

In addition to AACR2, the *MARC 21 Concise Format for Bibliographic Data* <http://lcweb.loc.gov/marc/bibliographic/ecbdhome.html>, and OCLC's *Bibliographic Formats and Standards* <http://www.oclc.org/oclc/bib/about.htm>, there are two other weapons that need to be in the AV cataloger's arsenal. The first is Nancy Olson's *Cataloging of Audiovisual Materials and Other Special Materials*. This fourth edition of the unofficial AV cataloger's "bible" features several major changes including two new format sections (interactive multimedia and Internet resources), the addition of MARC examples for each format, and of course updates that reflect the latest rule changes. The second is Richard Smiraglia's *Describing Music Materials: A Manual for Descriptive Cataloging of Printed and Recorded Music, Music Videos, and Archival Music Collections*. Though this book's emphasis is on musical works, the chapter covering sound recordings contains a wealth of information that should prove equally useful for non-music sound recordings. One especially nice feature in Smiraglia's book is the following recommended step-by-step description of the entire sound recording cataloging process:

1. Technical reading of the disc and container, to select the chief source of information;
2. Transcription of the title and statement of responsibility area from the chief source of information; only some statements may be transcribed into area 1 of the description;
3. Transcription of the publication, distribution, etc., data; this will include the label name, which is not necessarily the same as the name of the publisher; this also will include transcription of the dates of release or copyright of the *sound*;
4. Physical description of the recording;
5. Transcription of series data if appropriate;
6. Creation of the label name and number note;
7. Making other notes as appropriate.

Finally there are electronic mailing lists that AV catalogers should consider using on a regular basis. These electronic lists allow one to converse with many people in many locations at once on topics of mutual interest. Three of the most important lists to AV catalogers are: Autocat: the library cataloging and authorities discussion group; MLA-L: the list of the Music Library Association; and OLAC-List: the list of the Online Audiovisual Catalogers, Inc. All three of these lists are excellent for asking cataloging questions, exchanging ideas, and keeping current on the latest bibliographic and authority rule decisions and interpretations. Each of these lists also has an online archive that allows persons to search all the previous postings in the hopes of finding the answers they need.[3]

SOURCES OF INFORMATION

Chapter 6 of AACR2 states that the chief source of information for any sound recording is the specific item itself (i.e., disc, tape cassette, tape cartridge) and its label. Label is defined as "any permanently affixed paper, plastic, etc., label as opposed to the container itself, which may have data embossed or printed on it."[4] If one is dealing with a multi-part work and the items and their labels don't provide a collective title, then one should treat any accompanying textual material or container featuring a collective title as the chief source. Interestingly, 6.0B1 states that one should "prefer textual data to sound data." Basically, the item's label (accompanying material, container, etc.) should be preferred over anything actually recorded on the item. Finally, just like all other formats, any information not taken from the prescribed sources must appear within square brackets.

FIXED FIELDS

Unique fixed fields for non-music sound recordings in MARC21 include the following:[5]

Comp (Form of Composition)

Always coded "nn" (Not applicable. Not a musical sound recording.)

FMusic (Format of Music)

Always coded "n" (Not applicable. This code applies to recordings only.)

LTxt (Literary Text for Sound Recordings)

[blank] = Item is a musical sound recording
a = Autobiography
b = Biography
c = Conference proceedings
d = Drama
e = Essays
f = Fiction (Novels, short stories, etc.)
g = Reporting
h = History (May include historical dramas, historical poetry, etc.)
i = Instruction (How to . . .)
j = Instruction, language
k = Comedy, comedy routines
l = Lectures, speeches
m = Memoirs
o = Folktales
p = Poetry
r = Rehearsals of any nonmusical productions
s = Sounds (Nonmusical utterances and vocalizations that may or may not convey meaning; for example, sound effects, natural sounds [i.e., bird calls].)
t = Interviews
z = Other types of literary text

Type (Type of Record)

Always coded "i." (Nonmusical sound recording.)

PHYSICAL DESCRIPTION FIXED FIELD (007)

Though there are eight basic sound recording formats (discs, cylinders, cartridges, cassettes, sound-track films, player piano/organ rolls, wire recordings, and other), each with their own specific physical description fixed field codes, the majority of sound recordings in one's collections fall into three groups:

Discs (Both 33 1/3 and 78 rpm)

007 s $b d $d b $e (m, s, u) $f (m, s) $g (d, e) $h n $i n $n (d, e)

$e - Configuration of playback channels

m = monaural

s = stereophonic

u = unknown

$f - groove width/groove pitch

m = microgroove [33 1/3 rpm]

s = coarse [78 rpm]

$g - dimensions

d = 10 in.

e = 12 in.

$n - capture and storage technique

d = digital storage

e = analog electrical storage

Compact Discs

007 s $b d $d f $e (m, s, u) $f n $g g $h n $i n $k m $m e $n (d, e)

[$e and $n - same codes as for Discs]

Cassettes (Standard)

007 s $b s $d l $e (m, s, u) $f n $g j $h l $i c $m c $n (d, e)

[$e and $n - same codes as for Discs]

STANDARD NUMBER FIELDS (02X)

AACR2 Section 6.0B2 states that standard numbers can be taken from any source available. While many catalogers are familiar with the 020 (International Standard Book Number [ISBN]) field, they might not have worked with either the 024 (Other Standard Identifier) or 028 (Publisher Number) fields. The first indicator of a 024 field states what type of number it is, and is usually marked "1" for "Universal Product Code [UPC]." The second indicator is normally blank. The twelve digit UPC code is then entered in $a without any punctuation between the digits.

024 1 022917025006

The first indicator of a 028 field states what type of publisher number it is, and there are three distinct possibilities:

0 = Issue number (Identifies the issue or serial designation as assigned by the publisher to a specific recording or side of a recording. Located on the label, container, or accompanying material.)

1 = Matrix number (Identifies which master disc that this specific recording was pressed from. Inscribed into the disc itself.)

3 = Other music number (Any music publisher number that isn't the issue or matrix number.)

The second indicator determines whether or not a note or added entry is generated by one's local catalog. The choices are:

0 = No note, no added entry (the entry is neither displayed in the catalog record, nor is it indexed by the system)
1 = Note, added entry (the entry is both displayed in the catalog record and indexed by the system)
2 = Note, no added entry (the entry is displayed in the catalog record, but it is not indexed by the system)
3 = No note, added entry (the entry isn't displayed in the catalog record, but it is indexed by the system)

The publisher number is entered into $a just as it appears on the item. The source of the number appears in $b. This publisher source should be taken from the label.

028 02 TC 1115 $b Caedmon

MAIN AND ADDED ENTRY FIELDS (1XX, 7XX)

As with any format, main entry fields (1XX) take their information from the chief source, while added entry fields (7XX) are allowed to take their information from any source. There is, however, one optional subfield that often appears on non-music sound recording bibliographic records, and that is the relator code ($4). If one's catalog can support the relator code, one might consider utilizing it as an added service to their users. This is a three-letter code that indicates the relationship between the entry and the item. Below are those relator codes from the *OCLC-MARC Code Lists*[6] that are most likely to be found on a non-music sound recording:

Actor (act) = A person who principally exhibits acting skills in a musical or dramatic presentation or entertainment.
Author (aut) = A person or corporate body chiefly responsible for the intellectual or artistic content of a work. This term may also be used when more than one person or body bears such responsibility. *Use for* Collaborator and Joint author.
Commentator (cmm) = A person who provides interpretation, analysis, or a discussion of the subject matter on a recording, motion picture, or other audiovisual medium.

Compiler (com) = A person who produces a work or publication by selecting and putting together material from the works of various persons or bodies.

Composer (cmp) = A person who creates a musical work, usually a piece of music in manuscript or printed form.

Director (drt) = A person who is responsible for the general management of a work or who supervises the production of a performance for stage, screen, or sound recording.

Distributor (dst) = An agent or agency that has exclusive or shared marketing rights for an item.

Instrumentalist (itr) = A person who principally plays an instrument in a musical or dramatic presentation or entertainment.

Interviewee (ive)

Interviewer (ivr)

Moderator (mod) = The person who leads a program (often broadcast) where topics are discussed, usually with participation of experts in fields related to the discussion.

Musician (mus) = The person who performs music or contributes to the musical content of a work when it is not possible or desirable to identify the function more precisely.

Narrator (nrt) = The speaker who relates the particulars of an act, occurrence, or course of events.

Other (oth) = Relator codes from other formats which have no equivalent in MARC21 or for terms which have not been assigned a code.

Performer (prf) = A person who exhibits musical or acting skills in a musical or dramatic presentation or entertainment, if specific codes for those functions *(act, dnc, itr, voc, etc.)* are not used. If specific codes are used, *prf* is used for a person whose principal skill is not known or specified.

Recording engineer (rce) = A person who supervises the technical aspects of a sound or video recording session.

Singer (sng) = A person who uses his or her voice with or without instrumental accompaniment to produce music. A singer's performance may or may not include actual words.

Speaker (spk) = A person who participates in a program (often broadcast) and makes a formalized contribution or presentation generally prepared in advance.

Vocalist (voc) = A person who principally exhibits singing skills in a musical or dramatic presentation or entertainment.

Writer of accompanying material (wam) = A person who writes significant material which accompanies a sound recording or other audiovisual material.

TITLE STATEMENT FIELD (245)

As alluded to earlier, the title should be taken from the chief source of information. If it is taken from some other source, make sure to place the title within square brackets and then list this source in a 500 note. Next comes the General Material Designator [GMD] in $h, which is "[sound recording]." As for the statement of responsibility (245 $c), AACR2 section 6.1F1 informs us that one should "transcribe statements of responsibility relating to those persons or bodies credited with a major role in creating the intellectual content of the sound recording . . . as instructed in 1.1F." In other words, only enter a personal or corporate name as a statement of responsibility if the person's or body's contribution to the sound recording goes beyond performance, execution, or interpretation. Otherwise, they should be entered in a note.

245 14 The phantom of the opera $h [sound recording] / $c Gaston Leroux.

511 0 Read by Jeremy Nicholas and Peter Yapp.

Whether you place them in the title/statement of responsibility or notes field, one should provide added entries (7XX) for each name.

EDITION FIELD (250)

AACR2 section 6.2B1 instructs catalogers to transcribe edition statements as listed in section 1.2B. If one isn't sure, section 6.2B2 redirects one to section 1.2B3.

PUBLICATION, DISTRIBUTION, ETC. FIELD (260)

Sound recordings, whether they are musical or non-musical in nature, are very similar to all other formats except for the information entered in the date of publication, distribution, etc. subfield ($c). Richard Smiraglia states, "since 1971 by international convention the symbol Ⓟ has been used to indicate the copyright date of recorded sound."[7] Thus a letter "p" replaces that of "c" to represent a copyright date:

260 Los Angeles, CA : $b Dove Audio, $c p1997.

If the recording is unpublished, then the only information entered in the 260 field is the date field ($c) in brackets.

260 $c [1980]

PHYSICAL DESCRIPTION FIELD (300)

The sections of the physical description (300) field for sound recordings appear in the same order as in any other format. The first section ($a) covers the extent of the item in hand (i.e., 1 sound disc (45 min.), 2 sound cassettes (120 min.), while the second ($b) gives other physical details. These details include things like type of recording (digital or analog), playing speed (33 1/3 rpm, 7 1/2 ips, etc.), and number of sound channels (mono., stereo., quad.). However for sound recordings, the third section ($c) differs greatly from those of other formats in two distinct ways.

1. Aside from sound track films, the dimensions of sound recordings are given in inches rather than millimeters.
2. Dimensions are *not* given for either standard sound cassettes or player piano/organ rolls.

PLAYING TIME FIELD (306)

OCLC's *Bibliographic Formats and Standards* provides the following definition for this field:

> The duration of a sound recording. Use also for the duration of the performance of a music manuscript or printed music if the duration is on the item. Use six character positions in subfield $a. The six positions represent the duration of a work in hours, minutes, and seconds. Use field 500 to enter duration information as a note. In such cases, you may enter fields 306 and 500 in the same record.[8]

Since the same duration information is usually present in the 300 field, however, one could probably omit the 500 duration field. (See Appendix 2, lines 14-15.)

NOTE FIELDS (5XX)

The participant or performer note (511) contains the list of all participants, players, narrators, presenters, or performers on the sound recording. Make sure to also make additional entries in the 7XX fields. The summary note (520) is commonly used for videorecordings, films, realia, etc., but it can also be utilized for non-music sound recordings. As the label indicates, this field should contain a summary of the item's content. (See Appendix 2, line 21.) It is probably best to obtain the summary information from the item itself, but one could also take it from the container or any accompanying material. If you are quoting information from one of these sources, make sure to cite it directly after the quote.

SUBJECT HEADING FIELDS (6XX)

The subject heading "Audiobooks" is the authorized term for any recorded books, no matter the format (i.e., disc, cassette). Since the heading is referring to the item itself, make sure to place it in a genre/form field (655). The source of term subfield ($2) indicates where one has obtained the genre/form term. The codes themselves are taken from the *OCLC-MARC Code Lists* (e.g., lcsh = Library of Congress Subject Heading).[9]

CONCLUSION

Bibliographic control of non-music sound recordings will greatly benefit those collections owning this rich source of information. This article should provide the kind of guidance necessary to create accurate and complete bibliographic records by those catalogers lacking the experience and/or knowledge required to describe non-music sound recordings.

SELECTED RESOURCES

Archives of MLA-l@listserv.indiana.edu, 2000. <http://listserv.indiana.edu/archives/mla-l.html> [Accessed: November 24, 2000].

Autocat@listserv.acsu.buffalo.edu–Archives, 2000. <http://listserv.acsu.buffalo.edu/archives/autocat.html> [Accessed: November 24, 2000].

Gorman, Michael and Winkler, Paul W., eds., *Anglo-American Cataloguing Rules, 2nd ed., 1998 revision*. Chicago: American Library Association, 1998.

Library of Congress Network Development and MARC Standards Office. *MARC Standards,* 2000. <http://www.loc.gov/marc/marc.html> [Accessed: November 24, 2000].

OCLC. *Bibliographic Formats and Standards, 2nd ed.,* 2000. <http://www.oclc.org/oclc/bib/about.htm> [Accessed: November 24, 2000].

OLAC-list@listserv.acsu.buffalo.edu–Archives, 2000. <http://listserv.acsu.buffalo.edu/archives/olac-list.html> [Accessed: November 24, 2000].

Olson, Nancy B. *Cataloging of Audiovisual Materials and Other Special Materials: A Manual Based on AACR2, 4th ed.* Dekalb, Ill.: Minnesota Scholarly Press, 1998.

Smiraglia, Richard P., *Describing Music Materials: A Manual for Descriptive Cataloging of Printed and Recorded Music, Music Videos, and Archival Music Collections, 3rd ed.* Lake Crystal, Minn.: Soldier Creek Press, 1997.

NOTES

1. Susan Love, *Thomas Alva Edison,* May 1996. <http://www.minot.k12.nd.us/mps/edison/edison/edison.html> [Accessed: November 24, 2000].

2. Michael Gorman and Paul W. Winkler, eds., *Anglo-American Cataloguing Rules,* 2nd ed., 1998 revision (Chicago: American Library Association, 1998), 160-180.

3. Complete citations for each list are included in the Selected Resources section of this article.

4. *AACR2,* 162.

5. OCLC, *Bibliographic Formats and Standards–Fixed Field Elements,* 2000. <http://www.oclc.org/oclc/bib/ffflist.htm> [Accessed: November 24, 2000].

6. OCLC, *OCLC-MARC Code Lists, Chapter 4–Relator Codes,* 2000. <http://www.oclc.org/oclc/man/code/relate.htm> [Accessed: November 24, 2000].

7. *AACR2,* 165.

8. OCLC, *Bibliographic Formats and Standards–306 Playing Time,* 2000. <http://www.oclc.org/oclc/bib/306.htm> [Accessed: November 24, 2000].

9. OCLC, *OCLC-MARC Code Lists, Chapter 5–Source Codes,* 2000. <http://www.oclc.org/oclc/man/code/source.htm> [Accessed: December 10, 2000].

APPENDIX 1. Cassettes

```
OCLC: 36968270       Rec stat:   n
 Entered:  19970527   Replaced:  19970527   Used:  20000917
 Type: i     ELvl: I     Srce: d      Audn:       Ctrl:         Lang: eng
 BLvl: m    Form:       Comp: nn    AccM:       MRec:        Ctry: cau
 Desc: a     FMus: n    LTxt: f      DtSt: s     Dates: 1997,
  1 040    JBU $c JBU $d UPM
  2 007    s $b s $d l $e u $f n $g j $h l $i c $m c $n d
  3 020    0787111074 $c $25.00
  4 024 1   022917025006
  5 028 02  82450 $b Dove Audio
  6 049    UPMM
  7 100 1   Adams, Douglas, $d 1952-
  8 245 10  Dirk Gently's holistic detective agency $h [sound recording] /
$c Douglas Adams.
  9 260    Los Angeles, CA : $b Dove Audio, $c p1997.
 10 300    4 sound cassettes (ca. 6 hrs.) : $b analog, Dolby processed.
 11 306    060000
 12 511 0   Read by the author.
 13 500    Unabridged.
 14 500    Digitally mastered.
 15 520    After his friend is accused of murder, Detective Dirk Gently races throughout
the universe with a group of eccentric characters to save both the day and the human race.
 16 650  0  Gently, Dirk (Fictitious character) $v Fiction.
 17 655  7  Audiobooks. $2 lcsh
 18 655  7  Fantastic fiction. $2 gsafd
```

APPENDIX 2. Compact Discs

OCLC: 40424295 Rec stat: c
Entered: 19981117 Replaced: 20000202 Used: 20000809
Type: i ELvl: Srce: Audn: Ctrl: Lang: eng
BLvl: m Form: Comp: nn AccM: MRec: Ctry: gw
Desc: a FMus: n LTxt: f DtSt: s Dates: 1997,
1 010 98-708784
2 040 DLC $c DLC $d UPM
3 007 s $b d $d f $e u $f n $g g $h n $i n $k m $m e $n d
4 020 9626341181
5 028 00 NA211812 $b Naxos AudioBooks
6 028 00 NA211822 $b Naxos AudioBooks
7 043 e-fr---
8 050 00 Naxos AudioBooks NA211812
9 049 UPMM
10 100 1 Leroux, Gaston, $d 1868-1927.
11 240 10 Fantome de l'Opera. $l English
12 245 14 The phantom of the opera $h [sound recording] / $c Gaston Leroux.
13 260 [Germany?] : $b Naxos AudioBooks, $c p1997.
14 300 2 sound discs (2 hr., 38 min., 57 sec.) : $b digital ; $c 4 3/4 in.
15 306 023857
16 440 0 Classic literature with classical music. $p Classic fiction
17 500 Naxos AudioBooks: NA211812 (NA211812, NA211822).
18 500 An abridged recording of the book.
19 511 0 Read by Jeremy Nicholas and Peter Yapp.
20 500 Compact discs.
21 520 Presents the story of an elusive and grotesque "phantom" who abducts a beautiful opera singer into the labyrinthine bowels of the Paris Opera. A dramatic search for the missing girl leads to the truth about her strange captor.
22 650 0 Phantom of the Opera (Fictitious character) $v Fiction.
23 610 20 Opera de Paris $v Fiction.
24 650 0 Opera $z France $z Paris $v Fiction.
25 655 7 Audiobooks. $2 lcsh
26 700 1 Nicholas, Jeremy. $4 nrt
27 700 1 Yapp, Peter. $4 nrt

APPENDIX 3. Discs

OCLC: 6723017 Rec stat: c
Entered: 19800917 Replaced: 19960625 Used: 20000905
Type: i ELvl: I Srce: d Audn: Ctrl: Lang: eng
BLvl: m Form: Comp: nn AccM: MRec: Ctry: nyu
Desc: a FMus: n LTxt: f DtSt: s Dates: 1960,
1 040 MZN $c MZN $d OCL $d DVZ $d LLM $d OCL $d IVC $d BGU $d UPM
2 007 s $b d $d b $e u $f m $g e $h n $i n $n e
3 028 02 TC 1115 $b Caedmon
4 092 813 $b Po
5 049 UPMM
6 100 1 Poe, Edgar Allan, $d 1809-1849. $4 aut
7 245 10 Basil Rathbone reads Edgar Allan Poe $h [sound recording]
8 260 New York, N.Y. : $b Caedmon, $c [c1960]
9 300 1 sound disc (56 min.) : $b analog, 33 1/3 rpm ; $c 12 in.
10 306 005600
11 500 Title from container.
12 511 0 Basil Rathbone, reader.
13 505 0 The cask of Amontillado -- The facts in the case of M. Valdemar -- The pit and the pendulum.
14 520 Three tales from the American master of horror. The first recounts an intricate and deadly tale of revenge, while the second examines the boundary between life and death. The final track tells a story of torture and its effect on the human psyche.
15 650 0 American literature $y 19th century.
16 650 0 Short stories, American.
17 655 7 Audiobooks. $2 lcsh
18 700 1 Rathbone, Basil, $d 1892-1967. $4 prf
19 740 4 The cask of amontillado.
20 740 4 The facts in the case of M. Valdemar.
21 740 4 The pit and the pendulum.

Videorecording Cataloging: Problems and Pointers

Jay Weitz

SUMMARY. "Videorecording Cataloging: Problems and Pointers" assumes basic knowledge of MARC 21 and the AACR2 cataloging rules for videorecordings. Not intended to be a comprehensive review of videorecording cataloging, it instead concentrates on areas that have proven to be problems for catalogers. Included among the topics discussed are sources of information, when to input a new record, special issues regarding music videos, DVDs and other videodiscs, colorized versions, letterboxed versions, closed captioning and audio enhancement, treatment of certain types of titles, statements of responsibility and credits, field 007, dates, numbers associated with videos, genre headings, locally made videorecordings, "In" analytics, statements of responsibility, and collection level cataloging. *[Article copies available for a fee from The Haworth Document Delivery Service: 1-800-342-9678. E-mail address: <getinfo@haworthpressinc.com> Website: <http://www.HaworthPress.com> © 2001 by The Haworth Press, Inc. All rights reserved.]*

KEYWORDS. Cataloging of video recordings, descriptive cataloging–rules, MARC formats, Anglo-American cataloguing rules

Jay Weitz is Consulting Database Specialist, Metadata Standards and Quality Control Divisions, OCLC Online Computer Library Center, Inc., MC 741, 6565 Frantz Road, Dublin, OH 43017-3395 (E-mail: jay_weitz@oclc.org). He received his BA in English from the University of Pennsylvania (1975), his MLS from Rutgers University (1976), and his MA in Education from the Ohio State University (1981).

[Haworth co-indexing entry note]: "Videorecording Cataloging: Problems and Pointers." Weitz, Jay. Co-published simultaneously in *Cataloging & Classification Quarterly* (The Haworth Information Press, an imprint of The Haworth Press, Inc.) Vol. 31, No. 2, 2001, pp. 53-83; and: *The Audiovisual Cataloging Current* (ed: Sandra K. Roe) The Haworth Information Press, an imprint of The Haworth Press, Inc., 2001, pp. 53-83. Single or multiple copies of this article are available for a fee from The Haworth Document Delivery Service [1-800-342-9678, 9:00 a.m. - 5:00 p.m. (EST). E-mail address: getinfo@haworthpressinc.com].

© 2001 by The Haworth Press, Inc. All rights reserved.

INTRODUCTION

For nearly a decade, I've had the privilege of presenting videorecording cataloging workshops to catalogers from Chicago to Tokyo. The workshops revolve around questions that users have posed to me in my capacity as Visual Materials format specialist at OCLC. Some questions recur regularly, others evolve as our familiarity with a particular video format grows or as new formats supplant older ones. Just as often, the cataloging rules of AACR2 and the bibliographic format of MARC 21 (and its earlier manifestations) change, and with those changes come new, modified, or different answers.

This article is based on the content of the workshops. Like them, it is not meant to be comprehensive but instead concentrates on areas that have proven to be problems; that have generated questions, calls, letters, and e-mails; and that have caused catalogers confusion. A basic knowledge of AACR2 and the MARC 21 Visual Materials format is assumed, as is at least a general awareness of Visual Materials cataloging. The emphasis is on trying to be practical, to answer the sorts of everyday questions that plague catalogers as well as the occasional surprise that one has never encountered before. Because of the practical emphasis, we will generally avoid re-arguing, for instance, the recommendations of the Music Library Association's Working Group on Bibliographic Control of Music Video Material concerning main entry or the (admittedly fascinating) philosophical issues of Work versus Expression versus Manifestation versus Item. Some of these topics will be touched upon briefly, however.

Please note that the original videorecording cataloging workshop includes some thirty full bibliographic cataloging examples as well as many reproduced video labels and containers to illustrate the points made in the text. Due to reasons of space, reproducing more than a few of them here is not feasible.

A BRIEF HISTORICAL DIVERSION ON AACR2

In its move toward an integrated catalog, AACR2 attempted to keep the treatment of different kinds of materials parallel as much as possible. This had not always been the case: In AACR1, the first rule in the chapter on motion picture cataloging (this was the pre-video era, after all) said "Enter a motion picture under title." Period. The end.

Now, basically the same principles in the rules apply to all materials. Of course, the end result is most often exactly the same (that is, title main entry) since videos are usually of such mixed responsibility that a title main entry is usually the proper choice. But catalogers reach that conclusion by going through the same thought process as for, say, a book of mixed responsibility.

SOURCES OF INFORMATION

According to AACR2 7.0B1, the first choice for chief source of information is the item itself, in particular the title and credit (opening and/or closing) frames of the video. Those frames should be examined if at all possible. Nowadays, many if not most catalogers will have access to video tape and DVD players, but be aware that this is not universally the case. AACR2 recognizes this by making the second choice for chief source of information the integral container (for instance, the videocassette) and its label (or in the case of DVDs, the disc surface).

The fact that some catalogers will be able to examine title frames and others will not should make the cataloger extremely alert for differences in titles. As a colleague of mine is fond of saying, publishers are "not well behaved" and so are not particularly concerned with the consistency of information found in different places on a published item. When you find different titles cited on different parts of the same item, try to account for them and their sources in field 246 and other notes, as appropriate.

The 1998 revision of AACR2 included a small but significant addition to rule 7.0B2 for prescribed sources of information. For the edition; publication, distribution, etc.; and series areas, the container became another of the explicit prescribed sources; information taken from prescribed sources does not need to be bracketed.

WHEN TO INPUT A NEW RECORD

Although these guidelines for when to input a new record are based on those found in Chapter 4 of OCLC's *Bibliographic Formats and Standards,* 2nd edition (http://www.oclc.org/oclc/bib/chap4.htm), they are based on AACR2 and LC's application of AACR2. As such, they may serve as an aid in decision making even for non-OCLC members. Always remember that even when a new record is justified, it is not required. You always have the option of using an existing record, as long as you are aware of the implications (especially for resource sharing) of using a bibliographic record that does not accurately reflect your holdings.

Many of the differences that justify a new record are fairly obvious: black and white versus color (including colorized) manifestations of the same video; sound video versus silent; different videorecording formats that play on different machines (VHS, Beta, DVD, etc.); dubbed versus subtitled versions and other versions in different languages.

Videos that are of significantly different length would justify separate records, but sometimes differences in length can be difficult to determine. Often, a video will indicate different lengths on different parts of the item, for instance, an exact length on the label and an approximate length on the packaging. Sometimes the indicated duration will bear little resemblance to the actual playing time of a video, a fact that may not be discovered unless the video is actually timed by the cataloger. Use judgment in all such cases, and if there is some sort of length discrepancy that may confuse other catalogers, it may be useful to point it out in a note.

Further on in this article is a more detailed discussion of some of the problems with dates on videorecordings. Here, let us briefly point out that bibliographically significant changes or differences in publication dates usually justify separate records. You must be careful, however, to ignore dates that reflect merely changes in packaging design. (These sorts of design copyright dates often explicitly identify themselves as such.)

Among the most troublesome differences that may NOT justify a new record are the choices made by different catalogers about video publishers. In the 260 subfield $b section of OCLC's "When To Input A New Record," one murky guideline says: "Absence or presence of multiple publishers, distributors, etc., as long as one on the item matches one on the record and vice versa" does NOT justify a new record. The intention of this guideline is to remind catalogers that it is often difficult to differentiate publishers, distributors, and producers of videos. This is so not simply because of the welter of often ambiguous information that may be associated with any given video, but also because the definitions of "publisher," "distributor," and "producer" can be so jumbled. One may need to compare information found in statements of responsibility, in the publication, distribution, etc. area, and in notes to determine if the item in hand has the same (loosely-defined) "publisher" information as a record found online. Just as an example, compare the different treatments of some of the same "publisher" information in the four record excerpts in Figure 1.

Some of these records may actually represent the same published item, but information was interpreted differently by various catalogers.

FIGURE 1. Typical Publisher/Distributor/Producer Disputes

```
▶245 00  Ozawa ǂh [videorecording] / ǂc a film by David Maysles
... [et al.]
▶260     [S.l.] : ǂb CAMI Video ; ǂa N.J. : ǂb Distributed by
Kultur International Films, ǂc 1988, c1985.
▶300     1 videocassette (ca. 60 min.) : ǂb sd., col. ; ǂc 1/2
in.
▶538     VHS; stereo, hi-fi.

*****

▶245 00  Ozawa ǂh [videorecording] / ǂc a film by David Maysles
... [et al.] ; CAMI Video.
▶260     [Longbranch, N.J.] : ǂb Kultur, ǂc 1988, c1985.
▶300     1 videocassette (60 min.) : ǂb sd., col. ; ǂc 1/2 in.
▶538     VHS; stereo hi-fi.
▶508     David & Albert Maysles, filming team ; Susan Froemke,
producer ; Deborah Dickson, editor.

*****

▶245 00  Ozawa ǂh [videorecording] / ǂc a film by David Maysles
... [et al.]
▶260     [S.l.] : ǂb CAMI Video ; ǂa [New York] : ǂb Sony
Corporation of America, ǂc 1988, c1985.
▶300     1 videocassette (ca. 60 min.) : ǂb sd., col. ; ǂc 1/2
in.
▶538     VHS; stereo; hi-fi.

*****

▶245 00  Ozawa ǂh [videorecording] / ǂc a film by David Maysles
... [et al.]
▶260     [S.l.] : ǂb Sony Corporation of America, ǂc 1988,
c1985.
▶300     1 videocassette (ca. 60 min.) : ǂb sd., col. ; ǂc 1/2
in.
▶538     VHS.
▶500     Videocassette of the Cami Video release.
▶508     Producer, Susan Froemke.
```

Tend to err on the conservative side in such situations by editing to reflect your item when in doubt.

MUSIC VIDEOS: SPECIAL CONSIDERATIONS

A reading of AACR2 Rule 21.B2e and its Rule Interpretation along with the "Music Videos & Popular Music Folios" section of LCRI 21.23C suggests that performers cannot usually be considered the authors for most staged music videos that ostensibly tell a story, because responsibility is so diffuse. Straightforward concert videos may, however, sometimes qualify for entry under the name of a performing group or individual, when responsibility goes beyond "mere" performance, execution, etc.

This is reflected, more or less, in the findings of the Working Group on Bibliographic Control of Music Video Material of the Music Library Association's Bibliographic Control Committee, published as *Cataloging Musical Moving Image Material* in 1996. The Working Group's draft guidelines, which were circulated in various iterations from 1992 to 1995, generated considerable debate and led to the formation of an American Library Association Task Force on Music Moving Image Materials.

In its cover letter to the guidelines, the MLA Working Group chose to emphasize four points in particular:

- Those performing "technical" functions are not to be considered when determining the choice of entry.
- Unstaged performances should be entered much the same way as would an equivalent sound recording.
- Collections of performances on video should be entered the same way as equivalent sound recording collections.
- Added entries for music videos should correspond to those for sound recordings.

All of this is in line with LCRI 21.23C, which brings music videos and sound recordings into harmony with each other regarding choice of entry. AACR2 Rule 21.23C treats sound recordings (and so videos) containing works by different persons or bodies, and that have a collective title. If there is one principal performer, the item is entered under the heading for that performer. If there are two or three persons or bodies represented as principal performers, enter the item under the first named, with added entries for the others. If there are more than three persons or bodies represented as principal performers, or no principal performer, enter the item under title.

AACR2 Rule 21.23D treats sound recordings (and so videos) containing works by different persons or bodies, but that have NO collective title. Rule 21.23D1a covers instances where the performer's participation goes beyond "performance, execution, or interpretation" (generally, music in the so-called "popular" idiom); these are entered under the principal performer. Rule 21.23D1b covers instances where the performer's participation "does not go beyond that of performance, execution, and interpretation" (generally music in the so-called "classical" or "serious" idiom); these are entered under the heading for first work.

In cases of doubt (and especially when intellectual responsibility is diffuse), the safe option is to prefer entry under title. In this context, it may be useful to remember the distinction between "mixed" responsibility and "shared" responsibility. Mixed responsibility is where different persons or bodies contribute to the content through different activities (for instance, an author, an illustrator, an editor, a composer, a singer, a pianist, etc.). Shared responsibility is where two or more persons or bodies perform the same sort of activity in creating the content (for instance, several composers, several singers, several instrumentalists, etc.). Remember the trustworthy "Rule of Three": Where responsibility (such as principal performer) is shared by more than three persons or bodies, enter under title.

DVDs AND OTHER VIDEODISCS

Those of us who are of a certain age will recall the struggle among the various videocassette formats that began in the 1970s. Sony's Beta system was introduced in May 1975. Japan Victor Corporation's VHS system appeared in mid-1977. These two half-inch home video systems joined the 3/4 inch system that was already used widely since the early 1970s in industrial, broadcast, and educational settings, Sony's U-matic system. VHS eventually won that battle, although many libraries still have videos in the other formats, as well.

Something similar, but less dramatic and less public, has been taking place over the past two decades or more in the videodisc realm. Once there were twelve inch grooved CED (Capacitance Electronic Disc) discs that were read by a needle or stylus; this format faded after RCA discontinued producing its SelectaVision players in 1984. From 1978 until Pioneer abandoned them in mid-1999, twelve-inch grooveless laser optical videodiscs were a mildly popular medium and are still found in many libraries. They came chiefly in two varieties: standard play CAV (constant angular velocity) discs and extended play CLV (constant linear velocity) discs. There were also other videodisc types that came and went over the years, but they needn't concern us.

Today's fastest growing videodisc medium is DVD, first introduced to the market in March 1997. Depending on who you ask and where in the history of the medium you look, DVD stood for "Digital Video Disc" or "Digital Versatile Disc," but now it is just as self-identifying as VHS (which originally stood for "Video Home System"). Visually, video DVDs are indistinguishable from audio CDs or from CD-ROMs. Technically, DVDs are similar to CDs but DVDs have a considerably greater capacity than audio CDs, are often two sided, and rely heavily on compression to squeeze all that information onto their 4 3/4 inch diameter.

In general, the cataloging of any videodisc medium doesn't differ much from the cataloging of the common VHS cassette except in a few details. The GMD is still "videorecording." They are identified in the physical description as "videodisc(s)" with their correct diameter in inches ("4 3/4 in." for DVDs, "12 in." for most other CED and laser optical videodiscs) recorded in the 300 subfield $c. The particular videodisc format would be recorded in field 538 along with any important sound, color, and/or other physical characteristics called for in AACR2 Rule 7.7B10 (see Figure 2).

Where DVDs need special attention is in accounting for all the supplementary data, in addition to the re-issued film, that is so often available on the medium. DVDs may include additional language data (subtitles and/or dubbing in several languages), alternate takes and endings or even complete alternative versions of the whole film (studio cut vs. director's cut, widescreen vs. "altered to fit your TV screen"), formerly deleted scenes, documentary material, theatrical trailers, interviews, commentary, production notes, and on and on.

Language data (including closed captioning, subtitles, and dubbing) need to be clearly stated in a 546 field and reflected in the 041 field when appropriate. You may use a formal contents note (505) when the presentation of the material lends itself to that method, or an informal statement of contents in a 500 note when it doesn't. In some cases, content information may be suitable as part of a summary (520) note. Whenever the information is available, indicate the date of the original

FIGURE 2. DVD Cataloging Example

```
▶Type: g   ELvl: I  Srce: d  Audn:       Ctrl:       Lang: eng
 BLvl: m   Form:    GPub:     Time: 121  MRec:       Ctry: cau
 Desc: a   TMat: v  Tech: l  DtSt: s     Dates: 2000,
▶040      XXX ‡c XXX
▶007      v ‡b d ‡d c ‡e g ‡f a ‡g i ‡h z
▶020      0790744805
▶028 40   65091 ‡b Warner Home Video
▶041 1    eng ‡b frespa
▶245 00   Network ‡h [videorecording] / ‡c Metro-Goldwyn-Mayer ;
director, Sidney Lumet ; producer, Howard Gottfried ; screenplay,
Paddy Chayefsky.
▶260      Santa Monica, CA : ‡b Warner Home Video, ‡c c2000.
▶300      1 videodisc : ‡b sd., col. ; ‡c 4 3/4 in.
▶538      DVD.
▶546      English, with optional French and Spanish language
subtitles.
▶546      Closed captioned for the hearing impaired.
▶511 1    Faye Dunaway, William Holden, Peter Finch, Robert
Duvall, Wesley Addy, Ned Beatty, Arthur Burghardt, Bill Burrows,
John Carpenter, Jordan Charney.
▶508      Director of photography, Owen Roizman ; editor, Alan
Heim ; music, Eliot Lawrence.
▶500      Videodisc release of the 1976 motion picture by
Metro-Goldwyn-Mayer.
▶500      Special features include interactive quiz game, hidden
menu page, interactive menus, theatrical trailer, trivia and
production notes, scene access.
▶520      A satirical look at the politics and power struggles of
television executives as a network news anchorman turns the
tables on the "ratings".
▶505 0    Side A. Network (widescreen version) (121 min.) --
Side B. Network (standard version) (121 min.).
▶650  0   Feature films.
▶700 1    Chayefsky, Paddy, ‡d 1923-
▶700 1    Lumet, Sidney, ‡d 1924-
▶700 1    Gottfried, Howard.
▶700 1    Dunaway, Faye.
▶700 1    Holden, William, ‡d 1918-
▶700 1    Finch, Peter, ‡d 1916 Sept. 28-
▶700 1    Duvall, Robert.
▶710 2    Metro-Goldwyn-Mayer.
▶710 2    Warner Home Video (Firm)
```

release as a motion picture or original broadcast as a television program (plus any other relevant data) in a note.

One other major problem area with DVDs is the issue of dates. Because DVDs are so often released with substantial amounts of new, rediscovered, or extra material in addition to the original film itself (trailers, outtakes, documentaries about the making of the film, interviews with participants or scholars, multiple versions or cuts of the original film, and so on), they should often be considered entirely new published entities in respect to the dates. That means, unless a DVD consists only (or chiefly) of the original theatrical release, consider the Type of Date/Publication Status (008/06) to be "s" and record only the date of the release in hand in "Date 1." You should continue to include a note stating the date (and any other relevant information) about the original release, as appropriate. It remains up to cataloger's judgment how much new or different material actually qualifies for this treatment. If the only new material is a brief, original trailer for the film in question, for instance, you may want to ignore it for the purposes of date coding. Disregard advertising such as trailers for other films or products that might be tacked on to the item.

Some DVDs (and some DVD players) include an indication that they will play only in a certain region or regions. This is represented by the region number(s) superimposed on a world globe.

1. U.S., Canada, U.S. Territories
2. Japan, Europe, South Africa, and Middle East (including Egypt)
3. Southeast Asia and East Asia (including Hong Kong)
4. Australia, New Zealand, Pacific Islands, Central America, Mexico, South America, and the Caribbean
5. Eastern Europe (former Soviet Union), Indian subcontinent, Africa, North Korea, and Mongolia
6. China
7. Reserved
8. Special international venues (airplanes, cruise ships, etc.)

Use field 506 to record any such regional restrictions.

For DVDs and other videodiscs that consist of moving images, state the playing time as usual in parentheses (in the form "XX hr., XX min., XX sec." as necessary) in field 300 subfield $a following the specific material designation (see AACR2 7.5B2). If the item contains more than a single substantive work (such as an accompanying documentary, for instance), spelling out the durations in a general or contents note may be more useful. When a DVD or other videodisc consists of frames of still images, give the playing time if it is stated as such, or optionally, give the number of frames, if that is available.

An excellent and frequently updated source of information about DVDs is the "DVD Demystified: DVD Frequently Asked Questions (and Answers)" Web site at *http://www.dvddemystified.com/dvdfaq.html.*

PHYSICAL DESCRIPTION

Durations of videos are stated parenthetically in the 300 subfield $a, in the form of "XX hr., XX min., XX sec." AACR2 Rule 7.5B2 refers back to 1.5B4, which says:

- If the playing time is stated on the item, give it as it is stated.
- If the playing time is not stated on the item, but is "readily ascertainable," give it.
- If the playing time is neither stated nor readily ascertainable, the cataloger may optionally supply an estimated time. LCRI 1.5B4 says that Library of Congress practice is not to apply this option of estimating.

Otherwise, do not indicate the time.

The most significant aspect of the physical description is the videorecording system (VHS, Beta, U-Matic, DVD), although this designation does not belong in the 300 field. This vital information goes in field 538, following AACR2 Rule 7.7B10f. Putting it in the specialized 538 rather than the former practice of using the general 500 field, allows systems to designate the 538 as the first note, thereby placing the video system information in a suitably prominent place. AACR2 Rule 7.7B states, "Give a particular note first when it has been decided that note is of primary importance."

COUNTRY CODE

For motion pictures and videorecordings, the Country Code (008/15-17; OCLC Fixed Field "Ctry") has traditionally been coded for the country of the original film's production when that could be determined from the names of production companies in the statement of responsibility (245 subfield $c). This practice is really a leftover from the days when motion picture films were the dominant format. In those mostly pre-videorecording days, there were a relatively limited number of copies of each film in circulation; those films were generally not for sale nor were they available in most libraries. Several years ago, there was a MARBI discussion paper that dealt in part with bringing the coding of this element in the Visual Materials format into line with all other formats (that is, the Country Code corresponding to the place of publication, distribution, etc. in field 260 subfield $a). Although the policy has not officially changed in MARC 21, for most published videorecordings, it makes sense to code for the Country of the videorecording's publication as stated in field 260 subfield $a. The codes for the traditional country or countries of a film's production may, optionally, be included in field 044 (Country of Publishing/Producing Entity Code).

COLORIZED VERSIONS

Colorization of originally black-and-white films was a vogue in the 1980s and 1990s that seems to have faded in more recent years, but such videos are still out there being cataloged. A colorized video and the original black-and-white version of the same video are legitimately separate records. The fact that an item has been colorized needs to be brought out in the catalog record, so be sure that the 007/03 (OCLC 007 subfield $d) is coded for color, and that the 300 subfield $b also indicates color. Depending on how the information is presented on the item itself, a "colorized" edition statement of some kind may be appropriate. Otherwise, certainly indicate the fact of colorization in a 500 note (for instance, "Colorized version of the motion picture originally issued in black-and-white in 1955"). In some cases, when there is a disclaimer on the item about the colorization process, a quoted note may be useful (for instance, "This is a colorized version of a film originally marketed and distributed to the public in black and white. It has been altered without the participation of the principal director, screenwriter, and other creators of the original film"). Optionally in some catalogs, a uniform title for the film with the parenthetical "(Color version)" or "(Motion picture: Color version)" based on AACR2 Rule and LCRI 25.5B, might also be appropriate. As with other sorts of alternative versions of materials, be extremely careful about dates for colorized videos.

LETTERBOXED VERSIONS

Letterboxing is a technique used in video publishing to fit the wide rectangle of a motion picture image into the much more square space of a TV screen. Over the decades, film studios have used a variety of "aspect ratios" (numerical representations of the width-to-height ratio of the film image) for theatrical films, including standards as narrow as about 1.37:1 all the way to standards as wide as 2.35:1 and even 3:1. Because the average television screen has a ratio of roughly 1.33:1, the quick and dirty way to transfer a film to video was a technique known affectionately as "pan and scan." Only portions of the original image would fit on a TV screen (hence the common notice on videos, and notes in bibliographic records, that read "This film has been modified from its original version. It has been formatted to fit your TV"). Letterboxing, also known as "widescreen" format, usually means reducing the size of a video image so that the entire horizontal span fits onto the video screen, leaving black horizontal bands above and below the image proper. It's sort of ugly, especially on small television sets, but does a better job of retaining the integrity of the original film image. (There is an interesting and graphic explanation of the issue on the MGM Web site at *http://www.mgm.com/mgmhv/letterbox/*.)

Letterboxed or widescreen versions are treated similarly to colorized versions (see Figure 3). Depending on how the information is presented on the item itself, a "letterbox" or "widescreen" edition statement of some kind may be appropriate. Otherwise, certainly indicate that the item is letterboxed in a 500 note.

CLOSED CAPTIONING AND AUDIO ENHANCEMENT

Closed captioning consists of special subtitles in the same language as the audio portion of the video, traditionally included for the benefit of the hearing impaired, although captioning has proved useful in other contexts as well. "Closed" refers to the fact that the captions are hidden within many standard television broadcasts and videorecordings and require a decoder or otherwise specially-equipped television or VCR to make them visible. Captions usually appear as white letters against a black background. Captioning was developed during the 1970s, with the first closed captioned broadcasts taking place in March 1980. Closed captioned videos were first produced beginning in 1981. Much less common are open captions, which are permanently visible as part of the video image without the use of decoding equipment. You may find considerable information concerning captioning on the Web site of the National Captioning Institute (*http://www.ncicap.org/*).

The presence of closed captioning may be indicated on a video either explicitly with words or by any of a number of graphic means, the most common being the "CC" symbol, the "accented TV" symbol, or a stylized ear with a diagonal line though it (used mostly by the National Film Board of Canada). When a videorecording is determined to contain closed captioning, this should be mentioned in a 546 Language note ac-

FIGURE 3. Letterboxed Version Cataloging Example

```
▶Type: g   ELvl: M   Srce: d   Audn: g    Ctrl:       Lang: eng
 BLvl: m   Form:     GPub:     Time: 134  MRec:       Ctry: cau
 Desc: a   TMat: v   Tech: l   DtSt: p    Dates: 1991,1955
▶040      XXX ‡c XXX
▶007      v ‡b d ‡d c ‡e g ‡f a ‡g i ‡h z ‡i u
▶020      0792805232
▶245 00   Love me or leave me ‡h [videorecording] / ‡c MGM ;
Loew's Inc. ; director, Charles Vidor ; producer, Joe Pasternak ;
screenplay, Daniel Fuchs, Isobel Lennart.
▶250      Deluxe letter-box edition.
▶260      Culver City, Calif. : ‡b Turner Entertainment Co. : ‡b
Distributed by MGM/UA Home Video, ‡c c1991.
▶300      2 videodiscs (134 min.) : ‡b sd., col. ; ‡c 12 in.
▶538      LaserVision (CLV), digital sound.
▶511 0    Doris Day, James Cagney, Cameron Mitchell, Robert Keith,
Tom Tully.
▶508      Photography, Arthur E. Arling ; musical director, George
Stoll.
▶500      Videodisc release of the 1955 motion picture by Loew's
Inc.; renewed in 1983 by MGM/UA Entertainment Co.
▶500      "A Metro-Goldwyn-Mayer Picture".
▶520      Twenties singer Ruth Etting is befriended by a racketeer
who pushes her to the top but drives her to drink and despair in
the process.
▶600 10   Etting, Ruth, ‡d d. 1978 ‡v Drama.
▶650  0   Musical films.
▶650  0   Feature films.
▶700 1    Vidor, Charles, ‡d 1900-1959.
▶700 1    Pasternak, Joe, ‡d 1901-
▶700 1    Fuchs, Daniel, ‡d 1909-
▶700 1    Lennart, Isobel.
▶700 1    Day, Doris, ‡d 1924-
▶700 1    Cagney, James, ‡d 1899-1986.
▶700 1    Mitchell, Cameron, ‡d 1918-
▶700 1    Keith, Brian, ‡d 1921-
▶700 1    Tully, Tom.
▶700 1    Arling, Arthur E.
▶700 1    Stoll, Georgie, ‡d 1905-
▶710 2    Metro-Goldwyn-Mayer.
▶710 2    Loew's Incorporated.
▶710 2    Turner Entertainment Co.
▶710 2    MGM/UA Home Video (Firm)
```

cording to AACR2 Rule 7.7B2. It is also a good idea to bring out the presence of captioning in a subject heading such as "Video recordings for the hearing impaired" (sh87000886).

Because it is fairly easy to overlook an indication of the presence of captioning, some libraries do not include this note in bibliographic records. Generally speaking, do not create a new record for a captioned video if a record exists for the same item that does not mention captioning. You may input a separate record only in clear cases where BOTH captioned and uncaptioned versions of the same videorecording are known to exist. This information may be found in an explicit note in a bibliographic record or in such sources as video publisher or distributor catalogs.

"Audio enhanced" is the generic term for videorecordings specially altered for the visually impaired by including narrated descriptions of visual elements that do not interfere with the standard audio portion of the item. The most common variety of audio enhancement comes from the Descriptive Video Service or DVS. DVS is a specific service launched nationally in 1990 by the WGBH Educational Foundation. DVS, with permission, reissues special editions of videos with scenery, action, body language, graphics, and other visual elements verbally described for the visually impaired. For broadcast DVS programs, special equipment may be necessary, but DVS videorecordings require no special equipment for the audio enhancements to be heard. You can find out more about DVS on the WGBH Web site at *http://www.wgbh.org/wgbh/access/dvs/.*

Because DVS and other audio enhanced videos are truly separate bibliographic entities from the corresponding "standard" video, a new record will usually be justified. The audio enhancement information may be input as an edition statement if it is presented as such on the item. If the information is not already present as an edition statement, a 546 Language note indicating audio enhancement would be appropriate, according to AACR2 Rule 7.7B2. Because the DVS organization (or other responsible entity) will be represented as the producer/publisher/distributor of this described edition, an added entry for that group will usually be a good idea. As with captioned videos, you should bring out the presence of audio enhancement in a subject heading such as "Video recordings for the visually handicapped" (sh93003552).

SUMMARY NOTES

Because one cannot leaf through a video in quite the way one can leaf through a book, catalogers have discovered that summary notes can be extremely useful for library users. Especially since the advent of keyword indexing in local catalogs as well as in union catalogs such as OCLC's WorldCat, these summary notes can be rich source of free text "subject" information. It is especially important to provide a meaningful summary when the title of a video is less than informative about the nature of the item. Summary notes belong in field 520.

TELEVISION "SERIES" AND DEPENDENT TITLES

Thanks in part to the imprecision of the English language, one of the more difficult videorecording cataloging issues to grasp is the problem of television series and other sorts of dependent titles. First, we need to make a distinction between the common notion of the television "series" and the bibliographic "series." A television "series" can be anything from a multi-part dramatization of a novel to a weekly sitcom to an ongoing regular program of unrelated hour-long documentaries presented under the banner of a "series." In the context of broadcast or cable television, these are all "series" in the everyday sense, but not necessarily "series" in the bibliographic sense.

Bibliographically speaking (according to AACR2), a "series" is: "A group of separate items related to one another by the fact that each bears, in addition to its own title proper, a collective title applying to the group as a whole. The individual items may or may not be numbered." For videos, it is important to distinguish between items that were, incidentally, originally presented as part of some television "series" and items that are being published AS VIDEOS in a series devised by the video publisher. Remember that you are cataloging the published video that you have in hand, NOT the television program. Admittedly, because of the notorious misbehavior of publishers, these distinctions are not always crystal clear.

In cases where the video publisher appears to be presenting the television "series" as its own VIDEO series, that series name may legitimately be treated as a bibliographic series in 4XX and 8XX fields, as appropriate. When the video publisher appears NOT to be presenting the television "series" as its own video series, mention the previous broadcast or cable manifestation in a note (for instance, "Videocassette release of a production originally broadcast as an episode of the television program The American experience") and make a uniform title added entry (730) for the related television "series." In all cases, be sure to check the authority file first for the correct form of the series or uniform title.

Somewhat related to this is the issue of titles proper for video publications of television series. Keeping in mind the distinction between television "series" and video publisher series, there are a few useful guidelines to follow. If the individual part or episode title is distinctive, it is usually preferred as the title proper. Generally, tend not to use the television "series" title (as 245 subfield $a) with a dependent element (245 subfields $p and/or $n) when it can be avoided. This practice is found in *Archival Moving Image Materials* (AMIM), which serves as the basis for many LC records. But remember that AMIM was designed specifically for the cataloging of archival materials, as its title states, and was not really intended to be used for most commercially available items.

Here is what to do about titles proper when the television "series" is determined to be also the video publisher series. If only a small number of videos are involved or it is a limited, finite series, and each item has its own distinctive title, prefer individual entries under each distinctive title and a series entry (4XX/8XX). If one or more episodes lack a distinctive title (for instance, the episodes are simply numbered or have titles such as "Introduction" and "Conclusion"), you may use the series title in 245 subfield $a with subfields $p and/or $n, as appropriate.

STATEMENTS OF RESPONSIBILITY AND CREDITS

LC Rule Interpretations offer considerable guidance in trying to decide whether to include particular names in the statement of responsibility (245 subfield $c) or in the credits note (508). According to LCRI 7.1F1, those individuals and bodies with "overall responsibility" go in 245 subfield $c, including producers, directors, and writers.

Those who are deemed to have responsibility for only one segment or aspect of the work go in field 508. LCRI 7.7B6 lists some of those generally included here, among them photographers, camera people, cinematographers, animators, artists, illustrators, film editors, narrators, voices, composer of the film score, consultants, and advisers. At the same time, the LCRI suggests omitting such persons and bodies as assistants and associates, production supervisors and coordinators, project and executive editors, technical advisors and consultants, audio and sound engineers, writers of discussions and programs, and all others making on minor or purely technical contributions.

Don't agonize over making exceptions to either of these LCRIs, especially when the particular type of responsibility is important in relation to the content of the work. For example, the name of a rock group or performer who stars in a performance video may be given in 245 subfield $c, even though responsibility is limited to the performance. Likewise in a dance video, the names of the choreographer, the composer, and the dance ensemble may be appropriate in the 245 subfield $c.

How these decisions should be reflected in added entries is outlined in LCRI 21.29D. In essence, any person or body important enough to be mentioned in the 245 subfield $c statement of responsibility should probably have an added entry–producers, directors, and writers, especially. The LCRI states, "Do not make added entries for persons (producers, directors, writers, etc.) if there is a production company, unit, etc. for which an added entry is made, unless their contributions are significant." Given the exceptions, this appears NOT to apply to most theatrical films, student films, or other films in which the personal stamp of the main contributing individuals might conceivably be seen. Frankly, I'm not entirely sure where this exception might apply. A somewhat clearer exception is that when a person is considered solely responsible enough under AACR2 to be the main entry on a video, don't trace other persons unless they share responsibility with the person named in the main entry or their contributions are otherwise known to be significant.

Added entries should be made for all corporate bodies named in the publication, distribution, etc. area. All featured players, performers, and narrators should receive added entries, with two exceptions: If the main entry is for a performing group, don't trace individuals in the group unless their name appears in conjunction with, preceding, or following the group's name; if there are many players, trace only those most prominent in the chief source of information. Finally, make added entries for interviewers, interviewees, lecturers, and the like who are not chosen as the main entry.

DATES

For Visual Materials, dates are among the most difficult and confusing pieces of information to determine. For one thing, the item itself often has different sources for dates including the video image, the container, the cassette or disc label, and any accompanying material. Further complicating things is the fact that associated with any single item may be dates for a number of different bibliographic "events" including the original production, the original release as motion picture, the subsequent release as a video, and the copyright dates of package design or accompanying material. This last is particularly vexing for catalogers. Video publishers behaving badly often redesign the packaging for a videorecording and include a new copyright date for the revised design (and sometimes identify the date as such), confusing catalogers into thinking that this date has some bibliographic significance. Generally speaking, except in the absence of any other meaningful date, these "package design" sorts of dates should be ignored.

Although dates that appear in the chief source of information (that is, the video image itself or the integral label) are generally considered the most important, other factors MUST be considered. Especially consider the historical date of the first products in the particular videorecording format.

- Betamax machines were first sold in May 1975.
- VHS machines were first sold in September 1977.
- DVDs first became available in March 1997.

Any date for a videorecording that is earlier than the availability date of the respective recording format CANNOT possibly be considered a "publication" date. In cases where you find different or conflicting date information associated with a videorecording, a later date from a unifying element such as container MAY be more important than a date appearing in the chief source. By all means, account for other important dates (date of original recording or production, date of original release, etc.) in notes as appropriate.

For purposes of coding Type of Date/Publication Status (008/06; OCLC Fixed Field "DtSt"), consider the release of a work with identical content in a different medium, for instance a film released on video, to be Type of Date code "p" ("Date of distribution/release/issue and production/recording session when different"). In these coding terms, such an item is not considered to be a "re-release," which would need to be in the same videorecording medium. As noted in the earlier DVD discussion, an item that includes substantial additional material aside from the original film itself should be considered an entirely new published entity in respect to the dates coding, and so have Type of Date/Publication Status (008/06) "s," the date of the release in hand in "Date 1," and no date in "Date 2."

007

Originally designed for machine manipulation, field 007 ("Physical Description Fixed Field") was restructured into its present form in 1981, although it has continued to undergo changes. Some older and minimal-level Visual Materials records may lack a 007 field. If you wonder about the usefulness of the 007 field, be aware that OCLC uses certain 007 elements in its record matching algorithms for both the Visual Materials and Sound Recordings formats and for microforms. For videorecordings, the first character position (007/00; OCLC 007 subfield $a) is coded "v" for videorecording. The most common second character position (007/01; OCLC 007 subfield $b) codes are:

- d Videodisc (including DVD)
- f Videocassette (including Beta, U-matic, VHS)
- r Videoreel

Character position three (007/02; OCLC 007 subfield $c) is now considered undefined and should contain a blank, a fill character, or be omitted, depending upon your system. The most common fourth position (007/03; OCLC 007 subfield $d) codes are:

- b Black-and-white
- c Multicolored
- m Mixed (use, for instance, when the 300 field indicates "col. with b&w sequences")

Particularly important to code is the fifth position (007/04; OCLC 007 subfield $e) for the videorecording format. The specific format will also be stated explicitly in field 538. The most commonly used codes are:

- a Beta (1/2 in.)
- b VHS (1/2 in.)
- c U-matic (3/4 in.)
- g Laser optical (Reflective) videodisc (including DVDs and other laser-read videodiscs)[1]

The eighth position (007/07; OCLC 007 subfield $h) contains the code for the dimensions, that is, the width of the tape. There is currently no specific code for DVDs and other videodiscs, so the "other" code should be used for those media.

- o 1/2 inch (Beta, VHS)
- r 3/4 inch (U-matic)
- z Other (including DVDs and other videodiscs)

The ninth position was added in 1986 for "Configuration of playback channels." This should be coded based on a clear indication on the item itself:

- m Mono
- q Quad, multichannel, or surround
- s Stereo
- u Unknown (use when configuration of playback channels is not stated on the item)

For videorecordings, remember that an explicit statement of the playback configuration belongs in the 538 note rather than in the 300 field according to AACR2 Rule 7.7B10a.

NUMBERS

028

Since Format Integration in the 1990s, the publisher's videorecording numbers go in field 028, using first indicator value "4" (see Figure 4). Although this first indicator was new with Format Integration, the 028 field was already familiar to those who catalog Scores and Sound Recordings. The structure of the second indicator remains the same for generating notes and/or added entries; but be aware that different systems may have implemented compliance with the second indicator differently.

- 0 No note, no added entry
- 1 Note, added entry
- 2 Note, no added entry
- 3 No note, added entry

For videorecording records in OCLC, data in field 028 are programmed to print or display, if so coded, as the last note, after 5XX fields but before any 020 or 022/222. Remember to include the name of the video publisher in 028 subfield $b. In OCLC, information in subfield $b does not print or display in the generated note. In OCLC, videorecording numbers are indexed like all other numbers found in field 028.

037

Prior to Format Integration, videorecording numbers were placed in field 037 ("Source of Acquisition"). This field should now be used only for numbers such as the distributor's stock numbers. When using field 037, remember to include the name of the distributor in subfield $b. Unless the numbers are explicitly identified as such or there is some sort of mnemonic involved, it is sometimes difficult to differentiate videorecording publisher numbers from distributor's stock numbers. Generally, consider numbers that are not permanently affixed to the videorecording (for instance, numbers that are stamped on an item or that appear only in a distributor's catalog) as stock numbers.

020

Even though the "B" in ISBN stands for "Book," more and more ISBNs (International Standard Book Numbers) are appearing on videos. Often, they are labeled as such, but that is not always the case. Valid ISBNs are input in subfield $a and any canceled or invalid ISBN is input in subfield $z. Remember that ISBNs currently have ten digits. Don't confuse ISBNs with the twelve-digit Universal Product Code (UPC) or with the thirteen-digit International Article Number (or European Article Number, EAN), each of which should be coded in field 024.

024

Beginning with Format Integration, certain standard identifiers that did not already have their own defined field were assigned field 024, "Other Standard Identifier." The first indicator identifies the type of standard code found in the field. In all cases, valid numbers are input in subfield $a, any supplemental codes following the standard code are input in subfield $d, and any canceled or invalid number is input in subfield $z. All numbers in field 024 are entered without hyphens or spaces.

Use first indicator "1" for Universal Product Codes (UPC). UPCs usually appear as a bar code with twelve digits printed below. Transcribe all twelve digits, including the first character (the "Number System Character" or NSC) that appears outside and to the left of the bar code symbol, and the final check digit character that appears at the bottom right outside the bar code symbol.

Use first indicator "3" for International Article Numbers (also known as European Article Numbers or EANs). EANs are thirteen digits long. Transcribe all thirteen digits, including the left-hand digit that often appears outside of bar code symbol.

FIGURE 4. Cataloging Example with ISBN, UPC, and Videorecording Number

```
▶Type:  g    ELvl:  I   Srce:  d   Audn:  j     Ctrl:        Lang:  eng
 BLvl:  m    Form:      GPub:      Time:  030   MRec:        Ctry:  cau
 Desc:  a    TMat:  v   Tech:  c   DtSt:  s     Dates: 1987,
▶040        XXX ‡c XXX
▶007        v ‡b f ‡d c ‡e b ‡f a ‡g h ‡h o ‡i s
▶020        1557590060
▶024 1      017447804139
▶028 40     TT8041 ‡b Twin Tower Enterprises
▶092 0      784.218 ‡b CAR ‡2 20
▶245 00     Carnival of the animals ‡h [videorecording] / ‡c
produced for the Church of Jesus Christ of Latter-Day Saints by
Bonneville Productions ; produced and directed by Stanley P.
Ferguson  ; written by Stanley P. Ferguson.
▶260        Tarzana, CA : ‡b Twin Tower Enterprises, ‡c c1987.
▶300        1 videocassette (30 min.) : ‡b sd., col. ; ‡c 1/2 in.
▶538        VHS, stereo.
▶511 0      Starring Gary Burghoff ; featuring Kathryn Roos ; music
performed by the Mormon Youth Symphony ; musical director and
conductor, Robert C. Bowden ; guest pianists, Barlow Bradford,
Kay Bradford.
▶508        Director of photography, Art Wilder ; executive
producers, John G. Kinnear, Stephen B. Allen ; animation,
Kinney-Vallas Productions ; editor, Stephen L. Johnson.
▶518        Filmed on location at the San Diego Zoo and Sea World.
▶521        Primary grades through junior high school.
▶520        Presents a lighthearted romp through the zoo where
children enjoy the animals, the music of Saint-Sa¨ens, and the
humorous poetry of Ogden Nash.
▶650  0     Suites (Pianos (2) with instrumental ensemble)
▶650  0     Animals ‡v Songs and music ‡v Juvenile films.
▶650  0     Zoo animals.
▶700 1      Ferguson, Stan.
▶700 1      Kinnear, John G.
▶700 1      Allen, Stephen B.
▶700 1      Burghoff, Gary.
▶700 1      Roos, Kathryn.
▶700 1      Bowden, Robert C.
▶700 1      Saint-Sa¨ens, Camille, ‡d 1835-1921. ‡t Carnaval des
animaux.
▶700 1      Nash, Ogden, ‡d 1902-1971. ‡t Poems. ‡k Selections.
▶710 2      Bonneville Media Communications.
▶710 2      Church of Jesus Christ of Latter-Day Saints.
▶710 2      Mormon Youth Symphony.
▶710 2      Twin Tower Enterprises.
```

GENRE HEADINGS

Field 655 contains terms from standard published lists that indicate the genre, form, and or physical characteristics of the materials being described, what the item IS rather than what the item is ABOUT. In the context of videorecordings, "form" is defined as a broad category of works characterized by a particular format or purpose, for instance:

- Made for TV movies
- Editorials
- Game shows

In the context of videorecordings, "genre" is defined as a narrow category of fictional works characterized by recognizable conventions such as theme, plot formulas, character-type, icons. Examples include:

- Film noir
- Disaster drama
- Science fiction

Traditional subject headings and genre headings can supplement each other in your catalog, if your system is able to deal with field 655. LC's *Moving Image Materials: Genre Terms* by Martha M. Yee (1988) remains the standard genre term list for film and video materials. Another useful document is LC's "Moving Image Genre-Form Guide" (1998; accessible at *http://lcweb.loc.gov/rr/mopic/migintro.html*). Form and genre terms from the *Library of Congress Subject Headings* (LCSH) may also be coded as 655s, in addition to any topical headings. It may be appropriate to assign headings for any special aspect of the videorecording (for the sight or hearing impaired, for instance) and/or to identify motion picture genres (such as "Feature films," "Musical films," "Rock films"). In field 655, the second indicator "7" points to the source of the genre/form heading that is specified in coded form in subfield $2. The code for *Moving Image Materials* is "mim," that for "The Moving Image Genre-Form Guide" is "migfg," and that for LCSH is, not surprisingly, "lcsh."

With personal name (600), corporate name (610), meeting name (611), uniform title (630), topical (650), and geographic name (651) subject headings, form subdivisions may sometimes also be useful. These form subdivisions are now coded as subfield $v, again giving indication of what the item IS rather than what it is ABOUT. As with the genre headings themselves, the form subdivisions are applied as defined by existing thesauri or subject heading lists. When used, subfield $v is usually the final subfield in the subject heading field. When a term usually considered a form subdivision functions instead as a topical subdivision, it should be coded as a general subdivision, subfield $x. Considerable guidance on which subdivisions are generally considered to be form subdivisions can be found in LC's *Subject Cataloging Manual: Subject Headings* and in the LC Authority File.

LOCALLY MADE VIDEORECORDINGS

Although these guidelines for the bibliographic treatment of locally made videorecordings are intended specifically for OCLC users, they were devised in consultation with the Library of Congress and should be useful in other contexts as well. For OCLC users, the full OCLC guidelines constitute one section of the "Special Cataloging Guidelines" in OCLC's *Bibliographic Formats and Standards,* 2nd edition (p. 39-40 in the paper version, *http://www.oclc.org/oclc/bib/3_7.htm* online). Verna Urbanski's *Cataloging Unpublished Nonprint Materials* (1992) can also be an extremely useful document in treating these sorts of items.

There are three major varieties of locally made videorecordings: those that are locally produced, those that are locally reproduced, and those that are recorded from broadcast or satellite sources.

Locally Produced Videorecordings

Locally produced videorecordings include such items as lectures, local events, video theses and dissertations, class projects, and the like. They ordinarily exist as a unique copy or in a small number of multiple copies for local or limited distribution. The cataloger must often supply a title according to AACR2 Rule 7.1B2. Because these videos should be treated as unpublished materials, the 260 field will contain only the date of recording, provided that date is not already present in the 245 field. If the date of the recording already appears in the 245 field (for instance in a supplied title such as "Lecture delivered on July 5, 1996 . . . "), it should not be repeated in the 260 subfield $c; in such instances, the 260 would be totally blank.

Locally Reproduced Videorecordings

Locally reproduced videorecordings include such items as copies of motion pictures, other videorecordings, or other kinds of visual materials that are made with the permission of the publisher or distributor for such purposes as preservation or circulation. You have the options of using and editing an existing bibliographic record or you may input a new record, provided that a record for a locally made copy in the same videorecording format (VHS, Beta, etc.) does not already exist, regardless of its recording date.

If you can legitimately create a new record, retain the title, statement of responsibility, and publication information from the original record and use the GMD "videorecording" in the 245 subfield $h. Code the 007 and 300 fields for the reproduced copy in hand, and indicate the videorecording format of the copy in field 538. Don't forget to add a note indicating the original format. Be sure to include a note that specifies the date of the reproduction, the fact that it was done with permission, and the entity granting that permission. Code the Place of Publication, Production, or Execution fixed field (008/15-17; OCLC Fixed Field "Ctry") for the original, but the remaining fixed field elements for the reproduction. For a video copy of another videorecording, code the Type of Date/Publication Status (008/06; OCLC Fixed Field "DtSt") as "r." For a video copy of a motion picture or other visual material, code the Type of Date/Publication Status as "p." In both cases, enter the date of the reproduction in Date 1 and the date of the original in Date 2.

Off-Air Videorecordings

Off-air videorecordings are licensed copies of broadcast programs or programs transmitted by satellite. All off-air recordings are considered to be unpublished materials; broadcasting does not constitute publication. You have the options of using and editing an existing bibliographic record for a commercially available version of the recording, or you may input a new record, provided that a record for an off-air copy in the same videorecording format (VHS, Beta, etc.) does not already exist, regardless of its recording date or broadcast station.

If you can legitimately create a new record, retain the title, statement of responsibility, and publication information from the original record and use the GMD "videorecording" in the 245 subfield $h. Enter only the year of the off-air copy in field 260 subfield $c. Code the fixed field, the 007 field, and the 300 field for the off-air copy in hand, and indicate the videorecording format of the off-air copy in field 538. Include a note indicating that the recording was made under license and a note specifying the name of the broadcast station or satellite service and the date of the off-air recording.

"IN" ANALYTICS

It isn't often that one will need to use the technique called "In" Analytics for a videorecording, but it may occasionally come in handy in what LCRI 13.5 calls "very special cases." When a component part that is physically contained within a larger bibliographic entity is deemed to merit its own bibliographic description, "In" Analytics may be used. In a sense, it is moving down one bibliographic level from the whole item to, say, a chapter in a book, an article in a serial, or one work on a sound recording that includes multiple works. In this case, it involves cataloging an individual program on a videorecording that contains multiple programs. The practice is outlined in AACR2 Rule 13.5. For OCLC users, the full OCLC guidelines constitute one section of the "Special Cataloging Guidelines" in OCLC's *Bibliographic Formats and Standards,* 2nd edition (p. 36 in the paper version, *http://www.oclc.org/oclc/bib/3_4.htm online*).

Because the host item must be identified in order to locate the component part, the bibliographic record for the component part contains both fields to describe the component and fields to identify the host. Include the following elements, as needed, describing the analyzed component part:

- Title proper, other title information, statement of responsibility (245)
- Edition (250)
- Numeric or other designation (for serials, 362)
- Publication, distribution, etc. details (260)
- Extent and specific material designation, when appropriate, in terms of the physical position of the part within the whole (300)
- Other physical details

Bibliographic Level (Leader/07; OCLC Fixed Field "BLvl") should be coded "a" for "Monographic Component Part." The Country Code (008/15-17; OCLC Fixed Field "Ctry") should be coded to correspond with field 773 subfield $d (otherwise, as "xx" for "unknown"). The fixed field dates should reflect field 773 subfields $d or $g, as appropriate. The 260 field is not usually included unless the data differ from what is stated in the 773 field. In the 300 subfield $a, use the construction "on 1 videocassette" or "on 1 videodisc," as appropriate. When an intelligible note cannot be generated from the 773 field (and so, its first indicator is set not to display a note), use the 580 field, "Linking Entry Complexity Note," to explain the relationship between the component and the host.

Field 773, "Host Item Entry," describes the host item in just enough detail to locate it, including:

- Name and/or uniform title heading for the whole item, if appropriate (subfield $t corresponding to 130; subfield $a corresponding to 110, 110, or 111, with subfield $s if needed to correspond to 240)
- Title proper (subfield $t)
- Statement of responsibility, in rare cases when needed for identification (subfield $t)
- Edition statement (subfield $b)
- Numeric or other designation (for serials, subfield $g) or publication details (for monographs, subfield $d)

The use of the control subfield $7 (which indicates certain characteristics of the linked entry) is optional, but since each code is position-dependent, if any one position is coded, all preceding positions must also be coded. The use of the control subfield $w is also optional; it contains the control number of the host record. OCLC users should prefer the OCLC Number (prefaced with the MARC Code/NUC Symbol "OCoLC") over the Library of Congress Control Number (LCCN, prefaced with the MARC Code/NUC Symbol "DLC").

If no record exists for the host item, OCLC users should input one along with the record for any "In" Analytics. A host item may be analyzed selectively; it is NOT necessary to analyze a host item completely. Note that the Descriptive Cataloging Form (Leader/18; OCLC Fixed Field "Desc") values for the host record and any component part records do NOT have to match.

COLLECTION LEVEL CATALOGING

You may think of collection level cataloging as the opposite of "In" Analytics. Instead of giving access to a part of the larger whole, collection level cataloging takes a cue from the archival community, moving up one bibliographic level from the whole individual item. It allows you to gather together items that have not been produced, published, or distributed together. Such a record describes a collection defined by common provenance or by simple convenience, and is intended to be the most comprehensive record for the items collected. Such a collection must be arbitrarily formed by the cataloging agency; the practice is NOT to be used for collections published as collections. Bibliographic Level (Leader/07; OCLC Fixed Field "BLvl") code "c" (Collection) may be useful for groups of associated videorecordings (especially those that are locally made, including lectures, plays, concerts, etc.) for which some level of control and access is needed but for which individual records are not desired or cannot be justified.

Although the LCRI for Rule 1.4F10 (March 1986) was long ago incorporated into AACR2, the "interpretation" that accompanied it can still be a useful aid in dealing with collection level cataloging. If an unpublished collection of published items is cataloged as a unit, give in the publication, etc. area only the inclusive dates of publication, etc., of the items in the collection. Apply this also to unpublished collections containing a mixture of published and unpublished items. If all the items in the collection are from the same publisher, distributor, etc., give the place and publisher in a note.

NOTE

1. Editor's note: On June 16, 2001 MARBI restricted the definition of "g" to Laserdisc and approved a new code "v" for DVD. Use of the new code may begin once the MARC21 update is published and the new value is validated in online systems.

SELECTED BIBLIOGRAPHY FOR VIDEORECORDING CATALOGING

Berman, Sanford, ed. *Cataloging Special Materials: Critiques and Innovations*. Phoenix, AZ: Oryx Press, 1986.

Daily, Jay Elwood. *Organizing Nonprint Materials*. 2nd ed. New York, NY: Marcel Dekker, 1986.

Fecko, Mary Beth. *Cataloging Nonbook Resources: A How-To-Do-It Manual for Librarians*. New York, NY: Neal-Schuman, 1993.

Fritz, Deborah A. *Cataloging with AACR2R and USMARC: For Books, Computer Files, Serials, Sound Recordings, Video Recordings*. Chicago, IL: American Library Association, 1998.

Frost, Carolyn O. *Cataloging Nonbook Materials: Problems in Theory and Practice*. Littleton, CO: Libraries Unlimited, 1983.

Frost, Carolyn O. *Media Access and Organization: A Cataloging and Reference Sources Guide for Nonbook Materials*. Englewood, CO: Libraries Unlimited, 1989.

Hartsock, Ralph. *Notes for Music Catalogers: Examples Illustrating AACR 2 in the Online Bibliographic Record*. Lake Crystal, MN: Soldier Creek Press, 1994.

Intner, Sheila S., and Smiraglia, Richard P., eds. *Policy and Practice in Bibliographic Control of Nonbook Media*. Chicago, IL: American Library Association, 1987.

Intner, Sheila S., and Studwell, William E. *Subject Access to Films and Videos*. Lake Crystal, MN: Soldier Creek Press, 1992.

Library of Congress. AMIM Revision Committee. *Archival Moving Image Materials: A Cataloging Manual*. 2nd ed. Washington, DC: Library of Congress, 2000.

Library of Congress. Motion Picture, Broadcasting, and Recorded Sound Division. *The Moving Image Genre-Form Guide*, compiled by Brian Taves [et al.]. Washington, DC: Library of Congress, 1998. (*http://lcweb.loc.gov/rr/mopic/migintro.html*).

McCroskey, Marilyn. *Cataloging Nonbook Materials with AACR2R and MARC: A Guide for the School Library Media Specialist*. 2nd ed. Chicago, IL: American Association of School Librarians, 1999.

Music Library Association. Working Group on Bibliographic Control of Music Video Material. *Cataloging Musical Moving Image Material: A Guide to the Bibliographic Control of Videorecordings and Films of Musical Performances and Other Music-Related Moving Image Material With Examples in MARC Format*, edited by Lowell E. Ashley. Canton, MA: Music Library Association, 1996.

Olson, Nancy B. *Audiovisual Material Glossary*. Dublin, OH: OCLC Online Computer Library Center, 1988.

Olson, Nancy B. *Cataloging Motion Pictures and Videorecordings*. Lake Crystal, MN: Soldier Creek Press, 1991. With 1996 Update.

Olson, Nancy B. *Cataloging of Audiovisual Materials and Other Special Materials: A Manual Based on AACR 2*. 4th ed., edited by Sheila S. Intner and Edward Swanson. DeKalb, IL: Minnesota Scholarly Press, 1998.

Olson, Nancy B. *Cataloger's Guide to MARC Coding and Tagging for Audiovisual Material*. DeKalb, IL: Minnesota Scholarly Press, 1993.

Rogers, JoAnn V., and Saye, Jerry D. *Nonprint Cataloging for Multimedia Collections: A Guide Based on AACR 2*. 2nd ed. Littleton, CO: Libraries Unlimited, 1987.

Smiraglia, Richard P. *Describing Music Materials: A Manual for Descriptive Cataloging of Printed and Recorded Music, Music Videos, and Archival Music Collec-*

tions for Use with AACR2 and APPM. 3rd ed., rev. and enl. with the assistance of Taras Pavlovsky. Lake Crystal, MN: Soldier Creek Press, 1997.

Urbanski, Verna. *Cataloging Unpublished Nonprint Materials: A Manual of Suggestions, Comments, and Examples*. Lake Crystal, MN: Soldier Creek Press, 1992.

Weitz, Jay. *Music Coding and Tagging: MARC 21 Content Designation for Scores and Sound Recordings*. 2nd ed. Belle Plaine, MN: Soldier Creek Press, 2001.

Yee, Martha M. *Moving Image Materials: Genre Terms*. 1st ed. Washington, DC: Library of Congress, 1988.

The Microcomputer Revolution

Ann M. Sandberg-Fox

SUMMARY. With the introduction of the microcomputer in the 1980s, a revolution of sorts was initiated. In libraries this was evidenced by the acquisition of personal computers and the software to run on them. All that catalogers needed were cataloging rules and a MARC format to ensure their bibliographic control. However, little did catalogers realize they were dealing with an industry that introduced rapid technological changes, which effected continual revision of existing rules and the formulation of special guidelines to deal with the industry's innovative products. This article focuses on the attempts of libraries and organized cataloging groups to develop the Chapter 9 descriptive cataloging rules in *AACR2;* it highlights selected events and includes cataloging examples that illustrate the evolution of the chapter. *[Article copies available for a fee from The Haworth Document Delivery Service: 1-800-342-9678. E-mail address: <getinfo@haworthpressinc.com> Website: <http://www.HaworthPress.com> © 2001 by The Haworth Press, Inc. All rights reserved.]*

KEYWORDS. Cataloging of microcomputer software, descriptive cataloging–rules, Anglo-American cataloguing rules, Chapter 9, computer files, electronic resources

---

Ann M. Sandberg-Fox is a cataloging consultant in Fairfax, VT (E-mail: afox@globalnetisp.net). She was a member of the MARC Machine-Readable Data Files Format Working Group, as well as a member of the ALA ALCTS CC:DA task forces that were instrumental in developing guidelines for describing microcomputer software and interactive multimedia. She was also a member of the task force for harmonizing *International Standard Bibliographic Description for Electronic Resources ISBD(ER)* with Chapter 9 of *AACR2,* and served as the principal editor of the *ISBD(ER).*

[Haworth co-indexing entry note]: "The Microcomputer Revolution." Sandberg-Fox, Ann M. Co-published simultaneously in *Cataloging & Classification Quarterly* (The Haworth Information Press, an imprint of The Haworth Press, Inc.) Vol. 31, No. 2, 2001, pp. 85-99; and: *The Audiovisual Cataloging Current* (ed: Sandra K. Roe) The Haworth Information Press, an imprint of The Haworth Press, Inc., 2001, pp. 85-99. Single or multiple copies of this article are available for a fee from The Haworth Document Delivery Service [1-800-342-9678, 9:00 a.m. - 5:00 p.m. (EST). E-mail address: getinfo@haworthpressinc.com].

© 2001 by The Haworth Press, Inc. All rights reserved.

THE BEGINNING

Some twenty-five seemingly antediluvian years ago before the advent of the Internet and the World Wide Web, a few academic and research libraries had started to acquire mainframe data and program files, which in the parlance of the time were called "machine-readable data files" or MRDF. These files, for the most part, consisted of government-generated data, such as U.S. Census data, that were issued commercially or locally on magnetic tape for eventual transfer to other physical carriers that accommodated a particular institution's computer system or specialized research needs.

As with earlier technologies, such as films, microforms, and sound recordings, for instance, the problem of providing for the bibliographic control of MRDF was a primary concern. Could cataloging rules be developed and formulated to describe these materials? Yes, there had already been two attempts by the Association of Educational Communications and Technology and the Canadian Library Association, respectively, to include rules in their cataloging manuals for nonprint materials. However, responsibility for establishing principles and rules that would be compatible with *AACR* or its proposed revision was attributable to the formation and extensive work of the ALA Resources and Technical Services Division's (RTSD) Subcommittee on Rules for Cataloging Machine-Readable Data Files. This subcommittee, established in 1970, conducted its work over a five-year period, concluding with a final report submitted in Jan. 1976. Specific findings of the report were incorporated in Chapter 9, which was a new chapter added to Part I of the *Anglo-American Cataloguing Rules,* 2nd ed. *(AACR2)* (ALA, 1978).

Another issue in providing for the bibliographic control of MRDF was the compilation of a MARC format. Specialized formats, for instance, had already been compiled for music and maps. Could one be compiled within a timely framework for catalogers to use in creating catalog records applying the new *AACR2* Chapter 9 rules?

The response from the Library of Congress (LC) Network Development Office was "yes" along with an added bonus; unlike other specialized formats, the LC Network Development Office designed the MRDF format to incorporate multiple levels of information associated with a variety of products. In addition to automated catalog records, these included data inventories, sales catalogs, and union catalogs. Work on the MRDF format was initiated in 1979 and approved by MARBI in 1981. With cataloging rules and a MARC format in place, the bibliographic control of MRDF was assured, or so it seemed. What was not foreseen or could be anticipated were the rapid technological changes that were to occur throughout the century's remaining decades, effecting what might be described as two distinct revolutions–the microcomputer or PC revolution, which started in the early 1980s and continued throughout the decade and into the early 90s, followed by the Internet/Web virtual revolution, which started in the early 1990s and continues into this new millennium. The impact of these so-called revolutions from the library perspective of cataloging and, more broadly, from the perspective of bibliographic control measures, was such that the editor of this volume felt there was a need to discuss each topic separately. This article, therefore, will focus on the microcomputer revolution, taking into consideration the introduction of microcomputers in libraries and the attempts of libraries and organized groups to develop cataloging rules to describe the files that run on them. For the cataloging of Internet resources, see Nancy Olson's article, "Cataloging Remote Electronic Resources," in this publication. The following account highlights selected events and is not intended to be comprehensive. For a more complete history of the *AACR2* Chapter 9 rules and their evolution, the reader is encouraged to consult the references at the end of the article.

MICROCOMPUTERS AND THE NEW CHAPTER 9

With the introduction of the microcomputer in the 1980s, libraries began to acquire the machines and the software designed to run on them. However, unlike the few research and academic libraries acquiring mainframe data and programs, there were a considerable number of these libraries, many of which were school and public libraries. Much to their dismay, they discovered that the new Chapter 9 cataloging rules were not relevant for practical application to commercially produced software issued on floppy disks. Particularly contentious was rule 9.5, which called for the cataloger to formulate a "file description" rather than a physical description. Since, in the case of mainframe data and programs, the physical carrier was considered temporary and changeable, as noted earlier, the rule mandated that a description of the file or intellectual work be formulated in place of a physical description. If the physical carrier were to be identified, it would be given in the note area of the catalog record. Equally disconcerting was the general material designation (GMD) "machine-readable data file." Not only was it long, but considered confusing and misleading. The term "machine-readable," as originally conceived, embraced early data processing machines and optical character recognition (OCR) devices as well as the computer. The term "data file" embraced a broad definition that included any information, including the data stored in machine-readable form and the programs used to process it. Other aggravations included the recognition of an "adequate internal user label" as the chief source of information and, in its absence, the use of the documentation issued by the creator or producer of the file; the lack of rules for describing various physical carriers; and the lack of technical notes pertaining to system requirements that were so critical at the time for patrons selecting and using this material.

How best to resolve the problems and issues associated with the acquisition and use of this new generation of computers? The emphatic response of the national cataloging community was to provide guidance in the form of either new or revised cataloging rules. Already some school librarians had responded with the development of local guidelines for processing and incorporating microcomputer software in their collections. However, guidance at the national level was provided through the Cataloging Committee: Description and Access (CC:DA), which under the aegis of the Cataloging and Classification Section of RTSD, appointed a task force in 1983 to review Chapter 9 and identify specific problems and/or problem areas that needed to be addressed. After extensive deliberations, the task force submitted its final report, which resulted in the publication: *Guidelines for Using AACR2 Chapter 9 for Cataloging Microcomputer Software* (ALA, 1984), hereafter referred to as the *Guidelines*.

GUIDELINES FOR MICROCOMPUTER SOFTWARE

Although worded as mandated instructions, the *Guidelines* were optional; more importantly, they were not to serve as a substitute for Chapter 9 but, rather, to be used in conjunction with those rules, so that catalogers applying either or both sets of rules would conform to the national standard for cataloging. With two notable exceptions, the *Guidelines* received broad national acceptance by catalogers describing microcomputer files. The exceptions were the GMD and the file description (9.5); no consensus could be reached on either of these issues. Thus "machine-readable data file" was to continue in use, at least for the time being. In the case of the file description, a compromise was reached: the file description would be retained with the cataloger having the option to include a physical description of the carrier, e.g.:

> 1 program file on 1 computer disk

Additional options allowed for expanding the physical description to include the designation of sound and color, if appropriate, and dimensions, e.g.:

> 2 program files on 1 computer disk: sd., col. ; 8 in.

The following example illustrates the application of the *Guidelines* to a software title (Figure 1).

Experimental use of the *Guidelines* in the next couple of years reinforced the dissatisfaction of catalogers with these issues. Why not adopt a shorter, more relevant GMD or, for that matter, alternative GMDs that the cataloger could select to best identify the particular microcomputer file, e.g., "computer software" for system and application programs or "computer data" for census and survey data? And why not give a physical description in rule 9.5 as is the case with materials in the other special chapters in Part I of *AACR2?* Further, new physical carriers were being introduced at the time. What were mostly 8 inch floppy or mag-

FIGURE 1. Example of the *Guidelines for Using AACR2 Chapter 9 to Catalog Microcomputer Software*

Brumbaugh, Ken.
Minnesota agriculture [machine-readable data file] / author, Ken Brumbaugh. -- Version 8/20/79, Last update 80/9/29. -- St. Paul, Minn. : Minnesota Educational Computing Consortium, c1980.
1 program file on 1 computer disk: col. ; 5 1/4 in. -- (Minnesota Educational Computing Consortium social studies ; v. 2)

System requirements: Apple II; DOS 3.3; Applesoft; color TV monitor (preferred)
File name: Minnag.
Developed for the MECC Timeshare System, with adaptation for the Apple II by MECC staff.
Summary: An information retrieval program used to show geography as a determiner in the social and economic life of an area.
1. Agriculture--Minnesota. 1. Information storage and retrieval system. I. Minnesota Educational Computing Consortium. II. MECC Timeshare System. III. Title. IV. Title: Minnag. V. Series.

netic disks when the *Guidelines* were published had been superseded by 5 1/4 inch disks. The computer industry, meanwhile, was promising even smaller 3 1/2 inch floppy disks.

With the revision of *AACR2* which was then under way, the Joint Steering Committee for Revision of *AACR* (JSC) decided to include a revised Chapter 9, taking into consideration the existing rules and the *Guidelines,* along with the draft report of the Library Association/British Library Committee on *AACR2* entitled: *Study of Cataloging Computer Software: Applying AACR2 to Microcomputer Software* (British Library, 1984), and input from the Working Group on the International Standard Bibliographic Description for Machine-Readable Data Files, later renamed the *ISBD(CF)*. Subsequently, it published an offprint of a preliminary draft of the revised chapter rules: *Anglo-American Cataloguing Rules, second edition. Chapter 9, Computer Files* (ALA, 1987) with the intent of including a final version in the revised *AACR2,* which was scheduled to be published in 1988.

PRELIMINARY DRAFT OF REVISED CHAPTER 9

The preliminary draft introduced several significant changes, which served to establish the conceptual framework that was carried over in the final version included in the revised *AACR2* and in the subsequent 1998 revision of *AACR2* presently in use. The most significant change, or at least the most obvious, was in the title of the chapter from "Machine-Readable Data Files" to "Computer Files." This title change, in turn, was reflected in the change of the GMD to "computer file." Of the proposed GMDs, this was not a favored choice. Indeed, it was created and accepted in the end as a compromise for those who wanted to retain the original GMD, or a semblance thereof, and those who proposed a selection of alternative GMDs mentioned earlier.

Another significant change was the revised scope statement (9.0A) in which the two categories of computer files were defined: those available for "direct access" (on physical carriers, which the user could handle) and those available for "remote access" (not on physical carriers, which the user could not handle). The rationale for these categories became evident later in the rules with the implementation of a new "File Characteristics Area" (9.3) that was designed to accommodate the description of remote access files (e.g., mainframe data and program files at the time and, much later, Internet and World Wide Web resources) and the introduction of the "Physical Description Area" (9.5), at long last, to describe direct access files (e.g., microcomputer files on disks, etc.).

Still another significant change was the revised list of sources of information (9.0A), which identified the title screen as the chief source. Lacking the title screen, information was to be taken from other formally presented internal evidence, such as main menus or program statements. Of particular importance, especially for catalogers such as the author working at LC who had limited access to computers to check the title screen, was the allowance to use the physical carrier or its label in these circumstances.

With respect to notes, the system requirements note, which was introduced in the *Guidelines,* was carried over in the preliminary draft revision of Chapter 9. It was now made mandatory, and because of its importance it was sequenced to be the second note in the catalog record, following "Nature and scope." The following example illustrates application of the preliminary draft revised chapter (Figure 2).

Concluding the draft revised chapter was an appendix that proposed revised rules for accompanying material affecting 1.5E of *AACR2*. This proposed revision was added to help catalogers in understanding the changes demonstrated in some Chapter 9 examples. The revised text of the rule, however, was directed at recording items covered by Chapter 2, where in lieu of identifying the accompanying item by name, the cataloger was to use "v."

Catalogers had approximately two years during which they applied the revised chapter 9 rules experimentally. Most of the feedback was positive. The rules also enjoyed varied application. Particularly note-

FIGURE 2. Example of the Preliminary Draft Revised Chapter 9

Heaney, John.
The checkbook manager [computer file]. -- San Diego, CA : J. Heaney, c1989.
1 computer cassette.

System requirements: Timex Sinclair 1000; 16K.
Allows user to input up to 250 transactions of deposits and check issues.
Summary: A personal or business checking account program, which will store banking transactions, keep a running balance of the account, and sort transactions in a number of useful ways.

1. Accounting. 2. Finance, Personal. I. Title.

worthy was the Cataloging-In-Publication (CIP) Software Program, which LC had recently launched at the request of audiovisual catalogers. The author together with the CIP Office developed a data sheet and booklet of instructions for producers and publishers to use in reporting their software titles. Further, there was talk that LC was planning to open a new Machine-Readable Collections Reading Room (MRCRR), which would be made up of works deposited for copyright, supplemented with purchased applications, such as spreadsheets, word processors, and databases. Indeed, LC opened the MRCRR in July 1988 with a core collection of 250 titles, which the author had cataloged using the preliminary draft revised Chapter 9. Slowly, the collection grew and the catalog records produced in conjunction with applying the revised *AACR2* rules became available in LC's MUMS database as well as in OCLC.

NEW CHALLENGES

Even with the revised *AACR2* in place, however, catalogers of microcomputer files found themselves continually challenged by the rapid technological advances taking place. In several instances, special cataloging rules were inserted at the last minute to accommodate the idiosyncrasies of the technology. For instance, at the time the *Guidelines* were being prepared for publication, software was largely limited to running on a single make and model of computer. This was reflected in the *Guidelines,* which instructed the cataloger to record this information in the file description area, e.g.:

> 1 program file (Apple IIe) on 1 computer disk

However, producers had now started to make their software compatible for running on different makes and models of computers. As a result, at the last minute, an instruction was inserted in the *Guidelines,* which called for the cataloger to record this situation in a special "Also runs" note, e.g.:

> Also runs on: Osborne II or IBM PC, both with 48K and CP/M 2.2.

Both instructions, by the way, were omitted in the preliminary draft revised Chapter 9 rules; instead, catalogers were instructed to give such information in the system requirements note (9.7B1b). In another instance, when publication of the revised *AACR2* was imminent, software producers had started to issue their products on 3 1/2 and 5 1/4 inch floppy disks, both of which were inserted in a single package to accommodate the two different size disk drives that users may have with their machines. The question was: should the cataloger describe only one size disk in the physical description and provide a note about the other? If so, which size disk was to be described in which area? Again, at the last minute, JSC, in this case, added the instruction in 9.5D2 to give the dimensions for both sizes, starting with the smaller or smallest followed by the larger or largest size, e.g.:

> 3 computer disks; 3 1/2-5 1/4 in.

However, the biggest challenge to catalogers of microcomputer files was on the horizon and fast approaching. Just as microcomputers had exploded on the scene shortly after the publication of *AACR2* and the new Chapter 9, now a new revolutionary form of technology called "interactive multimedia" or just "multimedia" arrived soon after the 1988 revision of *AACR2* was published. As its name implies, the technology incorporated many types of media–text, graphics, animation, sound, and video in a single presentation, which was delivered on a variety of physical carriers, singly or in combination, such as floppy disks, optical discs, and videodiscs. At the 1990 Online Audiovisual Catalogers (OLAC) biennial meeting in Rochester, NY, the author in her workshop on cataloging computer files described several interactive multimedia titles made up of floppy disks and videodiscs that LC had acquired for the MRCRR, and she asked participants which chapter of *AACR2*–7 or 9–should be used as the basis for the description. While rule 0.24 called for basing the description on the "item in hand," in these cases, the cataloger had 2 major items in hand, each representing different technologies and different sets of cataloging rules associated with them. The participants could not reach a consensus, but there was a lively discussion, which resulted in an informal luncheon meeting held later at the conference hotel. This meeting, in turn, led to an organized meeting of cataloging experts, who met at the 1990 ALA annual meeting in Atlanta, GA. Under the leadership of Sheila Intner, who was on the faculty of the Graduate School of Library and Information Science at Simmons College, the group drafted an initial set of guidelines, and proposed that CC:DA appoint a task force to further study the problems of cataloging this material. This task force conducted its work from 1991-1992, and submitted a document that served as the starting point for a second task force, which CC:DA appointed in 1993. Within a year, this task force finalized a set of guidelines that was published and adopted nationally: *Guidelines for Bibliographic Description of Interactive Multimedia* (ALA, 1994), hereafter referred to as the *IM Guidelines* to distinguish them from the earlier *Guidelines.*

INTERACTIVE MULTIMEDIA GUIDELINES

Then, as now, questions were raised about the necessity–and validity–of special rules to catalog interactive multimedia. Specifically, was interactive multimedia a subclass of computer files in which case the *AACR2* Chapter 9 rules would apply, to be supplemented by special rules only as needed? Or was interactive multimedia, on the other hand, an identifiable class of material characterized by an integration of technologies–computer, sound, and videorecording, which required the development of its own set of rules, possibly to be added as a new chapter in *AACR2*? Assessing the extensive contents and detailed provisions from today's perspective, it would appear that they were intended to be added as a separate chapter in *AACR2,* although the Preface states that it left this matter to JSC to decide.

For catalogers using the *IM Guidelines,* it was particularly important that they understand the definition given in the text. In addition to the various physical carriers it could assume, interactive multimedia was also found to share certain salient characteristics. The definition enumerated two characteristics and stated that both must be exhibited in a work in order for it to qualify as interactive multimedia:

1. user-controlled, nonlinear navigation using computer technology; and
2. the combination of two or more media (audio, text, graphics, images, animation, and video) that the user manipulates to control the order and/or nature of the presentation.

To assist catalogers in determining the presence of these characteristics, the *IM Guidelines* contained a special "Additional help" section, which posed a series of questions and answers in the form of descriptive clues. For instance, to the question: "Does the work use computer technology?" the answer provided instructed the cataloger to consider whether the work required the use of a microcomputer, Level III or higher videodisc player, or a similarly sophisticated level of computer technology, in which case it would signify positive use. To the question: "Does the work offer nonlinear navigation?" the answer provided tells the cataloger this may be difficult to determine immediately, but a careful reading of the descriptive material on or accompanying the work can be instructive.

Further help beyond the *IM Guidelines* was available to catalogers through an ALCTS PreConference that was held at the 1994 ALA annual in Chicago, and through organized workshops sponsored by such groups as NELINET and FEDLINK. However, catalogers continually expressed difficulties in applying the definition. In addition, there was the new GMD "interactive multimedia," which some catalogers thought would be just as effective if shortened to "multimedia"; others expressed a hesitancy to using it, preferring "computer file" instead.

Also an issue of some concern was the introduction of the two different spellings: "disc" and "disk" to distinguish between optical and magnetic formats, respectively. The use of "disc" and the specific medium designation (SMD) "computer optical disc" to represent CD-ROMs in the *IM Guidelines* was at variance with the SMD given in rule 9.5B in the revised *AACR2,* which showed "computer laser optical disk." From the viewpoint of the task force that developed the *IM Guidelines,* "laser" was considered redundant and "disk" was determined to be more commonly associated with describing magnetic technology.

This critique of the *IM Guidelines,* however, did not diminish its usefulness particularly with respect to the diverse assortment of physical descriptions and related notes that were either not covered in *AACR2* or present only in random fashion in areas 5 and 7 of various *AACR2* chapters. For instance, because of the various physical carriers and playback equipment that may be required to access a particular work, the *IM Guidelines* allowed for the provision of multiple system requirements notes. The following example illustrates the use of these notes and other provisions in the *IM Guidelines* (Figure 3).

THE NEW ISBD(ER)

Over time, application of the *IM Guidelines* grew, but its future was uncertain. Its possible incorporation as a new chapter in a future edition of *AACR2* became doubtful following a decision of the *ISBD(CF)* Review Group, which had been formed to revise the first edition of the *ISBD(CF)* published in 1990. At it first meeting in April 1995, the group decided to treat interactive multimedia as a subclass of computer files. This meant that the rules and the GMD for computer files were applicable to works defined as interactive multimedia. More surprising, however, was the group's decision to replace the GMD "computer file" with "electronic resource." The group felt the latter term better repre-

FIGURE 3. Use of Multiple "System Requirements" Notes and Other Provisions in the *Guidelines for Bibliographic Description of Interactive Multimedia*

Biology encyclopedia [interactive multimedia] / HarperCollins. -- New York, NY: HarperCollins, c1991.
1 videodisc : sd., col. ; 12 in.
4 computer disks ; 3 ½ in.
1 table of contents/user's manual (104 p.) ; 28 cm.
1 barcodes book (154 p.) ; 28 cm.

System requirements for videodisc (Level I): Videodisc player that reads chapter codes and picture stops; television receiver or monitor; audio and video cables, or an RF cable.
System requirements for computer disks (Level III): Macintosh Plus or later; HyperCard 1.2.2 or later; hard disk with enough free space for the stack (3MBytes); HD backup; videodisc player with serial port (such as Pioneer 2200, 4200, 8000, 6000 series; Sony 1200, 1500, 2000; or Hitachi 9500, or other players that use the same commands); cable to connect the Macintosh modem to the videodisc player.
Title from videodisc label.
Title on computer disk labels: BioPedia HyperCard stack.
"A production of Nebraska Interactive Video, Inc., for Harper, Collins [sic] and Carolina Biological Supply Company"--User's manual.
Credits: Content developed by Charles Lytle and William Surver ; videodisc and HyperCard stack design by J. Mark Turner ; HyperCard stack programming by Helen Brooks.
Two-sided CAV laser videodisc that can be used as Level I without the computer or as Level III with the computer.
Summary: An interactive biology encyclopedia with videodisc containing 31 content chapters, more than 1500 photographic slides, over 1000 illustrations, and over 50 minutes of motion video. The HyperCard stack allows the user to access information on the videodisc.
ISBN 0-673-16331-1

1. Biology--Encyclopedias. I. Lytle, Charles. II. Surver, William. III. Turner, J. Mark. IV. Brooks, Helen. V. HarperCollins. VI. Nebraska Interactive Video, Inc. VII. Carolina Biological Supply Company. VIII. BioPedia HyperCard stack.

sented material available on the Internet and CD-ROMs; it was also considered to be a general term that patrons could easily understand. Subsequently, the review group and the ISBD were renamed *ISBD(ER)*. Among a number of other significant changes, which mostly affected the description of remote access files, the review group debated using the conventional terminology of "CD-ROM," "CD-I," and "Photo CD" in place of the given specific material designation (SMD) "optical disc." This had become an international issue with both librarians and patrons worldwide expressing the need for change. In the end, a compromise was reached whereby a cataloging agency had the option of adding the terminology in parentheses to the SMD, if desired, e.g.:

1 computer optical disc (CD-ROM)
2 computer optical discs (CD-I)

The publication of the *ISBD(ER)* in 1997 resulted in national cataloging agencies undertaking a review and update of their descriptive cataloging rules. In the U.S., CC:DA appointed a task force in fall 1997 to provide a detailed review of *AACR2,* noting where the rules, particularly in Chapter 9, were not in conformance, and proposing rule revisions that would harmonize the cataloging code with the *ISBD(ER),* where possible and feasible. After extensive–and intensive–review, the task force submitted a final report in August 1999 in which, among other decisions, it concurred with the *ISBD(ER):*

1. to include interactive multimedia as a category of computer files
2. to reaffirm its adoption of the new GMD "electronic resource"; and
3. to add "CD-ROM," "CD-I," and "Photo CD" in parentheses after the SMD "optical disc"

The report was approved by CC:DA and sent to JSC to be placed on its fall 1999 agenda.

JSC approved a number of the proposed revisions, but did not choose to be consistent with the *ISBD(ER)* in all cases. For example, instead of adding "CD-ROM" and other designated optical disc formats in parentheses to the SMD, it decided to allow catalogers to use the term optionally as an SMD, e.g.:

1 CD-ROM
2 Photo CDs

In addition, it added the example of a DVD:

1 DVD

This example has raised questions among catalogers as to its appropriateness in Chapter 9 or Chapter 7. Clarification seems warranted as DVDs come in different formats involving in some cases very different technologies. DVD-Video and DVD-ROM, for example, are a case in point with the former being more appropriately associated with Chapter 7 and the latter being associated with Chapter 9.

Following its fall 2000 meeting, JSC compiled all the rule revisions to Chapter 9 in a document that is now expected to be published, possibly in 2001. Many of these revisions have been available for comment and have been refined over time so that catalogers should not expect great surprises. However, whenever the newly "minted" Chapter 9 arrives, it will be welcome!

THE FUTURE

Alas, the future! After experiencing and enduring the volatility of the 1980s and early 90s, catalogers of microcomputer files have welcomed the present relatively stable period. Other than DVDs, there have been no new major physical carriers marketing commercial software and data since CD-ROMs were introduced, which can be traced to the 80s. While CD-ROMs currently dominate the market and the microcomputer software acquisitions of libraries, it is expected that DVDs will soon supersede them for reasons of their storage capacity, superb pictures, and superior technology. Software applications continue to proliferate in just about every conceivable area and field of study. Data now comes in gigabytes that no longer overwhelm users or their machines. Yes, the microcomputer revolution has been overtaken by the Internet/Web revolution, which is presenting its own bibliographic challenges to catalogers trying to describe and access these resources. Meanwhile, the fate of the microcomputer is being debated. Will there be a world without personal computers some day, as some predict? Or will the machines and their hardware and software components persist, but evolve into smaller and more portable devices yet to be invented? Is this present period merely a brief reprieve from a possible heady onslaught of new and innovative computers, physical carriers, and software that will challenge a future generation of catalogers to develop the needed guidance to ensure their bibliographic control? Perhaps the microcomputer revolution has slowed down, but it is too early for libraries to say it has stopped.

REFERENCES

American Library Association, Association for Library Collections and Technical Services, Committee on Cataloging: Description and Access. *Task Force on Harmonization of ISBD(ER) and AARC2: Final Report.* Chicago: American Library Association, 1999.

American Library Association, Resources and Technical Services Division, Cataloging and Classification Section, Committee on Cataloging: Description and Access. *Guidelines for Using AACR2 Chapter 9 for Cataloging Microcomputer Software*. Chicago: American Library Association, 1984.

American Library Association, Resources and Technical Services Division, Subcommittee on Rules for Cataloging Machine-Readable Data Files. *Final Report of the Cataloging Code Revision Committee, Subcommittee on Rules for Cataloging Machine-Readable Data Files*, mimeographed, 1976.

Anglo-American Cataloguing Rules, Second Edition. Chicago: American Library Association, 1978.

Anglo-American Cataloguing Rules, Second Edition. Chapter 9, Computer Files, Draft Revision. Edited, for the Joint Steering Committee for Revision of AACR, by Michael Gorman. Chicago: American Library Association, 1987.

Anglo-American Cataloguing Rules, Second Edition, 1988 Revision, prepared under the direction of the Joint Steering Committee for Revision of AACR. Chicago: American Library Association, 1988.

Association for Library Collections & Technical Services, Cataloging and Classification Section, Committee on Cataloging: Description and Access, Interactive Multimedia Guidelines Review Task Force. *Guidelines for Bibliographic Description of Interactive Multimedia*. Chicago: American Library Association, 1994.

Chapter 9, Electronic Resources, October 10, 2000 (4JSC/ALA/27/ALA follow-up/4/LC response/CCC rep response/2) (to be published).

Dodd, Sue A. and Ann M. Sandberg-Fox. *Cataloging Microcomputer Files: A Manual of Interpretation*. Chicago: American Library Association, 1984.

ISBD(ER): International Standard Bibliographic Description for Electronic Resources, revised from the *ISBD(CF): International Bibliographic Description for Computer Files*. Munchen: K.G. Saur, 1997.

Library of Congress, Network Development Office. *Machine-Readable Data Files: A MARC Format*. Washington, DC: Library of Congress, 1981.

Cataloging Remote Electronic Resources

Nancy B. Olson

SUMMARY. "Cataloging Remote Electronic Resources" provides a brief history of the development of cataloging rules for electronic resources, together with a thorough discussion of the descriptive cataloging of this material according to *AACR2*. Rules used for cataloging include an October 2000 draft of the new chapter 9 approved by the Joint Steering Committee for Revision of AACR (JSC). MARC 21 coding and tagging of the bibliographic records is also included. *[Article copies available for a fee from The Haworth Document Delivery Service: 1-800-342-9678. E-mail address: <getinfo@haworthpressinc.com> Website: <http://www.HaworthPress.com> © 2001 by The Haworth Press, Inc. All rights reserved.]*

KEYWORDS. Cataloging of electronic resources, electronic resources, MARC format, Anglo-American cataloguing rules

INTRODUCTION

One of the difficulties in cataloging any type of electronic resource is that of keeping up with rule changes. This chapter focuses on cataloging

---

Nancy B. Olson cataloged audiovisual and other special materials for 30 years at Minnesota State University, Mankato, retiring in 1999 as a Professor on the faculty there. She continues to teach workshops at the University of Pittsburgh, San Jose State University, and elsewhere as invited.

[Haworth co-indexing entry note]: "Cataloging Remote Electronic Resources." Olson, Nancy B. Co-published simultaneously in *Cataloging & Classification Quarterly* (The Haworth Information Press, an imprint of The Haworth Press, Inc.) Vol. 31, No. 2, 2001, pp. 101-137; and: *The Audiovisual Cataloging Current* (ed: Sandra K. Roe) The Haworth Information Press, an imprint of The Haworth Press, Inc., 2001, pp. 101-137. Single or multiple copies of this article are available for a fee from The Haworth Document Delivery Service [1-800-342-9678, 9:00 a.m. - 5:00 p.m. (EST). E-mail address: getinfo@haworthpressinc.com].

© 2001 by The Haworth Press, Inc. All rights reserved.

remote electronic resources using the *Anglo-American Cataloguing Rules, second edition, 1998 revision (AACR2)* and the MARC 21 bibliographic format. I do not address Dublin Core or the CORC project here; they are adequately addressed both online and in the literature, see, for example, the *Journal of Internet Cataloging*. Monographs, serials, and continuing publications are all included in this chapter.

HOW CATALOGING RULES ARE DEVELOPED

The Anglo-American cataloging rules are controlled by the international Joint Steering Committee for Revision of AACR (JSC). This group is made up of one representative each from the Library of Congress, the American Library Association (ALA), the British Library, the Library Association (British), the Canadian Committee on Cataloguing, and the Australian Committee on Cataloguing. Normally JSC meets once or twice a year to consider proposals for rule revision presented by any of the countries. They may ask for more information, reject a proposal, or refer the proposal to all the countries for comments before acting on it.

Catalogers in the United States submit proposals to the American Library Association Committee on Cataloging: Description and Access (CC:DA). This committee which meets twice a year, may act on a proposal, reject it, ask for more information, or form a committee or task force to look into the topic and report back, typically a year later. When CC:DA is in agreement, the resulting proposal is submitted to JSC for their consideration.

As you can see, this process is a lengthy one, though there have been attempts in recent years to accelerate the process.

THE MARC FORMAT

While the descriptive content of a bibliographic record is controlled by *AACR2*, the coding of that content for machine manipulation is done according to the MARC 21 bibliographic format. Changes are made to this format by the Library of Congress acting together with an ALA committee on Machine-Readable Bibliographic Information (MARBI). MARBI normally meets twice a year during ALA conferences.

HISTORY OF CATALOGING RULE DEVELOPMENT FOR ELECTRONIC RESOURCES

Development of rules for the cataloging of computer-related material began in the early 1970s and resulted in the appearance of chapter 9, "Machine-Readable Data Files" in *AACR2* (1978). This chapter was revised and published separately as, *Guidelines for Using AACR2 Chapter 9 for Cataloging Microcomputer Software* (ALA, 1984). These revisions were taken into account as the rules were revised for the chapter titled "Computer Files" in *AACR2,* 1988 revision. More revision was done for the 1998 revision of *AACR2*. These rules are now under major revision again and the new chapter, planned to be issued separately during 2001, will be called "Electronic Resources."

From the beginning of the effort to catalog electronic resources, one of the problems was that of form. The original electronic resources were stored on computer tape or punched cards or in memory of computers located in computer centers–access was through terminals in those computer centers and eventually located elsewhere on campuses. A patron did not handle any physical object but called for a file which was manually or electronically made available to a terminal for use. In chapter 9 of *AACR2* (1978) data files and program files were described; one was cataloging "data stored in machine-readable form and the programs used to process that data."

In the early 1980s small computers were being built for use in K-12 schools to run very simple programs–requiring a memory of 8 or 16 K. This software began to be distributed commercially on computer cassettes (they looked like, and sometimes were, sound tape cassettes) or on magnetic disks, 5 1/4 in. in diameter, enclosed in a tough paper sleeve. These commercial programs began to be accompanied by teacher's guides and user instructions. Now there were physical items to catalog and circulate. In chapter 9 of the 1988 revision of *AACR2,* a footnote to area 5 stated: "Do not give a physical description for a computer file that is available only by remote access. See 9.7B1c and 9.7B10." The information about files formerly carried in area 5 was moved to a new file description area, and notes were used about "mode of access" and physical description of the remote access file such as sound and color.

As minicomputers became more widely available from a great number of companies, and as memory capacity grew and computer software became more sophisticated, the number of commercially-available items grew explosively. Educational materials of all kinds became available. All kinds of office software (word-processing programs, spreadsheets, data base programs) became widely available. Game software became a big market. And libraries were collecting and circulating all of these materials.

Then the Internet began to be used widely in academic institutions, in the business world, at home, and in schools. Documents on all subjects became available online. Electronic journals appeared. Print materials became available electronically, and sometimes only online with the print product ceasing. These online monographs, serials, and continuing publications needed to be cataloged.

INTERNET CATALOGING PROJECTS

Aided by two grants from the U.S. Department of Education in 1991-1993 and 1994-1996, OCLC explored the possibilities of cataloging Internet resources. During the first project, cataloging guidelines using *AACR2* were developed and published online. These guidelines were tested during the second project with a second edition of the guide being published and distributed, both in print and online form. The Intercat database was established at OCLC to contain bibliographic records for Internet resources that we recataloged using the newly developed OCLC guidelines. Rule proposals were developed and presented to CC:DA as a result of these projects and proposals for changes to the MARC format were submitted to MARBI.

FRUSTRATIONS

While rules are being developed, the computer world is growing and changing. Rules have not been able to keep up with the current status of the computer industry, and catalogers and administrators have been increasingly frustrated by what were perceived by some as inadequate or outdated rules. An email on Sept. 27, 2000, by Debra Shapiro to the AUTOCAT electronic discussion list pointed out, "There are about 800 pages on the inadequacies of *AACR2R* for electronic, particularly networked electronic resources . . . by the Joint Steering Committee for the Revision of AACR, in two parts at: *http://www.nlc-bnc.ca/jsc/aacrdel.htm* and *http://www.nlc-bnc.ca/jsc/aacrde12.htm.*"

CURRENT EFFORTS AT RULE DEVELOPMENT

The *International Standard Bibliographic Description for Electronic Resources (ISBD(ER))* was published in 1997 after two years of revision and international review. It established a new name for the material previously called "machine-readable data files" or "computer files." It also set up an extensive list of terms to be used in area 3 of the bibliographic record–and we patterned the recommendations for area 3 in the OCLC Internet cataloging guidelines after those found in the *ISBD(ER)*.

An invitational JSC conference on the future of *AACR2* was held in the fall of 1997 in Toronto. In preparation for this conference an email discussion list was set up and there were calls for the revision of *AACR2* chapter 9, some revision to chapter 12 on seriality, changes to 0.24 on the basis for the bibliographic description, and to the structure of the rules themselves. There was also criticism of how slowly JSC acts in the rule revision process. These matters were all addressed during the conference with no decisions made, but some priorities were established.

JSC met in November 1998 and in October 1999 and considered recommendations of a CC:DA task force to bring *AACR2* chapter 9 into alignment with the *ISBD(ER)*. JSC endorsed many of these recommendations and planned a substantial revision of *AACR2* chapter 9, with final work to be done during their September 2000 meeting.

These plans were too optimistic. As an example, it was announced after the Brisbane meeting (Oct. 1999) that JSC had approved a recommendation that "the term 'disk' will be used throughout, rather than 'disk' and 'disc.' " This announcement caused a bit of a furor. CC:DA voted to reiterate its preference for distinguishing magnetic disks from optical discs, based on consistent usage in dictionaries in the field. It was also pointed out that optical discs are also spelled "disc" in the *AACR2* chapters on cataloging video discs and compact discs.

The major revision of chapter 12 on serials includes expansion to include all continuing resources, such as Web pages that change over time. As this revision has considerable impact on cataloging of electronic resources, both serial and continuing, neither revision (chapter 9 or chapter 12) can be done in isolation.

Meanwhile CC:DA, during the 2000 summer ALA, appointed a task force to examine areas 3 and 5 of chapter 9, and make recommendations as to where information about remote access files should go. This task force is scheduled to report to CC:DA during ALA's Annual Meeting in 2001. The task force will probably look also at area 5 for other types of special materials, as similar materials need to be treated in similar ways across the chapters of *AACR2*.

So the revision process continues, both nationally and internationally.

RULES USED IN THIS ARTICLE

The Canadians prepared a consolidation of revisions that have been approved by JSC to date. This report, dated October 10, 2000, was made available to the authors of papers for this publication by Barbara Tillett, Library of Congress representative to JSC, and we thank her for this courtesy. Our understanding is that this revised chapter will be made available through ALA Publishing in 2001. As explained above, areas 3 and 5 have not yet been changed, nor have any serial-related decisions been made. Changes that have been approved will be pointed out in the following sections.

Rules new to chapter 9 of *AACR2* are provided in this article along with discussion of both the new rules and the unchanged rules that are applicable to the cataloging of remote access electronic resources–monograph, serial, and continuing. The revision of chapter 9 "Electronic Resources," was kindly made available in draft form to those of us working on this text. However, more changes will be made before the revision process is complete, so the reader must be aware that this article which relies on the unpublished draft is not the final word in cataloging remote access electronic resources. For this, use the **published** revision of *AACR2* chapter 9.

SCOPE

The scope of the new chapter on electronic resources is as follows:

> 9.0A1. The rules in this chapter cover the description of electronic resources. Electronic resources consist of data (information representing numbers, text, graphics, images, maps, moving images, music, sounds, etc.), programs (instructions, etc., that process the data for use), or combinations of data and programs. Electronic resources often include components with characteristics found in multiple classes of materials so there will frequently be a need to consult other chapters. For example, in describing a serially-issued cartographic electronic resource, use chapters 3, 9, and 12.

> For cataloguing purposes, electronic resources may be treated in one of two ways depending on whether access is direct (local) or remote (networked). Direct access is understood to mean that a physical carrier can be described. Such a carrier (e.g., disc/disk, cassette, cartridge) must be inserted into a computerized device or into a peripheral attached to a computerized device. Remote access is understood to mean that no physical carrier can be handled. Remote access can only be provided by use of an input-output device (e.g., a terminal), either connected to a computer system (e.g., a resource in a network), or by use of resources stored in a hard disk or other storage device.

This rule makes it clear that only materials involving a computer or "computerized device" are to be considered electronic resources and cataloged by the rules of chapter 9.

MONOGRAPH, SERIAL, OR SOMETHING ELSE?

The first decision that must be made when cataloging an electronic resource is whether the item is a monograph or a serial–or a monographic set–or something like a loose-leaf publication. It is easy enough to spot a monograph–something published on a certain date and it is done.

But monographs can be published in multiple volumes, over many years–but the set is designed to be complete at some point. These monographic sets have a range of dates. Each volume may have its own title and be cataloged separately, or all cataloged together on one bibliographic record, with or without a contents note.

Serials, on the other hand, continue–when begun, there is no end planned. While the definition is being changed, at this writing it is still as published in *AACR2*–there must be a chronological and/or numeric designation on an issue for it to be considered, and cataloged, as a serial. These are now being called "continuing resources" in the rule revision process for *AACR2* chapter 12.

Then there are those electronic resources that change over time. This includes web sites, home pages, dynamic databases (e.g., OCLC online union catalog), and online services (e.g., Autocat). They are updated or revised irregularly or frequently or minute by minute, but none of these changes results in a title page with a chronological and/or numeric designation. There may be a note: "Last updated Dec. 17, 2000" or "Intended to be updated regularly" (with no indication that any updates actually occurred). No matter how much these may "feel" like serials, they are not serials by the current rules, so are to be cataloged much like the monographic sets.

So–first decide what remote access electronic resource you are cataloging. Is it a web site or something contained within a web site? Is it a serial, or a document from one issue of a serial? Is it a named column that appears regularly within a serial? Once you decide what you are cataloging, ignore all surrounding information unless or until needed for a note explaining where the document (or whatever) appears.

Is the item being cataloged a monograph, a serial, or something that is continuing but not a true serial? Once you make this decision be consistent in the treatment of the date in the 260, and notes about the item.

Remember a true serial carries a designation of volume and/or number and/or a chronological designation in a prominent position–if no such designation, it may be a continuing publication, but it is not a serial.

If the home page or list of items available on the web site contains something like "What's new"–that is an indication of a continuing publication, as it is being updated with news regularly or irregularly. Again, if no numeric and/or chronological designation is present, it cannot be cataloged as a serial.

SOURCES OF INFORMATION

There is some change in the rule about chief source of information, which is quoted in part as follows:

> 9.0B1. Chief source of information. The chief source of information for electronic resources is the resource itself. Take the information from formally presented evidence (e.g., title screen(s), main menus, program statements, initial display(s) of information, home page(s), the file header(s) including "Subject:" lines, encoded metadata (e.g., TEI headers, HTML/XML meta tags), and the physical carrier or its labels), including information that has been uncompressed, printed out, or otherwise processed for use. If the information in these sources varies in degree of fullness, prefer the source that provides the most complete information.

The rest of the rule is essentially unchanged.

AREA 1

TITLE AND STATEMENT OF RESPONSIBILITY AREA (MARC 245)

The major rule change made to this area is the change of the GMD to "electronic resource." There is a new provision to use the GMD "multimedia" or "kit" if the electronic resource "contains parts belonging to materials falling into two or more categories, and none of these is the predominant component."

For most remote access electronic resources, choosing the title proper is no more difficult than for any audiovisual or other special material. When the item has something that looks like a title page, the choices to be made for area 1 are obvious. For most documents or home pages or web sites or newsletters or journals there is an obvious (or fairly obvious) title. There may not be any other title information. There may not be a statement of responsibility. If so, don't try to construct one; use what is in the chief source. Notice the last statement in the quote above that directs the cataloger to choose the title found with the fullest information–this is helpful. Often titles are found in varying forms throughout a document, sometimes with fewer words, other times with abbreviations. When there is conflicting information, or variation in title, choose the the part of the item that gives the fullest information, and take the title and statement of responsibility information from that part. Give other forms of the title in 246 fields, if useful for retrieval.

Field 245 is to be an exact transcription of information found on the item.

```
245     Cataloging electronic resources $h [electronic
resource] : $b OCLC-MARC coding guidelines / $c by Jay
Weitz.
```

Remember we must always make a note stating where the title was found.

```
500     Title from caption of home page.
```

Serial cataloging tends to be briefer than other cataloging, partly because other title information, responsibility, publisher, etc., tend to change over time. One may choose to include only title proper in area 1, and, if considered important, put other information in notes for serials.

Varying Form of Title (MARC 246)

Varying forms of the title are given in field 246 if they represent the entire work, in field 740 if they represent only a part of the work. Field 246 may be used to correct a spelling error in a 245 title, or to spell out numbers, to use the word "and" instead of the ampersand symbol, or to create a title from some part of the 245 that a user might remember as the title. Field 246 may also be used for a parallel title, caption title, or other form of the title found on the item. There are many indicators available for use with field 246, and I refer you to the MARC 21 bibliographic format or the OCLC-MARC format document for these. There is no period used at the end of field 246.

```
246 00  OCLC-MARC coding guidelines
```

AREA 2

EDITION AREA (MARC 250)

Rule changes to this area applicable to remote electronic resources include adding an example for "Interactive version" and adding the following:

> 9.2B8. If a remote access electronic resource is frequently updated, omit the edition statement and give the information in a note (see 9.7B7).

If the file contains any word(s) or phrase(s) indicating the same information was or is available in a different form, treat that word or phrase as an edition statement and transcribe it exactly as found.

```
250      English edition.

250      Electronic version.
```

AREA 3

TYPE AND EXTENT OF RESOURCE AREA (MARC 256)

This area will be revised together with area 5 in the final phase of revising chapter 9 of *AACR2*. Options being discussed range from expanding the list of terms to omitting the area altogether; watch for decisions.

AACR2 states the type of file is given "when the information is readily available." The revised chapter has dropped this statement. The only terms listed in the new chapter are:

Electronic data
Electronic program(s)
Electronic data and program(s)

CONSER has chosen not to use this area. CONSER catalogers are required to use area 516 for similar information.

This area is required for remote access materials–if no physical description area is used, this area is to be used.

The list of terms in *ISBD(ER)* was modified for use in OCLC's Internet cataloging guidelines–these terms may be used when cataloging in OCLC until such time as final decisions are made to the area by JSC. The list below is from the Internet guidelines with the introductory word "computer" changed to the word "electronic."

- Electronic data
  - Electronic numeric data
    - Electronic census data
    - Electronic survey data
  - Electronic text data
    - Electronic bibliographic database
    - Electronic journal(s)
    - Electronic newsletter(s)
    - Electronic document(s)

Electronic image data
Electronic representational data
Electronic map(s) data
Electronic sound data
Electronic font data
Electronic program(s)
Electronic utility program(s)
Electronic application program(s)
Electronic CAD program(s)
Electronic database program(s)
Electronic spreadsheet program(s)
Electronic word processor program(s)
Electronic desktop publishing program(s)
Electronic game(s)
Electronic system program(s)
Electronic operating system program(s)
Electronic programming language(s)
Electronic retrieval program(s)
Electronic data and program(s)
Electronic interactive multimedia
Electronic online service(s)

AREA 3 (SERIALS)

NUMERIC AND/OR ALPHABETIC, CHRONOLOGICAL, OR OTHER DESIGNATION AREA FOR SERIALS (MARC 362)

This area is used for serial cataloging when cataloging from the first issue. It is used in addition to the type and extent of resource area and is given following that area, according to rule 0.25 in the recent changes to chapter 9.

```
362 0   Vol. 1, issue 1 (Aug. 1999)-
```

If one is cataloging from an issue other than the first, and if one knows when the serial began, that information is given in field 515, following the rule for note 12.7B8.

AREA 4

PUBLICATION, DISTRIBUTION, ETC. AREA (MARC 260)

The new rules include the following instruction:

> 9.4B2. Consider all remote access electronic resources to be published.

Place and Name of Publisher, Distributor, Etc.

One must always have a place of publication and the name of a publisher in area 4.

```
260 [Washington, DC] : $b Library of Congress,
```

If the cataloger cannot find any indication as to who published or distributed a remote access electronic resource, one might question whether the item is worth cataloging. Selecting remote access electronic resources is beyond the scope of this chapter, but sometimes the cataloger finds reason to question the value of an item while searching for cataloging information.

If, however, an item must be cataloged, but there is no place or name of publisher, follow directions in *AACR2* 1.4:

```
260     [S.l. : $b s.n.],
```

Date of Publication, Distribution, Etc.

For all remote access electronic resources, a note must be used giving the date the item being cataloged was viewed. See 9.7B22.

```
500     Description based on contents viewed Dec. 22,

2000.
```

Another new rule is:

> 9.4F4. If there is no publication, distribution, etc., date which applies to the item as a whole, and the item has multiple copyright dates which apply to various aspects of the production (e.g., programming, sound production, graphics, documentation), transcribe only the latest copyright date.
>
> Optionally, transcribe the other dates in a note (see 9.7B7) or in a contents note (see 9.7B18).

However, for a monograph, if the dates are given, but not as copyright dates, or as a mixture of copyright dates and publication or distribution dates, or as dates of updating, take the latest date as evidence of publication, distribution, etc., and use it in area 4 as an assumed date, in brackets.

```
260     Dublin, Ohio : $b OCLC, $c [1999].
```

For a monographic set, or a continuing publication that is not a serial, an open date or a range of dates are given in area 4.

```
260     Mankato, Minn. : $b Minnesota State University,
    $c 1997-
260     Washington, DC : $b Library of Congress, $c
1992-1998.
```

When cataloging a serial, no date is given in area 4 unless cataloging from the first issue. If one knows when the serial began, that information is given in field 515.

AREA 5

PHYSICAL DESCRIPTION AREA (MARC 300)

At the time of this writing, the physical description area is not used for remote access files. This may change.

AREA 6

SERIES AREA (MARC 4XX)

There is nothing unique about the series area when cataloging electronic resources.

```
490  0   Project Gutenberg etext
```

AREA 7

NOTE AREA (MARC 5XX)

There are about 30 possible notes, including some from the serials chapter and one from a recent LCRI. Notes may be combined if desired.

Some additional examples of notes have been added in the revision to Chapter 9.

9.7B1. Nature and scope, system requirements, and mode of access

9.7B1a. Nature and scope (MARC 500 or 516)

This note is used to give brief information on the nature or scope of the resource unless this is obvious from the rest of the description. If fuller information is needed about the resource, use the summary note instead of this note.

This note is coded in MARC field 500 in all other chapters of *AACR2*, but CONSER users are directed to use field 516 for nature and scope; they must always use a field 516.

```
500    Online auction site.

516    Electronic document.
```

9.7B1b. System requirements (MARC 538)

In the new chapter, an additional characteristic is added at the end of the list present in the 1998 *AACR2*: the type of any required or recommended hardware modifications.

Catalogers are directed to: "Make a note on the system requirements of the resource if the information is readily available. Begin the note with *System requirements:*. Give the following characteristics in the order in which they are listed below. Precede each characteristic, other than the first, by a semicolon." Many of these characteristics may be unknown for remote access electronic resources.

the make and model of the computer(s) on which the resource is designed to run
the amount of memory required
the name of the operating system
the software requirements (including the programming language)
the kind and characteristics of any required or recommended peripherals
the type of any required or recommended hardware modifications

```
538    System requirements: Adobe Acrobat
Reader.
```

9.7B1c. Mode of access (MARC 538)

The introductory phrase "Mode of access:" is now required.

```
538     Mode of access: World wide web.

538     Mode of access: Internet.
```

12.7B1. Frequency for serials (MARC 310)

The frequency of publication of a serial is given in this note.

```
310     Weekly.

310     Frequently updated.
```

9.7B2. Language and script (MARC 546)

Language and/or script of the spoken or written content is given in this note unless it is apparent from the rest of the description.

```
546     Available in English and Spanish.
```

Programming language, if known, is given in the system requirements note.

9.7B3. Source of title proper (MARC 500)

This note is required.

```
500     Title from title screen.

500     Title supplied by cataloger.
```

9.7B4. Variations in title (MARC 500, 246)

Other titles such as the title in an HTML header, or a file name or data set name, may be given, as may any variation of the title proper that is found on the item. These will normally be given in field 246.

```
246  1   $i Title in HTML header; $a American

Birding Association home page
```

9.7B5. Parallel titles and other title information (MARC 500, 246)

Parallel titles in another language are to be given in field 246 if a separate added entry is wanted for that title; the parallel titles will, of course, already be recorded in subfield b of field 245.

```
246 13  Legende etrealite : les heros historiques
et legendaires du Canada
```

Other title information not recorded in the title and statement of responsibility area, but considered important, may also be given here.

```
500     Some sections carry subtitle: His life and
times.
```

9.7B6. Statements of responsibility (MARC 500, 550, 536)

Names of people and/or corporate bodies not already named in area 1, but considered to be important, may be included here.

```
500     Copyright by Nancy B. Olson.
```

Information about the issuing body may be recorded in field 550.

```
550     Issued by ALA Reference and Adult Services
Division, Machine-Assisted Reference Section,
Direct Patron Access to Computer-Based Reference
Systems Committee.
```

Funding information maybe recorded in field 536.

```
536     Funded in part by the U.S. Department of
Education, Office of Library Programs, under the
College Library Technology and Cooperation Grants
Program.
```

9.7B7. Edition and history (MARC 500, 522, 567)

Notes about the edition and/or the history of the item are given here in field 500.

```
500     Originally available in print in 1993.
```

Geographic coverage of the item is part of the history of the file and may be given in field 522. A print constant is designed to display the introductory phrase: "Geographic coverage:".

```
522  County-level data from four Northwestern
states (Idaho, Montana, Oregon, Washington).
```

Methodology used in preparation of the file may be recorded in field 567.

```
567     Total civilian noninstitutional population
of the United States.
```

12.7B7. Relations with other serials (MARC 580, etc.)

Notes can be generated from MARC fields 765, 767, 770, 775, 776, 777, 780, 785, and 787 about the relationship of the item being cataloged to other items. These linking entries may have print constants. These linking entries do not take the place of added entry fields, and do not generate added entries.

If a free-text note is needed about the relationship of the item being cataloged to other serials, use field 580.

9.7B8. Type and extent of resource (MARC 500, 565)

Information about the type and extent of the resource is the information considered to be important, and is not found elsewhere in the description. This note will probably change as areas 3 and 5 are changed.

```
500     File in PostScript format.
```

Number of cases or variables making up the files may be recorded in field 565.

```
565     552 cases.
```

12.7B8. Numbering and chronological designation for serials (MARC 515)

Complex, irregular, or peculiar designations in serial numbering are given in field 515.

```
515     Numbering irregular.
515     Additional issues on special topics are
occasionally available.
```

9.7B9. Publication, distribution, etc. (MARC 500)

Information about publication, distribution, etc., not included in area 4 of the bibliographic record being created, but considered to be important, may be recorded here.

```
500     Available commercially from: Oxford Text
Archive, A-1300-A.
```

A date of release or transmittal may be recorded here.

```
500     "December 18, 2000."
```

9.7B10. Physical description (MARC 500)

For electronic resources available only by remote access, give details about color, sound, etc., here unless included in the summary. If the rules change to include area 5 for remote access electronic resources, this note will also change.

```
500     Displays in color; with stereo sound.
500     Document formatted into 27 pages.
```

9.7B11. Accompanying material (MARC 500, 556)

Documentation may be in a separate remote access file, or available in print from the publisher or originator of the electronic resource. Information about such material is given here.

```
500     Teacher's guide available in print from
the publisher.
```

Documentation such as code books is given in field 556.

```
556     Printed documentation available directly
from the originator of the file.
```

9.7B12. Series (MARC 500)

Information about series not already included in the series area may be given here.

```
500     Originally issued in series: American
national election study series.
```

9.7B13. Dissertations (MARC 502)

The standard dissertation note is given as appropriate.

```
502     Thesis (M.S.)--Minnesota State University,
Mankato. 2000.
```

9.7B14. Audience (MARC 521)

If the intellectual level of a resource, or its intended audience, is stated on the item, note it here.

```
521     For ages 8 and up.
```

1.7B15. References to published descriptions (MARC 510, 524, 581)

A note indicating where a serial item has been indexed is given in field 510.

```
510 0  Applied science and technology index.
```

The preferred citation of the materials being cataloged may be included in field 524.

```
524      Jennings M. Kent and Richard G. Niemi.
Youth-parent socialization panel study, 1965-1973.
Ann Arbor, Mich : Inter-university Consortium for
Political and Social Research, 1981.
```

Information about a publication based on the use, study, or analysis of the resource being cataloged is included in field 581.

```
581 8   The adjusted 1990 numbers are used as a
basis for the annual county population estimates
published in Current Population Reports Series
P-25 and P-26.
```

9.7B16. Other formats (MARC 530, 535)

Give details of other formats in which the content of the resource has been issued.

```
530      Also available on CD-ROM.
```

The location of the original or duplicates may be recorded in field 535.

```
535      Original document in archives of the
Minnesota Historical Society.
```

9.7B17. Summary (MARC 520)

A brief objective summary may be given in field 520, unless enough information for the user is available elsewhere in the bibliographic record. Information normally given in other notes may be included here as part of the summary.

```
520      Eight versions of a video game for 1-2
players. To survive, players use laser cannons to
destroy flying demons.
```

9.7B18. Contents (MARC 505, 500, 504)

A formal contents note is given in field 505.

```
505 0   1. Idaho -- 2. Montana -- 3. Oregon -- 4.
Washington.
```

This formal note may be enhanced with subfield codes for retrieval.

```
505 00  $g 1. $t Idaho -- $g 2. $t Montana -- $g
3. $t Oregon -- $g 4. $t Washington.
```

An informal contents note is given in field 500.

```
500     Includes selected articles from print
version; lacks illustrations.
```

A bibliography note is a type of contents note, given in field 504.

```
504     Includes bibliographic references.
```

9.7B19. Numbers (MARC 500)

Numbers that may be important and are not recorded elsewhere may be included in this note.

```
500     XY-2002
500     "RFC1251."
```

9.7B20. Copy being described, library's holdings, and restrictions on use (MARC 590, 506, 583)

Information about the copy being described or local holdings would be a local note so would go in field 590.

```
590     Only available to patrons on first three
terminals in Reference Area.
590     Not archived; only latest issue online.
```

Information about general restrictions on use is given in field 506.

```
506     Restricted to users at subscribing
institutions.
```

Notes about processing and reference actions may be recorded in field 583.

```
583     Destroy $c September 1.
```

9.7B21. "With" notes (MARC 501)

If more than one work is contained in an online electronic resource, and separate bibliographic records are made for each, a "With" note is made to connect these records. In note field 501, list the works other than those listed in field 245.

```
501     With: Uncle Sam's jigsaw -- U.S.
Constitution tutor -- Scramble.
```

9.7B22. Item described (MARC 500)

This note is added in the new rules with the directions that, for remote access resources, always give the date on which the resource was viewed for description.

```
500     Description based on contents viewed
Dec. 17, 2000.
```

1.7B22. Combined notes relating to the original (MARC 534)

This note is used to describe the original item represented by the electronic resource being cataloged.

```
534     $p Electronic text of: $a Sophocles. $t
The Oedipus trilogy / by Sophocles ; English
translation by F. Storr. $c Cambridge, Mass. :
Harvard University Press, 1912. $f (Loeb
Library).
```

1.7B22. (LCRI) Combined notes relating to their production (MARC 533)

The Library of Congress rule interpretation described later in this chapter gives the LC policy for describing an electronic reproduction of a book on the bibliographic record for the original. All the details about the electronic version are given in one note in field 533.

```
533     Electronic reproduction. $b Portland, OR.
: $c PNW Publications, $d 1998. $n Mode of
access: World Wide Web. $n System requirements:
Adobe Acrobat reader.
```

MAIN AND ADDED ENTRIES

There are no special rules for choice or form of main and added entries for remote access electronic resources. These entries are chosen just as for any other type of material being cataloged.

One must be careful to check the online authority file for the form of a personal or corporate name before using it in a bibliographic record.

SUBJECT ACCESS

There are no special guidelines for choosing subject headings, genre headings, or classification numbers for remote access electronic resources. There has been some discussion in the literature and on AUTOCAT, the electronic list for catalogers, about the need for giving classification numbers to materials not physically on shelves, but many agree that there is enough benefit for collection development to be able to group remote access works with other works available to students in a particular discipline to be worth the effort. Attaching holdings to such bibliographic records in OCLC may cause problems in a local system–as with any other process, one must know how it does or doesn't affect the local system before beginning a project.

Subject headings and genre headings should be used just as for other items in a library's collections.

MARC 21 CODING AND TAGGING

Field 856, Electronic Location and Access

Field 856 was developed during the first OCLC Internet cataloging project as a field to hold all information needed for access to the computer file being cataloged. It was hoped that this could eventually be a "button" that the user would push when viewing a bibliographic record that would take the viewer directly to the item being cataloged. Some of us laughed at the thought of this ever happening–now it is in use and taken for granted by our patrons.

Every remote access electronic resource must have an 856 field in the bibliographic record containing the electronic address, usually the URL, for the item being cataloged. The 856 field is repeatable.

There are many indicators and subfields available for field 856, so the reader is referred to the document titled *Guidelines for the Use of Field 856,* prepared by the Library of Congress, Network Development and MARC Standards Office. This document is revised periodically, so check for the newest version. The URL is *http://lcweb.loc.gov/marc/856guide.html.*

A typical URL appears in a bibliographic record as

```
856 40  $u http://lcweb.loc.gov/marc/856guide.html
```

Fields 006, 007, 008

A document from Network Development MARC Standards Office at the Library of Congress, *Relationship of Fields 006, 007, and 008,* explains that field 006 was developed during the format integration process to solve the problem of field 008 not being repeatable. (In OCLC bibliographic records, field 008 is displayed as the fixed fields.) Field 007 had long been used for special materials to hold codes for characteristics not included in field 008. Field 006 was to include characteristics that could not be included in a single field 008. For example, a serial videorecording with field 008 coded for a videorecording has no provisions for serial characteristics. Those serial characteristics could be recorded in field 006 in the same bibliographic record, and would become retrievable by local systems programmed to index the 006.

This solution worked for the local systems that made it work–in our system at Mankato State, for instance, we could qualify a search for video and retrieve the bibliographic record or qualify the search for serials and also retrieve the item–or search for a video serial and get it.

But many local systems did not want to do this work, or were unable to do it, or could not afford to do it. So . . .

What Workform to Use?

Meanwhile discussion was going on in some cataloging communities about content versus physical format. Map people felt the "mapness" of their items took priority over the physical form; a map coded as an electronic resource was still a map and should be cataloged on a map workform, with its computer characteristics expressed elsewhere. And those handling computer journals at the Library of Congress had cataloged them on book/serial workforms, because their check in procedures and other internal processing steps could not handle bibliographic records on computer workforms. These problems and others led to a new solution–that of cataloging what are now electronic resources on workforms representing the content of the item rather than the physical form, and adding whatever fields 006 and 007 may be necessary to code all the physical characteristics necessary for retrieval under the possible searches.

A series of documents were produced for our use in deciding which workform to use for any given bibliographic record. The two current guidelines are:

Cataloging Electronic Resources: OCLC-MARC Coding Guidelines, by Jay Weitz. Revised 2000 May 15 *www.oclc.org/oclc/cataloging/type.htm*

Guidelines for Coding Electronic Resources in Leader/06. Network Development and MARC Standards Office, Library of Congress. July 1, 1999. *lcweb.loc.gov/marc/ldr06guide.html*

These documents explain that the descriptive cataloging of the materials covered has not changed; only the workform chosen for the bibliographic record is changed. Fields 006 and 007 are required in all cases. The GMD "electronic resource" is to be used for all these materials.

A new code "s" has been added to the list for "Form of Item" in byte 23 of field 008 (a fixed field in OCLC); and in field 006 as appropriate. Code "s" (Electronic) is defined as:

> Item intended for manipulation by a computer. May reside in a carrier accessed either directly or remotely. May require use of peripheral devices attached to the computer. Do NOT use for items that do not require the use of a computer.

When cataloging an electronic resource that is a monographic document of any type, use the workform for books with field 006 for the computer characteristics and field 007 for additional physical characteristics.

When cataloging an electronic resource that is a serial document (journal, newsletter, etc.) that fits the current definition of serial by including a numeric and/or chronological designation, the serials workform is used, again with field 006 for the computer characteristics, and field 007 for additional physical characteristics.

The computer file workform is only to be used for computer software (including programs, games, fonts), numeric data, online systems or services, and computer-oriented multimedia. Fields 006 and 007 are added as appropriate.

Map items go on the map workform, music items on the music workform (scores or sound recordings as appropriate), visual materials go on the visual materials workform. In all cases fields 006 and 007 are added as appropriate.

Single Record or Separate Record?

Another practice under discussion is whether to catalog an electronic manifestation of a title on a separate bibliographic record or on the bibliographic record for the print version. This is also discussed in the OCLC-MARC guidelines cited above, with directions for both methods and discussion of other considerations. The CONSER guidelines permit the single record approach. OCLC prefers separate records, but permits single records. OCLC cautions users to check with your local system vendor and any network partners before choosing to use one approach or the other.

Monograph or Serial?

The OCLC-MARC guidelines also address the decision about coding an electronic resource as a monograph or as a serial. It is possible that the print form of a title will be cataloged as a serial, while the electronic version may be cataloged as a monograph. The guidelines list the following types of material as currently being excluded from cataloging as serials:

> Databases (including directories, A&I services, etc.),
> Electronic discussion groups (e.g., SERIALIST),
> Electronic discussion group digests (e.g., AUTOCAT digest),
> Gopher servers (e.g., LC-MARVEL),
> Online public access catalogs (e.g., OCLC, RLIN),
> Online services (e.g., America Online),
> Web sites (e.g., the CONSER home page).

Remember these and other decisions about creating bibliographic records for remote access electronic resources will change as the rules change. (See Appendix, Examples 1-3.)

Electronic Books

There has been a great deal of interest in the cataloging of electronic books, or ebooks. The Library of Congress issued a rule interpretation for rule 1.11A in *Cataloging Service Bulletin* no. 89 (summer 2000). This LCRI covers facsimiles, photocopies, and other reproductions, including electronic reproductions. It is reproduced below.

"1.11A. Facsimiles, Photocopies, and Other Reproductions.

Non-Microform Reproductions[1]

LC practice: Follow these guidelines for reproductions of previously existing materials that are made for: preservation purposes in formats other than microforms; non-microform dissertations and other reproductions produced "on demand"; and, electronic reproductions.

These guidelines identify the data elements to be used in the record for the reproduction, separate from the record for the original. For some electronic reproductions, however, LC may delineate details of the reproduction on the record for the original manifestation rather than create a separate record for the reproduction. LC catalogers should consult "Draft Interim Guidelines for Cataloging Electronic Resources" <http://lcweb.loc.gov/catdir/cpso/dcmb19_4.html> for more information (other cataloging agencies may have developed their own guidelines in this regard).

1. Transcribe the bibliographic data appropriate to the *original* work being reproduced in the following areas:

   title and statement of responsibility
   edition
   material (or type of publication) specific details
   publication, distribution, etc.
   physical description
   series

2. If appropriate, give in the title and statement of responsibility area the general material designation that is applicable to the format of the *reproduction* (cf. LCRI 1.1C)
3. Give in a single note (533 field) all other details relating to the *reproduction* and its publication/availability. Include in the note the following bibliographic data in the order listed:

   format of the reproduction
   dates of publication and/or sequential designation of issues reproduced (for serials)
   place and name of the agency responsible for the reproduction[2]
   date of the reproduction
   physical description of the reproduction if different from the original
   series statement of the reproduction (if applicable)
   notes relating to the reproduction (if applicable)[3]

   Apply rules1.4-1.7 for the formulation of the bibliographic data in the 533 field note. Enclose cataloger-supplied data in brackets. Omit the area divider (space-dash-space).
4. Use a physical description fixed field (007) applicable to the reproduction. For electronic reproductions, also supply information about the electronic location and access (856 field). (See Appendix, Examples 4-5.)

Footnotes:

1. A reproduction is a manifestation that replicates an item (or a group of items) or another manifestation (e.g., a reprint with no changes) that is intended to function as a substitute. The reproduction may be in a different physical form from the original. Reproduction is generally a mechanical rather than an intellectual process. The physical characteristics of the reproduction such as color, image resolution, or sound fidelity are influenced by the particular process used to create it, and therefore may differ from those of the original. Reproductions are usually made for such reasons as the original's limited availability, remote location, poor condition, high cost, or restricted utility. Cataloger judgment will be required to distinguish electronic reproductions from electronic republications or simultaneous publication in analog and digital form (only reproductions are covered by the LCRI). For example, an electronic reproduction produced using scanning techniques that results in a facsimile reproduction may be easily identified as a reproduction. Other non-facsimile electronic reproductions may also be considered under this LCRI when they purport to be a reproduction of the original and can serve as a surrogate for the original. Other cataloging agencies choosing to follow this LCRI may need to develop their own criteria for distinguishing reproductions from manifestations judged not to be reproductions. In cases of doubt, or in cases where there is inadequate information about the original on which to base a description, do not consider the electronic manifestation to be a reproduction.

2. Consider the "agency responsible for the reproduction" to be the agency that selected the material to be reproduced, arranged for reproducing the material, exercised control over production formats, has overall responsibility for quality, etc. If the agency is unknown, give "[s.n.]"; if place and agency are unknown, use "[S.l.: s.n.]." Transcribe also the name of the agency from which to secure copies or the agency that made the reproduction if the agency is named in one of the prescribed sources for the publication, distribution, etc., area of the reproduction.

3. Other cataloging agencies choosing to follow this LCRI may have compelling local reasons (e.g., data manipulation) for recording notes relating to the reproduction in other than the 533 field (e.g., system requirements (538), restrictions on access (506)).

Note: Items that are reproductions of materials prepared or assembled specially for bringing out an original edition (e.g., republished for inclusion in a collection, commemorative editions, published with new introductory material) are cataloged as editions, not as reproductions."

CONCLUSION

In this chapter I have explained how to catalog remote access electronic resources, going through the current rules bibliographic area by area, with examples for each. Remember, however, the rules will keep changing. While this chapter includes new rules not yet available to catalogers as of this writing, those rules will have been published by the time catalogers read this, and still more new rules will be in the process of approval. I anticipate that the process of development of new rules for *AACR2* for electronic resources and serials will take several years to complete, including the reconciliation of changes across the chapters of *AACR2*, and the possible major changes to rule 0.24. Meanwhile the computer world keeps changing and developing, so new forms of media may need cataloging.

When faced with the need to catalog a new material that does not seem to fit into a given chapter, go back to the basic rules in chapter 1 and whatever other rules seem to apply, and do the best you can. Your patrons need access to these new materials now, and it is up to you, the cataloger, to supply that need. Best of luck to you all, from a now-retired cataloger.

BIBLIOGRAPHY

This is not a historical bibliography, but a list of documents of current interest to those cataloging electronic resources.

AACR Related Documents

American Library Association. *Anglo-American Cataloguing Rules,* 2nd ed., 1998 rev. Chicago: American Library Association, 1998.

These are the basic rules for descriptive cataloging used internationally. Includes revisions approved between 1992 and 1996 by JSC but not previously published. Also includes *Amendments 1993,* those revisions approved by JSC in 1989, 1990, 1991, and 1992 and published by ALA in 1993.

American Library Association. *Anglo-American Cataloguing Rules,* 2nd ed., 1998 rev., Amendments 1999. Chicago: American Library Association, 2000. Available online at URL: *www.ala.org/editions/updates/aacr2.*

These are changes to the rules, agreed to by JSC in 1997 and 1998 and approved in 1999. Only available online or on CD-ROM.

"Chapter 9 Electronic Resources." 4JSC/ALA/27/ALA follow-up/4/LC response/CCC represponse/2. Unpublished JSC document dated October 10, 2000.

MARC 21 Related Documents

Network Development and MARC Standards Office, Library of Congress. *MARC 21 Format for Bibliographic Data.* Washington, DC: Library of Congress, 1999.

Official English version with full descriptions, examples, and guidelines. Base text dated February 1999; includes list of changes.

Network Development and MARC Standards Office, Library of Congress. *MARC 21 Concise Format for Bibliographic Data.* Washington, DC: Library of Congress, 1999. Available online at URL: *http://lcweb.loc.gov/marc/bibliographic/.*

Concise form of full publication, dated October 2000.

OCLC. *Bibliographic Formats and Standards,* 2nd ed. Dublin, Ohio: OCLC Online Computer Library Center, 1996- . Available online at URL: *http://www.oclc.org/oclc/bib/about.htm.*

Revised guide to machine-readable cataloging records in the OCLC union catalog. Last updated December 2000.

Weitz, Jay. *Cataloging Electronic Resources: OCLC-MARC Coding Guidelines.* Dublin, Ohio: OCLC. Available online at URL: *http://www.oclc.org/oclc/cataloging/type.htm.*

Revised Sept. 22, 2000.

Network Development and MARC Standards Office, Library of Congress. *Guidelines for Coding Electronic Resources in Leader/06.* Washington, DC: Library of Congress, 1999. Available online at URL: *http://lcweb.loc.gov/marc/ldr06guide.html.*

This document, dated July 1,1999, is "intended to assist MARC users in deciding how to code records for electronic resources in Leader/06 (Type of record) and Computer Files 008/26 and 006/09 (Type of computer file)."

Network Development MARC Standards Office, Library of Congress. *Relationship of Fields 006, 007, and 008: MARC21 Bibliographic Format.* Washington, DC: Library of Congress, 2000. Available online at URL: *http://lcweb.loc.gov/marc/formatintegration.html.*

Document dated April 21, 2000.

Network Development MARC Standards Office, Library of Congress. *Guidelines for the Use of Field 856.* Washington, DC: Library of Congress, 1999. Available online at URL: *http://lcweb.loc.gov/marc/856guide.html.*

Revised August 1999, this document includes all changes to MARC field 856 through the annual ALA conference held in June 1999.

Cataloging Documents

Olson, Nancy B., ed. *Cataloging Internet Resources: A Manual and Practical Guide,* 2nd ed. Dublin, Ohio: OCLC Online Computer Library Center, 1997. Also available online at URL: *http://www.purl.org/oclc/cataloging-internet/.*

Guidelines for cataloging Internet resources developed during a project partially funded by a grant from the U.S. Department of Education, and revised and tested during a second project with similar funding.

Beck, Melissa. *CONSER Cataloging Manual, Module 31: Remote Access Computer File Serials.* Washington, DC: Library of Congress, 1999. Available online at URL: *http://lcweb.loc.gov/acq/conser/module31.html.*

See the section: "What is a remote access computer file serial?" The CONSER guidelines differ in places from *AACR2,* though some differences are for experimental purposes.

IFLA Universal Bibliographic Control and International MARC Programme. *ISBD(ER): International Standard Bibliographic Description for Electronic Resources.* IFLA, 1999. Also available online at URL: *http://www.ifla.org/VII/s13/pubs/isbd.htm.*

The international standard for the bibliographic description of electronic resources, developed after several years of international review and revised from the *ISBD(CF): International Standard Bibliographic Description for Computer Files.*

Journal of Internet Cataloging: The International Quarterly of Digital Organization, Classification & Access. Binghamton, NY: The Haworth Information Press, 1997-

Issues v 4(1/2) are devoted entirely to CORC and entitled "CORC: New Tools and Possibilities for Cooperative Electronic Resource Description."

Library of Congress. *Cataloging Service Bulletin.* Washington, DC: Library of Congress, Summer 1978-

All LC rule interpretations are published in this quarterly bulletin, as are changes to subject heading subdivisions, and new or revised subject headings.

AUTHOR NOTE

Nancy B. Olson has been President of the Minnesota Library Association. Visiting Distinguished Scholar at OCLC, founder of the Minnesota AACR2 Trainers, founder of OLAC (OnLine Audiovisual Catalogers) and founder/owner of Soldier Creek Press. She has received both the Ester Piercy award (1980) and the Margaret Mann certificate (1999) from the ALCTS division of the American Library Association. She is the author of many works on, or related to, cataloging including the 15-volume set of *Combined Indexes to the Library of Congress Classification Schedules* (United States Historical Documents Institute, 1975), the annual cumulative *Cataloging Service Bulleting Index* (Soldier Creek Press, 1974-), *Cataloging of Audiovisual Materials and Other Special Materials* (Minnesota Scholarly Press, 1998) and numerous works on cataloging film, video, and electronic resources.

In retirement Nancy is enjoying her children and grandchildren and is busy with teaching, writing, genealogy, and sewing.

APPENDIX

EXAMPLE 1. Monograph

```
Type: a   ELvl: I   Srce: d   Audn: f   Ctrl:      Lang: eng
BLvl: m   Form: s   Conf: 0   Biog:     MRec:      Ctry: ohu
          Cont:     GPub:     LitF:     Indx: 0
Desc: a   Ills:     Fest: 0   DtSt: s   Dates: 2000,
006      mfd
007      c $b r $d a $e n
100 1    Weitz, Jay, $d 1953-
245 10   Cataloging electronic resources $h [electronic resource]
: $b OCLC-MARC coding guidelines / $c by Jay Weitz.
246 10   OCLC-MARC coding guidelines
256      Electronic document.
260      [Dublin, Ohio] : $b OCLC, $c 2000.
538      Mode of access: World Wide Web.
500      Title from caption, viewed Dec. 14, 2000.
500      "Revised 2000 May 15."
710 2    OCLC.
856 40   $u http://www.oclc.org/oclc/cataloging/type.htm
```

EXAMPLE 2. Continuing publication. Cataloged as open-entry monograph according to current rules.

```
Type: m   ELvl: I   Srce: d  Audn: f   Ctrl:     Lang: eng
BLvl: m   File: j   GPub: 0            MRec:     Ctry: nyu
Desc: a                      DtSt: m   Dates: 1995,9999
006      a f   0000
007      c $b r $d a $e n
245 00  OLAC $h [electronic resource] : $b Online Audiovisual
Catalogers, Inc.
246 10  Online Audiovisual Catalogers.
256      Electronic online service.
260      [United States] : $b OLAC ; $a [Buffalo, N.Y. : $b
State University of New York at Buffalo], $c 1995-
310      Updated frequently.
538      Mode of access: Internet.
500      Title from home page; viewed on Dec. 14, 2000 (last
updated: Aug. 12, 1999).
520      Web site for OLAC, an organization for catalogers of
audiovisual and other special materials. Includes information
about OLAC, its organization, officers, conferences, committees,
and awards, rationale for cataloging audiovisual and other
special materials, book reviews, and links to useful web sites.
650 0   Cataloging of nonbook materials.
710 2   On-Line Audiovisual Catalogers, Inc.
856 40  $u http//ublib.buffalo.edu/libraries/units/cts/olac/
```

APPENDIX (continued)

EXAMPLE 3. Serial

```
Type: a   ELvl: I   Srce: d   GPub:      Ctrl:      Lang: eng
BLvl: s   Form: s   Conf: 0   Freq:      MRec:      Ctry: ilu
          Orig:     EntW:     Regl: x    ISSN: 0
Desc: a   SrTp: p   Cont: 0   DtSt: c    Dates: 19uu,9999
006       mfd
007       c $b r $d a $e n
022       1056-6694
245 00    ALCTS network news $h [electronic resource]
256       Electronic newsletter.
260       Chicago, IL : $b Association for Library Collections &
Technical Services, American Library Association,
310       Irregular.
538       Mode of access: E-mail to subscribers.
500       Title from caption.
500       Available free to subscribers. Back issues available
through ALCTS web site. Only available in electronic form.
500       Description based on vol.20, no. 9 (Dec. 15, 2000);
viewed on Dec. 18, 2000.
710 2     Association for Library Collections & Technical Services.
856  0    ala.org $f AN2 $h listproc $i subscribe
```

EXAMPLE 4. [Given here in OCLC format rather than LC style]

```
007      cr
245 10   Introduction to United States government
information sources $h [electronic resource] / $c Joe
Morehead.
250      6th ed.
260      Englewood, Colo. : $b Libraries Unlimited, $c 1999.
300      xxv, 491 p. ; $c 25 cm.
440  0   Library and information science text series
504      Includes bibliographical references and indexes.
533      Electronic reproduction. $b Boulder, Colo. : $c
NetLibrary, $d 1999. $n Mode of access: World Wide Web. $n
Access restricted to NetLibrary subscribers.
856 4    $3 Display record $u
http:///www.netlibrary.com/summary.asp?ID=11187
```

EXAMPLE 5

```
007      cr
245 10   Breeding design considerations for coastal Douglas-
fir $h [electronic resource] / $c Randy Johnson.
260      Portland, OR : $b U.S. Dept. of Agriculture, Forest
Service, Pacific Northwest Research Station, $c [1998]
300      34 p. : $b ill. ; $c 28 cm.
500      Cover title.
500      "February 1998."
533      Electronic reproduction. $b Portland, OR : $c PNW
Publications, $d 1998. $n Mode of access: World Wide Web.
$n System requirements: Adobe Acrobat reader.
856 4    $u http:///www.fs.fed.us/pnw/pubs/qtr%5F411.pdf
```

Cataloging Three-Dimensional Artefacts and Realia

Nancy B. Olson

SUMMARY. "Cataloging Three-Dimensional Artefacts and Realia" assumes users have a basic knowledge of descriptive cataloging using the *Anglo-American Cataloguing Rules,* second edition (*AACR2*), and the MARC 21 bibliographic format. This article focuses on chapter 10 of *AACR2* and the special problems of cataloging materials such as games, toys, models and dioramas, realia, and three-dimensional art originals and reproductions. Some complete and some partial bibliographic records for these types of material are included. *[Article copies available for a fee from The Haworth Document Delivery Service: 1-800-342-9678. E-mail address: <getinfo@haworthpressinc.com> Website: <http://www.HaworthPress.com> © 2001 by The Haworth Press, Inc. All rights reserved.]*

KEYWORDS. Cataloging of realia, cataloging of models, cataloging of toys, cataloging of games, MARC format, descriptive cataloging-rules, Anglo-American cataloguing rules

Chapter 10 of the *Anglo-American Cataloguing Rules, second edition, 1998 revision (AACR2),* covers the descriptive cataloging of all

---

Nancy B. Olson cataloged audiovisual and other special materials for 30 years at Minnesota State University, Mankato, retiring in 1999 as a Professor on the faculty there. She continues to teach workshops at the University of Pittsburgh, San Jose State University, and elsewhere as invited.

[Haworth co-indexing entry note]: "Cataloging Three-Dimensional Artefacts and Realia." Olson, Nancy B. Co-published simultaneously in *Cataloging & Classification Quarterly* (The Haworth Information Press, an imprint of The Haworth Press, Inc.) Vol. 31, No. 3/4, 2001, pp. 139-150; and: *The Audiovisual Cataloging Current* (ed: Sandra K. Roe) The Haworth Information Press, an imprint of The Haworth Press, Inc., 2001, pp. 139-150. Single or multiple copies of this article are available for a fee from The Haworth Document Delivery Service [1-800-342-9678, 9:00 a.m. - 5:00 p.m. (EST). E-mail address: getinfo@haworthpressinc.com].

© 2001 by The Haworth Press, Inc. All rights reserved.

kinds of three-dimensional materials except for globes or cartographic relief models. This includes models, dioramas, games, braille cassettes, sculptures and other three dimensional art works (both originals and reproductions), exhibits, machines, and clothing. It also includes naturally occurring objects. There were no national or international rules for cataloging any of these materials before the development of *AACR2* in 1978.

For all these types of material, the chief source of information is the object itself together with any labels, accompanying material, and container. For complete cataloging rules consult the text of *AACR2*. Most of the rules in chapter 10 of *AACR2* are similar to those in other audiovisual-cataloging chapters, with the exceptions explained below.

The only Library of Congress Rule Interpretations for this chapter, other than one mentioned under the publication, distribution, etc., area below, are decisions made on options to the rules by the Library of Congress for their internal use. There are no special rules for these materials for choice or form of main or added entries. They are treated just as all other materials in the library for which they are being cataloged.

There are no special guidelines for subject headings or classification of these materials, though ALA committees have addressed this topic at times. Audiovisual materials should be classified and given subject headings just as are all other materials in the library for which they are being cataloged. In addition, one might want to consider adding genre access for the form of each object cataloged.

GENERAL MATERIAL DESIGNATIONS

The list of general material designations (GMD) that may be used in this chapter include:

art original
art reproduction
diorama
game
microscope slide
model
realia
toy

Each of these types of material will be defined and discussed in the following sections, with some complete examples given at the end of the chapter.

PUBLICATION, DISTRIBUTION, ETC. AREA AND MANUFACTURING

The only cataloging rules unique to chapter 10 are those for area 4 of the bibliographic record. Three-dimensional materials may be published or they may be manufactured; in either case they may be distributed by still another entity. Realia may be naturally occurring and have no publisher, manufacturer, or distributor. Rules in chapter 10 allow for any or all of these possibilities.

The pattern for area 4 information is as shown below:

```
    260      Place of publication : $b Name of publisher ; $a
Place of distribution : $b Name of distributor, $c Date of
publication/distribution $e (Place of manufacture : $f Name of
manufacturer, $g Date of manufacture).
```

As much or as little information as is available or as can be assumed is used in this area. If the information is assumed, it is placed within square brackets, even if within the parentheses of MARC subfields e, f, g.

Unpublished Three-Dimensional Artefacts

Handmade objects, three-dimensional art works, or unique materials that are not published would have only a date in the publication, distribution, etc., area, just as is done for dissertations and theses. The name of the maker/creator of the unpublished object goes in the statement of responsibility, bracketed only if not given anywhere on the item, but known by the cataloger. Any information about place of manufacture goes in a note rather than as place of publication, as the item is not published. This decision is reinforced by a Library of Congress rule interpretation published in *Cataloging Service Bulletin* 32 (Spring1986).

Realia

Real items may be collected, labeled, packaged, and distributed commercially, as are sets of rocks, seashells, and dried or preserved plant specimens. These items may also be collected by an individual or expedition and donated to a library, as was the alligator skin brought home by a missionary and given to our library many years ago. The commercially-packaged items have a normal area 4 following the pattern given above.

Any items collected from nature and donated to a library have no area 4 in the bibliographic record. There is no place of publication, distribution, or manufacture, no name of publisher, distributor, or manufacturer, and no date of publication, distribution, or manufacture for naturally-occurring objects. Information about who collected the items, where they were collected, and when they were collected goes into the note area.

PHYSICAL DESCRIPTION AREA

While the physical description area is similar to that found in any other bibliographic record, there are some differences.

Extent of Item

The name of the item being cataloged is given either using one of the GMD terms as a specific material designation, or by using the specific name of the item or names of the parts of the item:

```
1 toy

1 doll

1 action figure

3 finger puppets

1 game board, 6 playing pieces, 1 die
```

Number of pieces may be included as part of this subfield:

```
1 jigsaw puzzle (1,000 pieces)

1 game (1 board, 6 playing pieces, 1 die)

1 game (various pieces)
```

Here a note would be needed to explain "various pieces." It should give more detail about what the pieces are and about how many items there are of each.

Other Physical Details

The material of which the object is made is named when appropriate or when known.

If an item has more than two colors, use "col."; if it has one or two colors, the colors are named. For black-and-white objects, use "b&w."

```
1 statue : $b marble, tan

1 rock : $b brown and white

3 action figures : $b plastic and cloth, col.
```

Dimensions

Dimensions are given in centimeters, rounded up to the next whole centimeter. Multiple dimensions are given in the order height x width x depth, or as appropriate. A word may be added to a measurement as needed for clarity.

```
1 hand puppet : $b cloth, green and pink ; $c 26 x 16 cm.

1 cannon ball : $b lead, gray ; $c 10 cm. in diameter.

1 toy : $b wood, natural ; $c 26 x 34 x 16 cm.
```

Accompanying Material

Any printed material or other material accompanying chapter 10 items is treated as in any other chapter.

```
        24 rocks : $b col. ; $c 2 cm. cubes in box 28 x 20 x 4
cm. + $e 1 teacher's guide.
```

NOTES

Notes are extremely important when cataloging audiovisual material. Because the material cannot be examined before use as easily as can books shelved in open stacks, the user must rely on information contained in notes in the bibliographic record to decide if the item being described might be of use. *AACR2* chapter 1 lists 22 rules for notes, 17 of which are included in chapter 10. Any of the original 22, however, may be used if needed. Notes may be combined. Notes are to be used in the order given in the rules. Some of these notes have their own MARC codes, but most are coded as MARC field 500. Notes include:

10.7B1. Nature of the item (MARC field 500)
1. 7B2. Language of the item and/or translation or adaptation (MARC 546)
10.7B3. Source of title proper (MARC 500)
10.7B4. Variations in title (MARC 500)
10.7B5. Parallel titles and other title information (MARC 500)
10.7B6. Statements of responsibility (MARC 500)
10.7B7. Edition and history (MARC 500)
1.7B8. Material (or type of publication) specific details (Not applicable here)
10.7B9. Publication, distribution, etc. (MARC 500)
10.7B10. Physical description (MARC 500)
10.7B11. Accompanying material (MARC 500)
10.7B12. Series (MARC 500)
10.7B13. Dissertations (MARC 502)
10.7B14. Audience (MARC 521)
1.7B15. Reference to published descriptions (MARC 510)
1.7B16. Other formats (MARC 530 or 535)
10.7B17. Summary (MARC 520)
10.7B18. Contents (MARC 505, 500, or 504)
10.7B19. Numbers (MARC 500)
10.7B20. Copy being described, library's holdings, and restrictions on use (MARC 506, 583, or 590)
10.7B21. "With" notes (MARC 501)
1.7B22. Combined notes relating to the original (MARC 534)

TYPES OF MATERIAL

Art Originals, Art Reproductions

Three-dimensional works of art, whether original or reproductions, are cataloged by the rules in *AACR2* chapter 10. The bibliographic record for an original object would have only the date in MARC field 260, and would have the artist named in the statement of responsibility in field 245. Other details about the work of art and its creation would be given in notes.

The bibliographic record for a reproduction of a three-dimensional work of art would have a complete field 260 with the place and name of the publisher, manufacturer, and distributor included along with the date(s) related to the reproduction. Information about the original would be included in MARC field 534.

Dioramas, Models

Models are exact reproductions of an item, though they may be the exact size or larger or smaller than the original. A statement of the scale of the model is important and should be included as a note in the bibliographic description. Common types of models include architectural models, train models, models of flowers and their parts, and anatomical models and/or parts.

A diorama, commonly found in museums, is a scene containing many figures or items, all done to the same scale. Dioramas commonly include a background painted with an appropriate scene-as a diorama showing a wolf family set in a northern Minnesota forest. A model railroad with its setting would be a diorama.

Games

Games are cataloged by the rules in *AACR2* chapter 10. When cataloging games, it is important to include in notes information about how many players are needed, the age of the players, and the purpose of the game.

Toys

Because the GMD "toy" was not available for use until the 1988 revision of *AACR2*, records for toys can be found in OCLC and other databases with other GMDs, or without GMDs. Sometimes "realia" was used because these items are real toys, but that can be misleading (as when something with the title "Frog" is then given the GMD "realia"!).

Notes should be used to give the potential patron information about the age level appropriate for the toy, and perhaps some description of the purpose or intent of use. When cataloging puppets, one might also include whether the puppet is designed for a child's hand or an adult's, whether or not it can be used on the left hand, and what parts of the puppet are manipulated.

Realia

The term "realia" is used in *AACR2* for real items as opposed to reproductions, models, or toys. The real items may be manufactured, such as items of clothing, furniture, or weapons, or they may be handmade, such as quilts, handicrafts, or pottery. Handmade items, if not commercially packaged and distributed, would have only a date in MARC field 260.

This GMD is also used for naturally-occurring items (rocks, seashells, pressed flowers), whether packaged commercially or collected by an individual. Bibliographic records for naturally-occurring items that are not commercially packaged would not have a field 260, but would have notes about when and where they were collected, and by whom.

MARC FORMAT

Type code "r" is used for all chapter 10 material.

Type of material codes include:

- a art original
- c art reproduction
- d diorama
- g game
- p microscope slide
- q model
- r realia
- w toy
- z others-three-dimensional or realia, but not one of the above

There are no 007 fields for these materials.
Field 260 codes are shown in the example given earlier for area 4.

Processing for Circulation

Each item or object must be barcoded and given a call number label for circulation, and some must be packaged or repackaged as desired. It is not possible to make hard and fast rules about where a barcode or call number or other label is placed because these items vary so much in size and shape and composition. Sometimes we wired a piece of tag board or heavy sturdy paper to an object, and put all labels on that-we also reinforced the hole in the paper that the wire went through.

We sometimes made notes in the circulation record to tell the circulation people where the tattletape was hidden inside a puppet or toy so the correct area of the object could be "swiped" through the desensitizing machine. I opened seams and inserted tattletape into each puppet and doll and stuffed toy in our collection, and checked each one before sewing the seam closed. For some (such as a clam puppet) I used a round tattletape disc designed for CD-ROMs because the clam was not long enough in any dimension to accommodate a length of tattletape. We learned that we could not cut the tattletape, use the cut pieces, and have it function. Items with long tails usually got tattletape inserted into the tails!

Examples

1. Partial Bibliographic Record for a Mineral Specimen (Does Not Include Fixed Fields)

```
245 00  [Rhodochrosite specimen] $h [realia]
300     1 specimen : $b pink ; $c 7 x 9 x 6 cm.
500     Specimen of the mineral rhodochrosite showing
crystal structure; from Argentina.
500     Title supplied by cataloger.
655  7  Rhodochrosite.  $2 local
655  7  Mineral specimens.  $2 local
```

This item has no label or other information on it; it was purchased, just as collected, in a "rock" shop.

2. Partial Bibliographic Record for a Toy (Does Not Include Fixed or Variable Fields)

```
     245 00  Jesse Ventura, man of action $h [toy] : $b U.S. Navy
SEAL / $c Ventura for Minnesota, Inc.
     260     Minneapolis, MN : $b Toyboy Man, $c c1999 $e (China :
$f Formative Intl. Co. Ltd.)
     300     1 action figure : $b plastic and cloth, col. ; $c 32
cm. tall. in container 33 x 16 x 8 cm.
     500     Movable action figure of Jesse Ventura, Governor of
Minnesota, dressed as a U.S. Navy SEAL. Ventura served in Vietnam
as a Navy SEAL.
     521     For ages 5 and up.
     655  7  Action figures (Toys) $2 lcsh
     610 10  United States. $b Navy. $b SEALs.
     600 10  Ventura, Jesse.
     710 2   Ventura for Minnesota, Inc.
     710 2   Toyboy Man (Firm)
```

There were three action figures of Jesse Ventura issued in 1999-as the governor, as a U.S. Navy SEAL, and as a volunteer (high school) football coach. All used the same package (and the same UPC code). One side of the box carried the names of the three figures with brief descriptions. I decided this was the equivalent of a "list" title page common to scores, except there was no check mark or star by the title enclosed.

The name of the manufacturing company in China is given exactly as found on the package.

3. Complete Bibliographic Record for a Set of Games

Type: r ELvl: I Srce: d Audn: j Ctrl: Lang: eng
BLvl: m Form: GPub: Time: MRec: Ctry: cau
Desc: a TMat: g Tech: n DtSt: s Dates: 2000,

020 1575281112

024 1 794764013511

245 00 Harry Potter and the sorcerer's stone $h [game] : $b the game.

260 San Francisco, CA : $b University Games Corp., $c c2000.

300 7 games ; $c in container 31 x 43 x 8 cm.

500 Games based on book of the same name by J.K. Rowling.

500 "Includes 6 ¾ games."

500 Includes 6 interlocking game boards (each 26 x 26 cm.), 3 decks of cards (90 cards), 3 sorcerer's stone tokens, 117 game tokens, 1 double-sided spinner with arrow, 4 playing pieces with stands, 1 instruction booklet.

521 Ages 8 and up.

500 Games may be played in order on interlocking boards, or individually on separated boards.

505 0 1. Hagrid's challenge : Fluffy, the three-headed dog -- 2. Sprout's challenge : the Devil's snare -- 3. Flitwick's challenge : winged keys -- 4. McGonagall's challenge : wizard chess -- 5. Quirrell's challenge : the troll -- 6. Snipe's challenge : potions -- 6 3/4. The mirror of Erised and the sorcerer's stone.

655 7 Board games. $2 lcsh

655 7 Fantasy games. $2 lcsh

700 1 Rowling, J. K. $t Harry Potter and the philosopher's stone.

710 2 University Games Corporation.

One might want to add additional subject and/or genre headings.

I could have used a coded and tagged 505 to allow searching of the individual titles, but didn't feel that would be useful. I assume most patrons looking for this would search under Harry Potter.

The 700 contains the uniform title for this book-the original title as published in Great Britain. The authority file provides a cross reference to the title as published in the United States. In this bibliographic record we have access to the U.S. title through field 245.

For nine more examples, with illustrations, see my book, *Cataloging of Audiovisual Materials and Other Special Materials,* 4th ed. (Minnesota Scholarly Press, 1998).

AUTHOR NOTE

Nancy B. Olson has been President of the Minnesota Library Association, Visiting Distinguished Scholar at OCLC, founder of the Minnesota AACR2 Trainers, founder of OLAC (OnLine Audiovisual Catalogers) and founder/owner of Soldier Creek Press. She has received both the Esther Piercy award (1980) and the Margaret Mann certificate (1999) from the ALCTS division of the American Library Association. She is the author of many works on, or related to, cataloging including the 15-volume set of *Combined Indexes to the Library of Congress Classification Schedules* (United States Historical Documents Institute, 1975), the annual cumulative *Cataloging Service Bulletin Index* (Soldier Creek Press, 1974-), *Cataloging of Audiovisual Materials and Other Special Materials* (Minnesota Scholarly Press, 1998) and numerous works on cataloging film, video, and electronic resources.

In retirement Nancy is enjoying her children and grandchildren and is busy with teaching, writing, genealogy, and sewing.

Cataloging Kits

Nancy B. Olson

SUMMARY. The major problem in cataloging kits is that of identifying what is actually a kit according to *AACR2*-this problem is discussed, with examples given. The rules themselves are discussed and examples of kits are included. Sections also discuss processing these materials for circulation, weeding and preservation, and the future of kits. *[Article copies available for a fee from The Haworth Document Delivery Service: 1-800-342-9678. E-mail address: <getinfo@haworthpressinc.com> Website: <http://www.HaworthPress.com> © 2001 by The Haworth Press, Inc. All rights reserved.]*

KEYWORDS. Cataloging of kits, descriptive cataloging-rules, MARC 21 bibliographic format, Anglo-American cataloguing rules

WHAT IS A KIT?

The major problem with cataloging kits is that of deciding what a kit is. There have been conflicting definitions and/or usages over the years as explained by Jean Weihs in her article in this volume. The definition of kit/multimedia has been refined several times during the revisions of *AACR*, including explanations or expansions of the definition in various footnotes to rules.

Nancy B. Olson cataloged audiovisual and other special materials for 30 years at Minnesota State University, Mankato, retiring in 1999 as a Professor on the faculty there. She continues to teach workshops at the University of Pittsburgh, San Jose State University, and elsewhere as invited.

[Haworth co-indexing entry note]: "Cataloging Kits." Olson, Nancy B. Co-published simultaneously in *Cataloging & Classification Quarterly* (The Haworth Information Press, an imprint of The Haworth Press, Inc.) Vol. 31, No. 3/4, 2001, pp. 151-157; and: *The Audiovisual Cataloging Current* (ed: Sandra K. Roe) The Haworth Information Press, an imprint of The Haworth Press, Inc., 2001, pp. 151-157. Single or multiple copies of this article are available for a fee from The Haworth Document Delivery Service [1-800-342-9678, 9:00 a.m. - 5:00 p.m. (EST). E-mail address: getinfo@haworthpressinc.com].

© 2001 by The Haworth Press, Inc. All rights reserved.

CURRENT DEFINITION OF KIT

From *AACR2* (1998 revision):

1. An item containing two or more categories of material, no one of which is identifiable as the predominant constituent of the item; also designated "multimedia item" (q.v.).
2. A single-medium package of textual material (e.g., a "press kit," a set of printed test materials, an assemblage of printed materials published under the name "Jackdaw").

WHAT RULES APPLY?

The only rule in the *Anglo-American Cataloguing Rules, second edition, 1998 revision (AACR2)* specifically for kits is rule 1.10 for items made up of several types of material. This rule has several parts.

Rule 1.10A states that it "applies to items made up of two or more components, two or more of which belong to distinct material types"-it then goes on to give an example of a sound recording with a printed text.

So we are led to believe that two or more items are a kit. However, the rule goes on to have us make a distinction between items with one predominant component (1.10B), and items with no predominant component (1.10C). This distinction may be easy to make, or it may not. Though with so many titles now coming on CD-ROM (or being converted from separate types of media to a single CD-ROM), there may not be much need to worry about this because the concept of "kit" involves multiple physical items rather than multiple kinds of media on one physical item.

In any case, only when it has been determined that there is no predominant component, is it decided that the item to be cataloged is a kit. It may help in making this decision to consider whether the separate items, or some of them, could be used independently.

WHAT IS SPECIAL ABOUT CATALOGING A KIT?

An LC rule interpretation (LCRI) published in *Cataloging Service Bulletin* 84 (*CSB*) (Spring 1999) states that, "The chief source of information for kits is the item itself (including all components) together with the container and any accompanying material." The LCRI goes on to tell what to do if there is more than one title: "If the chief source includes more than one title, select as the title proper the one that collectively describes the contents as a whole. If there is more than one such unifying title, choose the one from a unifying piece (e.g., container or manual) that identifies the contents as a whole most adequately and succinctly."

The only area of the bibliographic record that is unique to cataloging kits is the physical description area. One may choose from three methods of description, depending on the kinds and numbers of material included, though an LCRI (*CSB* 84) says not to use the second method.

Rule 1.10C2a

One may give, in one statement, a list of how many of each kind of material is found in the kit. At the end of the statement, one may say the kit is in a container (or containers) and name the container(s) and give its dimensions.

```
    300     8 filmstrips, 4 sound discs, 8 charts, 10 posters,
34 identical elementary booklets, 1 secondary booklet, 1
teacher's guide ; $c in box 34 x 34 x 34 cm.
```

Rule 1.10C2b

If more detail is wanted to describe any of the items, one may use multiple lines of physical description. An LCRI (*CSB* 84) says not to use this method.

For many years multiple 300s were not possible in OCLC, so this method is not often seen. When we could only use one field 300, I sometimes used method "a" above with additional physical description in parenthesis as needed after each item name.

```
     300     8 filmstrips : $b col. ; $c 35 mm. + $e 4 sound
discs (analog, 33 1/3 rpm ; 12 in.)
     300     8 charts : $b b&w ; $c 28 x 22 cm.
     300     10 posters : $b col. ; $c 36 x 24 cm.
     300     34 identical elementary booklets (32 p. each) : $b
ill. ; $c 28 cm.
     300     1 secondary booklet (32 p.) : $b ill. ; $c 28 cm.
     300     1 teacher's guide (32 p.) : $b ill. ;  $c 28 cm.
     300     All in container 34 x 34 x 34 cm.
```

Rule 1.10C2c

When an item includes a very large number of parts, a simple statement may be used, such as

```
300     various pieces.
300     various pieces ; $c in box 34 x 28  x 10 cm.
300     37 items.
```

When one uses this technique, be sure to make a note in the bibliographic record indicating what kinds of materials are included, and put an accurate list inside or on the container if not already there, so the circulation people can check to see if the items are all present when checking the kit in or out and when doing inventory. The items may not need to be counted accurately (as when the total kit includes 1,000 red wooden beads, 1,000 black wooden beads, 30 white shoe strings, 1 teacher's guide) but the technician can make sure that enough are present for the kit to be used.

Rules 1.10C3, 1.10D

Rule 1.10C3 goes on to remind the cataloger of the need for notes explaining items within the kit such as individual titles, statements of responsibility for individual items, or any other aspect related to the kit as a whole or its parts.

Rule 1.10D provides the option of describing a single part of a multimedia item in a multilevel description, an option that LC says not to use in its LCRI (*CSB* 84).

MARC FORMAT FOR KITS

The Type code for kits is "o" while the Type of material code is "b."

There is no field 007 for a kit, though an 007 should be used for each item of film or sound material or electronic resource or map that may be found in the kit.

EXAMPLES OF KITS

A wide variety of materials are kits according to the *AACR2* definition. Already mentioned are a set of red and black wooden beads for stringing, together with a teacher's manual.

A complete assortment of materials for science experiments for a semester course at the 5th grade level would be a kit.

A set of textbooks, teacher's guides, workbooks, answer keys, etc., for K-8 language arts could be considered a kit under the second part of the *AACR2* definition. For this bibliographic record I would want to add field 006 for text if the bibliographic record was on a workform for a kit.

Many sets of curriculum materials now include audiovisual materials such as pictures, study prints, posters, videos, sound recordings, or electronic resources, in addition to the texts, teacher's guides, workbooks, resource guides, tests, etc. I would definitely catalog any such sets as kits, and add 006 and 007 fields as appropriate, together with contents notes and added entries for any individual titles included.

Jackdaws, mentioned in the second part of the *AACR2* definition, were a series of portfolios of reproductions of historical documents, each about a separate historical event. Each Jackdaw included about 50 pieces of paper that included facsimile reprints of broadsides, posters, maps, newspaper articles, tickets, census pages, pictures, etc. The Library of Congress did put these in their collections, but did them as textual material, on a type "a" (book) workform. They are, however, kits, as they each include several types of material, even though all are printed on paper.

THE FUTURE

True kits-those that fit the *AACR2* definition-are rarely encountered when cataloging for most libraries. As publishers convert titles formerly available as slide sets with narration, or in other media, to CD-ROMs, we are likely to see even fewer kits. I have encountered one CD-ROM that was originally available as a filmstrip with sound disc narration, then was converted to a set of slides with sound cassette narration, then a video (VHS) and then to CD-ROM; OCLC records were available for each format, and it was obvious by viewing these what had been done. None of these manifestations would be cataloged as kits by *AACR2*, though many AV people (and acquisitions people, and publishers) still refer to these packages as "kits." Because publishers of audiovisual material did not always include copyright dates on materials, watch out for such items where the outside packaging is new (and may carry a new date) but the content is old.

WEEDING AND PRESERVATION

If you are contemplating cataloging an existing collection, please consider weeding before cataloging. Many of these materials are now outdated technology, even though the content may still be accurate. All types of audiovisual material deteriorate-colors change or disappear, film becomes brittle and cracks, adhesive holding particles of magnetic media to their film backing loosens and the particles fall off and the backing gets brittle and breaks. Optical discs can crack or break and are easily scratched. Discard material in poor physical condition or with significant parts missing.

Even when the technology holds up, older materials show hairstyles and clothing styles that are out of date (try looking at some educational materials made during the early 1970s!) and cars and other vehicles are indications of the time period. These things are distracting when educational materials are shown to classes, and students tend to ignore any relevant content as they concentrate on the settings. Weed those materials that have out-of-date content and/or out-of-date settings.

PROCESSING FOR CIRCULATION

As with all audiovisual materials, individual pieces need labels, unless the items are too small to label. We at Mankato State sometimes had the campus printing service make labels when we needed more than 100 of one kind. A number of times we needed several thousand labels for big sets of materials.

The contents note near the date due slip becomes quite important during inventory (which we did annually) and when the item is checked out and again when it returns. The total number of items should be stated together with a breakdown of the exact items-the circulation people can do a quick count of items in a container; if the number matches the total no further check is needed. If the number does not match, then one must do an item by item comparison of the contents against the list.

Many times there are lots of identical pieces in a kit, such as the 1000 red wooden beads, or one pound of bean seeds, or 100 plastic drinking glasses (used in a science kit for mixing chemicals). As long as some of these items remain in the kit, one need not do an exact count or attempt to replace those missing. But when an important part of the contents is missing, such as a teacher's guide, one should attempt to replace it.

Sometimes kits need to be packaged, or repackaged. The circulation people or those in charge of a given collection might want items circulated individually instead of as a complete unit. The call number label on each of these might have to carry an additional line or two giving a word or phrase identifying the part labeled (teacher's guide, Grade 2 workbook), so that holding records can be distinguished one from another. Limitations of local systems may affect this decision.

CONCLUSION

Cataloging kits is no more difficult than cataloging any other type of audiovisual material-the problem is deciding whether or not you really have a kit to be cataloged.

AUTHOR NOTE

Nancy B. Olson has been President of the Minnesota Library Association, Visiting Distinguished Scholar at OCLC, founder of the Minnesota AACR2 Trainers, founder of OLAC (Online Audiovisual Catalogers) and founder/owner of Soldier Creek Press. She has received both the Esther Piercy award (1980) and the Margaret Mann certificate (1999) from the ALCTS division of the American Library Association. She is the author of many works on, or related to, cataloging including the 15-volume set of *Combined Indexes to the Library of Congress Classification Schedules* (United States Historical Documents Institute, 1975), the annual cumulative *Cataloging Service Bulletin Index* (Soldier Creek Press, 1974-), *Cataloging of Audiovisual Materials and Other Special Materials* (Minnesota Scholarly Press, 1998) and numerous works on cataloging film, video, and electronic resources.

In retirement Nancy is enjoying her children and grandchildren and is busy with teaching, writing, genealogy, and sewing.

HISTORY OF AUDIOVISUAL CATALOGING

A Somewhat Personal History of Nonbook Cataloguing

Jean Weihs

SUMMARY. Much of this history discusses the personal experience and recollections of the author, who since 1967 has been involved in the development of rules for nonbook cataloguing as an author of one of the works on which the AACR rules for nonbook materials are based, as a member of many cataloguing committees, and as chair of the Joint Steering Committee for Revision of AACR. Opposing points of view are described and reasons for actions taken are outlined. *[Article copies available for a fee from The Haworth Document Delivery Service: 1-800-342-9678. E-mail address: <getinfo@haworthpressinc.com> Website: <http://www.HaworthPress.com> © 2001 by The Haworth Press, Inc. All rights reserved.]*

Jean Weihs has worked in university, public, school, and special libraries as a reference librarian, a bibliographer, and a school librarian. However, most of her career has been involved in cataloguing, both as a practitioner and a teacher of librarians, library technicians, and school librarians in Canada and as a visiting professor in the United States. She represented the Canadian Committee on Cataloguing for nine years on the Joint Steering Committee for Revision of AACR, five of these as JSC Chair. She has held positions on 44 national and international committees, and has been the recipient of nine national and international awards.

[Haworth co-indexing entry note]: "A Somewhat Personal History of Nonbook Cataloguing." Weihs, Jean. Co-published simultaneously in *Cataloging & Classification Quarterly* (The Haworth Information Press, an imprint of The Haworth Press, Inc.) Vol. 31, No. 3/4, 2001, pp. 159-188; and: *The Audiovisual Cataloging Current* (ed: Sandra K. Roe) The Haworth Information Press, an imprint of The Haworth Press, Inc., 2001, pp. 159-188. Single or multiple copies of this article are available for a fee from The Haworth Document Delivery Service [1-800-342-9678, 9:00 a.m. - 5:00 p.m. (EST). E-mail address: getinfo@haworthpressinc.com].

© 2001 by The Haworth Press, Inc. All rights reserved.

KEYWORDS. Nonbook cataloguing, nonbook materials, nonprint cataloguing, nonprint materials, audiovisual cataloguing, audiovisual materials, cataloguing, descriptive cataloguing, Anglo-American Cataloguing Rules, Joint Steering Committee for Revision of AACR, JSC, media form subdivisions, media designations, general material designations, main entry

BACKGROUND

This article is not the definitive history of the cataloguing of nonbook materials. It will take a Ph.D. thesis to do justice to the topic. In my basement I have boxes and boxes of materials that I accumulated during my long years of involvement with nonbook cataloguing and a box of index cards with ca. 200 additional citations. I hope some diligent person will someday find these resources useful in his/her study of this history. When I read accounts or chronologies of the events in which I have been involved, I have found important events missing or not recalled as I remember them. Sometimes articles about other happenings have contradictory statements. For example, in one article by a Library of Congress staff member, two different dates are given for the beginning of the production of printed cards for motion pictures. Producing an accurate record of past events is a time consuming task. The time span allowed for development of this article did not permit the type of investigation required for a definitive study. Therefore, I had to make a decision about how much I could accomplish in the allotted time. I have decided that it might be important to record my remembrance of the events in which I had a part, so that a future researcher will have a fuller picture of this history. Therefore, many events in this article are not footnoted because they are personal recollections. I have also not footnoted statements that might cause embarrassment (such as the article by the Library of Congress staff member mentioned above).

In the 1960s "nonbook" usually referred to items not in the codex format; "nonprint" excluded items, such as microforms, that were essentially print; and "audiovisual" was used by audiovisual specialists, i.e., nonlibrarians. Since that time, these terms have come to be used interchangeably. Because both "nonbook" and "nonprint" are negative terms, various librarians and groups have tried from time to time to coin a positive term, such as those proposed by two British librarians. Brian Enright suggested the term "metabooks" and Malcolm Shifrin offered "materium/materia." None of the suggested terms found acceptance in the library profession. This article deals with the cataloguing of materials that are termed "nonbook" in its original meaning.

Lack of time and space does not permit the description of contributions made to the development of nonbook cataloguing by individuals and groups that were devoted to the cataloguing of specific types of materials, e.g., map cataloguing. This article is concerned with nonbook cataloguing developed by the general cataloguing community.

Two controversies were vigorously debated in the formative years of nonbook cataloguing: media designations (later called general material designations) and main entry with its associated questions of the classification of nonbook materials and the intershelving of books and nonbook materials. These will be discussed in separate sections of this article.

COLLECTIONS IN THE EARLY YEARS

I suspect that maps were the first nonbook materials in library collections. Surely there were maps in the libraries of Babylon and Alexandria and in many medieval libraries. Maps appear to have been the first nonbook items in the Library of Congress and the British Museum. The Library of Congress was founded on April 24, 1800, and in June 1800, L.C. ordered books from London. Charles Goodrum in his book *The Library of Congress* states that this initial order of books included "a special case tightly packed with maps."[1] When the Ordnance Survey of Great Britain started to publish maps in 1801, a copy of each map was deposited with the British Museum.

The earliest date I found in connection with nonbook materials organized for public circulation rather than use only in the library was 1889 when the Denver Public Library organized its picture collection for the use of its patrons. By 1897, the Library of Congress had pictures and photographs. Sound archives were found in Vienna in 1899. Sound recordings appeared in U.S. libraries around 1900, but exact dates are difficult to ascertain. Hoffman states that "the first documented record collection within the public library sector was begun in St. Paul, Minnesota . . . in 1913 or 1914."[2] National archives for sound recordings and for film were established both in the United States and Great Britain in 1935. Also, in 1935 it appears that there was a motion picture collection at the Museum of Modern Art in New York, although it did not become part of the general collection until after World War II.

By 1940 approximately twenty-five public libraries and several university libraries in the United States had nonbook collections; only two public libraries and no university libraries in Great Britain had nonbook collections available to the public. Nonbook materials did not appear in European libraries until the 1950s.

At this time most nonbook collections were single-medium collections, usually housed away from books, frequently in workrooms. The public was unaware of the existence of these collections and, in many cases, the library staff was nervous about the public "handling" what were considered to be fragile materials. Some librarians declared that nonbook materials would be subject to theft if left unprotected on open shelving. Other librarians considered nonbook items to be ephemeral.

The growth of nonbook materials in library collections began in the mid-1950s and accelerated in the 1960s, particularly in school libraries. This increase was largely due to the rise in government financing for education in both the United States and Canada. This was the golden age of education when educational innovation was backed by seemingly limitless funds. Educators were looking for materials for gifted students and materials that would help disadvantaged children, who appeared to respond to nonbook materials more readily than they did to books. In response to this growing demand, publishers and manufacturers flooded the market with nonbook materials in an increasing number of formats. When librarians and teachers realized the wealth of information contained in these new materials, the desire to integrate them into the general collection grew. If they were to be part of the general collection, these materials needed to be catalogued.

CATALOGUING HISTORY

The Early Years of Nonbook Cataloguing

There are sometimes conflicting and sometimes elusive clues in the search for the beginnings of nonbook cataloguing. For example, Arundell Esdaile, in his book *The British Museum Library*, states that the British Museum started cataloguing maps in 1841,[3] but rules for these materials were first published in 1897 in the British Museum's *Rules for Cataloguing*, which contained a brief one-page summary of the rules for the cataloguing of maps.[4] Obviously, cataloguers were struggling with what to do with "illustrative objects" in the early years of the twentieth century because in a book published in 1922, Dorcas

Fellows recognized problems that were still being debated forty years later:

> . . . if with the entries for books there could be included entries for illustrative objects also it would undoubtedly add greatly to the use . . . of available resources, both books and illustrative objects.[5]

The systematic cataloguing of sound recordings began around 1937 in some of the larger U.S. public and university libraries.[6]

When I first became involved with nonbook materials in the 1960s, their organization was haphazard. Some libraries treated these materials in the same manner as paperbacks, i.e., uncatalogued and housed randomly; other libraries stored them uncatalogued in workrooms. There were many reasons for this neglect. Many librarians were uncomfortable with nonbook formats. Patrons' demand for audiovisual services was not widespread. There was little catalogue copy or commercial cataloguing for nonbook materials, and the original cataloguing of nonbook materials was, and still is, a more time-consuming task than the similar cataloguing of books.

There were only a few guides and articles about the cataloguing of nonbook formats, so some libraries developed their own cataloguing rules for nonbook materials. As centralized and commercial cataloguing became more common, the need for standards emerged. School libraries developed standards at the district level and eventually at the state level. Unfortunately, each group worked in isolation, producing rules that differed from those developed elsewhere. Because commercial cataloguers were reluctant to adopt any particular standard, they developed their own rules.

One aspect of this bibliographic chaos was the difficulty of identifying nonbook materials for interlibrary loan. Librarians were aware that the bibliographic records in various catalogues might have had different criteria for the source of the title, which made the correct identification of a desired item problematic.

In 1952, the Library of Congress embarked on a project that was not completed until 1965-to draft rules for the cataloguing of the nonbook materials in their collection. Preliminary editions of *Rules for Descriptive Cataloging in the Library of Congress: Phonorecords, Rules for Descriptive Cataloging in the Library of Congress: Motion Pictures and Filmstrips,* and *Rules for Descriptive Cataloging in the Library of Congress: Pictures, Designs, and Other Two-Dimensional Representations* were published. Between 1953 and 1965 these rules were tested by working cataloguers, second preliminary editions published and tested, and eventually final editions appeared. The final versions were approved by the American Library Association's Descriptive Cataloging Committee and the appropriate committees at the Library of Congress. Despite their official acceptance, these rules caused problems for small libraries with nonbook collections, particularly libraries that wanted to list nonbook materials in the general public catalogue. These rules were designed for use at the Library of Congress where each type of nonbook format was housed separately and was described in a separate catalogue. Because of this particular L.C. arrangement, the three documents were developed by three different committees that did not coordinate their work. I make this latter statement without documented proof because one has only to look through the three publications to come to this conclusion. An example of this lack of coordination is discussed in the section below on general material designations.

The first edition of the *Anglo-American Cataloging Rules* (*AACR1*), published in 1967, was a disappointment to nonbook cataloguers. Part III, which dealt with nonbook materials, was based on the Library of Congress rules mentioned above. *AACR1* treated each medium separately without regard for integration in a general catalogue. For example, the rules for entry and description differed from medium to medium. If a Renoir painting was reproduced on a poster, the poster was entered under the name of the artist and was not given a medium designation. If the same painting was reproduced on a slide, the slide was entered under title and was assigned a medium designation. In addition, *AACR1* did not cover all the formats found in library collections. As a result, Part III was used by few librarians and criticized by many.

This is where my involvement with nonbook materials starts. In 1967, I was hired by a school board to catalogue the materials in its school libraries, including many types of nonbook materials. Up to that time, I had worked in libraries with few or no nonbook materials in their collections. I firmly believe that if you can read, you can do almost everything; so I went to the very extensive library at the University of Toronto's Faculty of Library Science. However, I found little to read and the little I found gave contradictory instructions. Next, I telephoned, or wrote to, librarians who had nonbook materials in their collections to ask for their help. After describing his or her cataloguing procedures, each person ended by telling me that these procedures were unsatisfactory.[7] I found the Library of Congress' bibliographic records confusing. I could not understand why descriptive cataloguing differed from medium to medium or why kits were catalogued as though they were filmstrips. (I later discovered that, because its collection guidelines did not include kits, L. C. made a policy decision to catalogue them according to the visual medium contained in the kit regardless of its relative importance to the other parts of the kit.)

I thought that I was too stupid to understand this cataloguing and that if I went to the American Library Association's conference, all would be clear. (I am unsure of the date of this conference; my best guess is 1968.) At the conference I asked questions about nonbook cataloguing at every cataloguing meeting I attended. One day in the middle of a meeting, I was handed a note from Sumner Spalding, the final editor of *AACR1* and Chief of the Descriptive Cataloging Division at the Library of Congress, whom I did not know at that time and who was like the god of cataloguing to me. He invited me to lunch! He was a charming man and we had a wonderful lunch. At the end of the meal he said to me that if I continued asking these questions, I would cause the Library of Congress to spend a million dollars. He knew that I was asking the right questions and that other cataloguers at the conference were starting to murmur. If the rules were to be changed to accommodate my concerns, L.C. would have to recatalogue much of its nonbook collection.

Sumner Spalding then told me the following story. The Council on Library Resources had allotted a sum of money to be spent over a period of five years for the development of a set of cataloguing rules that eventually became *AACR1*. The various committees working on the rules spent the bulk of the time working on the rules for entry and a lesser amount of time on the rules for description. This left a two-week period for the writing of Part III, "Non-Book Materials." Spalding locked himself in his office, took no telephone calls, consulted no one, and produced Part III in the two remaining weeks of the Council on Library Resources' grant. He stated that he had never catalogued nonbook materials and, therefore, was unfamiliar with any problems associated with these materials. The job had to be done before the money ran out and he did it. The most satisfactory chapter dealt with sound recordings because Spalding was a musician who understood this medium.

About this time I contacted Shirley Lewis and Janet Macdonald, who were then heads of the cataloguing departments of two local book and media wholesale companies, to suggest that we decide what rules would be used in the city of Toronto, so that at least in Toronto consistent rules would facilitate interlibrary loans. We started a small committee to work on the rules. The reaction to this work was astonishing. Within three months I received calls from many parts of North America asking about our work and inviting either me or the three of us to come to talk about nonbook cataloguing. In one year I was on thirty-nine flights. We were obviously people investigating "the right thing at the right time."

During this period the Department of Audiovisual Instruction (DAVI), a part of the National Education Association (later called the Association for Educational Communications and Technology), was also working on a manual for the cataloguing of audiovisual materials.[8] Because this was an association of audiovisual specialists, they had no interest in integrated catalogues or multimedia collections. Subsequently, DAVI representatives participated in the work of several library-related committees, and the fourth edition of this work titled *Standards for Cataloging Nonprint Materials* became one of the primary sources for the development of rules for nonbook materials in *Anglo-American Cataloguing Rules,* 2nd edition (*AACR2*).[9]

Pierce Grove recognized the need for an intensive dialog about nonbook cataloguing. He organized an institute that met for two weeks in August 1969 in Oklahoma and two additional weeks in conjunction with the American Library Association midwinter meeting in Chicago in January 1970 and the Association for Educational Communications and Technology conference in Detroit in April 1970.[10] The mixture of invited guest lecturers, who were noted authorities in their respective fields, and participants from the broad expanse of librarianship, all types of media centres, commercial cataloguing firms, and computer centres provided an impetus for several national organizations in the countries of the three AACR authors to establish committees to develop standards for the cataloguing of nonbook materials. The Institute was especially valuable in introducing nonlibrarians to cataloguing concepts. For example, the head of a large U.S. media centre that produced "catalogue records" was amazed to learn of the existence of cataloguing rules. His subsequent actions turned the records in his databank into ones that could be used by the broader cataloguing community.

After much investigation, Shirley Lewis, Janet Macdonald, and I concluded that all materials in a library should be catalogued according to rules based on the same cataloguing concepts, and, since most libraries would be unwilling to recatalogue their book collection, the rules for nonbook materials must fit into the principles of book cataloguing found in Parts I and II of *AACR1*. Our small committee agreed. The preliminary edition of *Nonbook Materials: The Organization of Integrated Collections* was published by the Canadian Library Association in 1970. This guide enabled libraries to have an integrated catalogue because the rules followed those for books as much as possible. *Nonbook Materials* was recommended by the Canadian Library Association Council and by the

American Library Association, Resources and Technical Services Division, Cataloging and Classification Section Executive Committee "as an interim guide for the cataloging of nonbook materials, with the proviso that a permanent ALA/CLA committee be established to work on any necessary revisions for the final edition and its supplements."[11] It was also officially adopted in Australia and unofficially by two South American countries. We invited comments on the book's contents and to our surprise and delight received about 250 letters, telephone calls, and personal communications from North America, the United Kingdom, the European continent, South America, and Saudi Arabia.

Nonbook Cataloguing in the 1970s

Following the American Library Association's proviso, the Joint Advisory Committee on Nonbook Materials was formed with representatives from the American Library Association including a Library of Congress representative, the Association for Educational Communications and Technology, the Canadian Library Association, the Educational Media Association of Canada, and the Canadian Association of Music Libraries. Dr. Margaret Chisholm, in later years a president of the American Library Association, was its chair. We examined all the comments sent to us about the preliminary edition and included those that were pertinent. One innovation in this edition of *Nonbook Materials* was the idea of entry under performer. The committee asked us to do this as a trial. It was a successful experiment, and this idea was later incorporated into *AACR2*. At the request of the Library of Congress representative, we included a sample card for a phonorecord that had been marketed in four different formats. The same bibliographic record could be used by a library that had one, two, three, or all of the formats by deleting the lines of physical description for the formats missing from their collection.[12] The Library of Congress had found this an economical way of cataloguing varying formats of the same item and wished to promote its use. It is interesting to note that since the International Conference on the Principles and Future of AACR, held in 1997, the concept of a single record for various formats is again being discussed. *Nonbook Materials: The Organization of Integrated Collections,* first edition, was one of the primary sources for the development of rules for nonbook materials in *AACR2*.[13]

The British also found Part III, "Non-book Materials" in *AACR1* inadequate. Because of the time pressure mentioned above, they were not able to give Part III the detailed scrutiny that they had devoted to Parts I and II.[14] The British announced their intention to investigate rules for nonbook materials and "to contribute the results of this work, alongside that of the Canadians, as a basis for the revision" of *AACR1* at a meeting convened by the Descriptive Cataloging Committee at the American Library Association's annual convention in Detroit in 1970.[15] The Media Cataloguing Rules Committee was established in 1970 with members from the library and audiovisual professions. "The committee was . . . in touch with other work and discussions on both sides of the Atlantic . . . In particular, information and ideas were exchanged with Jean Riddle Weihs and her colleagues in Canada."[16] *Non-book Materials Cataloguing Rules: Integrated Code of Practice and Draft Revision of Anglo-American Cataloguing Rules, British Text* was published in 1973 and was one of the primary sources for the development of rules for nonbook materials in *AACR2*.

In 1974 C.P. Ravilious completed *A Survey of Existing Systems and Current Proposals for the Cataloguing and Description of Non-book Materials Collected by Libraries, With Preliminary Suggestions for Their International Co-ordination,* as part of UNESCO's efforts to promote universal bibliographic control or UBC.[17] Based on these findings, the International Federation of Library Associations and Institutions (IFLA) established a committee, with Ravilious as its chair, to work on cataloguing rules for nonbook materials. The work of this committee resulted in the publication in 1977 of *ISBD(NBM): International Standard Bibliographic Description: Nonbook Materials*.[18] This work had some specific rules that differed from those in *AACR2* (in the list of general material designations, the physical description area, etc.), and was not widely used in North America.

The transition from *AACR1* to *AACR2* was eased for nonbook materials by the publication in 1975 of a revised and expanded version of chapter 12 (audiovisual media and special instructional materials)[19] and in 1976 of a revised chapter 14 (sound recordings).[20] The publication of *AACR2* in 1978 signaled the end of the basic development period for nonbook cataloguing rules because it provided rules for all types of materials, and bibliographic records for these materials could be integrated into a common catalogue if a library so desired.

Developments in the 1980s

A significant problem emerged in the 1980s-machine-readable data files. Official rules for machine-readable data files first appeared as chapter 9 in *AACR2*. These rules and the section on these materials in the first edition of *Nonbook Materials: The Organization of Integrated Collections* were based on the work done by the American Library Association's Descriptive Cataloging Committee Subcommittee on Rules for Cataloging Machine Readable Data Files,[21] originally established in 1970.[22] For various reasons, the Library Association Media Cataloguing Rules Committee was unable to do a detailed consideration of the draft chapter of special rules for the cataloguing of computer records prepared by one of its members, Ray Wall[23] or the American Subcommittee's draft. Therefore, rules for these materials were not included in *Non-Book Materials Cataloguing Rules*. When *AACR2* was published in 1978, machine-readable data files were found mostly in large research libraries and principally manipulated by main frame computers. Most libraries did not have such files and ignored chapter 9.

When computer software became part of library collections in the 1980s, cataloguers found it difficult, if not impossible, to apply the rules in chapter 9 to these materials. Their dissatisfaction resulted in action on both sides of the Atlantic. In the United Kingdom, the British Library commissioned a study that resulted in *Study of Cataloguing Computer Software: Applying AACR 2 to Microcomputer Programs,* by Ray Templeton and Anita Witten.[24] In the same year, an American Library Association committee produced *Guidelines for Using AACR 2 for Cataloging Microcomputer Software.*[25, 26]

Both these documents were criticized by working cataloguers, so the Joint Steering Committee for Revision of AACR (JSCAACR) and its constituent national committees went "back to the drawing board." I remember that some of the JSCAACR representatives themselves conducted their own research. For instance, I borrowed a large number of software disks from the Ontario Institute for Studies in Education Library and catalogued them at home using title screens as my chief source of information. The nonbook cataloguer at the Institute had catalogued the same items using only external sources, i.e., not booting them on a computer. In comparing our bibliographic records, we frequently found differences in the information given on the title screens and on the labels, packaging, and/or accompanying materials. This experience, also noted by other JSCAACR members, led to the requirement for computer files that the source of the title and the edition statement, if different from the source of the title, be listed in a mandated note.[27]

The most heated disagreements encountered in my years on JSCAACR were over the rules for computer files. Essentially two groups emerged: the "main frame group" whose members worked in large research libraries with main frame computers and the "software group" whose members were drawn mainly from public and school libraries and whose collections contained microcomputer software. The main frame group wanted the mandatory listing in the bibliographic record of the type of file and the number of records and/or bytes. The software group stated that this information was of no interest, and may even be confusing, to their users. JSCAACR compromised by establishing area 3, the "File Characteristics Area" and making it mandatory "when the information is readily available."[28] JSCAACR believed that this rule would satisfy both sides of the controversy. The main frame group would be required to list the file type and the number of records and/or bytes; the software group could ignore area 3 because the information was not readily available on microcomputer software. When *Anglo-American Cataloguing Rules,* second edition, 1998 revision (*AACR2R*) was published, to my surprise the Library of Congress interpreted this rule in a manner that I do not believe JSCAACR intended. L.C.'s bibliographic records for microcomputer software generally included file type because their cataloguers believed that it was usually easy to determine whether a disk contained data or programs or both. The other big controversy between the main frame group and the software group is discussed below in the section "General Materials Designations."

Because of the urgent need for rules for these materials now flooding into library collections, JSCAACR decided in 1987 to publish a preliminary draft of chapter 9 "to help bridge the gap between . . . the rules for the descriptive cataloguing of machine-readable files . . . [in] AACR2 . . . and the eventual publication of the final version in 1988."[29] This publication also provided an opportunity for input on the efficacy of the rules before they were embodied in *AACR2R*.

When *AACR2R* was published in 1988, JSCAACR anticipated that the rapid development of computer files would necessitate many rule revisions to chapter 9, but we (or at least I) did not foresee the advent of the Internet, a tale for the 1990s.

JSCAACR met in Toronto in March 1986 at the same time as IFLA Committee on Cataloguing's Working Group on the International Standard Bibliographic Description for Computer Files met in London, England. Each morning the chairperson, John Byrum, telephoned me from London to exchange information about the discussions and decisions taken by his committee that day and those of JSCAACR the previous day. The purpose of these transatlantic telephone calls was to reduce the potential for conflict in these two sets of rules. We were not totally successful in this endeavour due to the IFLA committee's need to harmonize its work with the other ISBDs and the somewhat different orientation between the IFLA committee's European members and the JSCAACR representatives. *ISBD(CF): International Standard Bibliographic Description for Computer Files* was published in 1990.[30]

JSCAACR representatives recognized that *AACR2* lacked rules for some materials.[31] One of these neglected media was holograms. Predictions about their acquisition by libraries had surfaced from time to time.[32] Some time in the first half of the 1980s (my files seem to suggest 1984), Michael Gorman (in the United States) and I (in Canada) individually tried to develop rules for the cataloguing of holograms. We both had the same frustrating experience. We both failed in this endeavour because the minds of physicists and librarians simply did not meet. We were unable to elicit from the physicists the specific information about the bibliographic nature of holograms that would aid in the construction of cataloguing rules. Neither of us continued to pursue this inquiry because libraries did not add holograms to their collections. Marc D'Alleyrand had announced in 1977 that he was writing *Rules for the Cataloging of Holograms,* but I was unable to obtain this work or to ascertain that it had ever been published.[33] The author did not reply to my inquiries. I also visited the stated publisher, the Museum of Holography in New York City, but the staff knew nothing of this manual. In a recent search of bibliographic databases, staff at the University of Toronto Faculty of Information Studies library failed to find evidence that this book had been published.

Brief mention might also be made of the *Multiple Versions Forum Report,* which "was convened . . . to arrive at a consensus on various aspects of constructing bibliographic records for items that are the same in content but differ in physical representation."[34] The forum concentrated, for the most part, on two-tier and three-tier bibliographic formats for print materials. I believed at the time that if its concepts had been accepted, the concepts must also have been applied to nonbook materials in order to maintain the integrity of the catalogue. However, the proposals did not progress beyond the discussion stage.

Cyberspace and the 1990s

The explosion in electronic publishing and networked information in the 1990s made the development of cataloguing rules for Internet resources the most important descriptive cataloguing activity in this decade. Many governments had ceased publishing some of their documents in paper copy and these were only available on the Internet, e.g., the twenty-five volume *Treasury Board Manual*. An increasing number of scientific reports could also only be found on a website. Research libraries felt a pressing need to make these resources available to their users through their public catalogues. Many individuals and groups were active in the developing rules for Internet resources. The most influential of these were OCLC, the National Library of Canada, the Association for Library Collections and Technical Services, and the International Federation of Library Associations and Institutions.

OCLC received two grants from the U.S. Department of Education to build a catalogue of Internet resources. Erik Jul was the manager of both projects. During the first grant (1991-1993) *Guidelines for Bibliographic Description of Internet Resources* were distributed to 100 participants, who catalogued items selected by the OCLC Office of Research.[35] "The resulting bibliographic records were examined and evaluated by OCLC, and comments and suggestions were compiled as the final research report was prepared. Suggested changes to the cataloguing rules and to the MARC format were forwarded to the appropriate committees of the American Library Association for their consideration."[36] The CC:DA Task Force on Cataloging Internet Resources submitted its report at the 1993 American Library Association Conference in New Orleans. At the end of this trial period the findings were edited by Nancy Olson and retitled *Cataloging Internet Resource: A Manual and Practical Guide*. During the period of the second grant (1994-1996), OCLC staff solicited comments, held a symposium, and attended many meetings to learn how effective these rules were. The second edition based on these findings was published in 1997.[37]

In June 1994 the National Library of Canada established the Electronic Publications Pilot Project "to acquire, catalogue, preserve and provide access to a small number of Canadian electronic journals and other representative publications available on the Internet."[38] The Electronic Collections Committee set up three teams, one of which was the Cataloguing Task Group. An interim report dated July 15, 1994, revised Aug. 29, 1994 (no longer available on the Internet), states that the group catalogued "chiefly electronic publications, but also including CD-ROMs . . . For descriptive cataloguing the group studied chapter 9, computer files, of . . . *AACR2*, OCLC's *Guidelines for Bibliographic Description of Internet Resources* and a variety of other articles and MARBI discussion papers." The final report, published in 1995 on the National Library's website, was not a manual of cataloguing rules, but rather a statement of policy and future direction for electronic publications in the Library's mandate. However, the experience gained in this project was transmitted informally to cataloguers and appropriate committees, such as the Canadian Committee on Cataloguing.

The rapid development of electronic resources also convinced IFLA in 1994 that a review of *ISBD(CF): International Standard Bibliographic Description for Computer Files* was needed despite its recent publication. The ISBD(CF) Review Group was formed with John Byrum, the chairperson of the ISBD(CF) working group, also appointed chairperson of the review group. The draft prepared by the ISBD(CF) Review Group was distributed to worldwide review. *ISBD (ER): International Standard Bibliographic Description for Electronic Resources,* published in 1997,[39] has had (and will have) a greater effect on the Anglo-American cataloguing rules than its predecessor, *ISBD(CF).*[40] ALCTS established the Task Force on Harmonization of ISBD(ER) and AACR2. JSCAACR has already accepted many provisions in the final report of the Task Force[41] including the change in general material designation from "computer file" to "electronic resource."

Not all cataloguing concerns in the 1990s were devoted to cyberspace items. In the beginning, the development of guidelines for the cataloguing of items that eventually came to be called interactive multimedia was a grassroots effort initiated by Sheila Intner. "The very first informal discussion took place at a luncheon table at the Online Audiovisual Catalogers' biennial conference in Rochester, New York, October 1990."[42] In June 1991 Intner invited about twenty cataloguing experts to an all-day meeting at the American Library Association conference in Atlanta to discuss the possibility of devising rules. She footed the bill for the room rental and catered lunch (we repaid her). She contacted several producers who supplied materials that the group could examine, unfortunately without the hardware to view them. Intner drafted the first version of the guidelines in November 1991 and wrote the proposal to CC:DA about the formation of a Task Force. The Task Force on Description of Interactive Media was established with Ben Tucker as its chairperson. Its report was delivered at the American Library Association's 1992 annual conference. The Interactive Multimedia Guidelines Review Committee was formed in 1993, with Laurel Jizba as its chairperson, to test the guidelines before their final publication in 1994.[43] *Guidelines for Bibliographic Description of Interactive Media* has been met with resistance in some quarters because it was argued that any item manipulated by a computer is interactive. JSCAACR has not as yet accepted interactive multimedia as a separate medium.

Nonbook Cataloguing in the Twenty-First Century

Many of the papers presented at the International Conference on the Principles and Future Development of AACR, held in Toronto in October 1997,[44] discussed concepts articulated in the IFLA study, *Functional Requirements for Bibliographic Records: Final Report*.[45] Since the conference, JSCAACR has commissioned studies of the conference delegates' recommendations, and, at this writing (October 2000), it appears that the Anglo-American cataloguing rules may undergo substantial change.

The winds of these changes were already in evidence before the conference. In late 1996 some staff members in the Cataloging and Support Office at the Library of Congress met to discuss the cataloguing treatment of materials that L.C. was digitizing from its own collections. This was "really an attempt to set a conceptual context and a common terminology for addressing electronic resources."[46] *Draft Interim Guidelines for Cataloging Electronic Resources* appeared on L.C.'s website at the end of December 1997.[47] It was based on the IFLA study, *Functional Requirements for Bibliographic Records: Final Report.* The Library of Congress' draft interim document did not deal with the cataloguing of Internet resources "because the collection development guidelines for remotely accessed electronic resources are only now beginning to be formulated."[48] In recent correspondence, David Reser states the L.C. cataloguers are primarily using the document "to provide guidance on the data elements to be used when LC has digitized the contents of items in its collection and needs to represent this fact on records that represent the original items, but they do provide other guidance on when to create a separate record for the digital manifestation."[49]

Metadata, a hot topic in the late 1990s, will undoubtedly have an effect on cataloguing rules in the early years of the new century. CC:DA appointed the Task Force on Metadata and the Cataloging Rules in 1995. Its final report deals not only with metadata and cataloguing, but also with the TEI header and the cataloguing rules, Dublin Core metadata and the cataloguing rules, Encoded Archival Description, and cataloguing problems with websites.[50]

SPECIAL ISSUES OF NONBOOK CATALOGUING

General Material Designations

Before the days of integrated catalogues, there were separate catalogues for each type of material. This was the accepted norm because nonbook materials were generally housed in a different section of the library, frequently stored in workrooms. No mention was made of general-material-designation-like terms in the 1949 publication of *Rules for Descriptive Cataloging in the Library of Congress*.[51] The beginnings of what would eventually be called "general material designations" appeared in 1952. I have noted above that in 1952 the Library of Congress embarked on three projects to draft rules for three types of nonbook materials: phonorecords, motion pictures and filmstrips, and pictures, designs and other three-dimensional representations. Each of the documents dealt (or did not deal) with the designation of format in totally different ways. *Rules for Descriptive Cataloging in the Library of Congress: Pictures, Designs, And Other Three-Dimensional Representations* contained no provision for designations.[52] Conversely, *Rules for Descriptive Cataloging in the Library of Congress: Motion Pictures and Filmstrips* directed a cataloguer to follow a title with "the explanatory phrase 'Motion picture' or 'Filmstrip' enclosed within parentheses."[53] Directions for the use of "germane terms for the physical medium of the work" were published in *Rules for Descriptive Cataloging in the Library of Congress: Phonorecords,* "in order to distinguish the aural from the visual forms of the same work."[54] These terms (phonocylinder, phonodisc, phonotape, phonowire, etc.) were to be listed in italics. No written directions were given for their placement. Presumably, cataloguers were to be guided by the examples, which showed the "germane term" placed after a uniform title without square brackets and, in the absence of a uniform title, placed after the title and enclosed in brackets. This is a clear demonstration of the lack of coordination between the three Library of Congress committees, probably a result of the segregation of different formats in the collection at the Library of Congress. Ronald Hagler noted that "the original purpose of the general material designation was not so much identification as file arrangement. It originated with the early rules for the cataloguing of sound recordings. Its position following the uniform title of a composition ensured that all entries for a recording would file in a group separate from the entries for the corresponding score or literary text."[55]

During the 1960s when many libraries began to add nonbook materials to their collections and to see the advantages of having bibliographic records for all materials in a single catalogue, the lack of media designations for all materials became a problem. Many libraries developed a scheme called colour coding in which there was a band of colour at the top of the catalogue card to denote a particular format, e.g., red for filmstrips, blue for sound discs, green for maps, etc. However, these colours were not standardized; each library chose its own colour scheme. This scheme became untenable when the number of nonbook formats exceeded the number of primary colours. The integrity of the colour stock could not be maintained when shades of colours must be used. However, some libraries hung on to colour coding long after other methods of indicating format were introduced, only abandoning them when card catalogues were discarded.

Media codes were another method of designating media. These generally consisted of two-letter codes used as the first part of a call number, e.g., RD for sound discs, PS for study prints. For example, the call number for a filmstrip titled "Mammals of the World" would have been FS 599 MAM. This also proved to be unsatisfactory because catalogue users were unfamiliar with the meaning of these codes. As a response to users' complaints, some libraries decided to use the full name of the medium in place of the codes, e.g., FILMSTRIP 599 MAM. Both of these schemes were developed for segregated shelving; neither was useful in libraries that wished to intershelve all their materials in one sequence.

Since many libraries rejected colour-coding and media codes, various organizations developed their own lists of media designations causing some media designation chaos in the cataloguing world. While the publication of *AACR1* in 1967 standardized some terms, it was a disappointment in this regard because media designations were not applied to all types of materials and not all media were included.

It was in response to the criticism from libraries wanting to have integrated catalogues that the Library of Congress and the National Library of Canada decided to develop a complete list of media designations. The British, one of the three-nation partners to the creation and revision of the Anglo-American cataloguing rules, did not want to be part of the decision-making because they disapproved of the concept of media designations. The National Library of Canada asked me to act on their behalf. Ben Tucker, then Acting Principal Cataloger at the Library of Congress, and I met at the Library of Congress in 1974 to establish an official list of media designations.

Our first decision was to develop a generic list of media designations that would minimize the disruption to library catalogues. This meant that the list of terms would be practical rather than theoretical or philosophical. Minimal disruption meant that all media designations currently in use (i.e., those listed in *AACR1* and terms commonly in use in the library profession as media designations for media lacking official terms) would be retained if they did not contravene the following guidelines that we formulated. General terms for designations should be selected to discourage a proliferation of terms when the technology of a particular type of material changed, but not so general as to be meaningless (e.g., record, film). Trade names must be avoided (e.g., microcard), and the terms must be in the singular to denote type of material rather than quantity. The terms also must be as understandable as possible to the library user. This latter guideline caused the major problem. In the 1950s, Jack Cooperman at the Library of Congress invented the prefix "phono," which became library jargon fairly meaningless to many catalogue users. At the time of our meeting, some audiovisual specialists were using the prefix "audio." (I remember at some meeting listening to a "how many angels dance on the head of a pin" type of conversation about whether our civilization owed more to the Greeks, hence "phonorecording" or more to the Romans, hence "audiorecording.") "Sound recording" was eventually selected because it was used by the U.S. Postal Service and a few other nonlibrary bodies, was acceptable to music librarians, and could be readily understood by the general public.

This list was formalized with the publication of *AACR2* in 1978 in which media designations were renamed general material designations. This was an occasion where the British and North Americans agreed to disagree because of their different attitudes to early warning signals in the bibliographic record and the different meanings of the same word on different sides of the Atlantic. For example, in the United Kingdom "kit" was something one carried on one's back while hiking and "pack" was a multimedia set, the reverse meaning of these terms in North America. British agencies were directed to use list 1 and North American agencies list 2. General material designations were made optional at the insistence of the British representatives to JSCAACR.

The greatest general material designation battle occurred over the term "machine-readable data file." This term was the choice of people working with main frame computers, mostly in large academic libraries, and was included in the list of general material designations in *AACR2*. The British preferred "machine-readable file" which they thought was a more inclusive term.[56] As school and public libraries began to collect and catalogue computer software in the 1980s, staff in these libraries complained that their users had no idea what "machine-readable data file" meant. They vigorously recommended that the general material designation be changed to "computer software" or to "software." This was adamantly opposed by the main frame people. Eventually, the JSCAACR decided on a compromise. The general material designation "computer file" was established by taking one word from each term supported by the adversarial groups-"computer" from the school and public libraries group and "file" from the main frame group.

Since that time there have been some additions to the list, mainly in the revisions packages published between *AACR2* editions. "Art reproduction," "braille," and "toy" were added between *AACR2* and *AACR2R*; "activity card" between *AACR2R* and *Anglo-American Cataloguing Rules,* 2nd edition, 1998 revision (*AACR2R-98*).

"Interactive multimedia," the general material designation recommended in *Guidelines for Bibliographic Description of Interactive Multimedia,*[57] has not yet been accepted by JSCAACR. The choice of this term was a vigorously debated topic by members of the committees that worked on this document. The first suggestions included "interactive media," "interactive multimedia," "interactive materials," and the qualifier "(interactive)" added to an appropriate general material designation, e.g., "videorecording (interactive)." Eventually the choice was narrowed to the first two, and drafts of the guidelines listed the one or the other at different times. One criticism of this general material designation is that it is frequently difficult to establish interactivity, particularly if a cataloguer is unable to play the item. The producers' descriptions on packaging are not reliable because producers believe that the word "interactive" on their products will increase sales, and many items are labeled "interactive" that prove not to be when used.

The cardinal principle on which all editions of AACR has been based, the requirement that the item in hand is the one to be catalogued, began to crack with the decision of the American Library Association, reflected in the Library of Congress rule interpretation,[58] directing that the original book be described with information about the microform placed in the note area. This concept was reinforced with the publication of *Guidelines for the Bibliographic Description of Reproductions* in which a hierarchical description is made with the original item in the primary position and the reproduction described secondarily.[59]

It may be that general material designations are slowly becoming more problematic as technology develops new formats and ways of manipulating information. For example, the general material designation "game" does not cover all games in a collection. Games are split two ways: those played on a computer are designated "electronic resource," the others as "game." A game can also be buried in the note area in flash card records because many flash card sets say "can also be played as a game." The same is true of other types of materials, such as technical drawings, which can be assigned the designation "technical drawing" or "microform" or "electronic resource." The same work of art can be "art original," "art reproduction," "electronic resource," "filmstrip," or "slide." The items that comprise a kit can now be found on a single CD-ROM. Should the latter be designated an electronic kit? Indeed, anything that can be photographed, microformed, digitized, or otherwise reproduced faces cataloguers with the dilemma of assigning a general material designation that is useful to their public.

The first edition of *ISBD(NBM)* proposed the use of dual general material designations, e.g. [Visual projection + Sound recording].[60] This was abandoned in the second edition. Some present-day cataloguers have expressed interest in this concept as a way of indicating to the catalogue user the nature of an item, e.g., for a computer game [electronic resource + game].

Despite the alternate list of general material designations in the various editions of *AACR2* for British use, most British libraries have steadfastly refused to use these designations, maintaining that their patrons should learn to read the complete bibliographic record. On the other hand, North American librarians have insisted on the need for general material designations listed early in the bibliographic record because they say their patrons rarely read the record beyond the title. This argument has less force than it once did. For many items, a catalogue user must read the bibliographic description, as the British advocate, to discover whether and what type of equipment is needed for the effective use of an item. The North American position will lose further ground if the current discussions about the move to catalogue the original rather than the item in hand are adopted. However, the elimination of the general material designation would bring other problems in its wake. The naming of media would then become a MARC prerogative, possibly subject to the whims of automated systems designers and their customers. As new nonbook formats were developed, this lack of a standard list of terms would be a fertile field for a return to the terminology chaos of earlier years.

Main Entry

Before the 1970s there were sharp differences of opinion about how nonbook items should be entered. For example, *Standards for Cataloging, Coding and Scheduling Educational Media* mandated title main entry.[61] While *Anglo-American Cataloging Rules, North American Text, Chapter 12 Revised, Audiovisual Media and Special Instructional Materials* allowed entry under author in some circumstances,[62] the Library of Congress and, consequently, many cataloguers, interpreted this very narrowly. Their rationale was that, in general, the intellectual responsibility for nonbook materials was diverse. Whereas authors were obviously responsible for the intellectual content of a book, more than three people usually contributed to the intellectual content of nonbook materials: cinematographers, caption or script writers, set designers, actors, composers, singers, etc. It would be difficult to establish any one of these as primarily responsible for intellectual content. Therefore, the rule of three, a long-standing principle found in *A.L.A. Cataloging Rules for Author and Title Entries* and in *AACR1* (now rule 21.6C2 in *AACR2R-98*), dictated title main entry for nonbook materials, with the exception of many sound recordings that were traditionally entered under composer.

Those that opposed title main entry as a general practice for nonbook items replied that there were many people who contributed to the intellectual content of a book that were not acknowledged in cataloguing because it was not the tradition in book publishing to highlight their skills. Editors, book designers, indexers, and foreword writers can all influence the accessibility of a book's content. Some people espoused the auteur theory of motion picture-making, stating that the practice of crediting everyone who had anything to do with the production gave a false impression of responsibility. These people claimed that the director was the person responsible for intellectual content, that the writers, cinematographers, etc., did exactly what the director told them to do. At one point, Shirley Lewis, Janet Macdonald, and I traveled around to various production companies to test the auteur theory. Staff in the production companies agreed that, indeed, one person was responsible for their products, but each company had a different idea who that person was. Most companies named either the director or the producer.

Title main entry advocates also argued that entry under title would also provide more economical cataloguing because a cataloguer would not have to spend time deciding on the person or organization responsible for the intellectual content of an item.

By and large, the proponents of title main entry were also proponents of segregated shelving, i.e., each medium housed by itself in a different part of the library. Some libraries had separate catalogues for each medium, and did not have to struggle with the problems of an integrated catalogue.

The Library Association Media Cataloguing Rules Committee proposed a system it called "unit entry." In this instance, there would be no main entry record. A basic record would be produced to which all appropriate headings would be added to create a set of bibliographic records for an item.[63] While this idea floated around the cataloguing community for a long time, it did not gain enough support for its serious consideration by international bodies.

My co-authors and I disagreed with the narrow interpretation of title main entry. We did agree that unit entry, if applied to book as well as nonbook materials, could be an acceptable method. However, we realized that libraries would probably reject the massive recataloguing this change would cause.

We came to the very firm belief that the same rules of entry must apply to all materials in a collection. Many nonbook materials did have the intellectual responsibility for an item clearly attributed to one, two, or three persons or bodies on appropriate sources of information. Even the occasional motion picture (the medium usually used as an example by the main entry advocates) was filmed, directed, written, etc., by three or fewer people.

Some nonbook materials had nondistinctive titles. Most librarians agreed that sound recordings of symphonies, concertos, etc., should be entered under composer and original works of art under artist. However, if such items were produced in another format, the title main entry rule was applied because it was considered that more people were involved in producing the intellectual content of the items.

This situation was especially frustrating to libraries that wanted to intershelve all their materials. These libraries wished to have all the items, nonbook materials as well as books, on the same subject by a particular person sit together on their shelves. These items would be given the same classification number but different Cutter numbers or letters depending on the first word of their titles. Consequently, the items would not stand together in the shelf sequence of a popular topic. The only remedy for this situation was for a library to develop a set of internal rules for applying Cutter numbers or author letters.

AACR2, published in 1978, put this controversy to rest when it mandated the same rules of entry for all materials. Even then, some cataloguers believed that all motion pictures and videorecordings were to be entered under title because it appeared that all Library of Congress records for these materials were entered in this manner. However, Ben Tucker stated that, although few in number, the Library of Congress did enter motion pictures and videorecordings under a personal name when appropriate.[64]

Media Form Subdivisions

The application of media form subdivisions was another controversy, albeit less serious than some of the others because it did not concern the basic concepts of cataloguing.

Some libraries stated that their clientele only searched for subjects in a particular format. For example, their catalogue users wanted to know what the library had in a motion picture format about polar bears, not about any of library's resources on polar bears. Adding general material designations to appropriate subject headings was a convenience to these users because their search could be confined to contiguous records in the catalogue, thus saving users from the need to look through all the subject records for the main topic.

Other libraries were opposed to the addition of media form subdivisions because they wished to emphasize that information came in a variety of formats. They believed the subject headings with media form subdivisions might limit catalogue users, that looking through all the bibliographic records on a topic would expose users to sources of information beyond their perceived needs.

This controversy was resolved when the American Library Association Resources and Technical Services Division Board of Directors adopted "Guidelines for the Subject Analysis of Audiovisual Materials," which suggested the optional use of media form subdivisions and that these subdivisions should be taken from general material designations. This gave an official sanction to libraries, which either used, or did not use, media form subdivisions in their catalogues. These Guidelines were published in the second edition of *Nonbook Materials: The Organization of Integrated Collections*.[65] In 1987, when I asked Karen Muller, Executive Director of the Resources and Technical Services Division, for permission to reprint the Guidelines in the third edition of *Nonbook Materials: The Organization of Integrated Collections*, she was surprised to discover that through some oversight the Guidelines had never appeared in any American Library Association publication.

The only place they have been published is in the second and third editions of *Nonbook Materials.*[66]

Subject Analysis for Nonbook Materials

The application of subject headings and classification numbers to nonbook materials could also be difficult. While currency and precision can be problems for the subject analysis of all materials, they are greater problems for nonbook materials. Many nonbook formats can be produced more quickly than books. For example, a videorecording about a recent disaster can be on library shelves long before a book on the same topic. Standard lists of subject headings and classification schemes are slow to produce new terms and numbers, particularly in the days before the Internet. The subject content of some nonbook items can be very specific. I remember trying to assign classification and subject headings to a filmloop that demonstrated how to throw a baseball. Subject heading lists and classification schemes were developed for books, and most books do not deal with single concepts.[67]

Because many nonbook formats were not, and are not, easily browsed, it was, and is, particularly important that appropriate subject headings be used.

The subject analysis problems associated with nonbook materials have eased since the advent of sophisticated automated catalogues. Now the catalogue user is able to access information in the bibliographic record that was much more difficult to find in the early days of nonbook cataloguing.

CONCLUSION

I started this article by stating that a definitive history of nonbook materials would take the time and diligence needed for a Ph.D. thesis. Even though I understood this, I leave the topic with a sense of frustration and of a job inadequately done. There are so many documents in my basement that throw light on different aspects of nonbook cataloguing, such as Paul Winkler's personal critique of the Library Association's *Non-Book Materials Cataloguing Rules* or the letter to me from Peter Lewis, chair of the committee that developed these rules, comparing them with the first edition of *Nonbook Materials: The Organization of Integrated Collections* and explaining why he believes the British rules are a better solution. I have tried to describe the "main street" of nonbook cataloguing, and not to stray into side issues that could become whole articles in themselves. I hope that these side issues will be investigated by someone in the years to come.

I feel very lucky to have been a participant in the development of nonbook cataloguing. It has been interesting, challenging, and fun. I have only one regret. I turned down Sumner Spalding's offer to succeed him as editor of AACR, because I was overwhelmed by the task. I later regretted this decision. The library world, however, has profited from my timidity. Michael Gorman has made a far, far better editor than I would have been. During my years on the Joint Steering Committee for Revision of AACR, I worked with or consulted Michael, Ronald Hagler, and Ben Tucker. These three men have a grasp of cataloguing concepts and issues that few have equaled, and part of the success of AACR should be attributed to them.

I am also aware of the many librarians who contributed to nonbook cataloguing in various ways and who are not mentioned in these pages. I have not forgotten you, and I hope that someday you will tell your own tales.

REFERENCES

1. Charles Goodrum, *The Library of Congress* (New York: Praeger, 1974), 11.

2. Frank W. Hoffmann, *The Development of Library Collections of Sound Recordings* (New York: Marcel Dekker, 1979), 2.

3. Arundell Esdaile, *The British Museum Library: A Short History and Survey* (London: Allen & Unwin, 1946), 216.

4. A.H. Chaplin, *GK: 150 Years of the General Catalogues of Printed Books in the British Museum* (Aldershot, England: Scolar Press, 1987), 82.

5. Dorcas Fellows, *Cataloging Rules with Explanations and Illustrations*, 2nd ed. rev. and enl. (New York: H.W. Wilson, 1922), 263.

6. Library of Congress, Descriptive Cataloging Division, *Rules for Descriptive Cataloging in the Library of Congress: Phonorecords*, preliminary ed. (Washington, D.C.: Library of Congress, 1952), iii.

7. There were attempts to deal with the cataloguing of nonbook materials during the 1950s and early 1960s. See Margaret Chisholm, "Problems and Directions in Bibliographic Organization of Media," in *Reader in Media, Technology and Libraries*, ed. by Margaret Chisholm with Dennis D. McDonald (Englewood, CO: Microcard Editions Books, 1975), 350-69.

8. National Education Association, Department of Audiovisual Instruction, *Standards for Cataloging, Coding and Scheduling Educational Media* (Washington, D.C.: 1968).

9. Alma M. Tillin and William J. Quinly, *Standards for Cataloging Nonprint Materials*, 4th ed. (Washington, D.C.: Association for Educational Communications & Technology, 1976).

10. The sixty-eight papers by forty-nine specialists are published in Pearce S. Grove and Evelyn G. Clement, eds., *Bibliographic Control of Nonprint Media* (Chicago: American Library Association, 1972).

11. Jean Riddle Weihs, Shirley Lewis and Janet Macdonald in consultation with the CLA/ALA/AECT/EMAC/CAML Advisory Committee on the Cataloguing of Nonbook Materials, *Nonbook Materials: The Organization of Integrated Collections*, 1st ed. (Ottawa: Canadian Library Association, 1973), vii.

12. Ibid., 23.

13. *Anglo-American Cataloguing Rules*, 2nd ed., prepared by The American Library Association, The British Library, the Canadian Committee on Cataloguing, The Library Association, The Library of Congress, ed. Michael Gorman and Paul W. Winkler (Chicago: American Library Association; Ottawa: Canadian Library Association, 1978), xi.

14. Library Association, Media Cataloguing Rules Committee, *Non-Book Materials Cataloguing Rules: Integrated Code of Practice and Draft Revision of Anglo-American Cataloguing Rules*, British Text, Part III, Working Paper, no. 11 (London: National Council for Educational Technology with the Library Association, 1973), 2. In a letter to Jean Weihs, dated 14 March, 1973, Phillip Escreet, Chair of the Library Association Cataloguing Rules Committee stated his approval of the fact that this document was published without the endorsement of his committee. Because of the pressure work before the committee, the document would have received only a superficial examination.

15. Ibid., 3.

16. Ibid., 4.

17. C.P. Ravilious, *A Survey of Existing Systems and Current Proposals for the Cataloguing and Description of Non-Book Materials Collected by Libraries, With Preliminary Suggestions for Their International Co-ordination* (Paris: UNESCO, 1975). My copy has the notation "Distribution: limited"; therefore, this document may not be widely available.

18. International Federation of Library Associations and Institutions, Committee on Cataloguing, Working Group on the International Standard Bibliographic Description for Non-Book Materials, *ISBD (NBM): International Standard Bibliographic Description: Non-Book Materials* (London: IFLA International Office for UBC, 1977).

19. *Anglo-American Cataloging Rules, North American Text, Chapter 12 Revised, Audiovisual Media and Special Instructional Materials* (Chicago: American Library Association, 1975).

20. *Anglo-American Cataloging Rules, North American Text, Chapter 14 Revised, Sound Recordings* (Chicago: American Library Association, 1976).

21. Weihs, Lewis, and Macdonald, *Nonbook Materials*, 1st ed., 46.

22. Sue A. Dodd, *Cataloging Machine-Readable Data Files: An Interpretive Manual* (Chicago: American Library Association, 1982), xv.

23. Library Association, *Non-Book Materials Cataloguing Rules*, 4.

24. Ray Templeton and Anita Witten, *Study of Cataloguing Computer Software: Applying AACR 2 to Microcomputer Programs*, Library and Information Research Report, no. 28 (London: British Library, 1984).

25. American Library Association, Committee on Cataloging: Description and Access, *Guidelines for Using AACR2 for Cataloging Microcomputer Software* (Chicago: American Library Association, 1984).

26. For much fuller details about the background to the development of this publication see Nancy B. Olson, "History of Organizing Microcomputer Software," in *The Library Microcomputer Environment: Management Issues*, ed. Sheila S. Intner and Jane Anne Hannigan (Phoenix: Oryx Press, 1988), 22-28.

27. For details about activities of American Committees in this period see Ibid., 28-30.

28. *Anglo-American Cataloguing Rules*, 2nd ed., 1988 revision, prepared under the direction of the Joint Steering Committee for Revision of AACR, ed. Michael Gorman and Paul W. Winkler (Ottawa: Canadian Library Association; London: Library Association Publishing; Chicago: American Library Association; 1988), 228.

29. *Anglo-American Cataloguing Rules, Second Edition, Chapter 9, Computer Files*, draft rev., ed. Michael Gorman for the Joint Steering Committee for Revision of AACR (Chicago: American Library Association; Ottawa: Canadian Library Association; London: Library Association, 1987), iii.

30. International Federation of Library Associations and Institutions, Committee on Cataloguing, Working Group on the International Standard Bibliographic Description for Computer Files, *ISBD(CF): International Standard Bibliographic Description for Computer Files* (London: IFLA Universal Bibliographic Control and International MARC Programme, 1990).

31. Ronald Hagler, "Nonbook Materials: Chapters 7 Through 11," in *The Making of a Code: The Issues Underlying AACR2*, ed. Doris Hargrett Clack (Chicago: American Library Association, 1980), 83.

32. Monty M. Maxwell, "Unconventional Photographic Systems: How Will They Change Your Library?" in *Reader in Media, Technology and Libraries*, ed. Margaret Chisholm with Dennis D. McDonald (Englewood, CO: Microcard Editions Books, 1975), 96-101.

33. Marc R. D'Alleyrand, "Holograms: Putting the Third D into the Catalog," *Wilson Library Bulletin*, 51, no. 7 (May 1977), 746-50.

34. *Multiple Versions Forum Report: Report from a Meeting Held December 6-8, 1989, Airlie, Virginia* (Washington, D.C.: Network Development Office and MARC Standards Office, Library of Congress, 1990), 3.

35. *Guidelines for Bibliographic Description of Internet Resources*, draft, November 1992. Typescript.

36. Nancy B. Olson, ed., *Cataloging Internet Resources: A Manual and Practical Guide* (Dublin, Ohio: OCLC, 1995). Typescript. Foreword, pages not numbered.

37. Nancy B. Olson, ed., *Cataloging Internet Resources: A Manual and Practical Guide*, 2nd ed. (Dublin, Ohio: OCLC, 1997).

38. National Library of Canada, Electronic Publications Pilot Project Team and Electronic Collections Committee, *Electronic Publications Pilot Project (EPPP): Final Report, June 1996* (*www.nlc-bnc.ca/pubs/abs/eppp/e-report.pdf*).

39. *ISBD(ER): International Standard Bibliographic Description for Electronic Resources* (Munich: K.G. Sauer, 1997).

40. A good description of the changes can be found in: Ann Sandberg-Fox and John D. Byrum, "From ISBD(CF) to ISBD(ER): Process, Policy, and Provisions" *Library Resources and Technical Services* 42, no. 2 (April 1998): 89-101.

41. Association for Library Collections and Technical Services, Task Force on Harmonization of ISBD(ER) and AACR2: *Final Report*, August 9, 1999, rev. September 2, 1999 (*www.ala.org/alcts/organization/ccs/ccda/tf-harm1.html#report*).

42. Association for Library Collections and Technical Services, The Interactive Multimedia Guidelines Review Task Force, *Guidelines for Bibliographic Description of Interactive Multimedia* (Chicago: American Library Association, 1994), ix.

43. Ibid., viii-ix.

44. Jean Weihs, ed. *The Principles and Future of AACR: Proceedings of the International Conference on the Principles and Future Development of AACR, Toronto, Ontario, October 23-25, 1997* (Ottawa: Canadian Library Association; London: Library Association Publishing; Chicago: American Library Association, 1998).

45. IFLA Study Group on the Functional Requirements for Bibliographic Records, *Functional Requirements for Bibliographic Records: Final Report* (Munich: K.G. Sauer, 1998).

46. Letter to Jean Weihs from David Reser, Cataloging Policy and Support Office, Library of Congress, January 8, 1998.

47. Library of Congress, Cataloging Policy and Support Office, *Draft Interim Guidelines for Cataloging Electronic Resources*, 12/24/97 (*lcweb.loc.gov/catdir/cpso/elec_res.html*).

48. Ibid.

49. Letter to Jean Weihs from David Reser, Cataloging Policy and Support Office, Library of Congress, May 22, 2000.

50. Association for Library Collections and Technical Services, Task Force on Metadata and the Cataloging Rules, *Final Report*, August 21, 1998 (*www.ala.org/alcts/organization/ccs/ccda/tf-tei2.html*).

51. Library of Congress, Descriptive Cataloging Division, *Rules for Descriptive Cataloging in the Library of Congress* (Washington, D.C.: Library of Congress, 1949).

52. Library of Congress, Descriptive Cataloging Division, *Rules for Descriptive Cataloging in the Library of Congress: Pictures, Designs, and Two-Dimensional Representations*, preliminary ed. (Washington, D.C.: Library of Congress, 1959). N.B. no further editions were published.

53. Library of Congress, Descriptive Cataloging Division, *Rules for Descriptive Cataloging in the Library of Congress: Motion Pictures and Filmstrips*, 1st ed. (Washington, D.C.: Library of Congress, 1965), 7.

54. Library of Congress, Descriptive Cataloging Division, *Rules for Descriptive Cataloging in the Library of Congress: Phonorecords*, 2nd preliminary ed. (Washington, D.C.: Library of Congress, 1964), 2. N.B. no final edition was published.

55. Hagler, "Nonbook Materials," 80.

56. Jean Weihs, "Microcomputer Software Cataloguing: Some Differences of Opinion," *School Libraries in Canada* 6, no. 2 (winter 1986): 25.

57. Association for Library Collections and Technical Services, *Guidelines for Bibliographic Description of Interactive Multimedia*, 7.

58. This was not a rule interpretation made by the Library of Congress. This *AACR2* rule reversal was the result of a vote taken by the Committee on Cataloging: Description and Access at the American Library Association Midwinter meeting in Washington in 1981. CC:DA asked L.C. to disseminate this A.L.A. decision. It has done so

through its rule interpretations (email communication from Ben Tucker, Jan. 8, 2001). [*Editor's note*: *For another account of these events, see Edward Swanson, A Manual of AACR 2 Examples for Microforms* (*Lake Crystal, Minn.: Soldier Creek Press, 1982*), *i-ii.*]

59. Association for Library Collections and Technical Services, Committee on Cataloging: Description and Access, *Guidelines for the Bibliographic Description of Reproductions* (Chicago: American Library Association, 1995).

60. International Federation of Library Associations and Institutions, *ISBD(NBM)*: *International Standard Bibliographic Description*: *Non-Book Materials*, 14.

61. National Education Association, Department of Audiovisual Instruction, *Standards for Cataloging, Coding and Scheduling Educational Media*, 1-4.

62. *Anglo-American Cataloging Rules, North American Text, Chapter 12 Revised, Audiovisual Media and Special Instructional Materials*, 4-5.

63. Jean Riddle Weihs, "The Standardization of Cataloging Rules for Nonbook Materials: A Progress Report-April 1972," *Library Resources and Technical Services*, 16, no. 3 (summer 1972), 309-10.

64. This statement was made in personal conversation and at a meeting. I cannot recall the time or place.

65. Jean Weihs, with Shirley Lewis and Janet Macdonald in consultation with the CLA/ALA/AECT/AMTEC Advisory Committee on the Cataloguing of Nonbook Materials, *Nonbook Materials*: *The Organization of Integrated Collections*, 2nd ed. (Ottawa: Canadian Library Association, 1979), 127.

66. Jean Weihs, with the assistance of Shirley Lewis and in consultation with the CLA/ALA/AECT Advisory Committee on the Cataloguing of Nonbook Materials, *Nonbook Materials*: *The Organization of Integrated Collections*, 3rd ed. (Ottawa: Canadian Library Association, 1989), 132.

67. For a more detailed account of the subject analysis problems related to nonbook materials, see Jean Weihs, "Access to Nonbook Materials: The Role of Subject Headings and Classification Numbers for Nonbook Materials," in *Policy and Practice in Bibliographic Control of Nonbook Materials*, ed. Sheila S. Intner and Richard P. Smiraglia (Chicago: American Library Association, 1987), 53-63, and Jean Riddle Weihs, "Problems of Subject Analysis for Audio/visual Materials in Canadian Libraries" *Canadian Library Journal* 33, no. 5 (October 1976), 453-455.

SUBJECT ACCESS ISSUES

The *Thesaurus for Graphic Materials*: Its History, Use, and Future

Arden Alexander
Tracy Meehleib

SUMMARY. The Library of Congress' *Thesaurus for Graphic Materials (TGM)* is one of the major thesauri used for indexing visual materials. Developed by the Library's Prints and Photographs Division (P&P) in the 1980s, the thesaurus has become an essential tool for numerous libraries, archives, and historical societies that catalog images, in the United States and abroad. This article will trace the history, development, and current use of *TGM* in P&P and other institutions, and take a look at its future, addressing subject indexing guidelines and principles along the way.

Arden Alexander, MLS, is Visual Materials Cataloger and Co-Editor of the *Thesaurus for Graphic Materials,* Prints and Photographs Division, Library of Congress (E-mail: aale@loc.gov). Tracy Meehleib, MLS, is National Digital Library Visual Materials Cataloger, Prints and Photographs Division, Library of Congress, and Co-Editor of the *Thesaurus for Graphic Materials* (E-mail: tmee@loc.gov).

The authors wish to acknowledge the valuable contributions of previous editors Elisabeth Betz Parker, Jackie Dooley, Helena Zinkham, Barbara Orbach Natanson, and Sarah Rouse, who have been key in the development of the *Thesaurus for Graphic Materials* and in the field of visual materials cataloging.

This paper originated as a presentation, "Visual Materials Cataloging in the Prints and Photographs Division," given by the authors and Lucia Rather, former Director for Cataloging, at the Library of Congress, July 15, 1998, and co-sponsored by the Library of Congress' Cataloging Policy and Support Office and the Subject Cataloging Working Group.

[Haworth co-indexing entry note]: "The *Thesaurus for Graphic Materials*: Its History, Use, and Future." Alexander, Arden, and Tracy Meehleib. Co-published simultaneously in *Cataloging & Classification Quarterly* (The Haworth Information Press, an imprint of The Haworth Press, Inc.) Vol. 31, No. 3/4, 2001, pp. 189-212; and: *The Audiovisual Cataloging Current* (ed: Sandra K. Roe) The Haworth Information Press, an imprint of The Haworth Press, Inc., 2001, pp. 189-212.

KEYWORDS. Visual materials cataloging, subject cataloging, subject indexing, image retrieval, thesaurus/thesauri, *Thesaurus for Graphic Materials (TGM)*, image cataloging, picture cataloging, photographs, prints

INTRODUCTION

The Library of Congress' Prints and Photographs Division (P&P) has custody of roughly fourteen million images, dating from the fifteenth century to the twenty-first century, and encompassing a wide variety of subjects and formats, including documentary and art photography; fine prints; architectural, design, and engineering drawings; posters; and popular and applied graphic arts. Division reference librarians, catalogers, curators, and technicians are responsible for providing access to this extensive image collection. The holdings are international in scope, though particularly rich in Americana, and comprise corporate and individual archives, personal collections, and single items.

Visual literacy and the demand for images have increased substantially over the past several decades. Studies indicate that, among a variety of libraries and archives, the most frequent approach to image retrieval is by subject (image content).[1] Division statistics confirm these documented trends. Each month, P&P addresses more than 4,000 research queries with subject queries predominating.[2]

To provide access given the range and magnitude of our holdings, P&P catalogers incorporate and employ traditions from the library, museum, and archives fields. We evaluate and decide-for each project-what the appropriate processing and cataloging treatment will be for a given group of materials, i.e., whether or not the images merit minimal- or full-level cataloging and whether or not the images should be cataloged at the item-, group-, and/or collection-level. Based on project decisions, P&P catalogers create item-level, group-level, collection-level catalog records, and finding aids, frequently using some combination of these four methods to facilitate access to materials. This "blended cataloging" approach allows us to gain broad control over our holdings at the group level as well as specific control over individual images (especially high-demand images, images used in exhibits, or images with high intrinsic and/or market value) at the item level.

Because picture researchers are interested in subject content (the information communicated, conveyed, or documented in an image) as well as genre and format (the processes, techniques, and materials used to produce the image), P&P catalogers identify both the "subject or topical content" of an object as well as the "form and genre" of the object, indexing for both in the catalog record. P&P catalogers draw the majority of their subject indexing vocabulary from two principal sources: *Thesaurus for Graphic Materials I: Subject Terms (TGM I),* which contains subject or topical headings, and *Thesaurus for Graphic Materials II: Genre and Physical Characteristic Terms (TGM II),* which contains form and genre terms.[3]

HISTORY AND DEVELOPMENT OF TGM

TGM I originated in 1980, when P&P cataloger Elisabeth Betz Parker produced a consolidated list of subject headings that had been in use for over fifty years in the Division's manual files and local subject heading lists. The typed list, *Subject Headings Used in the Library of Congress Prints and Photographs Division (SHP&P),* synthesized the subject headings that the Division had used to arrange and index its images. It was an unpublished, in-house document. The same year, the American National Standards Institute (ANSI) published its *Guidelines for Thesaurus Structure, Construction, and Use,*[4] which provided a model for subject heading lists and how they should function. In addition, Lexico, a thesaurus software package designed to facilitate the construction and maintenance of an automated subject heading file, became available.[5] In 1983 P&P took advantage of these developments and began to convert *SHP&P* from a list into a thesaurus, using the new ANSI guidelines and Lexico software. During this process, P&P dropped proper names that had been included in *SHP&P* and instituted a policy of using the *Library of Congress Subject Headings (LCSH)*[6] and the *Library of Congress Name Authority File (LCNAF)* for proper name headings.

Initially, P&P evaluated the possibility of using other subject indexing tools, such as the *LCSH* and the *Art & Architecture Thesaurus (AAT)*[7] because the Division anticipated integrating its records with the rest of the Library's automated records.[8] However, the Division concluded that neither *LCSH* nor *AAT* were appropriate for large, general collections of visual materials. *LCSH,* with over 200,000 terms developed primarily to accommodate textual materials, included terms that when applied to images seemed to overlap conceptually.[9] *LCSH* also lacked terms for the kinds of subjects frequently depicted in visual materials, which are typically too specific to be the topic of a book, for example, "Yin yang (Symbol)," "Moonlight," and "Corn husking." On the other hand, *AAT*, developed by the Getty Art History Information Program, contained roughly 120,000 terms focusing on art and architecture in the Western world, but lacked terms for abstract concepts-often represented in allegorical prints, cartoons, and posters-as well as terms for people and activities, all necessary for cataloging large and diverse image collections.[10]

Consequently, P&P decided to continue to develop its own subject heading list, and, in the interest of making the vocabulary as consistent as possible with other existing subject indexing tools, to draw from *LCSH*, *AAT*, and the *Legislative Indexing Vocabulary (LIV)*[11] as principal sources for new terms. Ultimately, the Division's objective was to create a thesaurus that would be in step with current standards, efficient to use (for catalogers and researchers), and compatible with other established subject indexing tools.

TGM II originated in 1980 as well, when P&P began a project to expand and integrate several informal genre and physical description lists to create a form and genre thesaurus for visual materials cataloging. This work was prompted by several factors: the Independent Research Libraries Association's (IRLA) recommendations to develop a form and genre thesaurus appropriate for rare books and special collections, the addition of new data fields to the MARC format, especially for terms indicating genre and physical characteristics, and the noted lack of a standardized vocabulary source for indexing forms and genres of visual materials.[12] P&P applied the new ANSI guidelines and thesaurus software in this effort as well.

In the late 1980s the Library of Congress published and distributed both thesauri. Initially, the thesauri were issued separately. *TGM II*, the form and genre thesaurus, appeared first, in 1986, under the title *Descriptive Terms for Graphic Materials: Genre and Physical Characteristic Headings (GMGPC)*.[13] A year later, in 1987, the subject term thesaurus was published under the title *LC Thesaurus for Graphic Materials: Topical Terms for Subject Access (LCTGM)*.[14] Then, in 1995, updated versions of the two were published together in one volume under the new title *Thesaurus for Graphic Materials (TGM)*.[15] Cross references for *TGM II* form and genre terms were added to *TGM I* in the 1995 publication, reflecting their roles as companion documents. That same year, *TGM* was included in *Cataloger's Desktop*, a CD-ROM cataloging tools package issued by the Library of Congress.[16]

A year later, in 1996, the Library loaded a new version of the Lexico thesaurus software onto a stand-alone terminal in the Division, which enabled P&P to launch both thesauri on the Web-*TGM I* in 1996 and *TGM II* in 1997. The upgraded thesaurus software also allowed us to incorporate new terms, edit existing terms, and update the *TGM* Web and ftp sites on a monthly basis. These new updating and editing capabilities greatly improved the efficiency and flexibility of thesaurus maintenance. Most recently, in 1999, *TGM* data moved into the latest Java-based version of Lexico, further increasing updating and editing capabilities.[17] Now, in 2000, the Web versions of the thesauri can be edited with corresponding changes appearing instantly. The most up-to-date versions of *TGM I* and *TGM II* reside on an LC server and can be accessed directly or via the Library of Congress Thesauri homepage, or through P&P's homepage.[18] In addition, ASCII files of *TGM* terms can be easily downloaded from the *TGM I* and *TGM II* homepages, and lists of recently proposed and newly added terms can be viewed there as well.

TGM: STRUCTURE, SYNTAX, CODING, AND SUBDIVISION PRACTICES

TGM I and *TGM II* have become internationally used tools in the field of visual materials cataloging. As collection-driven thesauri, they continually evolve in relation to what subjects, forms, and genres are being cataloged by P&P as well as by other *TGM* users. *TGM I* provides a controlled vocabulary for describing a broad range of subjects depicted in images, including subject terms for activities, objects, occupations, events, concepts, and structures. It contains more than 6,300 authorized terms with approximately 5,000 cross references.[19] Several hundred terms are added each year. Recent cataloging has produced new terms such as "Body painting," "Desert islands," "Bazookas," "Lame duck," and "Diapers."

TGM II contains controlled vocabulary for genre terms, which describe categories of material such as "Advertisements," "Landscapes," and "Portrait photographs," and for form terms, which describe the physical attributes of an image and the techniques employed to produce the image, for example, "Drawings," "Lithographs," and "Gelatin silver prints." *TGM II* has more than 600 authorized terms with more than 450 cross references. Each year, two or three terms are added to *TGM II*. The difference in annual growth rate between the two thesauri is attributable to the fact that *TGM I* is collection-driven and new terms are generated as they arise in cataloging projects, whereas *TGM II* was thoroughly researched at the outset in order to create an extensive form and genre thesaurus for still pictures.

Designed to function as a tool for both catalogers and researchers, *TGM I and TGM II* contain abundant scope notes and cross references (Figure 1). Following the ANSI guidelines, terms are established based on common usage, American spelling conventions, natural language word order, and literary warrant. They are listed alphabetically, with authorized and unauthorized terms (cross references) interfiled. Authorized terms appear with their corresponding unauthorized terms (UF), broader terms (BT), narrower terms (NT), and related terms (RT). Concrete objects are established in the plural (e.g., "Pearls"), abstract concepts in the singular (e.g., "Evolution"), and activities as gerunds (e.g., "Cycling"). Compound terms appear in natural language order (e.g., "Olive trees"), and compound terms united

FIGURE 1. Entry for the term "Civil rights," showing its associated terms, relationships, and location in the hierarchy-from the Web version of *Thesaurus for Graphic Materials.*

Civil rights
--|country or state|--|city|

Public Note	Search also under the subdivision --CIVIL RIGHTS used with names of ethnic, racial, and regional groups and classes of persons (Appendix A).
Catalogers Note	Used in a note under CIVIL LIBERTIES and CIVIL RIGHTS DEMONSTRATIONS.
Used For	Civil rights movements Freedom from discrimination Rights, Civil
Broader Term	Civil liberties
Narrower Term	Children's rights Gay rights Veterans' rights Women's rights
Related Term	Abolition movement Civil rights demonstrations Civil rights leaders Discrimination Integration Legal aid Minorities Segregation Slavery

Hierarchy
<<(2) Liberty
<(1) Civil liberties
Civil rights
>(1) Children's rights
>(1) Gay rights
>(1) Veterans' rights
>(1) Women's rights
>>(2) Women's suffrage

with the symbol "&" are used when two terms are commonly represented together visually (e.g., "Bathtubs & showers," "Good & evil"). Qualifiers in parentheses differentiate homographs, e.g., "Buttons (Fasteners)" versus "Buttons (Information artifacts)." Facet indicators document how a term may be subdivided for added specificity and are displayed in brackets (e.g., "Iceboats"--[nationality]--[country or state]--[city]).

Both *TGM I* and *TGM II* work well with other descriptive cataloging tools used for cataloging images, namely *Anglo-American Cataloguing Rules* (*AACR2*)[20] and *Graphic Materials,*[21] which extends *AACR2* for descriptive cataloging of historical and original still pictures. The *MARC 21 Format for Bibliographic Data*[22]-a standard for communicating bibliographic data in machine readable form-can be used with of all of these tools. When creating MARC records, terms from *TGM I* are entered in the subject field (650) in subfield a. The indicator 7 and the subfield 2 with the code "lctgm" are used to indicate that *TGM I* is the source of the term. Similarly, terms from *TGM II* are entered in the genre/form field (655), in subfield a, and the indicator 7 and the subfield 2 with the code "gmgpc" are used to indicate that *TGM II* is the source of the term. Terms from both *TGM I* and *TGM II* may be subdivided to indicate additional subject information and to subarrange files of headings. P&P uses the following subdivision pattern: general subdivisions are entered in subfield x; geographic subdivisions are entered in subfield z; chronological subdivisions are entered in subfield y; and the source of term is entered in subfield 2, as illustrated in Figure 2 below.

TGM I: SUBJECT INDEXING GUIDELINES AND PRINCIPLES

P&P has developed guidelines and principles, discussed in more detail in the introductions to *TGM I* and *TGM II,* to steer catalogers through the challenging process of selecting subject headings for images. Like book cataloging, visual materials subject cataloging consists of two parts: first, subject analysis; second, selection of terms from a thesaurus. Book catalogers determine subjects by examining titles, tables of contents, and other written material. However, picture catalogers encounter many images that have little or no accompanying textual documentation and must be analyzed visually.

During subject analysis, the visual materials cataloger must decide which aspects of the picture are important to index in order to provide optimal access. First, the cataloger determines the major focus of the image. For the image titled "Moonlight, St. John's River, Florida" (Figure 3), the

FIGURE 2. Example of P&P subdivision and MARC-coding practices for subject (650) and form/genre (655) fields. [Two Czechoslovakian families, who arrived in New York, on the Holland-America liner Vendaam, enroute to Montreal . . .], Associated Press photograph, 1939. Library of Congress, P&P (call no. NYWTS - SUBJ/GEOG - Refugees--General, neg. no. LC-USZ62-115089).

SUBJECT:
650 -7 $aFamilies $zNew York (State) $zNew York $y1930-1940. $2lctgm
650 -7 $aImmigrants $xCzechoslovakian $zNew York (State) $zNew York $y1930-1940. $2lctgm

FORM/GENRE:
655 -7 $aGroup portraits $y1930-1940. $2gmgpc
655 -7 $aPortrait photographs $y1930-1940. $2gmgpc
655 -7 $aPhotographic prints $y1930-1940. $2gmgpc

cataloger selected the terms "Moonlight" and "Rivers," which are both mentioned in the title and are the most prominent elements of the image. The boats and docks are not depicted clearly enough to warrant subject headings. If an image has no title, the cataloger must rely solely on visual elements. For example, an untitled architectural rendering of boats tethered to a dock near a lighthouse is indexed with "Lighthouses" and "Boats."

FIGURE 3. "Moonlight, St. John's River, Florida," c1886 by George Barker. Library of Congress, P&P (call no. LOT 3282-3, neg. no. LC-USZ62-122064).

SUBJECT:

Rivers--Florida--St. John's River--1880-1890
Moonlight--1880-1890

FORM/GENRE:

Photographic prints--1880-1890

A poster produced by the WPA's Federal Art Project, advertising a recreation program in Illinois, is more challenging (Figure 4). Although baseball, volleyball, and basketball are all clearly depicted, the cataloger chose the index terms "Sports" and "Recreation" to reflect the general topic of the poster. Our goal is to provide rich subject access relating to the main element(s) of the image. The large number of pictures we catalog and the need to provide timely records generally prevent exhaustive indexing, although some images do warrant the indexing of visually less prominent aspects. For example, a photograph of Civil War officers with a woman cooking in the background is indexed with "Women" as well as "Military officers" because images of women's activities during the Civil War are sought after and rare.

FIGURE 4. "Athletics--W.P.A. recreation project, Dist. No. 2," 1936-1939. Library of Congress, P&P (call no. POS - WPA - ILL. H385, no. 1, neg. no. LC-USZC2-5192).

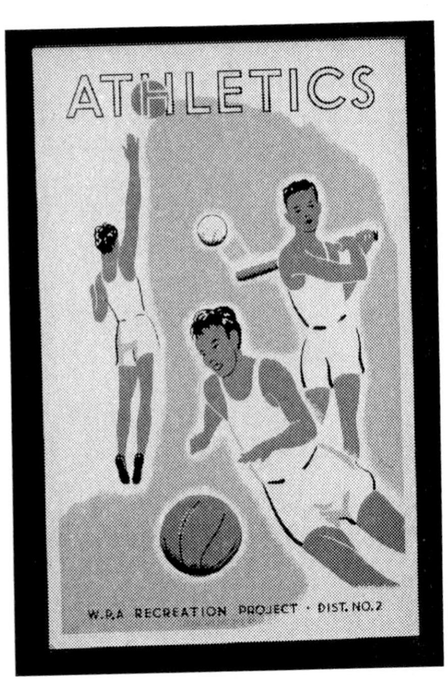

SUBJECT:
Recreation--Illinois--1930-1940
Sports--Illinois--1930-1940

FORM/GENRE:
Posters--1930-1940
Screen prints--Color--1930-1940

Each image is carefully examined for significant places, people, or events. While photographs of Abraham Lincoln, or well-captioned pictures of World War II battles, may suggest obvious subject headings, others-especially political cartoons and images of less well-known events with sparse documentation-are more difficult to catalog. In these cases, the cataloger may need to perform additional research to provide accurate subject headings. For example, the title "The bullet scarred American Legation from barricaded City Wall - Forbidden City and Coal Mountain in the distance, Peking, China" does not identify the conflict depicted in the corresponding image. Research revealed that this scene occurred during the Boxer Rebellion. Thus, the *LCSH* authorized name for this conflict, "China--History--Boxer Rebellion, 1899-1901," was included in the record. Without research, crucial access points can be unintentionally excluded.

Picture catalogers, like book catalogers, carefully read captions, titles, and other accompanying textual material for subject heading clues. These materials must be thoroughly examined because, in some cases, they contain conflicting, misleading, or inaccurate information. A cataloger presented with a photographic postcard captioned "US troops surrounding the Indians on Wounded Knee battlefield" might assume that the image depicts the tragic massacre of 1890. However, according to reference sources, this image does not document the actual massacre, but instead shows a filmed reenactment performed twenty-three years later. Thus, the cataloger assigned the subject headings "Historical reenactments" and "Film stills," in addition to the name for the event.

Images portray specific objects, but some also possess additional themes or contexts that are important to acknowledge. In addition to indexing what an image is "of," the subject cataloger must also index what an image is "about."[23] For example, a political cartoon from 1870 showing an octopus with its tentacles around New York City Hall is "of" an "Octopus" and "City & town halls" but "about" "Corruption."

A comparison between two photographs also illustrates this concept. Figures 5 and 6 depict boys swimming, and both could be indexed with the same subject headings. However, the caption on the back of Figure 5 reveals that the image shows a lake set aside in the 1940s by the North Carolina State Park Service for the sole use of African Americans. Thus, the cataloger becomes aware of the larger context of this image-the subject of segregation-and the terms chosen for this image are "Swimming" (of) and "Segregation" (about).

Although it is important to index for context, catalogers should avoid projecting any subjectivity into an image and corresponding catalog record. One of P&P's most famous images "Migrant Mother" (Figure 7), taken by Dorothea Lange in 1936, is captioned "Destitute peapickers in California, a 32 year old mother of seven children." The cataloger chose the subject terms, "Migrant agricultural laborers," "Mothers & children," and "Poor persons." Although it might have been tempting to index for other concepts, such as "Worry," "Distress," and "Social classes," the cataloger could not verify the feelings of the mother, nor the intent of the photographer, therefore, these terms were not applied. On the other hand, a record for a cartoon showing wealthy capitalists on a raft being carried by workers

FIGURE 5. "Park for Negro citizens," Acme photograph, 1945. Library of Congress, P&P (call no. LOT 13094, no. 58, neg. no. LC-USZ62-116926).

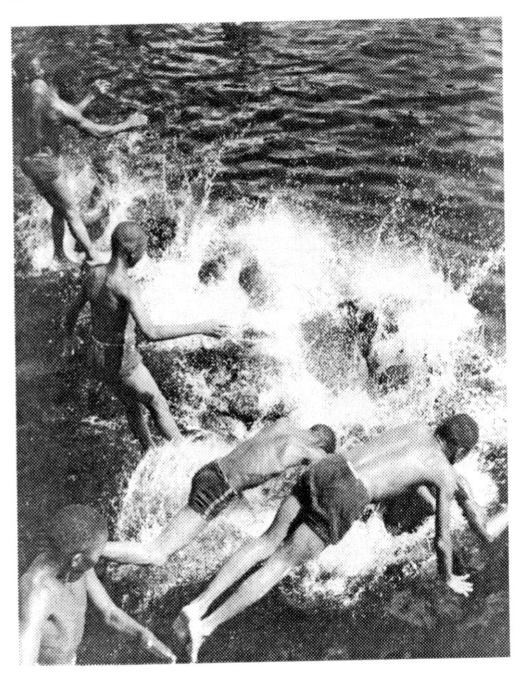

SUBJECT:
African Americans--Sports--1940-1950
Swimming--North Carolina--1940-1950
Segregation--North Carolina--1940-1950

FORM/GENRE:
Photographic prints--1940-1950

is indexed with the term "Social classes" because it is clearly the cartoonist's intended topic and the main point of the image (Figure 8). The cataloger's goal should always be to apply accurate, verifiable headings.

Unlike book catalogers, visual materials catalogers use subject terms for symbolic representations. The image in Figure 9, titled "The Cactus," is an example of a genre known as formation photographs. This photograph depicts military personnel assembled to form their regimental insignia, a cactus. The cataloger selected the topical terms "Military personnel" and

FIGURE 6. "The swimming pool, Glenwood Springs, Colo.," by Louis Charles McClure, 1900-1920. Library of Congress, P&P (call no. SSF - Swimming pools, neg. no. LC-USZ62-100201).

SUBJECT:

Swimming--Colorado--Glenwood Springs--1900-1920
Swimming pools--Colorado--Glenwood Springs--1900-1920

FORM/GENRE:

Photographic prints--1900-1920

"Cactus" because, although the image is not of a real cactus, it is symbolic of one.

After subject analysis is completed, the cataloger selects appropriate subject terms following the principle of specificity. For each image the most specific applicable index terms are selected. For example, for an image of a woman playing a banjo, the cataloger chooses the term "Banjos" rather than the broader term "Stringed instruments." Catalogers generally avoid double indexing-including a term and its broader term in the same record-except where it is advised by *TGM* or where a proper name is used as

FIGURE 7. "Destitute peapickers in California, a 32 year old mother of seven children," photograph by Dorothea Lange, 1936. Library of Congress, P&P (call no. Item in FSA-OWI Collection J-339168, neg. no. LC-USZ62-95653).

SUBJECT:
Migrant agricultural laborers--California--1930-1940
Mothers & children--California--1930-1940
Poor persons--California--1930-1940

FORM/GENRE:
Group portraits--1930-1940
Portrait photographs--1930-1940
Photographic prints--1930-1940

a heading.[24] For example, under the term "Brewing industry" *TGM* advises double indexing the physical plant under "Industrial facilities" (or one of its NTs). An image featuring the Waldorf-Astoria in New York is indexed with the proper name heading "Waldorf-Astoria Hotel (New York, N.Y.)" and the topical term "Hotels" so that a researcher interested in hotel architecture in New York City does not have to know the specific names of hotels in order to find relevant images.

Following subject analysis and term selection, P&P catalogers opt to further specify subject matter by adding appropriate geographic and chro-

FIGURE 8. "The protectors of our industries," cartoon by Bernhard Gillam, published in *Puck*, Feb. 7, 1883, p. 368. Library of Congress, P&P (call no. Illus. in AP101.P7, neg. no. LC-USZC4-3108).

SUBJECT:
Capitalists & financiers--United States--1880-1890
Social classes--United States--1880-1890

FORM/GENRE:
Editorial cartoons--1880-1890
Periodical illustrations--1880-1890
Lithographs--1880-1890

nological subdivisions. For example, in Figure 3, the term "Rivers" is geographically subdivided by "Florida" and "St. John's River." P&P catalogers tend not to use a separate geographic name field (651), but instead rely on geographic subdivisions to bring out place names, an exception being when an image is an overall view of a place, for example, an aerial photograph of London.

The usual practice in P&P is to subdivide chronologically by the decade span that encompasses the date of creation and depiction. Thus, the terms

FIGURE 9. "The Cactus, regimental insignia [of the] 35th Infantry, formed by the regimental personnel in Schofield Barracks, T.H. June 25th, 1933," c1993 by R. L. Dancy. Library of Congress, P&P (call no. SSF - Formations--1933, neg. no. LC-USZ62-100362).

SUBJECT:
Cactus--1930-1940
Military personnel--1930-1940

FORM/GENRE:
Formation photographs--1930-1940
Photographic prints--1930-1940

"Recreation" and "Sports," used in the record for the poster created between 1936 and 1939 (Figure 4), are subdivided by the date span "1930-1940." This method allows researchers to search for topics within specific decades or time spans, for example, images of children in the 1920s. For images created after the event depicted, the chronological subdivision reflects the event depicted rather than the date the image was created. For example, the heading "Campaigns & battles" is appropriately subdivided by 1240-1250, not 1830-1840, for a drawing made in 1837 illustrating the death of a German prince in battle in 1241.

Unlike book catalogers who employ a fairly liberal use of general topical subdivisions, P&P catalogers use general topical subdivisions (found in the appendices to *TGM I*) with only four categories of proper names: (1) Names of ethnic, racial, regional groups, and classes of people; (2) Names of persons; (3) Names of wars; and (4) Names of corporate bodies and named events. These subdivisions divide large files of records so researchers can refine their searches on topics of interest. For example, more than 2,000 P&P online records are indexed with the term "Indians of North America." The general subdivision "Dance" was added to the proper name heading in 124 of these records to allow for more precise access to this broad topic (Figure 10). Specific topical headings are frequently used in addition to subdivided proper names. In this example, the terms "Ceremonial dancers" and "Body marking" were applied in addition to the subdivided proper name heading "Indians of North America--Dance."

In contrast to items that are cataloged individually and receive specific headings, when P&P creates catalog records at the group level, we use general subject headings and avoid indexing for every topic. For example, P&P's NAACP collection includes approximately 5,000 images on a variety of topics including civil rights demonstrations, school integration, court cases, and portraits of leaders and members. Terms used in the collection-level record are more general, for example, "African Americans," and "Civil rights leaders." In other words, the "focus changes from a greater degree of specificity with the single item to a more general one with a collection."[25]

TGM II: SUBJECT INDEXING GUIDELINES AND PRINCIPLES

Before selecting appropriate *TGM II* terms, the cataloger must correctly identify the photographic or print format of the item being cataloged. The cataloger needs to know how to distinguish an engraving (Figure 10) from a screenprint (Figure 4).[26] The cataloger also identifies relevant genre categories, such as "Formation photographs" (Figure 9) or "Portrait photographs" (Figure 7). As with topical term indexing, specificity is important. P&P has established a general policy that, for full-level cataloging projects, narrower terms (if available and known) are used, whereas, for minimal-level cataloging projects, where limited research time is available for identifying specific physical media, broader terms are chosen. For example, "Photographic prints" was selected instead of "Gelatin silver prints" for the image in Figure 5. If a cataloger is uncertain about the specific format of the item being cata-

FIGURE 10. "Dance of the Indians of the Mission of St. Joseph in New California," engraving by Letitia and Elizh. Byrne, 1814. Library of Congress, P&P (call no. FP - XIX - B995, no. 1, neg. no. LC-USZ62-116522).

SUBJECT:

Indians of North America--Dance--California--1810-1820
Ceremonial dancers--California--1810-1820
Body-marking--California--1810-1820

FORM/GENRE:

Engravings--1810-1820

loged, he or she should select a broader term, e.g., "Prints" or "Photographic prints," for the sake of accuracy. Like *TGM I* terms, *TGM II* terms can be subdivided, but with fewer options. All terms are subdivided by date of creation, and can also be subdivided by nationality of the creator, as well as by general subdivisions, such as "Reproduction" or "Color" (Figure 4).

TGM II terms are used as topical terms when appropriate. For example, a photograph of a child looking at a circus poster is indexed with the *TGM II* term "Circus posters," used as a topical term, in the subject field (650), instead of the genre/form field (655). The photograph is "of" a circus poster, not a physical example of one.

More examples of P&P catalog records are available and can be viewed online via the Prints & Photographs Online Catalog (PPOC), the Library of Congress OPAC, and the National Digital Library/American Memory Web sites.[27]

TGM USE IN OTHER INSTITUTIONS

TGM I and *TGM II* are used in many libraries, historical societies, archives, and federal agencies. Institutions as varied as the National Library of Ireland, the Western History and Genealogy Department of the Denver Public Library, the North Dakota State University Institute for Regional Studies, the New York Historical Society, the National Park Service Museum Management Program, and the Defense Virtual Library Project at the Department of Defense have used *TGM* in past and present cataloging projects. We conducted an informal survey among these *TGM* users to get a sense of how the thesauri are currently being used outside the Library of Congress.[28] Our questionnaire, along with examinations of catalog records created by *TGM* users, reveals a diversity of practices.

TGM I and *TGM II* are commonly used in conjunction with other thesauri. Some institutions employ *TGM I* and *TGM II* as their primary tools for subject indexing pictures, along with *LCSH* and *LCNAF* for proper name headings, similar to P&P practice. Others have chosen to use *LCSH* or *AAT*, consulting *TGM I* and *TGM II* only when appropriate terms are not found in these other sources. The principal reason given for using *LCSH* over *TGM* is the need to integrate records for visual material records with records for textual materials.

Subdivision practices vary widely. Some institutions follow the general, geographic, and chronological subdivision practices described in *TGM*. Others use only general or geographic subdivisions, subdivide geographically and use a geographic name field (651) in addition to the geographic subdivision, do not subdivide at all, or rely on a geographic name field (651) or a hierarchical place name (752) to provide access to the geographic aspect.

Users take full advantage of the fact that *TGM* is available in multiple formats. Some prefer using the *TGM* Web sites, some the print edition, some the *Cataloger's Desktop*. Others use a combination, for example, they use the print edition primarily, but consult the Web version when desired vocabulary is not located in the print edition.

TGM editors accept term proposals from P&P staff as well as from other cataloging institutions (Figure 11). Many institutions, such as the Denver

FIGURE 11. Example of a submitted *TGM I* proposal form for the addition of the term "Tide pools."

TGM I TERM PROPOSAL FORM

✓ Accepted
☐ Rejected
Initials/Date

Proposed by : Anne Mitchell
Date : 10/10/1999
Material : Charles & Ray Eames

OPTIONS:

✓ Add a term : Tide pools
☐ Delete a term :
☐ Change a term :
☐ Other :

SOURCES:

LCSH : i
LIV : o
AAT : o
OTHER : –

i = Identical
o = Omitted
c = Same concept
d = Different meaning
x = Non-postable

FACET NOTES:

☐ [country or state]
✓ [country or state]-[city]
☐ [nationality]-[country or state]-[city]
☐ [nationality]

SCOPE NOTES:

✓ PUBLIC NOTE (PN): Pools left by ebbing tides.
☐ CATALOGERS NOTE (CN):
☐ HISTORY NOTE (HN):

RELATIONSHP	TERM	TGM	+/–
USE FOR (UF)	Tidepools		
BROADER TERM (BT)	Bodies of water		
	Natural phenomena		
NARROWER TERM (NT)			
RELATED TERM (RT)	Aquatic animals		
	Seas		
	Waterfronts		

Public Library and the New York Public Library, have greatly enriched the vocabulary by making use of this process. For example, the terms "Opium dens," "Adobe houses," "Three monkeys (Motif)," "Goldmining equipment," "Working dogs" and "Light bulbs" were all generated by cataloging projects at other institutions.

The level of indexing in records tends to differ among *TGM* users, with some institutions indexing more exhaustively than P&P. For example, the

Institute for Regional Studies at North Dakota State University (NDSU) includes the index term "Electric lighting" in the record for an image of a millinery shop with a lighting fixture suspended from the ceiling, although the focus of the picture is women trying on hats. This detailed, analytical cataloging strategy can be appropriate for some institutions and collections, but factors such as the size of a catalog or the presence of a cumbersome backlog can make this approach untenable for larger institutions. By indexing each element of a picture, the quantity of records retrieved for a single topic can also be overwhelming. In catalogs that can distinguish the primary subject focus of an image from the mere occurrence of an object in the image, indexing of all elements is less hazardous.

While most known *TGM* users appear to be "traditional" library and archival institutions, a number of private sector commercial companies have inquired about downloading *TGM* to use in their own image databases and other systems, or have incorporated *TGM* into commercial database management products. Because *TGM* is in the public domain, it is a fruitful (and inexpensive) source of vocabulary for these types of applications.

Information scientists and researchers have also found creative uses for *TGM.* Andrew Gordon, currently a researcher at the IBM T. J. Watson Research Center, used *TGM* to produce a powerful browsing interface called Déjà vu.[29] To create this program, Gordon broadened *TGM's* traditional thesaurus links (BTs, NTs, and RTs) by constructing an expanded network of term sets based on activities such as "flying in a passenger airplane" or "working as a miner in an underground mine." Déjà vu used these term sets to navigate and access different image collections. For several years Déjà vu was used as a customized browsing system and public interface for photographic collections at NDSU, linking *TGM* terms to online records and video laser disc images.[30] Using *TGM* as an example, another researcher, Stanley Rice (owner of Autospec, Inc.), has discussed the inadequacies of using a collection-driven thesaurus for any kind of long-term subject access, stating that "as time goes on, whatever the superimposed hierarchical or data-oriented index schemes that may be added, they are progressively less clear to searchers."[31]

CONCLUSION

What lies ahead for *TGM?* In the near future, the Web versions of *TGM I* and *TGM II* will continue to be the most up-to-date forms of the thesauri available. In addition, the thesauri will continue to be available on *Cataloger's Desktop,* which is updated quarterly. However, P&P has no plans to update the printed edition. P&P's eventual goal is to link terms in the online version of *TGM I* and *TGM II* to corresponding catalog records carrying digital images to create a seamless web of access to our visual material subject matter.

Conversion of *TGM* terms to the MARC format has been discussed by several institutions. Availability of *TGM* in MARC would greatly assist catalogers and make it easier for institutions to incorporate *TGM* directly into their online catalogs. In addition, users would benefit from easier access to *TGM* vocabulary in their online searching. Cross references integrated into search queries could guide users from "Nuclear power" to "Atomic power," for example, or, from "Farming" to all of its narrower terms, enabling researchers to explore visual resources more fully. Our survey demonstrated that most institutions that use *TGM* also index using other thesauri. One user proposed incorporating *TGM* terms into *LCSH* or *AAT*. This approach would be advantageous in that it would eliminate the need to use multiple thesauri, but the ease and efficiency of using a smaller vocabulary would be lost.

TGM has enabled researchers to seek visual materials in ways formerly available only for textual holdings. Ongoing development of the thesaurus should ensure its continued relevance to visual materials cataloging. Experiments in targeted browsing systems and technologies, such as those of Andrew Gordon and Stanley Rice, and other content- and semantic-based retrieval projects-including some that use digital images as subject queries-may prove to enhance image retrieval in imaginative and cogent ways, possibly transcending language-based retrieval systems.[32] Until then, subject access to visual materials appears to be best accomplished by combining a controlled vocabulary, such as *TGM*, for subject query retrieval, with digital browsing capabilities for image selection.

NOTES

1. Linda H. Armitage and Peter G.B. Enser, "Analysis of User Need in Image Archives," *Journal of Information Science* 23 (4), 1997: 287-299. Also see Karen Collins, "Providing Subject Access to Images: A Study of User Queries," *American Archivist*, 61(1), 1998: 36-55.

2. Prints and Photographs annual statistics and Barbara Orbach Natanson, P&P reference librarian, interviewed by authors, Washington, DC, 18 August 2000. Also see Elisabeth Betz Parker, "Controlled Vocabulary for Indexing Original and Historical Graphic Materials," *Terminology for Museums: Proceedings of an International Conference held in Cambridge, England, 21-24 September 1988*, (Cambridge, UK: The Museum Documentation Association with the Assistance of the Getty Grant Program, 1990): 254.

3. Published together in Library of Congress, Prints and Photographs Division, *Thesaurus for Graphic Materials*, (Washington, DC: Library of Congress, 1995). Web versions of *TGM I* and *TGM II* are available via the Library of Congress Thesauri homepage

<*http://lcweb.loc.gov/pmei/lexico*> or directly <*http://lcweb.loc.gov/rr/print/tgm1*> and <*http://lcweb.loc.gov/rr/print/tgm2*>.

4. American National Standards Institute, *American National Standard Guidelines for Thesaurus Structure, Construction, and Use: Approved June 30, 1980,* (New York: ANSI, 1980). ANSI Z39.19-1980.

5. Lexico is distributed by PMEI, 7900 Wisconsin Avenue, Suite 201 Bethesda, Maryland 20814 <*http://www.pmei.com/info.html*>.

6. Library of Congress, Cataloging Policy and Support Office, *Library of Congress Subject Headings,* 23rd ed., 5 vols., (Washington, DC: Library of Congress, Cataloging Distribution Service, 2000).

7. Toni Petersen, *Art & Architecture Thesaurus,* (New York: Oxford University Press, 1990). <*http://shiva.pub.getty.edu/aat_browser*>.

8. P&Ps automated records were fully integrated with the rest of the Library's records in August of 1999 when LC implemented its new online catalog.

9. For example, we recently cataloged an image about ecumenism. We decided to add the term "Ecumenism" to *TGM I,* instead of one of the more specific *LCSH* terms dealing with this topic *(LCSH* offers the following terms: "Christian union movements," "Councils and synods, Ecumenical," "Creeds, Ecumenical," "Ecumenical liturgies," and "Ecumenical movement," listing the latter term as the UF for "Ecumenism"). Because the image was about ecumenism in a broad sense, not an ecumenical movement, none of the *LCSH* terms seemed adequate for or appropriate to our cataloging needs. We could, however, see a future cataloging use for the term "Ecumenism."

10. Later editions of *AAT* are more international in scope and include numerous occupational headings for people.

11. Library of Congress, Congressional Research Service, *Legislative Indexing Vocabulary: The CRS Thesaurus,* 20th ed., (Washington, DC: Library of Congress, 1991). The web version is available via the Library of Congress Thesauri homepage <*http://lcweb.loc.gov/pmei/lexico*> or directly <*http://lcweb.loc.gov/pmei/lexico?db=LIV*>.

12. Discussed more fully in the introduction to *TGM II.* Also see Helena Zinkham, Patricia D. Cloud, and Hope Mayo, "Providing Access by Form of Material, Genre, and Physical Characteristics: Benefits and Techniques," *American Archivist,* 52, 1989: 300-319.

13. Helena Zinkham and Elisabeth Betz Parker, eds., *Descriptive Terms for Graphic Materials: Genre and Physical Characteristic Headings,* (Washington, DC: Library of Congress, 1986).

14. Library of Congress, Prints and Photographs Division, *LC Thesaurus for Graphic Materials: Topical Terms for Subject Access,* (Washington, DC: Library of Congress, 1987).

15. Library of Congress, Prints and Photographs Division, *Thesaurus for Graphic Materials,* (Washington, DC: Library of Congress, 1995).

16. Library of Congress, *Cataloger's Desktop,* (Washington, DC: Library of Congress, Cataloging Distribution Service, 1994-).

17. Lexico is a platform independent system that is Javabased, Web server-thin client architecture-compliant and can be accessed and manipulated over the Internet.

18. Prints and Photographs Division homepage <*http://lcweb.loc.gov/rr/print*>.

19. For an in-depth analysis of the nature of the vocabulary and a discussion of its comparative strengths and weaknesses see Corinne Jörgensen, "Image Indexing: An Analysis of Selected Classification Systems in Relation to Image Attributes Named by Naïve Users," *Annual Review of OCLC Research,* 1999 <*http://www.oclc.org/oclc/research/publications/review99/jorgensen/*>.

20. *Anglo-American Cataloguing Rules,* 2nd ed., 1998 revision, (Chicago: American Library Association, 1998).

21. Elisabeth W. Betz, *Graphic Materials: Rules for Describing Original Items and Historical Collections,* (Washington, DC: Library of Congress, 1982). 1996 version online *<http://www.tlcdelivers.com/tlc/crs/grph0199.htm>*.

22. Library of Congress, Network Development and MARC Standards Office, *MARC 21 Format for Bibliographic Data,* 2 vols., (Washington, DC: Library of Congress, Cataloging Distribution Service, 1999).

23. For further discussion of "of" and "about" see Sara Shatford's classic article "Analyzing the Subject of a Picture: A Theoretical Approach," *Cataloging & Classification Quarterly,* 6(3), 1986: 39-61.

24. Discussed more fully in the introduction to *TGM I,* Section II.D.

25. Elisabeth Betz Parker, "Controlled Vocabulary for Indexing Original and Historical Graphic Materials," *Terminology for Museums: Proceedings of an International Conference held in Cambridge, England, 21-24 September 1988,* (Cambridge, UK: The Museum Documentation Association with the Assistance of the Getty Grant Program, 1990): 254.

26. Several useful reference works on print and photograph identification methods are: Bamber Gascoigne, *How to Identify Prints: A Complete Guide to Manual and Mechanical Processes from Woodcut to Ink Jet,* (London: Thames and Hudson, 1986); William M. Ivins, Jr., *How Prints Look,* rev. and exp. ed., (Boston: Beacon Press, 1987); Gordon Baldwin, *Looking at Photographs, A Guide to Technical Terms,* (Malibu, CA: J. Paul Getty Museum in association with British Museum Press, 1991); James M. Reilly, *Care and Identification of 19th-Century Photographic Prints,* (Rochester, NY: Eastman Kodak Co., 1986).

27. P&P Online Catalog *<http://lcweb.loc.gov/rr/print/catalog.html>*; Library of Congress Online Catalog *<http://catalog.loc.gov>*; National Digital Library, American Memory homepage *<http://memory.loc.gov>*.

28. *TGM* users with whom P&P corresponded were asked the following questions: (1) Do you use *TGM* now? If so, how? For example, do you use *TGM* in conjunction with other cataloging thesauri and tools-e.g., *LCSH, LC Name Authority File, Art & Architecture Thesaurus,* etc.? (2) Have you used TGM in the past? If so, how? Did you use it differently then than you do now? (3) Do you follow P&P subdivision guidelines described in *TGM* or do you have your own subdivision practices? (4) Do you use the paper edition, the Web site, or both? (5) If you use TGM terms in catalog records that are available on the Web, please list relevant Web site addresses-or send us sample records if possible. (6) Do you currently propose new terms to *TGM?* (7) Do you anticipate using TGM differently in any future projects? If so, how?

29. Andrew Gordon, "The Design of Knowledge-Rich Browsing Interfaces for Retrieval in Digital Libraries," (Ph.D. diss., Northwestern University, 1999).

30. John Bye, Institute for Regional Studies, North Dakota State University, interviewed by authors, 6 December 2000.

31. Stanley Rice, "Conceptual Filtering of Image Collections," copyright 1999 *<http://www.cruzio.com/~autospec/access1.htm>* (21 August 2000).

32. For an interesting and thought-provoking discussion on the inherent limitations of using language-based subject indexing for access to non-textual materials see Elaine Svenonius, "Access to Nonbook Materials: The Limits of Subject Indexing for Visual and Aural Languages," *Journal of the American Society for Information Science,* 45(8), 1994: 600-606.

Providing Better Subject Access to Nonprint Fire Emergency Materials for Illinois Firefighters

Lian Ruan

SUMMARY. The Illinois Fire Service Institute Library (FSI Library) has the most comprehensive and popular nonprint fire emergency collection in Illinois. Besides providing descriptive cataloging for nonprint materials, the Library assigns in-depth subject terms and modified Library of Congress Classification to the catalog records. The Library reviewed its subject list and found numerous inconsistencies and duplications, because catalog records are acquired from sources using different subject vocabularies. The Library began a project in August 1999 to map the Library of Congress Subject Headings (LCSH), Medical Subject Headings (MeSH) from the National Library of Medicine, and

Lian Ruan is Director/Head Librarian, Illinois Fire Service Institute, University of Illinois at Urbana-Champaign.

The author is grateful for the Institute's continual support; to Professor Pauline Atherton Cochrane, Professor Emeritus at the Graduate School of Library and Information Science, University of Illinois at Urbana-Champaign, for her stimulating discussions and suggestions during the study; for inFIRE (international Fire and Information Reference Exchange, a worldwide fire libraries consortium) members' generous support; for Yan Xu and Guang Hu, graduate assistants; and to the Illinois Secretary of State's Office and the Illinois State Library for awarding the FSI Library the 1999 LSTA (Library Service and Technology Act) Mini-grant, Bring in An Expert, and the 2000 LSTA Full Year Grant, in July 1999 and January 2000, respectively, to partially fund this research project.

[Haworth co-indexing entry note]: "Providing Better Subject Access to Nonprint Fire Emergency Materials for Illinois Firefighters." Ruan, Lian. Co-published simultaneously in *Cataloging & Classification Quarterly* (The Haworth Information Press, an imprint of The Haworth Press, Inc.) Vol. 31, No. 3/4, 2001, pp. 213-235; and: *The Audiovisual Cataloging Current* (ed: Sandra K. Roe) The Haworth Information Press, an imprint of The Haworth Press, Inc., 2001, pp. 213-235. Single or multiple copies of this article are available for a fee from The Haworth Document Delivery Service [1-800-342-9678, 9:00 a.m. - 5:00 p.m. (EST). E-mail address: getinfo@haworthpressinc.com].

© 2001 by The Haworth Press, Inc. All rights reserved.

other fire vocabulary systems. The project developers created FireTalk, a new FSI thesaurus with a mix of LCSH, MeSH terms (identified as such), plus more specific fire science terms. FireTalk is used with the Library's Online Public Access Catalog at the Institute's website to enhance retrieval of relevant bibliographic citations and facilitate multiple database searching. *[Article copies available for a fee from The Haworth Document Delivery Service: 1-800-342-9678. E-mail address: <getinfo@haworthpressinc.com> Website: <http://www.HaworthPress.com> © 2001 by The Haworth Press, Inc. All rights reserved.]*

KEYWORDS. Subject access, nonprint fire emergency materials, outreach program, firefighters (Illinois), FireTalk, FSI thesaurus

NONPRINT FIRE EMERGENCY COLLECTION

The Illinois Fire Service Institute, University of Illinois at Urbana-Champaign, a statutory State Fire Academy, established the FSI Library in 1990 as an in-house library to support the training and teaching of the Institute's major programs, including Fire Fighting, Hazardous Materials (HazMat), Counter-Terrorism, Rescue, Investigation and Fire Prevention, Industrial Fires, and Emergency Medical Services (EMS). The Library has served the local fire departments throughout Illinois from time to time in the early 1990s. The Library's subject strengths are arson investigations, fire fighting, hazardous materials, counter-terrorism, rescue, fire education, fire safety, fire services management, emergency management, Emergency Medical Services (EMS), and general training. The various types of library information (i.e., book, periodical, videotape, transparency/overhead, slide, CD-ROM, training outlines, etc.) have been identified as needed by firefighters in the field.

According to the 1999 Illinois Office of State Fire Marshal statistics, there are 42,675 firefighters with a 20% turnover rate. Among 1,293 fire departments, the characteristics of the Illinois fire service say that 6% of all fire departments are paid firefighters, 65% are volunteer/paid-on call, 15% are combined (mixing volunteer and paid) and 14% are other. Because the turnover rate is high, and more than half of firefighters are volunteers, providing ongoing training and furnishing the most up-to-date training information at low or no cost become crucially important to maintain a well-prepared firefighting force to protect citizens' lives and property from fire and other dangerous hazards. Since the Institute was designated as the State Fire Academy in 1981, it has been able to reach about 33% of Illinois firefighters. In 1997, under the new Vision 2000 for the Future, the Institute's goal is to find the best ways to reach *every* Illinois firefighter with the training, education, and *information* he/she requires each year.

The FSI Library initiated and conducted a survey in 1998 among all fire departments in Illinois with a 46% response rate.[1] Among many key findings, the survey showed there are 305 survey respondents whose organization has a library. Only 3% own more than 500 titles; 48% own fewer than 50. Among the 31 County Firefighters' Association libraries, there are 3% with titles over 500, and 32% less than 50. Few have nonprint materials. Nine percent answered that they had no personnel working in the department libraries, 10% had non-library professionals, and none had librarians. Apparently, local information resources are fragmented, unbalanced, and lack professional support for acquisitions, organization, and access. The respondents also favored nonprint materials (e.g., videotapes, transparencies, CD-ROMs) over other training formats, when asked to identify which best meets their local training needs. Although nonprint materials are reported as the most widely used teaching aids for fire service instructors, they are extremely expensive to purchase and difficult to maintain, citing price and security reasons. For example, a six-videotape series, *Fire Investigation* (National Fire Protection Association, *http://www.nfpa.org*), costs non-members $1,203 and members $1,083. A single videotape, *Introduction to Hazardous Chemicals* (Emergency Film Groups, *http://www.efilmgroup.com*), costs $395. A CD-ROM with curriculum called *Essentials of Firefighting* (International Fire Service Training Association, *http://www.ifsta.org*) costs $820. Ninety-three percent of the respondents supported the Institute's plan to establish the Library's Outreach Program, which would aim to provide no-cost library and information services and programs to every Illinois firefighter, especially those who lack funding and resources, such as small and/or volunteer fire departments in under-served urban and rural communities. Since 1998, the Library has devoted more than half of its collection development budget to nonprint materials, covering a wide range of subject areas in the fire emergency field. Nonprint materials now make up more than one-third of the Library collection, which is the largest and most popular nonprint collection for fire emergency training in Illinois.

The 1998 survey also revealed that a majority of fire departments have access to the statewide online system, ILLINET. Therefore, the

Library decided to broaden its capability to serve every community in Illinois via interlibrary loan (ILL) and other outreach activities. In 1998, the FSI Library obtained Full Membership in the Lincoln Trail Libraries System (LTLS), one of Illinois's 12 regional libraries systems and began systematic ILL procedures, thus becoming a "special public library." The Library loans materials, including nonprint items, to firefighters throughout Illinois via ILL at no charge and has received positive feedback from both fire emergency service and library communities.

The ability to reach the widely dispersed clientele of Illinois firefighters was made more feasible with electronic access to the FSI Library's multi-media collection and services. Developing a fully electronic infrastructure has enhanced access to the FSI Library. The Library OPAC (Online Public Access Catalog) uses the software called inMagic WebPublisher (*http://www.inmagic.com*) to post the catalog of the *entire* library collection at the Institute's web site (*http://www.uiuc.edu/unit/IFSI/*). The Library uses the World Wide Web with a web-based search engine for accessing the Library OPAC. Anyone with web access can access the Library 24 hours a day, 7 days a week. The Library responds to interlibrary loan requests and other correspondence during regular business hours.

The Library is planning to integrate the catalog for this highly specialized collection into the statewide library online system (LTLS LSSAP-LINC). This will mean that the holdings of the FSI Library could be retrieved as the result of a system-wide search of library catalogs. In this way, firefighters or small libraries without World Wide Web access could search the Library's holdings.

CATALOGING NONPRINT FIRE EMERGENCY MATERIALS

The FSI Library follows the *Anglo-American Cataloguing Rules, 2nd ed. 1998 rev.* (*AACR2*) and catalogs nonprint materials with a detailed level of specification. The catalog records for nonprint materials often include abstracts and note fields. The Library has either obtained permission from publishers to use their summary information or has created its own annotations. Both the abstracts and note fields are searchable by keyword in the OPAC. There is a collation field for physical description of the items, as the user would expect, and the Library always adds the publication date to the title field. Subject entries appear in the record after the title field, and are occasionally followed by a Subject Name field for popular acronyms and other names. For videotapes, the Library includes running time in the collation field. Figures 1-4 show the coding of cataloging fields for videotape, slide program, CD-ROM, and transparency/overhead.

Through reference services and Internet outreach training workshops, the FSI Library found that fire service personnel appreciate more in-depth indexing using technical fire terminology. As JoAnn V. Rogers suggests: "Those who catalog nonprint materials must understand not only the physical characteristics and the content of the materials, but also the types and amount of information that the user will need to identify the material."[2] The FSI Library keeps users' needs in mind and intends to assign as many subjects as possible from title, segment, abstracts, and note fields for nonprint materials. When information from title, segment, abstracts and note is not enough, the Library views the videotapes or goes through the slides, transparencies and CD-ROMs. Selection of subject terms is based on anticipated user queries. The following catalog record (Figure 5) shows the level of subject specificity the FSI Library wants to achieve in order to better meet information needs of end users.

Classification number is another method to represent the FSI Library's subject analysis work. The Library uses the *Library of Congress*

FIGURE 1. Coding of Cataloging Fields for Videotape

Record Type: Video

Call Number: TH9145 .N59F514 1981

Title: Fire fighting strategy, 1981

Subject: Firefighting operations // Strategies // Fire attack // Fireground command // Personnel // Fireground communications // Media relations

Publisher: Film Communicators

Date: c1981

Collation: 1 VHS or 3/4' videotape (24:00 min.).

Availability: Available on Interlibrary Loan

Abstract: Lists and describes the sequences of eight basic steps in firefighting operations. Discusses bases for decisions in attack plans. Strategy includes a systematic method of dealing with fire emergencies, identifying phases of firefighting operations and providing a logical sequence for performing them. Strategy should also include a designated command, properly positioned personnel, effective communications and the clear, previous designation of back-up tasks such as dealing with the news media.

FIGURE 2. Coding of Cataloging Fields for Slide Program

Record Type: Slide

Call Number: TH9336 .E31 1984 Unit 1

Title: Engine and ladder company operations, Unit I: engine company operations, part 1, 1984

Subject: Engine company operations // Ladder company operations // Ladder companies // Engine companies

Subject Name: NFPA SL-120

Collation: 80 slides: col. + 1 cassette + 1 presentation.

Publisher: National Fire Protection Association

Date: c1984

Availability: Available on Interlibrary Loan

FIGURE 3. Coding of Cataloging Fields for CD-ROM

Record Type: CD-ROM

Call Number: T55.3 .H3M100C 1997

Author: Noll, Gregory G. // Hildebrand, Michael S.

Title: Hazardous materials, managing the incident, interactive CD-ROM, 1997

Subject: Hazardous materials incidents // Hazardous materials

Collation: 1 CD-ROM + 2-p. instruction + 1 24-p. user's manual.

Publisher: Hildebrand & Noll Associates

Date: c1997

Availability: Available on Interlibrary Loan

Classification scheme (*LCC*). When LCC numbers are too general to reflect the FSI Library's highly specialized collection, the Library provides further subdivisions to a LCC number by assigning a subject number from Cutter tables. For example, the Library uses TH9360 .R68 for ropes and TH9360 .P90 for pumps. The Library assigns different class numbers to different audiovisual media, for example, TH9383 .L20 for

FIGURE 4. Coding of Cataloging Fields for Transparency/Overhead

Record Type: Transparency

Call Number: TH9323 .F77In10 1980

Title: Handling hose, 1980

Subject: Fire hoses // Hoses

Subject Name: IFSTA 200

Collation: 24 transparencies (24 overlays): col. ; 22 x 28 cm.

Publisher: Oklahoma State University

Date: c1980

Availability: Available on Interlibrary Loan

FIGURE 5. Catalog Record for Videotape

Record Type: Video

Call Number: TH9360 .F74T23 1990 #4

Author: Brennan, Tom.

Title: High security devices: roll-down metal doors and scissor gates, part 4 of the forcible entry video series, 1990

Subject: Forcible entry // High security devices // Security systems // Roll down metal doors // Doors // Gates // Scissor gates // Fire incidents

Publisher: Fire Engineering

Date: c1990

Collation: 1 VHS videotape (20 min.) + 1 brochure.

Availability: Available on Interlibrary Loan

Note: Copy 2 without brochure.

Abstract: Recognizes the scissor gate and roll-down metal door configurations. Shows when to cut the lock and door. Discusses dangers unique to fire incidents with high security devices. Describes details of construction and the different types of operations. Provides techniques in cutting the roll-down metal door and scissor gate.

videotape on ladders, and TH9383 .L30 for transparency on ladders. Date of publication is also added to make the call number complete and distinguish editions of the same work.

Security and preservation concerns cause the Library to separate nonprint materials from print materials and shelve nonprint materials by the medium (for example with videotapes in one area and CD-ROMs in another).

THE PROBLEMS FOR SUBJECT ACCESS WHEN MULTIPLE VOCABULARIES ARE USED

The previous section describes how the FSI Library catalogs nonprint materials by offering great detailed level of description, modifying LCC, and assigning in-depth subject indexing to meet the end user's needs for bibliographic information.

The bibliographic records in the FSI Library nonprint catalog have subject headings from multiple sources, including LCSH, MeSH, the National Emergency Training Center's Learning Resource Center (NETC) Subject List, as well as from other specialized and locally developed word lists. The Library compiled one subject index from these various sources but did not resolve differences. Before becoming a part of the statewide online system, both LTLS (Lincoln Trail Libraries System) and FSI Library believed that the FSI Library should evaluate the non-LCSH subject headings used by the Library and map the vocabulary to LCSH, the standard vocabulary for the statewide system.

In many university libraries, two primary cataloging units, one in a subject area (e.g., health sciences library), and one in the general university library, would respectively assign MeSH and LCSH headings. These headings would be indexed separately and appear in different MARC (Machine-Readable Cataloging) fields. A good example of this process is Weintraub's description of the cataloging system at the University of California at San Diego Library.[3] In contrast, the FSI Library generates its own subject headings, as well as assigning Library of Congress Subject Headings (LCSH) and they all appear in the subject field of the catalog record. Catalogers have concerns about the limitations of LCSH and the Sears List of Subject Headings for the subject analysis of nonprint materials.[4] Weihs pointed out in 1987 that LCSH did not incorporate new topics fast enough, and the terms were not specific enough for the indexing of nonprint materials.[5] There is almost universal agreement about the difficulty of using LCSH for subject retrieval in specialized fields.[6]

The primary challenge in subject searches of library catalogs, whether online catalogs or card catalogs, is finding the proper form of the subject term. Smith and Cochrane suggest that multiple vocabulary catalogs can cause difficulties for searchers.[7] When gateways link to multiple databases, subject searching problems are further complicated because each database may use a different vocabulary. Limiting the search to one subject heading system at a time can result in a failure to retrieve all relevant materials, and even sequential searching of each database will not necessarily lead to full recall, because of inconsistencies and lack of knowledge of how the terms were used for the items cataloged. Often users unconsciously select an inappropriate index to search and retrieve few or no successful hits. On the other hand, as Olson and Strawn point out, a universal search of a mixed-system vocabulary can result in duplication of headings, incomplete or partial retrieval, conflicts between headings of one system and "search under" references in the other, and confusion of terms that have one meaning in one system and quite another in the second.[8] Keyword searching in title and abstract fields alone is not the answer, as Figure 1 (Coding of Cataloging Fields for Videotape) shows. If *fire fighting* was searched, this record would be retrieved by title word, but other records on *firefighting operations* would not be retrieved if neither title nor abstract keywords spelled the word correctly.

Strategies have been developed for coping with multiple vocabularies in the online catalog. Chaplan and Mandel have suggested that there are three methods-mapping, merging and switching.[6,9] The first strategy, as Chaplan states, is to map or link terms directly from one vocabulary to another, or to multiple vocabularies. In a map, the terms in one vocabulary are listed, with an indication of what the equivalent terms are in the other vocabulary. There may also be an indication of whether the term is identical, a synonym, or holds some other relationship to the term in the second vocabulary.[6] Olson and Strawn point out this method of integrating subject systems is accomplished by: (a) mapping terms and headings from one system to corresponding headings in another system; (b) adding the mapping data to authority records; and (c) enhancing the library management system software so that mapping data in authority records can be used to develop syndetic structures that relate the systems smoothly and consistently, enhancing subject retrieval.[8] Another strategy, as Chaplan explains, is to merge vocabularies as " . . . simply combining terms in their original form, with their accompanying cross references and term relationships, from two or more vocabularies into a single alphabetical list, with indications of which vocabulary contains the term."[6] A third strategy is to automatically switch, or transform, the terms from one vocabulary into those of another.[6]

Chaplan and Olson and Strawn both used the mapping techniques. Chaplan mapped Laborline Thesaurus terms to LCSH,[6] while Olson and Strawn mapped MeSH and LCSH.[8]

THE SOLUTIONS

In order to meet the challenge discussed in the previous section, the FSI Library applied, in April 1999, for the LSTA (Library Service and Technology Act) Mini-grant, Bring in an Expert, offered by the Illinois Secretary of State's Office and the Illinois State Library. The Library received the award in July 1999 and hired Professor Pauline Atherton Cochrane, an expert in subject access, to evaluate subject access in the FSI Library catalog. Professor Cochrane helped formulate procedures for evaluating the Library's subject index vocabulary and showed the Library how to develop a thesaurus with a map of relevant MeSH, LCSH, and other vocabulary terms in the file. She trained the project developers, FSI Head Librarian and her graduate assistant, in thesaurus review and maintenance. The project began during the Library's LSTA 2000 Full Year Grant in 2000 and continues as an ongoing project.

After working with Professor Cochrane, the project developers undertook several projects.

1. Create FireTalk, a thesaurus of approved subject headings with syndetic structure (UF, BT, NT, RT) and mapping information (showing origin of term and match, if any, in other vocabularies like MeSH, LCSH). For this, the Library purchased MultiTes software. This thesaurus becomes a subject authority file for the cataloger to use when validating headings from catalog records with LCSH, MeSH, and other subject headings.

The project developers knew from the file of reference queries and e-mail requests that the subject vocabulary used to access the Library nonprint collection would have to include such terms as: arsonists, fire causes, fire department management, fire safety, firefighting operations, juvenile firesetters, industrial fires, hazardous materials, hazardous materials awareness, hazardous materials operations, live burn training, public education, self contained breathing apparatus, vertical rescue operations, etc. Since LCSH does not provide these terms, the developers have included them in FireTalk and created the necessary syndetic structure, as shown in Figure 6. Regardless of whether the user searches title, subject, or keyword, the specificity of subject terms found in a catalog record (such as in Figure 1) will provide access to the controlled vocabulary mechanisms in the thesaurus which relate these terms to other related, broader and narrower terms.

2. Convert subdivisions to thesaurus terms or place them in another field, such as Subject Place, Subject Name, Subject Date, and Record Type, as in the example shown in Figure 7.

3. Review all class numbers used in the FSI Library's catalog records, with the aim of using them as subject access routes.

4. Develop specifications for the subject mapping across vocabularies in the various databases the Library uses. This could help the cataloging practices and display of the Library OPAC.

FIGURE 6. Example of Syndetic Structure in FireTalk

FIREFIGHTING OPERATIONS

TT 06 Firefighting operations

BT Firefighting operations

NT Fire companies

Fire operations

Firefighting equipment

Incident command systems

Rural firefighting operations

Structural firefighting operations

Suburban firefighting operations

Wildland firefighting operations

RT Fire investigations

Hazardous materials

Rescue operations

UF Fire fighting operations

FIGURE 7. Sample Record for Record Type, Subject Place and Subject Date

Record Type: *Video*

Call Number: SD421.4 .F51F514 1991

Title: Fire in the hills: the Oakland story, 1991

Subject: Wildland fires

Subject Place: *Oakland (California) // Berkeley (California)*

Subject Date: *1991*

Collation: 1 VHS videotape (22:00 min.) + 1 booklet.

Publisher: National Interagency Fire Center

Date: c1991

Availability: Available on Interlibrary Loan

5. Produce printed and web-based versions of FireTalk so that it can be distributed to FSI Library users and other fire science libraries around the world.

Project 3, 4 and 5 are not yet fully completed.

The FSI Library's FireTalk maps topics from multiple vocabulary sources, including subject heading lists from LCSH, MeSH, National Emergency Training Center's Learning Resource Center (NETC), and New York State Academy of Fire Science Library's periodical indexing system (New York). The map data exists as a database using MultiTes. If a FireTalk term is found in any of the listed source vocabularies, the entries in the printed and web-based thesauri indicate the source (see Figure 8).

When the technology allows, the Library will implement switching between the vocabularies, but for now our main objective is to produce a single subject authority list with an indication of what the equivalent terms are in the other vocabularies.

CREATING FireTalk-THE NEW FSI THESAURUS[10]

To produce a single subject authority list and complete the project tasks described in the previous section, Professor Cochrane and the project developers reviewed the *original card file* of subject headings and subdivisions in the FSI Library catalog records. The list contained 3,000

FIGURE 8. Sample Record with Mapping Data in FireTalk Thesaurus

FIREFIGHTERS (NETC, New York, FSI)
TT 01 Management
BT Fire department personnel (NETC, FSI)
NT Forest firefighters (FSI)
Marine firefighters (FSI)
Rural firefighters (FSI)
Volunteer firefighters (NETC, New York, FSI)
Women firefighters (NETC, New York, FSI)
RT Fire officers (NETC, New York, FSI)
UF Firefighter
Fire fighters (LCSH)
Fire fighter
Firemen

unique terms. Headings came from MeSH, LCSH, were locally produced, or of unknown origin. Some headings were proper names or geological terms. There had been no apparent preference given to either MeSH or LCSH headings, nor there had been any attempt to resolve inconsistencies between them. A card file of all subject headings had been kept with some broader terms (BT) or related terms (RT). In the card file, RT meant the other term assigned when a video or other type of material had this same heading. The call number used was also recorded (see Figure 9).

This card system was helpful when a similar heading appeared for a new item, but failed because it was not maintained. Evaluation of the list revealed a confusing sprawl of unrelated terms, inconsistent use of singular and plural forms, inverted and uninverted styles, the use of compound phrases and main terms, plus subdivisions to express the same concept.

The project developers decided to follow the American National Standard, *Guidelines for the Construction, Format, and Management of Monolingual Thesauri* (ANSI/NISO Z39.19-1994),[11] and took the following steps to convert LCSH-like headings into thesaurus terms.

FIGURE 9. Record from Old Subject Authority Card File

FIREFIGHTERS-VIDEOS

RT Training

Women firefighters

(TH9123 .T68 Firefighters

T9505 .H83 Training

TH9123 .W84 Women firefighters)

1. Relocated terms and subdivisions. The format moved to the "Record Type" (i.e., type of material) field in the bibliographic record (see Figure 10) and was used to create a Record Type pop-up table on the OPAC with a list including Video, Slide, Transparency, CD-ROM, etc. The project developers chose to use Record Type as the format field name in order to match it with the National Emergency Training Center's Learning Resource Center OPAC (*http://www.lrc.fema.gov*) Record Type field name.

2. Moved geographical headings and proper names. Such headings were placed in a separate "Subject" field and accessed by indices of "Subject Name," "Subject Place," and "Subject Date" in the OPAC. For example, Hackensack Fires was used for Subject Name; July 1, 1988 was used for Subject Date; and Hackensack (New Jersey) was used for Subject Place (see Figure 11). The indices are particularly useful for incidents and investigation report searches. The Word Wheel, a built-in feature of inMagic WebPublisher, provides users with a browsable list in an alphabetical order, but only in the chosen field. To do a general keyword search in all fields of the record, the user must do keyword or multiple searches.

FIGURE 10. Pop-Up Table for Type of Material

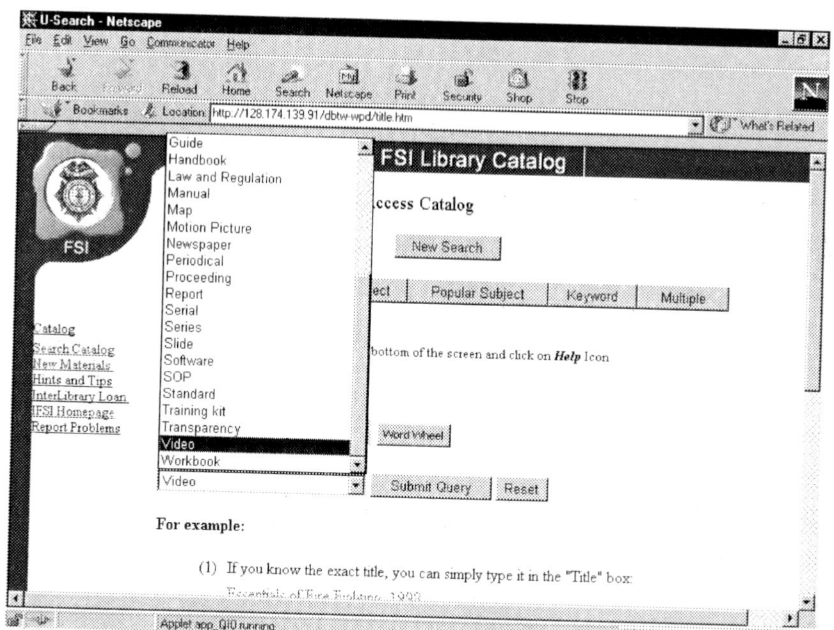

3. Established Broad Subject Categories for subject terms. These categories reflect the Institute's major academic areas of fire and emergency services (in the thesaurus record they are called TT-Top Terms). The list of subject terms in each category could be automatically generated and form a "micro thesaurus," which is useful for screening and reviewing those terms with FSI faculty (see Figure 12).

The project developers reviewed each term in a category to establish all Used For, BT, NT and RT terms associated with it. As needed, the developers added scope notes and collected information about the existence of the term (in whatever form found) on other lists, such as MeSH or LCSH.

When the developers are satisfied that the terms are part of a good hierarchical structure, they will meet with each Program Director at the Institute to discuss the particular section of the thesaurus that covers their subject area, and to be open to suggestions for improvement. The developers will also review the Library Reference Request Database to study how the end users made requests in each category. This review

FIGURE 11. Subject Search

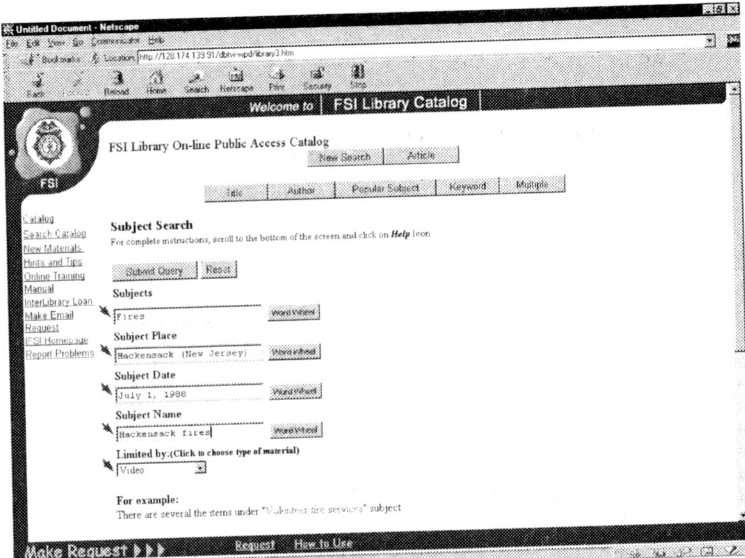

will help establish the entry vocabulary (UF terms) that will improve access to the Library nonprint collection for OPAC users.

In making decisions, the project developers routinely consulted American National Standard, *Guidelines for the Construction, Format, and Management of Monolingual Thesauri*, the MeSH Tree Structures, several medical dictionaries, handbooks in fire emergency fields, and IFSTA (International Fire Service Training Association) manuals. With the help of the KWOC printouts and hierarchical displays easily available using the MultiTes software, the project developers checked the treatment of similar terms and the logical structure of the relationships. The hierarchical display for each term does not include RT and UF portions of the thesaurus. The number of dots before the terms in the display indicates the depth of the hierarchy. For example, in Figure 13, Changes, Fire department management, and Fire service management are narrow terms under Management. Organizational changes, Alliances, Cooperation and Fire services are still narrower terms under each of these terms, respectively.

FIGURE 12. Subject Category/Top Term List and Example of Thesaurus Record

SUBJECT CATEGORY / TOP TERM	TOP TERM NUMBER
General	00
Management	01
Public Education	02
Fire Prevention and Inspections	03
Hazardous Materials	04
Emergency Communications	05
Firefighting Operations	06
Arson and Fire Investigations	07
Rescue and Search Operations	08
Training	09
Emergency Management (Natural Disasters)	10
Counter-Terrorism	11
Emergency Medical Services (EMS)	12
Industrial Fires	13

A. Subject Category / Top Term

EXPLOSIVES
TT 04 Hazardous Materials
NT Combustible liquids

B. Example of Thesaurus Record

FIGURE 13. KWOC and Hierarchical Display

KWOC (Key Word Out of Context)	Hierarchical Display (Partial)
MANAGEMENT Communication in management Compensation management Conflict management Fire department management Fire service management Management Management games Personnel management Risk management Stress management Total quality management	MANAGEMENT . Changes . . Organizational changes . Fire department management . . Alliances . . . Partners . . . Partnerships . . Consolidation . Fire service management . . Cooperation . . . Interagency cooperation . . Fire services . . . Fire information services . . . Metropolitan fire services . . . . Metropolitan fire departments . . . Rural fire services . . . . Rural fire departments

MAPPING FROM FireTalk TO OTHER WORD LISTS

The previous section described how the project developer created FireTalk, the FSI thesaurus. The vocabularies, which the project developers selected for retrospective mapping in FireTalk, include: the 1999 edition of the Library of Congress Subject Heading (LCSH), the 2000 Medical Subject Headings from the National Library of Medicine (MeSH), the 1999 National Emergency Training Center's Learning Resource Center Subject Terms (NETC), and the 1999 New York State Academy of Fire Science Library's Subject Terms used in the periodical indexing system (New York).

The project developers began with the assumption that each term in FireTalk was probably derived from MeSH, LCSH, or was locally established. Beginning with the first word in FireTalk, the developers sought a matching term in LCSH, MeSH, New York, and NETC. If there was no match, the developers looked for cross references or alternative headings derived from the developer's experience and knowledge of the field. When a match was found, the developers made note of it (see example in Figure 8) and, as needed, the project developers noted relevant cross-references, broader or narrower headings, and related headings. If more than one heading was relevant, all were noted. The developers looked up each alternative heading in the sources to determine whether it was relevant and to seek additional cross-references or headings. To determine matches of meanings, the terms found elsewhere were looked for in the FireTalk's structured display, to check for scope notes or the context of the term in the thesaurus structure. No attempt was made to seek matches that could be made by Boolean combinations of two or more headings.

The general principle followed here is to identify and map one-to-one correspondences between LCSH, MeSH, FSI, New York and NETC main headings. In order to map a LCSH and MeSH heading onto each other, the headings must be co-extensive; one cannot be broader or narrower than the other. The existing hierarchical structure is relied on to direct a user from a known heading to a broader or narrower heading.

For near-matches, the project developers have so far found problems in the following two categories:

1. Terms with similar meaning but differ in;

a) Word order or phrasing;

Example 1
- Stoves, Wood (LCSH)
- Wood, Stoves (FSI)

Example 2
- Building, Fireproof (LCSH)
- Fireproof building (FSI)

b) Spelling;

Example 3
- Fire fighters (LCSH)
- Firefighters (FSI) (NETC) (New York)

Example 4
- Emergency Treatment (MeSH)
- Emergency medical care (FSI) (NETC) (New York)

c) Singular vs. plural form;

Example 5
- Hose (LCSH)
- Hoses (FSI) (NETC) (New York)

In a number of cases, the same noun was used but one system used the singular form while the other used the plural. The plural form might represent a class of objects (e.g., a class of chemical compounds), and the singular form the most common or best-known member of that class. Unfortunately, often the heading in the singular form is used to represent the entire class of objects.

The project developers generally mapped singular and plural headings, unless evidence in the authority records indicated that no mapping should be made. The developers followed the guidelines for Singular and Plural Forms in 3.5 "American National Standard, Guidelines for the Construction, Format, and Management of Monolingual Thesauri," which says that terms can be divided into two categories: count nouns and noncount (mass) nouns. The guidelines for singular and plural based on these categories apply to the formulation of both descriptors and entry terms.

The choices for the approved FireTalk terms in the above examples are: Wood stoves, Fireproof buildings, Firefighters, Emergency medical care, and Hoses. Appropriate use and/or used for references were made, and mapping information was recorded.

2. Terms that differ but are somewhat similar in meaning;

Example { Fire extinction (LCSCH)
Firefighting operations (FSI) (NETC)
Fire-fighting tactics (New York) }

The choice for the approved FireTalk term is Firefighting operations, with appropriate use and/or used for references and mapping information.

The project developers went beyond the "use for" or "see" reference structure found in either MeSH or LCSH and considered that those headings already constructed were valid access points, even if they were no longer authorized headings, for example, Search operations. Previously used terms that were found in the FSI Library catalog records were also cross-referenced, so that the mapping database could change those records during an update of the file or provide the searcher with clues and links between terms.

MeSH proved quite capable of handling specific medical topics in fire science. LCSH handled only general concepts related to fire science. NETC and New York provided more detailed terms in the fire science field. The project developers noticed that neither MeSH nor LCSH authorizes more specific terms, yet professionals and lay people alike make heavy use of them.

Headings are properly and consistently capitalized in FireTalk's mapping information, giving preference to the LCSH form. For MeSH headings, all significant words in the headings are capitalized; in LCSH, only the first word in the heading is capitalized. Local headings, comprising mostly names of persons, places or dates, are retained as Subject Name, Subject Place, or Subject Date.

In place of the original FSI list of 3,000 headings, the new FireTalk thesaurus presents 5,000 approved entry terms or lead-in vocabulary. The link from the OPAC to "FireTalk, FSI Thesaurus," is rudimentary at present. The project developers plan to suggest improvements to both the Library OPAC and MultiTes vendors to make the interface more user-friendly and transparent. Navigation between the thesaurus display needs to be facilitated.

The project developers use FireTalk when performing original and copy cataloging. FireTalk allows the developers to validate the terms used in cataloging and see how LCSH, MeSH, and other local vocabulary terms have been mapped to FireTalk. The FireTalk Thesaurus also facilitates multiple database searching and is provided in an alphabetical and hierarchical display for OPAC users. The developers will continue mapping terms as new headings are added.

In addition to providing subject searching by Subject, Subject Place, Subject Date, Subject Name (all with Word Wheels), the Library OPAC also has provided a "Popular Subject" term menu screen, with links to key information by category (Figure 14). This feature targets users by their broad subject interests.

BENEFITS OF FireTalk PROJECT

Today, the FSI Library provides its patrons with an improved subject access tool. Though the process of mapping and development of a thesaurus is extremely labor-intensive and time consuming, it is necessary if the Library is to establish some consistency and integrity in the sub-

FIGURE 14. Popular Subject Search

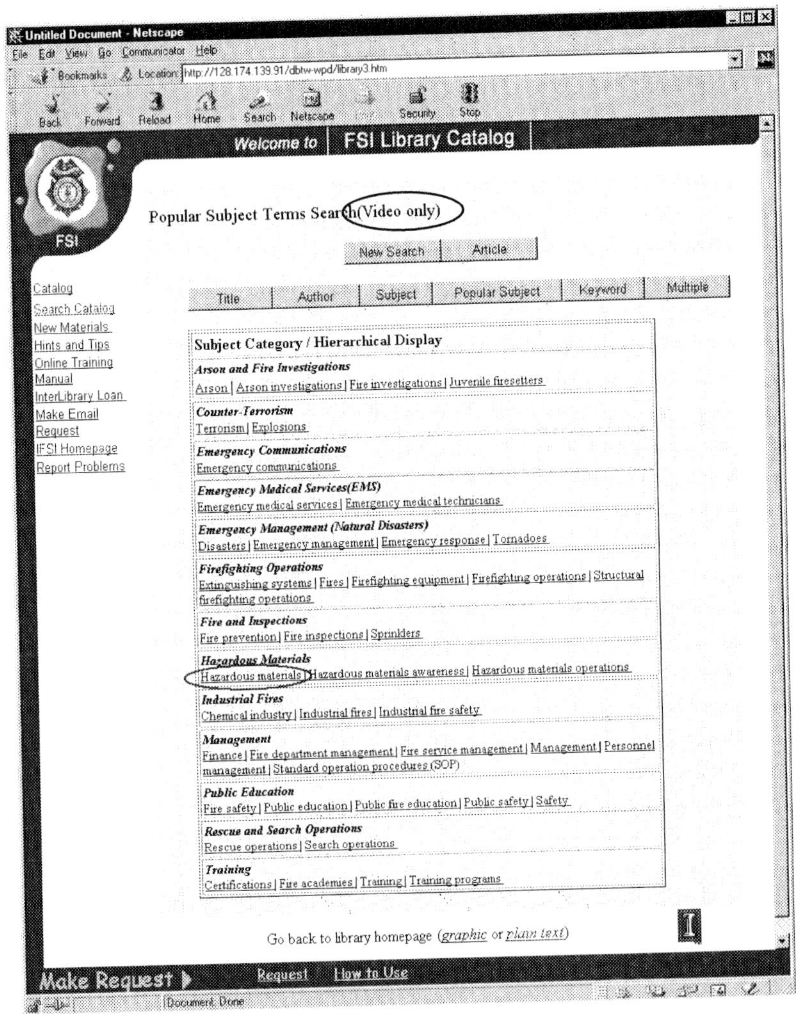

ject access mechanisms in OPACs and gateways that cross several vocabularies.

FireTalk developers hope the procedures followed during this review of subject access mechanisms in the FSI Library will be useful to others who acquire catalog records from various sources and need to guide their users doing subject searches. The revision of the Library subject headings to include a Record Type (i.e., type of material) pop-up table in the OPAC along with Subject, Subject Name, Subject Place and Subject Date has proven especially helpful to those searching for nonprint materials.

REFERENCES

1. Lian Ruan, "Reaching Out to Underserved Illinois Firefighters: Results of a Survey Project." Paper presented at the annual conference of inFIRE, Montour Falls, New York, May, 1999. Available online from URL: *http://www.wpi.edu/Academics/Library/InFire//Conferences/1999/.*

2. JoAnn V. Rogers, *Nonprint Cataloging for Multimedia Collections, a Guide Based on AACR2* (Littleton, Colo.: Libraries Unlimited, Inc., 1982), 23.

3. Tamara S. Weintraub, "The Dual-Thesaurus Catalog: MeSH and LCSH." *Technicalities* 12, no. 12 (1992): 10-12.

4. Ingrid Hsieh-Yee, *Organizing Audiovisual and Electronic Resources for Access, a Cataloging Guide* (Englewood, Colorado: Libraries Unlimited, Inc., 2000), 87.

5. Jean Weihs, "Access to Nonbook Materials: The Role of Subject Headings and Classification Numbers for Nonbook Materials," in *Policy and Practice in Bibliographic Control of Nonbook Media*, edited by Sheila S. Intner and Richard P. Smiraglia (Chicago: American Library Association, 1987), 53-63.

6. Margaret A. Chaplan, "Mapping Laborline Thesaurus Terms to Library of Congress Subject Headings: Implications for Vocabulary Switching." *Library Quarterly* 65, no.1 (1995): 39-61.

7. Marilyn J. Smith and Pauline Atherton Cochrane, "Creating Better Subject Access with Multiple Vocabularies: Upgrading the Subject Heading List for the Alzheimer's Association." *Library Resources and Technical Services* 43, no.1 (1999): 53-58.

8. Tony Olson and Gary Strawn, "Mapping the LCSH and MeSH Systems." *Information Technology & Libraries* 16 (March 1997): 5-19.

9. Carol A., Mandel, *Multiple Thesauri In Online Library Bibliographic Systems* (Washington, DC: Cataloging Distribution Service, Library of Congress, 1987), 72.

10. *FireTalk, FSI Thesaurus* will be published in print and electronic format. For more information, contact Lian Ruan by phone at 217/333-8925 or by e-mail at L-ruan@uiuc.edu.

11. American National Standard, *Guidelines for the Construction, Format, and Management of Monolingual Thesauri* (Bethesda, Md.: NISO Press, 1994).

Two Genre and Form Lists for Moving Image and Broadcast Materials: A Comparison

Martha M. Yee

SUMMARY. *The Moving Image Genre-Form Guide* and *Library of Congress Subject Headings* are compared as sources of genre or form terms for moving image and broadcast materials. Based on the findings of this comparison, it is recommended that any library, media collection or archive that uses LCSH for the provision of topical subject access to moving images and broadcast materials strongly consider using LCSH for genre and form access to moving images and broadcast materials as well. A number of recommendations are made for improving LCSH as a tool for form and genre access to moving image materials and an exhaustive list of LCSH terms which are *examples of* a form or genre is appended. *[Article copies available for a fee from The Haworth Document Delivery Service: 1-800-342-9678. E-mail address: <getinfo@haworthpressinc.com> Website: <http://www.HaworthPress.com> © 2001 by The Haworth Press, Inc. All rights reserved.]*

Martha M. Yee is Cataloging Supervisor, UCLA Film and Television Archive since 1983. She has a PhD in Library and Information Science from UCLA and did her dissertation on moving image versions. She is currently Vice Chair/Chair Elect of the Cataloging and Classification Section of the Association for Library Collections and Technical Services.

Greta de Groat and David Miller were kind enough to read this article in draft form and to offer many suggestions for ways to improve it. Lisa Kernan, a most welcoming and knowledgeable public service librarian at the UCLA library that collects film and television literature (the Arts Library), did some research for the author, who was unable to get to the library due to a bus strike. The author alone is responsible for any errors that may remain, of course.

[Haworth co-indexing entry note]: "Two Genre and Form Lists for Moving Image and Broadcast Materials: A Comparison." Yee, Martha M. Co-published simultaneously in *Cataloging & Classification Quarterly* (The Haworth Information Press, an imprint of The Haworth Press, Inc.) Vol. 31, No. 3/4, 2001, pp. 237-295; and: *The Audiovisual Cataloging Current* (ed: Sandra K. Roe) The Haworth Information Press, an imprint of The Haworth Press, Inc., 2001, pp. 237-295. Single or multiple copies of this article are available for a fee from The Haworth Document Delivery Service [1-800-342-9678, 9:00 a.m. - 5:00 p.m. (EST). E-mail address: getinfo@haworthpressinc.com].

© 2001 by The Haworth Press, Inc. All rights reserved.

KEYWORDS. Genre headings for motion pictures, genre headings for radio programs, genre headings for television programs, cataloging of motion pictures, cataloging of television programs, cataloging of radio programs, subject headings-motion pictures, subject headings-radio programs, subject headings-television programs, motion pictures-terminology, radio broadcasting-terminology, television broadcasting-terminology

INTRODUCTION

Two genre/form lists for moving image materials are currently in use in the United States, one a specialized list developed by the Motion Picture, Broadcasting and Recorded Sound Division at the Library of Congress, *The Moving Image Genre-Form Guide* (henceforth referred to as MIGFG),[1] and the other the Library of Congress Subject Headings list itself (henceforth referred to as LCSH).[2] LCSH is a general purpose list developed primarily for print materials, including books about moving image materials. Headings are added to the list as needed in the cataloging of materials collected by libraries and archives that use LCSH, many of which do collect moving image materials. LCSH has evolved gradually over the last century by means of the accretion of headings just described. In contrast, MIGFG was designed specifically to provide form and genre access to moving image materials, and was created rather rapidly over the last several years; in other words, it is not the product of many years of gradual accretion as LCSH is.

This article constitutes a critique of these two currently used sources of headings for the provision of access to genre and form in collections of moving image materials, as well as a comparison to an earlier list that MIGFG replaced but that is still used by some moving image collections in the United States, *Moving Image Materials: Genre Terms* (henceforth referred to as MIM).[3]

The following questions are raised and discussed: Are some of the headings in each of the two lists actually topical subject headings in disguise? Do some of the headings express concepts other than form or genre, such as audience, type of broadcast or distribution, filmmaker, point of view, production cost, style, series, fictitious character or time slot? Are the headings as specific and direct as they could be? Are the headings consistent in their facet analysis and citation order? Do the headings obey literary warrant? Do the number and grammatical part of speech of each heading follow standard usage and are they consistent?

Are the syndetic structures (cross references) adequate and consistent? Are all useful genre and form terms for moving image materials included in each list? Can the headings be integrated easily into heading displays that draw headings from a number of different sources of headings? And finally, does either list contain headings that create categories into which so many moving image titles fall that they become virtually unusable for direct searching?

In this article, genre is defined as a widely recognized category of fictional moving image and/or broadcast works characterized by recognizable conventions such as common themes, narrative formulae, character-types, settings, and, for moving image works, even visual characteristics (characteristic lighting, set design, props or icons); a genre may be associated with a particular subject, but the fact that a work deals with that particular subject is not a necessary or sufficient reason to consider that work to be in the genre. Form is much more nebulous than genre; unlike genre, it is not limited to fictional materials and not associated with particular content or subject matter; instead, it is often linked to distribution and presentation formats, as in the case of features, shorts, wide-screen films, television series and television specials, or to particular methods of production, as in the case of cartoons, live shows and documentaries. In a sense, one could define form negatively as any category of moving image and/or broadcast works that is of interest to users of these materials and is not a genre, as defined above.

A QUICK REVIEW OF THE NATURE OF GENRE AND FORM ACCESS

In theory, we assign the genre heading 'Western films' to a bibliographic record for a film that *is* a western (i.e., *an example of* a western), not a film that *depicts* the making of westerns or is *about* westerns. We distinguish this type of heading by putting it into a 655 field in the MARC 21 format. A film *about* or *depicting* the making of westerns would be assigned the same heading in a 650 (topical subject heading) field, rather than a 655 field.

It should be noted, however, that although LCSH contains many genre and form headings appropriate for adding to films or programs that are *examples of* a category, rather than *works about* a category, current practice is not to distinguish between these headings and regular topical subject headings using MARC 21 tags: all go into 650 fields.

The Library of Congress (LC) does have plans to identify the genre/form and other *examples of* headings, and begin placing them in 655 fields. The *Authority Data Elements Implementation* page maintained by the Cataloging Policy and Support Office of the Library of Congress contained the following statement on July 27, 2000: "Creation of authority records for form/genre headings in 155 fields and more widespread assignment of form/genre terms in 655 fields of bibliographic records will occur in future stages of the form/genre implementation plan and may be phased in by format or discipline. The Library is not yet projecting any specific dates for these future stages of implementation."[4] For a history of recent developments in the provision of genre and form access to materials in U.S. libraries, see Hemmasi, Miller and Lasater, 2000.[5]

LC's practice concerning works about a genre or form of film or television program is to add the subdivision '--History and criticism' to the 650 topical subject heading for the form or genre; e.g.:

> Western films--History and criticism.

There is a good deal of inconsistency across subject areas or academic disciplines, however, in the way LCSH uses heading structure to distinguish between works *about* a genre or form and *examples of* a genre or form. Compare and contrast the following, for example:

> 'Opera' (*works about*) and 'Operas' (*examples of*); headings linked by scope notes
>
> 'Gangster films--History and criticism' (*works about*) and 'Gangster films' (*examples of*); no see also references or scope notes to link a main heading with one of its subdivisions
>
> 'Photography' (*works about*) and 'Photographs' (*examples of*); no see also references or scope notes to link headings, or to alert users to one broader form subdivision ('--Pictorial works') that includes many *examples of*
>
> 'Cartography' (*works about*) and 'Maps' (*examples of*); headings linked by scope notes
>
> 'Computer war games' (same heading for both *works about* and *examples of*)

It is possible that use of the same heading for both *works about* and *examples of* is the technique most likely to guarantee that all users of all catalogs are presented with a choice between *works about* and *examples of*, or allowed to view both, if desired. After all, any time the two headings differ, there is a chance the user will find one and not the other. However, the technique of using the same heading for both concepts functions well only if catalogers differentiate between them by means of MARC 21 tagging (655 for *example of* and 650 for *works about*) *and* only if systems use the difference in tagging to drive displays, qualifying one or both of the headings with display constants, for example.

EXAMPLE:
Computer war games (*works about*)
Computer war games (*examples of*)

If systems simply lump all *works about* and *examples of* together into one alphabetical list, the result is likely to be more confusing than helpful. For further discussion of effective displays of *works about* and *examples of* see Yee and Layne, 1998.[6]

Sometimes it is not that easy to tell whether a moving image work being cataloged consists of an *example of* or a *work about*. Consider a televised baseball game, for example. Is a televised baseball game:

a. an *example of* a baseball game (the thing itself) (655)

OR

b. a *depiction* of a baseball game (650)

This may be the same problem as that presented by a play adapted into a screenplay and filmed; the film is generally considered a new work because of the added cinematographic authorship functions. Therefore, the film work itself may not be an *example of* a play, but may rather *depict* or *contain* a performance of a play. (See the work of the ALCTS CC:DA Task Force on Works Intended for Performance, 1996-1997, for more discussion on this question.)[7] However, perhaps a "mere recording" of a performance of a play on a moving image format actually *is* an *example of* a play?

There are other LCSH headings for types of performance or event that can be filmed or televised, raising the same question about whether such a filmed or televised performance or event is an *example of* such a performance or event (655) or *depicts* such a performance or event (650); see Appendix 4 for a list of such headings.

Sometimes the *works about* are given a heading that means a process or discipline, such as 'Photography' or 'Cartography,' above. There are motion picture processes as well, which can be seen in related *examples of*. *Examples of* 'Wildlife cinematography' can be seen in 'Wildlife films,' both LCSH headings. This raises questions about other headings that perhaps need counterparts for *examples of*. If 'Wide-screen processes (Cinematography)' is meant to be used for books about wide-screen processes, does another heading need to be created for the wide-screen films themselves? Two other similar headings in LCSH are:

Computer animation (*about*? or *examples of*? or both?)
Underwater cinematography (what heading for *examples of*?)

In contrast to LCSH, MIGFG was not designed to provide access to works *about* particular moving image genres and forms, only to *examples of* them. Thus the complexities described above are avoided with MIGFG. On the other hand, this means MIGFG does not attempt to help users who are interested in both westerns and, for example, documentary films and programs about westerns.

GENRE/FORM vs. TOPICAL SUBJECT HEADINGS

The first question we want to ask is the following: Are some of the headings in each of the two lists actually topical subject headings in disguise? Any film, television program or radio program on a topic could potentially be given both an *about* heading and an *example of* heading that virtually duplicate each other, if the *example of* heading means essentially 'films about' whatever the topic is. For example, if you have a film about abortion, you could give it a topical subject heading for 'Abortion' (the *about* heading) and a genre/form heading for 'Films about abortion' (the *example of* heading). This would double the size of our subject/genre/form indexes without providing any added service for users.

The most valuable genre and form headings are those that identify categories independently of subject matter. For example, the western or the gangster film are well-known examples of genre film, characterized by recognizable conventions such as common themes, narrative formulae, character-types, settings, and even visual characteristics (characteristic lighting, set design, props or icons). A documentary about the Oregon Trail is not a western, since it does not follow the conventions of the western genre. A documentary about Al Capone is not a gangster film, since it does not follow the conventions of the gangster film genre. Adding the genre headings only to the records for the films that truly are genre films allows users to limit their searches to these films only, rather than having to go through every film about a topical subject associated with a particular genre of interest, looking for those films that are genre films.

There are a number of headings in the MIGFG list that seem to be topical subject headings in the form of genre/form headings rather than to represent true genres as defined above, and therefore have the potential of causing duplicate entry under both a topical heading and a genre/form heading for the same concept. See Appendix 5 for a list of headings in the MIGFG genre list that might more usefully be converted to topical subject headings.

LCSH, too, contains some topical subject headings disguised as *example of* headings. For example, the heading 'Science films' is used for films about science. Since thousands of other topics are dealt with simply by adding the topical heading to the record for a film, rather than by constructing a heading in the format '[topic] films,' it is hard to see why an exception is made for films about science. See Appendix 6 for other such headings in LCSH. One has to wonder how the user benefits from having a film about Christmas listed under both 'Christmas films' and 'Christmas.' LCSH has never allowed headings to be subdivided by physical format, such as 'Christmas--videocassettes,' 'Christmas--audiocassettes,' etc., probably from a desire to avoid "segregating" nonbook materials from books on the same subject. One suspects that headings such as 'Christmas films' represent the insinuation of physical format into the headings themselves in compensation for the inability to subdivide by physical format.

Is there perhaps a need to better relate the following types of heading for catalog users:

a. [topic] in motion pictures [for works that discuss how the topic is handled in motion pictures]
b. [topic] [when added to non-fiction motion pictures]
c. [topic] $v Drama. [when added to fictional motion pictures]

b. and c. being *examples of* motion pictures that address the topic as opposed to *works about* motion pictures that address the topic? For example, would the user who found the heading 'AIDS (Disease) in motion pictures' realize that under that heading will be found books that discuss how AIDS has been handled in motion pictures, but that under the heading 'AIDS (Disease)' will be found actual documentary films about AIDS, and under 'AIDS (Disease)--Drama' will be found fictional films about AIDS? Complex see references under the '[topic] in . . . ' headings might be helpful, at least in systems that are capable of displaying such complex see references . . . Unfortunately, online public access catalogs currently do a rather poor job of providing users with access to the wealth of useful information already found in cross references and notes on LCSH authority records.

GENRE/FORM vs. AUDIENCE, TYPE OF BROADCAST OR DISTRIBUTION, FILMMAKER, POINT OF VIEW, PRODUCTION COST, STYLE, SERIES, FICTITIOUS CHARACTER OR TIME SLOT

The second question we want to ask is: Do some of the headings in the two lists express concepts other than form or genre, such as audience, time slot, fictitious characters or type of broadcast or distribution? Both LCSH and MIGFG include other types of *examples of* headings that are neither genre nor form headings nor topical subject headings:

1. Films Made for a Particular Audience (Women, Children, African Americans, Etc.)

In Appendix 7 can be found a list of terms in both lists that provide access to moving image materials by the intended audience. Intended audience is not always easy to determine and judgments as to potential audience on the part of the cataloger can be very subjective, so this kind of indexing is bound to be somewhat haphazard; however, it is so popular among users of moving image materials, and intended audience can have such a profound effect on form and genre, that it is probably worth doing our best to provide this type of access, even though most libraries and archives cannot afford to do the extensive research that would be necessary to provide truly comprehensive and accurate information about this aspect of moving image and broadcast works. If we were to commit ourselves to providing this type of access, however, we would need to use a much more extensive list of group-as-audience headings than is currently available (see Appendix 7).

Since it is possible that this type of access could verge on the offensive when the intended audience at the time of release or broadcast consisted of an ethnic group that has been the target of racism, it might be better to explore other means than subject/genre/form headings to provide this type of access. For example, byte 22 of the 008 field in the MARC 21 format[8] is defined as 'target audience.' Of course, 26 letters of the alphabet do not allow much latitude for coding the various ethnic groups that have been intended audiences for motion pictures and television programs over the course of history, but use of MARC 21 coding of some type might provide cleaner and, arguably, less offensive access to this type of information than adding headings such as 'Motion pictures for African Americans,' 'Motion pictures for Jews in the United States,' or 'Motion pictures for Chinese-Americans' to LCSH.

2. Type of Broadcast or Distribution (e.g., Cable, Home Movie or Video, Etc.)

Historically, the two classic methods of distribution for these materials were theatrical distribution (film) and broadcasting (television and radio); at the present time we should probably also include cable, satellite, home video distribution (although distribution for home use actually goes much further back in history than the videocassette revolution and encompasses 16 mm. film distribution), and Internet distribution. The two lists under discussion show significant differences in approach to the distinction among distribution mechanisms.

LCSH establishes three terms:

EXAMPLES:

Western films
Western radio programs
Western television programs

MIGFG list uses form subdivisions (of which, more below):

EXAMPLES:

Western--Feature.
Western--Television series.

It is not possible in either list to provide access by distribution mechanism to moving image materials distributed as home videos, to moving image materials broadcast on cable or by satellite, or to moving image materials distributed over the Internet.

The earlier list, MIM, used the same heading for both television and film whenever possible:

EXAMPLE: Westerns

Could it be that this latter approach is the best in the long term, when possible, given the current and on-going change in distribution mechanisms for moving image materials? If we find that films and television programs are all eventually distributed over the Internet along with other types of moving image, will we then be constricted by having to choose between calling each title either a 'film' or a 'program'?

3. Films Made by a Filmmaker That Belongs to a Particular Group of People (Women, Children, African Americans, Etc.)

LCSH EXAMPLE: Films by children

Rather than using topical subject headings attached to bibliographic records to provide this kind of access, it might be more useful to develop ways to add topical subject headings to authority records for persons and corporate bodies, so that users interested in filmmakers belonging to a particular group could first search authority records to pull together the filmmakers that fall into the category of interest (African American women choreographers, for example), and then ask to see the bibliographic records attached to each authority record of interest, in order to see the films of each person of interest. David Bearman has been advocating the provision of this type of access to authority records for years (see Bearman and Szary, 1987,[9] and Bearman, 1989[10]).

4. Point of View

LCSH EXAMPLES:
Feminist films
Populist films

Monograph catalogers generally avoid trying to analyze point of view in this fashion because it is so subjective and can be so controversial. One person's feminist film is another person's sexist film and another person's propaganda (see also the discussion below concerning whether or not propaganda headings in LCSH are meant to be used for *examples of*). Consider where this trend could lead . . . Also add Communist films? Leftist films? Racist films? Right wing films? Religious right films?

5. Unfinished

LCSH EXAMPLES:
Unfinished animated films
Unfinished motion pictures

This is a somewhat odd category, but might be of interest to some users.

6. Cost, Production Values

LCSH EXAMPLES:
B films
Low budget motion pictures
Low budget television programs

It can sometimes be difficult for catalogers to judge whether or not a film or program was low budget, but there is no question that moving image scholars are interested in these categories, as can be seen in the literary warrant experiments in Appendix 3.

7. Styles, Movements

LCSH EXAMPLE:
New wave films

The area of styles and movements is another area in which judgements of catalogers and catalog users can be highly subjective and not always in sync, but access by style or movement would undoubtedly be useful, and would probably become more reliable over time, as scholars come to agreement about which films have a given style or resulted from a given movement.

8. Series?

See Appendix 8 for a list of LCSH headings that would seem to indicate a pattern of using topical subject headings to provide access to films in a series. Since many films in series don't carry series statements and are inconsistently numbered if at all, but rather reveal themselves by means of their titles and release dates, it is possible that this is a useful kind of access; however, it may be that it simply duplicates access that is provided by both title access and fictitious character access, the latter discussed further below. An example of such a series is:

A Nightmare on Elm Street (1984)
A Nightmare on Elm Street, Part 2: Freddy's Revenge (1985)
A Nightmare on Elm Street 3: Dream Warriors (1987)
A Nightmare on Elm Street 4: the Dream Master (1988)
A Nightmare on Elm Street: the Dream Child (1989)

(Titles were taken from *Leonard Maltin's 1999 Movie & Video Guide*.)

9. Fictitious Characters

LCSH seems to have established a pattern of creating topical subject headings for fictitious characters, as well as genre/form headings for films about these fictitious characters. For example the following pairs of headings are in LCSH:

James Bond films
vs.
Bond, James (Fictitious character)

Tarzan films
vs.
Tarzan (Fictitious character)

This seems repetitious. While there is no question of the value of fictitious character access (see Yee and Soto[11]), it hardly seems necessary to duplicate every fictitious character heading with potentially three more headings in the form of '[fictitious character] films,' '[fictitious character] television programs,' and '[fictitious character] radio programs.' Perhaps this is another case where the desire for access by physical format or media (the Tarzan films as opposed to the Tarzan novels) is being allowed to distort genre/form access. Other LCSH headings of this type are listed in Appendix 9.

10. Time Slot (Television or Radio); e.g., Daytime, Prime Time

Neither list provides a mechanism to allow users of television or radio materials to search by time slot, which could be very useful for some types of research, although it would create large, unusable categories for direct searching in a collection of any size. Time slot might more usefully be employed as a subdivision (see below).

SPECIFICITY AND DIRECTNESS

The principles of specificity and directness that underlie most Anglo-American subject heading practice call for entering a work directly under the topic it discusses (or in this case, the genre or form it represents), instead of entering it under a broader topic (not specific) or a broader topic broken down hierarchically until the specific topic is reached, as in an alphabetico-classed catalog (not direct). The *ALA Glossary of Library and Information Science* defines 'specific entry' as "The representation of a work or bibliographic item in a catalog or index under a subject heading or descriptor that is coextensive with its subject content."[12] The same source defines 'coextensive subject indexing' as "the assignment of a subject heading, descriptor, or class number to a document which is neither broader nor narrower than the subject of the work(s) contained in the document." For further discussions of the principles of directness and specificity, see Svenonius, 1976,[13] and Haykin, 1951.[14]

The third question we want to ask is: Are the headings in the two lists under consideration as specific and direct as they could be? The creation of genre and form terms that begin with the terms 'Motion picture,' 'Radio,' or 'Television' has the effect of classing together everything distributed in a certain way (and/or distributed in a certain physical format) before breaking down this broad class by more specific genre or form. This has a particularly unfortunate effect in collections that specialize in film, radio or television moving image and broadcast materials, in that it creates huge clumps of records at the same points in the alphabet, and probably not under the entry terms that would be expected by users of specialist catalogs.

This is one area in which MIGFG and MIM are both clearly superior to LCSH, which has too many headings beginning with the word 'motion picture,' 'radio,' or 'television' for a collection that specializes in collecting moving image materials. See Appendix 10, Section A for a list of the problem headings, and Appendix 10, Section B for suggestions for ways to make them more direct, using media terms as qualifiers only when it is necessary to do so in order to disambiguate homonyms.

MIGFG, too, has inconsistencies in this regard, however; for example, compare the following:

Game (for game shows)
vs.
Television mini-series

Why is the term 'television' necessary? What other field uses the term 'mini-series'? If television terms are felt to need special identification in a list in which film terms predominate, why not 'television game'? Other similar phrases (used in MIGFG for subdivisions, rather than as main headings) can be found in Appendix 10, Section C.

FACET ANALYSIS AND CITATION ORDER

The ALA Glossary defines 'facet' as "1. In classification, the set of subclasses produced when a subject is divided by a single characteristic. 2. Any of a number of aspects of a subject." Further discussion of the concept of facet as applied to subject headings can be found in Svenonius, 1979.[15] Some of the facets of genre headings that might be assigned to moving images include audience and method of distribution. If the heading 'Animated television westerns for children,' existed, it could be said to have a technique facet (animation as opposed to live action), a method of distribution facet (broadcast on television as opposed to theatrically distributed) and an audience facet (for children, as opposed to for women or for scientists, etc.), in addition to the genre facet itself (westerns as opposed to cop shows or science fiction).

Citation order refers to the order in which facets occur in any given heading. In linear left-to-right files, citation order affects the way in which a particular heading gathers together like materials. Thus, in the fabricated heading above, the term 'animated,' since it is first in the citation order, has the effect of first gathering together all works in the catalog by technique. The animated works are then broken down by method of distribution ('television'), genre ('westerns') and finally, at the tail end of the citation order, audience ('for children'). Further discussion of citation order can be found in Svenonius, 1979.[16]

The fourth question we want to ask about the two lists under examination is: Are the headings consistent in their facet analysis and citation order? LCSH often has inconsistent citation order when one compares headings for the same type of genre or form distributed differently (published as texts vs. broadcast on television or radio vs. theatrically distributed).

LCSH EXAMPLES:
Campaign debates vs. Speeches, addresses, etc. vs. Radio addresses, debates, etc.
Children's films vs. Television programs for children and Radio programs for children
Comedy films vs. Television comedies and Radio comedies
Puppet films vs. Puppets in television

MIGFG does not overtly state this in its introduction, but it was actually specifically designed to be a faceted uniterm thesaurus similar to the *Art and Architecture Thesaurus (AAT)*.[17] By design, therefore, MIGFG is cleaner with regard to facet analysis and citation order, in that the main headings tend to be single terms or uniterms (e.g., 'Gangster') that usually represent either a genre or a form (but see the section above concerning topical subject access disguised as genre/form access), which are then subdivided either by form, if motion picture (e.g., 'Gangster--Feature'), or by distribution mechanism and then form, if television (e.g., 'Gangster--Television series'). In this case, the extremely rigid approach to facetting, consistent use of uniterms and citation order characteristic of faceted uniterm lists lead to a rather artificial language that probably does not correspond to the terms commonly used by those who consult our catalogs (see the section on literary warrant below and the experiments in Appendix 3). It is probably more likely that a user will search under 'westerns' than 'western feature,' or 'gangster films' than 'gangster feature.'

It can be observed from the above discussion, by the way, that the principle of consistent citation order can easily come into conflict with the principle of literary warrant, or the preference for the name by which a genre or form is commonly known. This is not too surprising when one considers that natural language does not tend to adhere to consistent citation order.

COMPOUND HEADINGS

Sometimes LCSH will use a compound heading consisting of two terms joined by 'and.' It has been criticized for this in the past, since this type of heading does not tend to be as specific as it might be (see above). Classic LCSH compound headings of the past have included 'Boats and boating,' and 'Labor and laboring classes.' The last example is a heading that had to be broken out into more than one heading eventually because so many books were written about just labor, or just the laboring classes. The following compound genre form heading in LCSH is problematic:

Detective and mystery films

Not all mysteries have characters that are detectives, and detective films and programs have spun off into subgenres, such as gentleman detective films and programs, and hardboiled detective films and programs. The compound heading in LCSH makes it very difficult for the user interested only in hardboiled detective films, for example, to find them, lumped in as they are with gentleman detective films, detective-less mysteries and so forth.

LITERARY WARRANT

The principle of literary warrant refers to the practice of deriving the language of a subject heading from the literature it is being used to index. If a concept is known by more than one term or set of terms, the term or set of terms most often used by writers of books or articles on that concept is chosen, and cross references are made from the others. The theory is that the principle of literary warrant provides a method by which the term commonly known by library users for a particular concept can be chosen for the subject heading used in catalogs for works about that concept. More extensive discussion of the concept of literary warrant can be found in Svenonius, 1979,[18] and Haykin, 1951.[19]

The fifth question we want to ask about the two lists under consideration is: Do the headings obey literary warrant? MIGFG contains a bibliography of sources consulted, but the headings themselves do not seem to follow the forms found in these sources, since there are a number of instances in which MIGFG does not seem to use the vocabulary in common use in the field of motion picture and television studies as documented by citations of actual publications. We have discussed above the artificial and rigid citation order and faceted uniterm language maintained by MIGFG that prevents headings from corresponding to commonly used terminology. None of the sources listed in the MIGFG bibliography use the terms 'Western--Feature' or 'Gangster--Feature,' for example. Appendix 3, Section C lists additional terms in MIGFG that do not seem to be commonly used among film and television scholars, as documented in Appendix 3, Sections A and B.

LCSH also has a number of genre and form headings that do not seem to employ commonly used terms (see Appendix 3, Sections A, B and D). In LCSH, which is normally based on literary warrant at the time a particular heading is being established, the commonly used forms often seem to become distorted due to a desire to include some term in the heading that denotes physical format, media, or method of distribution (see discussion above). Perhaps if that is the reason for the deficiencies with regard to literary warrant, a better approach would be to use the commonly used term, but then qualify it by format/media/method of distribution.

NUMBER AND GRAMMATICAL PART OF SPEECH

Our sixth question is: Do the number and grammatical part of speech of each heading in each list follow standard usage and are they consistent? In MIGFG, use of the singular form does not match common usage, or standards such as the NISO[20] and ISO[21] standards. Users ask "what musicals do you have?" not "what musical do you have?"

The *Subject Cataloging Manual: Subject Headings* meant to accompany LCSH and explain its application does not directly address the question of number and grammatical part of speech. However, the examples given in the section on 'constructing headings' (15) in the unit on assigning and constructing subject headings (H180) follow NISO and ISO standards in that count nouns are expressed as plurals and noncount nouns and names of abstract concepts are expressed in their singular forms.[22]

MIGFG is not based on any national or international standards for subject heading or thesaurus construction. Notably, headings are sometimes in adjectival form (e.g., 'Ethnographic') and sometimes in singular noun form (e.g., 'Dark comedy') while existing standards call for use of the plural noun form in most cases.

Also, there are some strange juxtapositions in MIGFG; for example, compare the following:

Religion
vs.
Religious

It is doubtful that users will know or be able to guess what the difference between these two headings is.

SYNDETIC STRUCTURE

Our seventh question is: Are the syndetic structures adequate and consistent in both lists? The MIGFG syndetic structure (*see* and *see also* references) to lead users from terms in common use to the somewhat arcane and artificial language employed by the list is much less extensive than the syndetic structure in LCSH. This is unfortunate, since one of the advantages of a uniterm system such as MIGFG over a phrase heading system like LCSH is that the former can use each uniterm consistently, and make cross references to it from all synonyms. In LCSH, for example, some headings use the term 'film,' as in 'Gangster films,' and some headings use the term 'motion picture,' as in 'Motion picture serials.' Because LCSH is not a uniterm system, one of those terms cannot be chosen with a cross reference from the other, as could potentially be done in a uniterm system like MIGFG. Of course, the other side of the coin is that in MIGFG one can't make a phrase cross reference of the type 'Gangster films, USE Gangster--Feature.'

One of the major strengths of LCSH is its powerful syndetic structure, which links narrower genres to broader ones that encompass them, as well as linking the heading for a *work about* a genre to the heading for *examples of* the genre. However, over time, the LCSH syndetic structure has become inconsistent. Some LCSH syndetic structure problems are detailed in Appendix 11.

The relationship between a process heading such as 'Wildlife cinematography' and the heading for *examples of* the process ('Wildlife films') in LCSH was discussed above, as were better ways to link related concepts such as linking the heading for books about how a topic is treated in films with the heading for films that treat that topic.

MISSING HEADINGS

Our eighth question is: Do both lists include all useful genre and form terms for moving image materials commonly found in moving image and broadcast material collections and commonly studied by scholars? MIGFG lacks many specific genre and form headings that used to be available in MIM, many of which are also available in LCSH. Appendix 12, Section A, lists genre and form headings that were in MIM but are not in the MIGFG list. There are a few genres and forms that are dealt with in MIGFG but are not yet in LCSH, however, and genre/form headings for these probably should be submitted via SACO. These are listed in Appendix 12, Section B.

An important thing to note about LCSH in regard to this question of inclusivity is the powerful edge it has over MIGFG because of the SACO (Subject Authority Cooperative) program, by means of which users of the list can submit genre or form headings as they are needed. Another powerful edge it has is that it is maintained over time by a coordinated effort between a large editorial staff and a large cataloging staff that routinely sees the moving image literature as it is published, and so will become aware of new genre and form categories as they are written about in the published literature.

MIGFG, on the other hand, as a more fully faceted list than LCSH, does to that degree allow users of the list to create headings by constructing them out of the uniterms listed in each facet rather than making them wait to have headings established as heading strings. It may take longer for new genre facets to be established, however, due to the lack of a large editorial staff.

INTEGRATABILITY INTO HEADINGS DISPLAYS

Our ninth question is: Can the headings in each list be integrated easily into heading displays that draw headings from a number of different sources of headings? MIGFG is incompatible with LCSH and no attempt was made to map between the two. Obviously, LCSH, as a single list that integrates topical subject headings with genre and form terms, and as a list on which many other existing lists has been modelled, has the edge over MIGFG in this regard. When a genre or form heading is added to LCSH, its relationship to related headings, such as the heading used for works about that genre or form, is usually demonstrated by means of syndetic structure, scope notes, subdivision and the like. Integration won't be perfect until LC gets around to designating those headings that belong in X55 fields in the MARC 21 format, but the list is very usable even now in this regard, since the structure of the headings themselves already tends to make the differentiation. LCSH is also rich in headings for related performing arts genres and forms such as those for music, dance and theater, that can easily be recorded using moving image or broadcast media.

Faceted lists like MIGFG are inherently difficult to integrate with other systems. The full power of a faceted list is not felt unless it is implemented using software that allows users to change the citation order at will to meet their research needs. Unfortunately, such software is not widely available, and is not usually integrated with online public access catalog software that is designed to be used with static heading strings in MARC 21 fields. Thus, in practice, a faceted system such as MIGFG and AAT must either be used independently of the online public access catalog, or, if it must be integrated into existing catalogs, it must be used with the rigid citation order that we have seen in MIGFG. Thus users usually are not given the flexibility and power that should be their reward for putting up with the artificiality of the language in faceted systems.

HUGE CATEGORIES

A tenth question is whether either list contains headings that create categories into which so many moving image titles fall that they become virtually unusable for direct searching. Appendix 13 contains a list of headings from both lists that would be likely to create such huge categories. If all of the headings in LCSH listed in Appendix 13 were to be designated as suitable for use as *example of* headings (655), they would create rather large categories in a moving image collection of any size. It is doubtful whether many users would want to directly search such large categories, although they would be of undoubted use for either limiting searches or subdividing large files (see section below on the potential for more subdivision of genre and form headings for moving image materials). The heading for 'Foreign films' is rather interesting. How would this heading be applied in Canada? Could we share records with them?

Both lists include headings for concepts such as romance, adventure or suspense:

MIGFG:
Adventure
Romance

LCSH:
Adventure films

When you consider the fact that practically every commercially released dramatic feature length film ever released has elements of romance, adventure and suspense in its plot line, you will see that such headings will quickly become so bloated as to be useless. There probably are a fair number of people who come into a public library media collection looking for "a good love story" or "a good adventure." They would probably be better off with a good reference librarian than with a catalog that gave them a massive A to Z list of every single film and television program in the collection that included a love story or an element of adventure.

The scope note on the term 'Adventure' in MIGFG reveals that in fact it is meant to be much more narrowly applied than just to any film or program that concerns an 'adventure.' In fact, it is used as a synonym for 'Swashbuckler'; the latter term has considerably more literary warrant for this concept (see Appendix 3), so would probably be preferable, especially given the broad meaning that the term 'adventure' has for most users. For example, the book by Tony Thomas on adventure films[23] has a much broader definition than that found in the MIGFG list, such that 'Adventure films' encompasses disaster films, fantasy, science fiction, war films, and westerns.

PHYSICAL FORMAT ACCESS

There is a little bit of evidence in LCSH of a desire to use subject headings to provide access to physical format categories of moving image materials; the headings in Appendix 14 are included in LCSH, although it may be that they are intended only for use on *works about* not *examples of*. There are also some terms in LCSH that are used for physical elements of moving image materials, also listed in Appendix 14.

There is an undoubted need for better access to physical format and element information in moving image collections. There are many types of users, including archivists in other institutions working on preservation projects, who would find it useful to be able to survey categories such as IB Technicolor prints held, and wide-screen or 3-D titles held. One huge obstacle to providing such access, however, is the lack of standardization in use of physical format terminology; from one lab to the next and one archive to the next, the same terms are used to mean different things. Also, a good deal of physical format information is already encoded in MARC 21 records in the 007 fields in both holdings and bibliographic records; the potential of this encoded information for providing better access to physical format information to our users has been largely untapped by current systems. For more discussion of this topic, see Yee and Layne.[24]

QUESTIONS ABOUT LCSH APPLICATION

It is not clear to the author whether the headings listed in Appendix 15 can legitimately be used as *example of* headings for moving image materials. It seems possible that some of them are the rare headings that do not follow the usual LCSH pattern of breaking a topic down into physical format or medium categories by adding a term such as 'films' or 'programs.'

It is also not clear whether the headings listed in Appendix 16, Section A, can be used as *example of* headings (655) for moving image materials, or whether they are intended to be used only for *works about* or only for monographs and serials? Can 'Television broadcasting of . . . ' headings be used as *example of* type headings (655)? Or only for *works about*? If it is legitimate to use these headings as *example of* type headings, why this form of heading? Why not 'Animated films (Television),' 'Court proceedings (Television),' etc. (See the headings listed in Appendix 16, Section B.)

Normally, headings of the type '[topic]--In motion pictures' can only be used as topical headings; that is, for example, the heading 'Suspense in motion pictures' can only be used for books written about suspense films, not for suspense films themselves. However, is it possible that the 'in' headings listed below can be used as *example of* type headings (655)? (See H910 in the *Subject Cataloging Manual,* for example.[25])

> Radio in religion [x-ref from Religious radio]
> Television in religion [x-ref from Religious television, Televangelism; use for religious television programs?]

Compare with Religious broadcasting, Religious films. Other questionable 'in' headings are listed in Appendix 16, Section C.

Another question arises concerning the use of subdivisions under the heading 'Advertising' for *examples of* commercials on particular products. For example, can the LCSH heading 'Advertising--Cigarettes' be used as an *example of* heading for a TV commercial for Marlboro Cigarettes, or is it meant to be used only for *works about* cigarette advertising?

And finally, can headings in the form 'Motion pictures--[country]' or 'Motion pictures, [nationality]' be used as *example of* headings to provide the access to films by country of origin that is much desired by our users? The following could all be extremely useful if validated for use as *example of* headings:

Motion pictures--Africa
Motion pictures--France
Motion pictures--Japan

Motion pictures, African
Motion pictures, French
Motion pictures, Japanese

However, few of us would want to make use of 'Motion pictures--United States' and 'Motion pictures, American' in this fashion! Also, the distinction between films shown outside a country ('Motion pictures, African') and films shown inside the country ('Motion pictures--Africa') might not be that useful, and might be difficult to apply in practice. Another potential approach to providing access to moving images by nationality might be to use geographic subdivisions on genre and form headings, as discussed below.

SACO WORK TO BE DONE

Here at UCLA we are submitting headings from MIM that are not yet present in LCSH by way of the SACO program. We would like to encourage other catalogers of moving image materials to submit genre and form headings and cross references as well so that cooperatively we can improve the cataloging that we are sharing with each other. In addition to allowing us to add needed headings, this method could be used to submit more scope notes for existing headings, including scope notes that incorporate information currently only available in the *Subject Cataloging Manual,* considering that the latter is rarely made available for consultation by reference librarians or catalog users.

MORE POTENTIAL FOR USE OF SUBDIVISIONS WITH GENRE/FORM HEADINGS?

In MIGFG form subdivisions may be used to distinguish a genre as used in a film ('Feature' or 'Short'), as opposed to a genre as used in a television program (given television form subdivisions, such as 'Television series.')

EXAMPLES:
Western--Feature
Western--Television series

Form subdivisions can also be used to distinguish a genre as used in an animated short from the same genre as used in a live-action feature.

EXAMPLES:
Western--Short--Animation
Western--Feature

Genre and form headings in LCSH can already be subdivided geographically. It could be quite useful to subdivide LCSH genre headings several other ways (especially in large files), for example, by:

language subdivisions
chronological subdivisions for genres that are quite different over time, e.g., 1950s film noir vs. 1990s film noir
form subdivisions for categories such as cartoon westerns or parodies of westerns ('Westerns--Cartoons,' and 'Westerns--Parodies.')
time slot for broadcast materials, e.g., daytime, prime time format, such as 'series' or 'special' for broadcast materials, or 'feature' or 'short' for films

CONCLUSION

In comparing these two lists, we have found that both seem to include a certain number of headings that are actually topical subject headings disguised as *example of* headings (655), although proportionately, MIGFG has many more of these than LCSH. Both lists contain *example of* headings that index categories other than genre/form, such as audience, filmmaker and the like; since most of these headings are useful, that should be considered beneficial, although in some instances there may be more efficient and more accurate ways to provide the desired type of access than using genre/form headings. MIGFG has headings that are more direct than does LCSH, which has many headings that begin with the terms 'Motion picture,' 'Radio,' and 'Television.' MIGFG has a much more rigid citation order than LCSH, to the extent that it works against literary warrant. LCSH headings adhere to literary warrant much more than do MIGFG headings, that is, LCSH headings are much more likely to correspond to the terminology actually used by scholars and researchers in the moving image and broadcasting field. LCSH follows a standard approach to number and grammatical parts of speech in its headings (plural nouns for genre/form headings), while MIGFG is very idiosyncratic and unpredictable in this regard, sometimes using adjectives and sometimes nouns, and seeming to prefer the singular to the plural. LCSH has a much more powerful syndetic structure than does MIGFG. MIGFG is missing many more genre and form headings that used to be present in MIM than is LCSH, which means, surprisingly, given its specialist nature, that MIGFG is less comprehensive than LCSH. LCSH is given a further edge with regard to inclusivity by the SACO program that allows users of the list to submit new genre and form headings as they are needed, and by the large editorial staff it has available to maintain the list over time. It is much easier to integrate LCSH genre and form headings into displays of LCSH topical subject headings (such as those used for works about a particular genre) than it is to integrate MIGFG headings into such displays. LCSH is also rich in headings for related performing arts genres and forms such as those for music, dance and theater, all of which can easily be recorded using moving image or broadcast media. Both lists contain headings that are likely to create huge unmanageable groupings over time if used as *example of* headings for moving image material.

RECOMMENDATIONS FOR MOVING IMAGE COLLECTIONS

Based on these findings, it is recommended that any library, media collection or archive that uses LCSH for the provision of topical subject access to moving image and broadcast materials strongly consider using LCSH for genre and form access to moving images and broadcast materials as well, placing the appropriate LCSH terms in 655 fields (with $2 subfields containing the code *lcsh*) when they are being used for *examples of* a form or genre, rather than works about it. An exhaustive list of such terms present in LCSH at the time this article was written can be found in Appendix 1. This list should be used with care, however, as LCSH is a constantly growing and evolving list, and Appendix 1 will necessarily become out of date as time passes.

RECOMMENDATIONS FOR REVISION OF LCSH

In order to improve LCSH access to moving image genres and forms, it is further recommended that LCSH be revised as follows:

1. Use the same form of heading for *works about* as is used for *examples of*. Use MARC 21 tagging (650 vs. 655) to distinguish between the two different uses of the same genre/form heading. Rely on system designers of OPACs to communicate the distinction to users at the point of display. Broaden this approach to cover all types of form and genre access in all disciplines so that the approach is consistent and predictable for both system designers and users.
2. Write clear scope notes to identify the meaning of a genre/form heading when tagged as 650, and its meaning when tagged as 655. How should this heading be used for *works about* the form or genre? How should this heading be used for *examples of* the form or genre? How should this heading be used for works that *depict* or *contain* a work in this form or genre?
3. Eliminate headings such as 'Science films' and 'Historical films' that are topical subject headings disguised as *example of* headings. Instead, encourage people to use topical headings such as 'Science' and 'History' to provide broad subject or disciplinary access to moving image materials.
4. Because of the massive change that is occurring in the way moving images are distributed, it is recommended that wherever possible, type of broadcast or distribution be eliminated from genre/form headings; for example, convert 'Western films,' 'Western radio programs,' and 'Western television programs' to 'Westerns.'
5. Initiate projects to add topical subject headings to authority records for persons and corporate bodies. Encourage OPAC designers to provide topical subject access to authority records

such that users can identify, for example, authority records for persons who are African American women choreographers, and then proceed to view works by and about the desired group that are linked to these authority records.

6. Avoid the further creation of redundant headings for moving image series.
7. Avoid the further creation of *example of* headings for films with fictitious characters of the type 'Tarzan films.' Prefer instead to establish a heading for the fictitious character, e.g., 'Tarzan (Fictitious character).'
8. In order to honor the principle of directness, revise all genre/form headings that begin with 'Motion picture . . . ,' 'Radio . . . ,' or 'Television . . . ' to either remove the media term altogether, or, when necessary to disambiguate homonyms, to replace it with a media or method of distribution qualifier.
9. Split the compound genre heading 'Detective and mystery films' to allow separate access to 'Detective films' and 'Mysteries (Motion pictures).'
10. Revise existing genre/form headings that do not correspond to current literary warrant as recommended in Appendix 3.
11. Make the recommended changes to the syndetic structure discussed above and in Appendix 11.
12. Eliminate the heading 'Adventure films,' and prefer use of 'Swashbucklers' instead.
13. Make a decision about the value of providing access to physical format categories by means of subject headings. If it is deemed desirable to do so, incorporate many more *example of* headings for physical format categories relevant to moving image materials.
14. Write clear scope notes or application pages in the *Subject Cataloging Manual,* as appropriate, to clarify whether headings such as 'Anthologies,' 'Puppets in television,' 'Television broadcasting of . . . ' and 'Radio in religion' can be used as *example of* headings for moving image materials.
15. Explore the possibility of establishing more free-floating subdivisions for moving image and broadcast form and genre headings, such as form or format subdivisions, radio and television time slot subdivisions, and chronological subdivisions.

NOTES

1. Library of Congress, Motion Picture/Broadcasting/Recorded Sound Division, *The Moving Image Genre-Form Guide* (February, 1998), *<http://lcweb.loc.gov/rr/mopic/migintro.html>*.

2. *Library of Congress Subject Headings,* 22nd ed. (Library of Congress: Cataloging Distribution Service, 1999).

3. Martha M. Yee, *Moving Image Materials: Genre Terms,* 1st ed. (Washington, D.C.: Cataloging Distribution Service, Library of Congress, 1988).

4. *Authority Data Elements Implementation,* Cataloging Policy and Support Office, *<http://lcweb.loc.gov/catdir/cpso/authimp.html>*.

5. Harriette Hemmasi, David Miller and Mary Charles Lasater, "Access to Form Data in Online Catalogs," From Catalog to Gateway-Briefings from the CFFC, *ALCTS Newsletter Online* 10, no. 4 (Feb. 2000), *<http://www.ala.org/alcts/alcts_news/v10n4/v10n4onepage.html>*.

6. Martha M. Yee and Sara Shatford Layne, *Improving Online Public Access Catalogs* (Chicago: American Library Association, 1998), 148, 183-187, 201-203.

7. ALCTS CC:DA Task Force on the Cataloging of Works Intended for Performance, *Documents* (1996-97), *<http://www.ala.org/alcts/organization/ccs/ccda/tf-wks1.html>*.

8. *MARC 21 Concise Format For Bibliographic Data,* 1999 English ed., *<http://lcweb.loc.gov/marc/bibliographic>*.

9. David Bearman and Richard Szary, "Beyond Authorized Headings: Authorities as Reference Files in a Multi-Disciplinary Setting," in *Authority Control Symposium (1986: New York, N.Y.), Papers Presented During the 14th Annual ARLIS/NA Conference, New York, N.Y., Feb. 10, 1986,* Karen Muller, ed. (Tucson, Ariz.: Art Libraries Society of North America, 1987), 69-78.

10. David Bearman, "Authority Control Issues and Prospects," *American Archivist* 52 (Summer 1989): 286-299.

11. Martha M. Yee and Raymond Soto, "User Problems with Access to Fictional Characters and Personal Names in Online Public Access Catalogs," *Information Technology and Libraries* 10, no. 1 (March 1991): 3-13.

12. *The ALA Glossary of Library and Information Science* (Chicago: American Library Association, 1983).

13. Elaine Svenonius, "Metcalfe and the Principles of Specific Entry," in *The Variety of Librarianship: Essays in Honour of John Wallace Metcalfe,* ed. by W. Boyd Rayward (Library Association of Australia, 1976), 171-189.

14. David Judson Haykin, *Subject Headings: a Practical Guide* (Washington, D.C.: U.S. Government Printing Office, 1951).

15. Elaine Svenonius, "Facets as Semantic Categories," in *Klassifikation und Erkenntnis II: Proceedings der Sektionen 2 und 3 "Wissendarstellung und Wissensvermittlung" der 3. Fachtagung der Gesellschaft für Klassifikation e.V. Königstein/Ts., 5.-6. 4. 1979,* Redaktion, Wolfgang Dahlberg (Frankfurt: Gesellschaft für Klassifikation e.V., 1979), 57-78.

16. Ibid.

17. *The Art & Architecture Thesaurus Browser,* Version 3.0 (updated June 26, 2000), *<http://shiva.pub.getty.edu/aat_browser/>*.

18. Svenonius, 1979.

19. Haykin.

20. *Guidelines for the Construction, Format and Management of Monolingual Thesauri,* ANSI/NISO Z39.19-1993 (Bethesda, Maryland: NISO (National Information Standards Organization) Press, 1994). NISO 3.5.1: "Count nouns are names of objects or concepts that are subject to the question 'How many?' but not 'How much?' These should normally be expressed as plurals." 3.5.2, "Noncount nouns are names of materials or substances that are subject to the question 'How much?' but not 'How many?' These should be expressed in the singular."

21. *Documentation-Guidelines for the Establishment and Development of Monolingual Thesauri,* ISO 2788-1986 (E) (Switzerland: International Organization for Standardization, 1986). ISO 6.2.1: "An indexing term should preferably consist of a noun or a noun phrase." 6.3.2.1, "count nouns . . . should be expressed as plurals." 6.3.2.2, "the names of abstract concepts . . . should be expressed in their singular forms."

22. Library of Congress, Cataloging Policy and Support Office, *Subject Cataloging Manual: Subject Headings,* 4th ed. (Washington, D.C.: Cataloging Distribution Service, Library of Congress, 1991-).

23. Tony Thomas, *The Great Adventure Films* (Secaucus, N.J.: Citadel Press, 1976).

24. Yee and Layne.

25. *Subject Cataloging Manual.*

BIBLIOGRAPHY

The ALA Glossary of Library and Information Science. Chicago: American Library Association, 1983.

ALCTS CC:DA Task Force on the Cataloging of Works Intended for Performance. *Documents.* 1996-97. *<http://www.ala.org/alcts/organization/ccs/ccda/tf-wks1.html>. <http://www.ala.org/alcts/organization/ccs/ccda/tf-wks2.html>.*

Authority Data Elements Implementation. Cataloging Policy and Support Office. *<http://lcweb.loc.gov/catdir/cpso/authimp.html>.*

Bearman, David. "Authority Control Issues and Prospects." *American Archivist* 52 (Summer 1989): 286-299.

Bearman, David and Richard Szary. "Beyond Authorized Headings: Authorities as Reference Files in a Multi-Disciplinary Setting." In: *Authority Control Symposium (1986: New York, N.Y.). Papers Presented During the 14th Annual ARLIS/NA Conference, New York, N.Y., Feb. 10, 1986.* Karen Muller, ed. Tucson, Ariz.: Art Libraries Society of North America, 1987. pp. 69-78.

Discussion Paper no. 83, USMARC Authority Records for Genre/Form Terms. *<http://lcweb.loc.gov/marc/marbi/dp/dp83.html>.*

Documentation-Guidelines for the Establishment and Development of Monolingual Thesauri. Switzerland: International Organization for Standardization, 1986. (ISO 2788-1986 (E)).

Guidelines for the Construction, Format and Management of Monolingual Thesauri. Bethesda, Maryland: NISO (National Information Standards Organization) Press, 1994. (ANSI/NISO Z39.19-1993).

Haykin, David Judson. *Subject Headings: a Practical Guide.* Washington, D.C.: U.S. Government Printing Office, 1951.

Hemmasi, Harriette, David Miller and Mary Charles Lasater. "Access to Form Data in Online Catalogs." (From Catalog to Gateway-Briefings from the CFFC). *ALCTS Newsletter Online* 10, no. 4 (Feb. 2000). *<http://www.ala.org/alcts/alcts_news/v10n4/v10n4onepage.html>.*

Library of Congress. Motion Picture/Broadcasting/Recorded Sound Division. *The Moving Image Genre-Form Guide.* February, 1998. *<http://lcweb.loc.gov/rr/mopic/migintro.html>.*

Library of Congress. Cataloging Policy and Support Office. *Subject Cataloging Manual: Subject Headings.* 4th ed. Washington, D.C.: Cataloging Distribution Service, Library of Congress, 1991- .

Library of Congress Subject Headings. 22nd ed. Library of Congress: Cataloging Distribution Service, 1999.

MARC 21 Concise Format For Bibliographic Data. 1999 English ed. *<http://lcweb.loc.gov/marc/bibliographic>.*

Program for Cooperative Cataloging SACO Home Page. <http://lcweb.loc.gov/catdir/pcc/saco.html>.

Proposal no. 95-11, Definition of X55 Fields for Genre/Form Terms in the USMARC Authority Format. <http://lcweb.loc.gov/marc/marbi/1995/95-11.html>.

Svenonius, Elaine. "Design of Controlled Vocabularies." In: *Encyclopedia of Library and Information Science,* v. 45, supplement 10. New York: Marcel Dekker, 1990. pp. 82-109.

Svenonius, Elaine. "Facets as Semantic Categories." In: *Klassifikation und Erkenntnis II: Proceedings der Sektionen 2 und 3 "Wissendarstellung und Wissensvermittlung" der 3. Fachtagung der Gesellschaft für Klassifikation e.V. Königstein/Ts., 5.-6. 4. 1979.* Redaktion, Wolfgang Dahlberg. Frankfurt: Gesellschaft für Klassifikation e.V., 1979. pp. 57-78.

Svenonius, Elaine. "Metcalfe and the Principles of Specific Entry." In: *The Variety of Librarianship: Essays in Honour of John Wallace Metcalfe.* ed. by W. Boyd Rayward. Library Association of Australia, 1976. pp. 171-189.

Yee, Martha M. and Sara Shatford Layne. *Improving Online Public Access Catalogs.* Chicago: American Library Association, 1998. pp. 148, 183-187, 201-203.

Yee, Martha M. *Moving Image Materials: Genre Terms.* 1st ed. (Washington, D.C.: Cataloging Distribution Service, Library of Congress, 1988).

Yee, Martha M. and Raymond Soto. "User Problems with Access to Fictional Characters and Personal Names in Online Public Access Catalogs." *Information Technology and Libraries* v. 10, no. 1 (March 1991): 3-13.

Yee, Tom. *LC Report to ALA ALCTS CCS Subject Analysis Committee (SAC) Subcommittee on Form Headings/Subdivisions Implementation.* [Reports of Feb. 17, 1997 through June 26, 1998 can be found at: *<http://www.pitt.edu/~agtaylor/ala/>.*

APPENDIX 1

GENRE AND FORM HEADINGS FOR FILM, TELEVISION AND RADIO IN LCSH

Rev. August 20, 2000

[It is not yet clear to the author whether all of the starred (*) headings are meant to be used as *example of* headings (655); the uncertainties about the application of these headings are all discussed in the text of the article.]

3-D films
Actualities (Motion pictures)
Adventure films
Advertising--Motion pictures
Advertising--Television programs
*Advertising, Political
Amateur films
Andy Hardy films
Angélique films
Animal films
Animated films
Animated television programs
*Anthologies
Audience participation television programs
B films
Baseball films
Beach party films
*Beauty contests
Bible films
Biographical films
Biographical television programs
Book review radio programs
Bowery Boys films
*Burlesque (Theater)
*Campaign debates
*Campaign speeches
Caper films
Carry On films
Charlie Chan films

APPENDIX 1 (continued)

Children's films
Christmas films
Cisco Kid films
City symphonies (Motion pictures)
Clay animation films
College life films
Comedy films
*Computer animation
Cop shows
*Dance [and more specific headings beneath]
*Debates and debating
Detective and mystery films
Detective and mystery television programs
Disaster films
Documentary films
Documentary radio programs
Documentary television programs
Dracula films
*Drama [and more specific headings beneath; UF Plays]
*Editorials
Epic films
Erotic films
Erotic videos
Experimental films
Exploitation films
Fantasy comedies (Motion pictures)
Fantasy films
Fantasy television programs
*Farces
Feature films
Feminist motion pictures
*Film adaptations
Film noir
Films by children
Films for the hearing impaired
Films for the visually handicapped
*Foreign films
*Foreign language films
*Forums (Discussion and debate)

Frankenstein films
Game shows
Gangster films
Gay erotic videos
Godfather films
Godzilla films
Haunted house films
Haunted house television programs
Heimatfilme
Historical films
Historical television programs
Hopalong Cassidy films
Horror films
Horror radio programs
Horror television programs
Hospital films
Hospital television programs
Indiana Jones films
Industrial films
*Interviews
James Bond films
Jungle films
Jungle television programs
Juvenile delinquency films
*Lectures and lecturing
Live television programs
Lone Ranger films
Loop films
Low budget motion pictures
Low budget television programs
Magazine format television programs
*Male striptease
Motion picture errors
Motion picture remakes
Motion picture sequels
Motion picture serials
Motion picture soundtracks
Motion picture trailers
*Motion pictures
*Motion pictures--Sound effects
*Motion pictures--[country]

APPENDIX 1 (continued)

*Motion pictures, [nationality]
Motion pictures for men
Motion pictures for women
*Motion pictures in advertising
*Motion pictures in propaganda
Mummy films
*Music [and more specific headings beneath]
Music videos
Musical films
Nature films
New wave films
Newsreels
Nightmare on Elm Street films
Novelty films
*Operas
*Oral interpretation of fiction
*Oral interpretation of poetry
Our Gang films
Outtakes
Planet of the Apes films
Police films
*Popular music [and more specific headings beneath]
Populist films
*Press conferences
Prison films
*Propaganda
Puppet films
*Puppets in television
Quiz shows
*Radio adaptations
*Radio addresses, debates, etc.
Radio comedies
*Radio in religion
*Radio plays
*Radio programs
*Radio programs--[country]
Radio programs for children
Radio programs for the blind

Radio programs for youth
Radio programs, Musical
Radio programs, Public service
Radio serials
Reality television programs
*Religious broadcasting
Religious films
*Revues
Road films
*Roasts (Public speaking)
Rock videos
Rural comedies
Rushes (Motion pictures)
Samurai films
*Satire
Science fiction films
Science fiction radio programs
Science fiction television programs
Science films
Science television programs
Screen tests
Screwball comedy films
Sherlock Holmes films
Short films
Silent films
Singing commercials
Snuff films
Soap operas
*Sound motion pictures
*Speeches, addresses, etc.
Sports films
Spy films
Spy television programs
Star Trek films
Star Trek television programs
Star Wars films
*Stand-up comedy
*Storytelling
Street films
Striptease
Super-8 motion pictures

APPENDIX 1 (continued)

Superman films
Swashbuckler films
Talent shows
Talk shows
Tarzan films
*Television adaptations
Television advertising
Television and family (x-ref from Television programs for the family)
*Television broadcasting--Auditions
*Television broadcasting--Awards
*Television broadcasting--Sound effects
*Television broadcasting--Special effects
*Television broadcasting of animated films
*Television broadcasting of court proceedings
*Television broadcasting of films
*Television broadcasting of music
*Television broadcasting of news
*Television broadcasting of sports
Television comedies
Television dance parties
*Television in propaganda
*Television in religion
Television mini-series
Television musicals
Television pilot programs
*Television plays
Television programs
*Television programs--[country]
*Television programs, Foreign
Television programs, Public service
Television programs for children
Television programs for women
Television serials
Television specials
*Television weathercasting
Three Stooges films
Tom and Jerry films
Torchy Blane films
Trapalhões films
Travelogues (Motion pictures)
Trick films

True crime television programs
Unfinished animated films
Unfinished motion pictures
Vampire films
Variety shows (Television programs)
*Vaudeville
Video art
Video recordings for children
Video recordings for the hearing impaired
Video recordings for the visually handicapped
War films
*Weather broadcasting
Werewolf films
Western films
Western radio programs
Western television programs
*Wide-screen processes (Cinematography)
Wildlife films
Young adult films
Zombie films
Zorro films
Zorro television programs

APPENDIX 2
BIBLIOGRAPHY OF REFERENCE SOURCES FOR MOVING IMAGE AND BROADCAST MATERIALS GENRE/FORM TERMS

Beaver, Frank Eugene. *Dictionary of film terms*. New York: Twayne, 1994. (BEAVER)

Brown, Les. *Les Brown's Encyclopedia of Television*. 3rd ed. Detroit: Gale Research, 1992. (BROWN)

Ellmore, R. Terry. *NTC's Mass Media Dictionary*. Lincolnwood, Ill.: National Textbook Co., 1991. (NTC)

Ensign, Lynne Naylor and Knapton, Robyn Eileen. *The Complete Dictionary of Television and Film*. New York: Stein and Day, 1985. (ENSIGN)

Halliwell's Filmgoer's and Video Viewer's Companion. 10th ed. ed. by John Walker. New York: HarperPerennial, 1993. (HALLIWELL'S)

Handbook of American Film Genres. ed. by Wes D. Gehring. New York: Greenwood Press, 1988. (HANDBOOK)

Katz, Ephraim. *The Film Encyclopedia*. 2nd ed. New York: HarperCollins Publishers, 1994. (KATZ)

APPENDIX 2 (continued)

Library of Congress. Recorded Sound Reference Center. *Genre Terms*. *<http://www.lcweb.loc.gov/rr/record/gen.html>*.

Lopez, Daniel. *Films by Genre: 775 Categories, Styles, Trends, and Movements Defined, with a Filmography for Each*. Jefferson, N.C.: McFarland, 1993. (LOPEZ)

Oakey, Virginia. *Dictionary of Film and Television Terms*. New York: Barnes & Noble, 1983. (OAKEY)

The Oxford Companion to Film. ed. by Liz-Anne Bawden. New York: Oxford University Press, 1976. (OXFORD)

Penney, Edmund F. *The Facts on File Dictionary of Film and Broadcast Terms*. New York: Facts on File, 1991. (FACTS ON FILE)

Robertson, Patrick. *Guinness Movie Facts & Feats*. Enfield: Guinness, 1988. (GUINNESS)

APPENDIX 3
LITERARY WARRANT EXPERIMENTS

A. TERMS THAT MAY NEED TO CHANGE TO MATCH LITERARY WARRANT

B movies

'B movie(s)' (the term in MIM) occurs in 58% of the summaries of articles in English in the Autumn 1998 edition of *International Film Archive CD-ROM* (IFA-CD), containing the *International Index to Film Periodicals,* and 10% of the titles; it occurs in 80% of book titles on the topic in the UCLA collection.

'B film(s)' (the LCSH term) occurs in only 3% of titles and 7% of summaries; it occurs in only 20% of book titles on the topic in the UCLA collection.

Other terms that also occur:
'B feature(s)' (3% of summaries)
'B picture(s)' or 'B pix' (3% of titles and 7% of summaries)
'B(s)' (14% of titles)
'B' [plus another genre term, e.g., B westerns] (3% of titles and 10% of summaries)

BEAVER: B-picture

Bloopers

This form is not indexed at all in IFA-CD.

MIM: Bloopers

LCSH: Motion picture errors

NTC: Blooper

College comedies

This genre is not indexed at all in IFA-CD.

The UCLA collection contains one book on the topic (*The Movies go to College: Hollywood and the World of the College-life Film*)

MIM: College films and programs
LCSH: College life films
MIGFG: College

LOPEZ: Campus musicals (See references or AKAs: College campus musicals; College musicals)

Commercials

'Commercial(s)' (the term in MIM) occurs in 66% of the summaries of articles in English (IFA-CD) and 24% of the titles; it occurs in 26% of titles on the topic in the UCLA collection

'Advertising' occurs in .5% of the titles and .5% of the summaries

'Television advertising' (the LCSH term) does not occur in any title or summary; it occurs in 38% of titles on the topic in the UCLA collection

'Television commercial(s)' (the MIGFG term) does not occur in any title or summary, although a close equivalent, 'TV commercial(s),' occurs in 5% of titles, and 28% of summaries; it occurs in 30% of titles on the topic in the UCLA collection

Total use of 'Commercial(s)' (Commercials and Television commercials combined): 29% of the titles (IFA-CD) and 94% of summaries; 56% of titles in the UCLA collection

Other terms that also occur in IFA-CD:
'Ad(s)' (6% of titles)
'Advert(s)' (1% of summaries)
'Advertisement(s)' (1% of summaries)
'Blurb(s)' (.5% of titles)
'Commercial ad(s)' (.5% of summaries)
'Commercial spot(s)' (1% of titles)
'Spot(s)' (5% of titles)
'Telefilm(s)' (.5% of titles)
'TV ad(s)' (.5% of titles)

APPENDIX 3 (continued)

'TV advertisement(s)' (1% of titles)
'TV commercial(s)' (5% of titles, 28% of summaries)
'TV spot(s)' (1% of titles)

Other terms that also occur in book titles in the UCLA collection:
'Campaign commercials' (2% of titles)
'Political campaign commercials' (3% of titles)
'Political commercials' (1% of titles)
'Presidential campaign commercials' (1% of titles)
'Political advertising on television' (4% of titles)
'Public service advertising' (1% of titles)
Presidential television advertising' (1% of titles)

NTC: Commercial; Commercial ad; Commercial announcement

Detective films

'Detective film(s)' (the term in MIM) occurs in 67% of the summaries of articles in English (IFA-CD) and 22% of the titles; it occurs in three titles of monographs in the UCLA collection.

'Private eye film(s)' (also a term in MIM) occurs in the form of 'private detective films' in 11% of the summaries of articles in English (IFA-CD) and in the form of 'hardboiled detective film(s)' in 11% of summaries of articles in English.

BEAVER: Detective film; Mystery-thriller; 'Whodunit, a colloquial term for a mystery or detective film . . . '
LOPEZ: Private detective film (see references or AKAs Detective film, Investigative film, P.I. film, Private eye film, Shamus movie); Adventurer detective film; Amateur detective film; Detective comedy films; Private eye films; Sherlock Holmes films
NTC: Mystery, Whodunit

The following monographs refer to 'detective film(s)' and variants in the text as follows:

The BFI Companion to Crime. Berkeley: University of California Press, 1997. "Private-eye movies"-entry under Private Eyes.

Cocchiarelli, Joseph J. *Screen sleuths: a Filmography*. New York: Garland, 1992. "sleuthing films"-p. xi. "mystery film built around a sleuthing subplot"-p. xiii. "detective mysteries"-p. xiv.

Everson, William K. *The Detective in Film*. Secaucus, N.J.: Citadel Press, 1972. "the detective film"-p. 2.

Langman, Larry and Daniel Finn. *A Guide to American Crime Films of the Forties and Fifties*. Westport, Conn.: Greenwood Press, 1995. "the detective genre"-p. ix.

Langman, Larry and Daniel Finn. *A Guide to American Silent Crime Films*. Westport, Conn.: Greenwood Press, 1994. "the detective film"-p. ix, xiv.

Parish, James Robert and Michael R. Pitts. *The Great Detective Pictures*. Metuchen, N.J.: Scarecrow, 1990. "the detective film"-p. ix.

Musicals

'Musical(s)' (the term in MIGFG and MIM) occurs in 56% of the summaries of articles in English (IFA-CD) and 23% of the titles; it occurs in the titles of 20% of monographs on the subject in the UCLA collection.

'Musical film(s)' (the LCSH term) occurs in only 3% of titles and 7% of summaries; it occurs in the titles of 12% of monographs on the subject in the UCLA collection.

Other terms that also occur:
'Hollywood musical(s)' (7% of titles and 12% of summaries; the titles of 28% of monographs on the subject in the UCLA collection)
'Screen musical(s)' (1% of summaries)
'Musical cinema' (1% of summaries)
'Film musical(s)' (10% of titles and 15% of summaries; the titles of 12% of monographs on the subject in the UCLA collection)
'Filmusical(s)' (1% of titles and 1% of summaries)
'Movie musical(s)' (1% of titles; the titles of 20% of monographs on the subject in the UCLA collection)
'Musical comed(y/ies)' (3% of summaries)
'Musical picture(s)' (the titles of 4% of monographs on the subject in the UCLA collection)
'Motion picture musical(s)' (the titles of 4% of monographs on the subject in the UCLA collection)

BEAVER: Musical film
ENSIGN: Musical (See references or AKAs: also Musical film, Musical comedy)
GUINNESS: Musicals
LOPEZ: Musical (See references or AKAs: Film musical, Musical comedy film, Musical film, Music film, Song-and-dance film, Songfest film)
NTC: Musical, Musical comedy
OXFORD: Musicals

Screwball comedies

This genre is not indexed at all in IFA-CD.

APPENDIX 3 (continued)

'Screwball comedy films,' the term used in LCSH, occurs in the titles of 17% of monographs on the subject in the UCLA collection

'Screwball comedies' occurs in the titles of 83% of monographs on the subject in the UCLA collection

MIM: Sophisticated comedies
LCSH: Screwball comedy films
MIGFG: Screwball comedy; Sophisticated comedy
BEAVER: Screwball comedy

Shorts

'Short(s)' (the term in MIGFG and MIM) occurs in 36% of the titles of articles in English (IFA-CD) and 6% of the summaries; it occurs in the titles of 15% of monographs on the subject in the UCLA collection.

'Short film(s)' (the LCSH term) occurs in 21% of the titles and 83% of the summaries. It should be noted, however, that since the heading used in IFA-CD is 'Short films', the summary writers are probably influenced by the term they have just assigned in the indexing process. However, it also occurs in the titles of 78% of monographs on the subject in the UCLA collection.

'Short subject(s)' occurs in the titles of 10% of the titles on the subject in the UCLA collecction.

BEAVER: Shorts (see references or AKAs: Short subjects)
GUINNESS: Shorts and documentaries
KATZ: Short subject (see references or AKAs: also Short)
NTC: Short

Situation comedies

'Situation comed(y/ies)' (the term in MIGFG and MIM) occurs in 12% of the titles of articles in English (IFA-CD) and 63% of the summaries; it occurs in the titles of 29% of monographs on the subject in the UCLA collection.

'Sitcom(s)' occurs in 28% of the titles and 63% of the summaries; it occurs in the titles of 21% of monographs on the subject in the UCLA collection.

'Television comed(y/ies)' (the LCSH term) does not occur in any of the titles or summaries in IFA-CD; it appears in the titles of 38% of monographs on the subject in the UCLA collection (as compared to the 50% that use either 'situation comedy' or 'sitcom').

NTC: Situation comedy

Spy films

'Spy films' (the term in LCSH and MIM) occurs in 100% of the titles of articles in English (IFA-CD); it occurs in the titles of 83% of monographs (as either 'spy films' or 'spy pictures') on the subject in the UCLA collection.

'Espionage films' (the term in MIGFG) occurs in no article titles in English (IFA-CD) and in the titles of only 17% of monographs on the subject in the UCLA collection.

ENSIGN: Spy film
LOPEZ: Spy film (see references or AKAs: Cloak and dagger drama, Espionage film, Secret agent film, Secret Service drama, Spy thriller)
OAKEY: Spy film

Swashbucklers

'Swashbuckler films,' the term used in LCSH, does not occur in any of the titles or summaries in IFA-CD, nor does it appear in any book titles.

'Swashbucklers,' the term in MIM, occurs in the titles of 75% of monographs on the subject in the UCLA collections.

LOPEZ: Swashbuckler (see references or AKAs: Swashbuckling film, Sword-fight film); Chivalric films (see references or AKAs: Chivalric epics); Cloak and sword romances (see references or AKAs: Cape and sword films); Oriental swashbucklers; Pirate films; Righter-of-wrongs films

TV movies

'TV movie(s)' occurs in 19% of the summaries of titles of articles in English (IFA-CD) and 10% of the summaries; it occurs in the titles of 47% of monographs on the subject in the UCLA collection.

'Television broadcasting of films' (the LCSH term) does not occur in any of the titles or summaries.

Made for TV movie(s) (the MIM term) occurs in 10% of titles and 15% of summaries; it occurs in the titles of 11% of monographs on the subject in the UCLA collection.

'Television feature(s)' (the MIGFG term) does not occur in any of the titles or summaries.

Other terms that also occur:
'Films for TV' (2% of titles (IFA-CD)
'Films made for TV' (4% of summaries (IFA-CD); titles of 5% of monographs on the subject in the UCLA collection)
'Films shown on TV' (2% of summaries)
'Made-for-television releases' (titles of 16% of monographs on the subject in the UCLA collection)
'Made for TV film(s)' (17% of summaries)
'Made-for-TV movies' (titles of 11% of monographs on the subject in the UCLA collection)

APPENDIX 3 (continued)

'Made for TVs' (2% of titles)
'Movies for TV' (titles of 5% of monographs on the subject in the UCLA collection)
'Movies made for TV' (titles of 16% of monographs on the subject in the UCLA collection)
'Tele-feature(s)' (titles of 5% of monographs on the subject in the UCLA collection)
'Telefilm(s)' (6% of titles, 5% of summaries)
'Television films' (titles of 5% of monographs on the subject in the UCLA collection)
'TV drama' (2% of summaries)
'TV feature film(s)' (2% of summaries)

BEAVER: Made-for-television movie
LOPEZ: Television movie (See references or AKAs: Made-for-TV movie, Movie-for-TV, Movie made-for-television, Telefeature, Telefilm, TV movie, TVM, Vidpic)
NTC: Made for television; Television motion picture; Telefilm (See references or AKAs: Movie for television; Television film; Made-for-television movie)

Westerns

'Western(s)' (the term in MIGFG and MIM) occurs in 87% of summaries of articles in English (IFA-CD) and 41% of titles; it occurs in titles of 75% of monographs on the subject in the UCLA collection.

'Western film(s)' (the LCSH term) occurs in only 5% of titles and 11% of summaries (IFA-CD); it occurs in titles of only 23% of monographs on the subject in the UCLA collection.

Other terms that also occur:
'Western movie(s)' (2% of titles and 1% of summaries (IFA-CD); titles of 2% of monographs on the subject in the UCLA collection)
'Movie western(s)' (1% of titles (IFA-CD); titles of 2% of monographs on the subject in the UCLA collection)
'Shoot-em-ups' (titles of 2% of monographs on the subject in the UCLA collection)

BEAVER: Western (see references or AKAs: Horse opera, Oater)
BROWN: Western
ENSIGN: Western; Oater, "a slang expression for a cowboy (Western) film"
FACTS ON FILE: Westerns
GUINNESS: Westerns

HALLIWELL'S: Westerns
KATZ: Horse opera, "slang for a Western movie, usually applied to a standard B picture. Also known as 'horse opry,' 'oater,' or 'sagebrusher.'
LOPEZ: Western (see references or AKAs: Cowboy film, Western film)
NTC: Horse opera, "a slang term for a western; also called an oater."
OAKEY: western film (movie), western
OXFORD: western films; the western

Women's films

'Women's film(s)' occurs in 58% of summaries of articles in English (IFA-CD) and 8% of summaries; it occurs in titles of 100% of monographs on the subject in the UCLA collection.

'Motion pictures for women' (the LCSH term) does not occur in any of the titles or summaries in IFA-CD, or in any monograph titles at UCLA.

'Women' (the MIGFG term) does not occur in any of the titles or summaries.

'Melodrama' (the MIM term) occurs in 8% of summaries.

Other terms that also occur:
'Woman's film(s)' (42% of titles and 25% of summaries)
'Woman's picture(s)' (8% of titles and 8% of summaries)
'Women's cinema' (8% of summaries)

BEAVER: Melodrama differently defined (as films that "seek to engage the emotions of the audience and provide thrills; the form has been popular . . . particularly in mystery thrillers and westerns; . . . characters are often one-dimensional, appearing in action plots in which good eventually triumphs over evil")
HANDBOOK: Melodrama ("perhaps the most consistently agreed-upon feature of film melodrama is that it emphasizes the 'domestic' or 'maternal' elements of family life")
LOPEZ: Weepie (See references or AKAs: Five-handkerchief film, Four handkerchief picture, four-hankie pic, Hankie pic, Sobby, Sob-story, Tear-jerker, Three-hanky soap opera, Weeper, Weepy)
NTC: Sob story; (See references or AKAs: Sob stuff); Tearjerker. Melodrama differently defined (as "a script or play that depends primarily on plot action. Loosely, melodrama is to tragedy what farce is to comedy.")

B. TERMS THAT MAY NOT HAVE LITERARY WARRANT AT ALL

Adventure (MIGFG)

There is only one article in English on 'adventure films' listed in IFA-CD, and that article is a review of a book entitled *The Romance of Adventure: the*

APPENDIX 3 (continued)

Genre of Historical Adventure Movies, by Brian Taves, who, coincidentally, compiled MIGFG.

Prehistoric (MIGFG)

The term 'prehistoric' is not used in any of the article titles in English and in only one summary (one that mentions 'prehistoric animals') listed in IFA-CD. Titles of articles include:

Creating dinosaurs for Baby
Death of an epic
Jurassic Park. When dinosaurs rule the box office
ILM's digital dinosaurs tear up effects jungle
Shooting for an A on My science project
Theme park and variations

Perhaps a better approach would be to use subject headings such as 'Dinosaurs--Drama.'

Speculation (MIGFG)

This concept is not indexed at all in IFA-CD.

C. TERMS IN MIGFG THAT DO NOT APPEAR TO BE COMMONLY USED AMONG FILM AND TELEVISION SCHOLARS

adventure
espionage
prehistoric
speculation
television feature (for TV movie)

D. TERMS IN LCSH THAT DO NOT APPEAR TO BE COMMONLY USED AMONG FILM AND TELEVISION SCHOLARS

B films (*not* B movies)
College life films (*not* College comedies or College comedies (Motion picture)
Comedy programs (*not* Situation comedies or Situation comedies (Television)
Motion picture errors (*not* Bloopers or Bloopers (Motion picture)
Motion pictures for women (*not* Women's films]

Musical films (*not* Musicals or Musicals (Motion picture) and Musicals (Television))
Screwball comedy films (*not* Screwball comedies or Screwball comedies (Motion picture))
Short films (*not* Shorts or Shorts (Motion picture))
Swashbuckler films (*not* Swashbucklers or Swashbucklers (Motion picture))
Television advertising (*not* Commercials or Commercials (Television))
Television broadcasting of films (*not* TV movies?))
Western films (*not* Westerns or Westerns (Motion picture) and Westerns (Television))

APPENDIX 4
LCSH HEADINGS FOR TYPES OF PERFORMANCE OR EVENT THAT CAN BE FILMED OR TELEVISED

Beauty contests [can this be used for televised beauty contests, or newsreel coverage of a beauty contest?]
Burlesque (Theater) [can this be used for burlesque performances on film or TV?]
Campaign debates [can this be used for televised or broadcast campaign debates?]
Campaign speeches [can this be used for televised or broadcast campaign speeches?]
Debates and debating [can this be used for televised or broadcast debates?]
Forums (Discussion and debate) [can this be used for televised or broadcast forums?]
Male striptease [only for *works about* or also for actual performances as recorded in moving image form?]
Press conferences [can this be used for televised or broadcast press conferences?]
Radio addresses, debates, etc. [can this be used for speeches and debates broadcast over the radio?]
Roasts (Public speaking) [can this be used for actual roasts when televised or broadcast?]
Speeches, addresses, etc. [can this be used for televised or broadcast speeches?]
Stand-up comedy [can this be used for actual performances when filmed, televised or broadcast?]
Vaudeville [can this be used for actual vaudeville performances when filmed, televised or broadcast?]

APPENDIX 4 (continued)

Dramatic music
Music
Popular music
Musical genres and forms (listed as narrower terms under 'Dramatic music,' 'Music' and 'Popular music') as performed on film or broadcast on radio or television, e.g.:
- Big band music
- Christmas music
- Gospel music
- Jazz
- Operas

Dance
Dance genres and forms (listed as narrower terms under 'Dance') as performed on film or broadcast on television, e.g.:
- Ballet
- Hula (Dance)
- Jitterbug (Dance)

Plays

"Play" genres (listed as narrower terms under 'Drama'), such as:
- Detective and mystery plays
- Farces
- Puppet plays
- Radio plays
- Television plays

APPENDIX 5
HEADINGS IN THE MIGFG LIST THAT MIGHT MORE USEFULLY BE CONVERTED TO TOPICAL SUBJECT HEADINGS

Adventure (Nonfiction) [use 'Adventure and adventurers' and the narrower terms under it for specific adventures such as 'Safaris' and 'Shipwrecks']
Animal [use 'Animals--Drama' (650) or specific types of animal, such as 'Dogs--Drama' (650)]
Aviation [use 'Aeronautics--Drama' (650)]
Disability [use 'Handicapped--Drama' (650)]
Ethnic (Nonfiction) [use 'Ethnic groups' (650), or better, perhaps, use the name of the specific group the film is about; see also discussions below about audience]
Ethnographic [use 'Ethnology' (650), or better, perhaps, use the name of the specific group the film is about]
Family [use 'Family--Drama' (650)]
Historical [use 'History--Drama'(650)]
Medical (Nonfiction) [use 'Medicine' (650)]
Political [use 'Politics, Practical--Drama' (650)]
Religion [use 'Religion' (650)]
Religious [use 'Religion--Drama' (650)]
Social guidance [use 'Teenagers--Conduct of life' (650)]
Social problem [use 'Social problems--Drama' (650)]
Sports [use 'Sports--Drama' (650)]
Sports (Nonfiction) [use 'Sports' (650)]
Survival [use 'Survival after airplane accidents, shipwrecks, etc.--Drama' (650)]
Yukon [use 'Yukon River Watershed (Yukon and Alaska)--Drama' (651)]

APPENDIX 6
OTHER LCSH EXAMPLES OF TOPICAL SUBJECT HEADINGS BEING TREATED AS *EXAMPLE OF* HEADINGS

Baseball films (not 'Baseball' and 'Baseball--Drama')
Christmas films (not 'Christmas' and 'Christmas--Drama')
Historical films (not 'History' or 'United States [or some other country]--History' and 'History--Drama' or 'United States--History--Drama')
Historical television programs
Sports films (not 'Sports' and 'Sports--Drama')

APPENDIX 7
AUDIENCE HEADINGS IN BOTH LISTS

MIGFG:
Children's
Ethnic
Women
Youth

LCSH:
Children's films
Films for the hearing impaired
Films for the visually handicapped
Motion pictures for men
Motion pictures for women
Radio programs for children
Radio programs for the blind
Radio programs for youth
Television and family (x-ref from Television programs for the family)
Television programs for children
Television programs for women
Young adult films

APPENDIX 8
EXAMPLES OF TOPICAL SUBJECT HEADINGS BEING USED IN LCSH TO PROVIDE ACCESS TO FILMS IN A SERIES

Carry On films
Nightmare on Elm Street films
Planet of the Apes films
Star Trek films
Star Wars films

APPENDIX 9
EXAMPLES OF FICTITIOUS CHARACTER HEADINGS BEING USED AS *EXAMPLE OF* HEADINGS IN LCSH

Andy Hardy films
Angelique films
Bowery Boys films
Charlie Chan films
Cisco Kid films
Dracula films
Frankenstein films
Godfather films
Godzilla films
Hopalong Cassidy films
Indiana Jones films
James Bond films
Lone Ranger films
Our Gang films
Sherlock Holmes films
Superman films
Tarzan films
Three Stooges films
Tom and Jerry films
Torchy Blane films
Zorro films
Zorro television programs

APPENDIX 10
GENRE AND FORM HEADINGS THAT ARE NOT DIRECT, WITH SUGGESTIONS ON HOW TO EDIT THEM TO MAKE THEM SO

A. LCSH genre and form headings that are not direct. Starred headings (*) are discussed further in the section that discusses questions about LCSH application:

LCSH headings:

Motion picture errors
Motion picture remakes
Motion picture sequels
Motion picture serials
Motion picture soundtracks
Motion picture trailers
*Motion pictures--Sound effects
Motion pictures for men
Motion pictures for women
*Motion pictures in advertising
*Motion pictures in propaganda

*Radio adaptations
Radio addresses, debates, etc.
Radio comedies
*Radio in religion
*Radio plays
Radio programs for children
Radio programs, Musical
Radio programs, Public service
Radio serials

*Television adaptations
Television advertising
Television and family (x-ref from Television programs for the family)
*Television broadcasting--Auditions
*Television broadcasting--Awards
*Television broadcasting--Sound effects
*Television broadcasting--Special effects
*Television broadcasting of animated films
*Television broadcasting of court proceedings
*Television broadcasting of films
*Television broadcasting of music
*Television broadcasting of news

*Television broadcasting of sports
Television comedies
Television dance parties
*Television in propaganda
*Television in religion
Television mini-series
Television musicals
Television pilot programs
Television plays
Television programs, Public service
Television programs for children
Television programs for women
Television serials
Television specials
*Television weathercasting

B. The LCSH genre and form headings listed in Section A would be more consistent with the principle of directness if they were established with the term commonly used for the concept as the entry term, and with media terms used as qualifiers only when necessary to disambiguate homonyms, such as 'serials' and 'sequels' which have different meanings in other fields, as follows:

Advertising (Motion picture), or, even better because with better literary warrant? Theater advertising
Errors (Motion picture), or, even better because with better literary warrant, Bloopers
Men's films (instead of Motion pictures for men)
Propaganda films
Remakes
Sequels (Motion picture)
Serials (Motion picture)
Sound effects (Motion picture)
Soundtracks (Motion picture)
Trailers (Motion picture)
Women's films (instead of Motion pictures for women)

Adaptations (Radio)
Addresses, debates, etc. (Radio)
Children's radio programs
Comedies (Radio)

APPENDIX 10 (continued)

Musical radio programs
Plays (Radio)
Public service radio programs
Religious radio programs
Serials (Radio)

Adaptations (Television)
Advertising (Television), or, with even better literary warrant, Commercials
Animated films on television
Auditions (Television)
Awards (Television)
Children's television programs
Comedies (Television)
Court proceedings on television
Dance parties (Television)
Films on television, or with even better literary warrant, TV movies
Mini-series (Television)
Musicals (Television)
Music on television
News on television, or with even better literary warrant, News programs (Television)
Pilot programs (Television)
Plays (Television)
Propaganda (Television)
Public service television programs,
Religious television
Serials (Television)
Sound effects (Television)
Special effects (Television)
Specials (Television)
Sports on television, or with even better literary warrant, Sports programs (Television)
Television programs for the family
Weathercasting (Television)
Women's television programs

C. MIGFG subdivisions that are not direct:

Television commercial
Television feature
Television pilot
Television series
Television special

APPENDIX 11
LCSH SYNDETIC STRUCTURE PROBLEMS

'Motion picture errors' not linked to the Motion picture syndetic structure
'Tarzan films' and 'Jungle films' are not linked as related terms
'Adventure films' should link to 'Swashbuckler films,' 'Tarzan films' and 'Jungle films' (the latter currently a narrower term) as related terms, as well as 'Disaster films,' 'Fantasy films,' 'Science fiction films,' 'War films,' and 'Western films' (see discussion below in the section on Huge categories)
'Dracula films' and 'Vampire films' are not linked as related terms
'Zombie films' should link upwards to 'Horror films,' not 'Motion pictures'
'Charlie Chan films' should link upwards to 'Detective and mystery films' (as 'Sherlock Holmes films' do)
'Documentary mass media' links to television but not to radio or film
'Wildlife cinematography' should link to 'Wildlife films'

APPENDIX 12
MISSING GENRE AND FORM HEADINGS IN BOTH LISTS

A. MIM GENRE AND FORM HEADINGS MISSING IN MIGFG:

NOTE: starred genre/form headings are also in LCSH; nonstarred genre/form headings are also missing from LCSH:

Army comedies
*Audience participation programs (LCSH: Audience participation television programs)
Award presentations
*B movies (LCSH: B films)
*Beauty contests
*Bloopers (LCSH: Motion picture errors)
Cinema vérité
Creature films
*Debates
Detective films and programs
*Epics (LCSH: Epic films)
*Fantasy comedies (LCSH: Fantasy comedies (Motion pictures)
Gambling films
Invisible man films
*Live shows (LCSH: Live television programs)
Monster films
*Mummy films

APPENDIX 12 (continued)

Navy comedies
*Novelties (LCSH: Novelty films)
Panel discussions
Panel shows
*Plays (LCSH: Drama)
*Press conferences
Private eye films and programs
*Quiz shows
Readings
*Remakes (LCSH: Motion picture remakes)
Rock and roll musicals
*Rural comedies
*Sequels (LCSH: Motion picture sequels)
*Sound effects (LCSH: Motion pictures--Sound effects; Television broadcasting--Sound effects)
Stock shots
Superhero films and programs
*Swashbucklers (LCSH: Swashbuckler films)
*Talent shows
*Theater advertising (LCSH: Motion pictures in advertising?)
Theater announcements
*Trailers and promo's (LCSH: Motion picture trailers; Advertising--Television programs)
*Vampire films
*Vaudeville
*Werewolf films
*Zombie films

B. MIGFG GENRE AND FORM HEADINGS MISSING IN LCSH:

Aviation (MIM: Aerial combat films and programs)
Buddy
Chase
Dark comedy
Fallen woman
Home shopping
Journalism (MIM: Reporter films and programs)
Legal (MIM: Legal films and programs, but Courtroom films and programs may have more literary warrant)
Martial arts (MIM: Martial arts films and programs)
Reality-based (this may be rather hard to scope, though)
Singing cowboy
Slapstick comedy (MIM: Slapstick comedies)
Slasher (MIM: Psychopath films and programs)
Trigger

APPENDIX 13
HEADINGS THAT WILL PRODUCE HUGE CATEGORIES

MIGFG:
Adaptation
News
Television

LCSH:
Feature films
Film adaptations
Foreign films
Foreign language films
Motion pictures
Radio adaptations
Radio programs
Short films
Sound motion pictures
Television adaptations
Television broadcasting of news
Television programs

APPENDIX 14
LCSH TERMS FOR PHYSICAL FORMAT CATEGORIES AND PHYSICAL ELEMENTS OF MOVING IMAGE MATERIALS

The following headings are included in LCSH, although it may be that they are intended only for use on *works about* not *examples of*:

Super-8
Sound motion pictures

There are also some terms in LCSH that are used for physical elements of moving image materials:

Credit titles (Motion pictures, television, etc.)
Motion pictures--Sound effects
Outtakes
Rushes (Motion pictures)
Television broadcasting--Sound effects

APPENDIX 15:
LCSH HEADINGS NOT LIMITED BY MEDIA THAT MAY BE APPLICABLE TO MOVING IMAGE MATERIALS

Anthologies [use for anthology films? anthology television programs?]
Editorials [use for the editorial segments of television news?]
Interviews [use for interviews in newsreels and on television?]
Lectures and lecturing [use for lectures recorded by means of moving image?]
Oral interpretation of fiction [use for readings of fiction on film, television or radio?]
Oral interpretation of poetry [use for readings of poetry on film, television or radio?]
Propaganda [use for *examples of* or only for *works about*?]
Revues [use for performances of revues on film or television as well as for music for revues?]
Satire [use for satirical films or radio or television programs?]
Stand-up comedy [use for performances on radio or television or on film?]
Storytelling [use for performances on radio or television or on film?]

APPENDIX 16
LCSH HEADINGS THAT ARE AMBIGUOUS CONCERNING WHETHER THEY CAN BE USED AS *EXAMPLE OF* HEADINGS

A. GENERAL LIST

Film adaptations [use for all films that have been adapted from previously published works in another medium, e.g., based on a novel?]
Motion pictures--Sound effects [use for *examples of* or only for *works about*?]
Motion pictures in propaganda [use for *examples of* or only for *works about*?]
Puppets in television [use for television programs that use puppets or broadcast performances of puppet shows?]
Radio adaptations [use for all radio programs that have been adapted from previously published works in another medium, e.g., based on a novel?]
Religious broadcasting [use for *examples of* or only for *works about*?]
Television adaptations [use for all television programs that have been adapted from previously published works in another medium, e.g., based on a novel?]
Television broadcasting--Auditions [use for *examples of* or only for *works about*?]
Television broadcasting--Awards [use for *examples of* awards ceremonies such as the Academy Awards, or only for *works about*?]
Television broadcasting--Sound effects [use for *examples of* or only for *works about*?]
Television broadcasting--Special effects [use for *examples of* or only for *works about*?]
Television in propaganda [use for *examples of* or only for *works about*?]
Television weathercasting [use for *examples of* or only for *works about*?]
Weather broadcasting [use for *examples of* or only for *works about*? use for radio weather reports, but use Television weathercasting for television weather reports?]
Wide-screen processes (Cinematography) [use for *examples of* or only for *works about*?]

B. TELEVISION BROADCASTING OF . . . HEADINGS

Television broadcasting of animated films
Television broadcasting of court proceedings
Television broadcasting of films [meant for TV movies?]
Television broadcasting of music
Television broadcasting of news [meant for TV news programs?]
Television broadcasting of sports

C. OTHER QUESTIONABLE 'IN' HEADINGS

Motion pictures in advertising [question: use for theater advertising?]
Motion pictures in propaganda [question: should this be used for propaganda films? See also 'Propaganda']
Television in propaganda [question: should this be used for propaganda films? See also 'Propaganda' below . . .]

AV AND AV USER GROUPS BY LIBRARY TYPE

Scholars and Media: An Unmixable Mess of Oil and Water or a Perfect Meld of Oil and Vinegar?

Sheila S. Intner

SUMMARY. Reviews the setting in which nonprint materials collections have been housed and used, namely, the academy, and its traditions of collecting these materials. Compares older data on the state of nonelectronic nonprint media collections in academic libraries with more recent reports and freshly-collected data obtained in 2000 at the Eighth Biennial Conference of Online Audiovisual Catalogers, to see if any trends are discernible. Then, superimposes findings from a review of recent literature on the impact of the Internet on collection development

Sheila S. Intner is Professor, Graduate School of Library and Information Science at Simmons College, Boston, MA, where she teaches cataloging and classification, collection development, professional writing, and other courses. She served as Editor of *Library Resources & Technical Services* for four years and Editor of *Technicalities* for nine years. Professor Intner was elected an American Library Association Councilor at Large and President of the Association for Library Collections & Technical Services, and was awarded the Margaret Mann Citation and the OnLine Audiovisual Catalogers Annual Award.

[Haworth co-indexing entry note]: "Scholars and Media: An Unmixable Mess of Oil and Water or a Perfect Meld of Oil and Vinegar?" Intner, Sheila S. Co-published simultaneously in *Cataloging & Classification Quarterly* (The Haworth Information Press, an imprint of The Haworth Press, Inc.) Vol. 31, No. 3/4, 2001, pp. 297-312; and: *The Audiovisual Cataloging Current* (ed: Sandra K. Roe) The Haworth Information Press, an imprint of The Haworth Press, Inc., 2001, pp. 297-312. Single or multiple copies of this article are available for a fee from The Haworth Document Delivery Service [1-800-342-9678, 9:00 a.m. - 5:00 p.m. (EST). E-mail address: getinfo@haworthpressinc.com].

© 2001 by The Haworth Press, Inc. All rights reserved.

and interprets what it indicates about the collection of electronic resources. Finds that traditional nonprint materials have not gained an important share of collections while newer electronic resources have achieved an important collection share in just a few years, and it is increasing. The developments facilitate the work of the institution and confer a positive value on librarians doing the job. Attention to materials in older forms of nonprint media continues to shrink as some become obsolete and others are digitized, crossing over into the world of electronic resources. If the trend to digitize traditional nonprint materials continues, it should have a positive effect on the accessibility and potential use of all media by scholars and teachers alike. *[Article copies available for a fee from The Haworth Document Delivery Service: 1-800-342-9678. E-mail address: <getinfo@haworthpressinc.com> Website: <http://www.HaworthPress.com> © 2001 by The Haworth Press, Inc. All rights reserved.]*

KEYWORDS. Audiovisual materials, library collections, academic libraries, nonprint media

INTRODUCTION

When the author was first asked to write about collections of nonprint media in academic libraries, she thought it would be a straightforward task to examine published data about library holdings for the current year and one or more previous years, see what a comparison of the statistics for the various years suggested, and write it down. Two things shattered that pleasant dream: first, the published data she had expected to find were not available for the current year; and, second, the entire environment has changed dramatically in the several years prior to this writing, but the changes aren't yet reflected in libraries' reports about their holdings. Regarding the latter issue, the fact that electronic resources are not "held" as items librarians can hold in their hands and store on library shelves may result in our never being able to determine exactly who has access to which online resources or how many online resources individual libraries "collect" for their users.

For better or worse, the approach had to be rethought. The author decided to begin by reviewing the setting in which nonprint materials collections were housed and used, namely, the college or university, and traditions of collecting. Next, she used some of the older data that were available for the first part of an assessment of the state of nonprint media collections in academic libraries, augmented it with freshly-collected data obtained at the Eighth Biennial Conference of Online Audiovisual Catalogers,[1] and looked to see if a comparison of the two bodies of data suggested any trends. That was the skeleton of the assessment. Last, having recently examined literature on the impact of the Internet on collection development for another study,[2] she tried to put some flesh on the skeleton by superimposing what that body of literature and study seemed to say about the collection of electronic resources. The article below follows this framework.

THE WORK OF THE ACADEMY

The academy has always been about scholarship, whether it was fulfilling its teaching role or its research mission. The most highly regarded form of teaching is that of the master scholar initiating a cadre of acolytes into doctoral-level studies, who absorb his (or her) ideas, after which they serve their master and themselves by validating and perpetuating those ideas in pursuing scholarly careers of their own. The system is well-described, albeit briefly, by James Gleick in *Genius,* biography of physicist Richard Feynman, a brilliant physicist who participated in the Manhattan project and later became a professor at the California Institute of Technology; and the description was echoed by novelist Saul Bellow in his recent novel, *Ravelstein,* whose title character is a University of Chicago professor.

Gleick writes, "At universities a graduate student, unlike an undergraduate, was as much hired as admitted to a department; he would be paid for teaching and research and would be on a track for promotion. Furthermore, graduate departments considered themselves responsible to the industries they fed . . . that conducted most research in the applied sciences . . . . "[3] In his novel, Bellow suggests that Ravelstein's former students, later known in their own right, supported their teacher, quite literally, and describes how closely they kept in contact. The story's narrator, Chick, says: "But Ravelstein knew the value of a set. He had a set of his own. Its members were students he had trained in political philosophy and longtime friends. Most of them were trained as Ravelstein himself had been trained, under Professor Davarr and used his esoteric vocabulary. Some of Ravelstein's older pupils now held positions of importance on national newspapers. Quite a number served in the State Department. Some lectured in the War College or worked on the staff of the National Security Adviser. One was a protége of Paul Nitze. Another, a maverick, published a column in the *Washington Times*. Some were influential, all were well informed; they were a close group, a community. From them Ravelstein had frequent reports, and when he was at home he spent hours on the telephone with his disciples."[4] When Bellow's fictional portrayal is paired with Gleick's real description of faculty mentoring in the field of physics, one realizes they do not exaggerate the power of professors to mold more than their narrow scholarly fields in ways few laypersons would imagine.

The foregoing raises the question, how does one advance to become a Professor? Ask junior faculty members on any campus and the answer will be "through research and publication." Gleick, after relating how Feynman's first publication was the result of work he, Feynman, did on a problem bothering one of his professors, after which they wrote it up together, goes on to say, "[Professor] Vallarta let his student [Feynman] in on a secret of mentor-protége publishing: the senior scientist's name comes first."[5] Under the circumstances, is it any wonder that scholarship-in the form of research and publication-are the principal endeavors of academe? The big question on campuses today is whether publication in electronic journals carries the same weight as in traditional printed scholarly journals. Some university committees making decisions on faculty appointments, tenure, and promotion say "yes"; others say "no." No matter how likely it is that all of them will eventually come around and accept electronic publication, few junior faculty want to be the ones to suffer the rejection of the naysayers in the interim.

What has all this to do with nonprint media materials in academic libraries? The connection is direct and real: the mission of these libraries is to support the activities of their institutions, namely, research and teaching (aka scholarship). If both are inextricably bound up in the world of printed publications, one could expect that print would dominate the collections. This was, indeed, the case before 1990. Beginning around 1990, however, the maturation of computerized networks facilitated nearly instantaneous scholarly communication (though not necessarily publication, at first) and, subsequently, forays into electronic publishing. Let's go back a little more than a decade to the 1970s and 1980s, to see where the collection of nonprint media stood at that time and how it developed before the Internet era.

NONPRINT RESOURCES IN LIBRARIES: TRADITIONS OF THE 1970s

This author conducted a doctoral research study about nonprint media materials and cataloging in 1980 and 1981, disseminating the results in a 1984 book. Although her research was focused on public libraries, she discussed the state of academic library collections briefly as part of a general background about media in libraries. She reported on three studies: (1) Boyd Ladd's 1975 national survey, done under the auspices of the National Commission on Libraries and Information Services, which aimed to document how well the then-current holdings of public, school, and academic libraries met existing standards for various types of materials;[6] (2) Doris Cruger Dale's study of media cataloging and classification in 100 randomly selected two-year community colleges;[7] and (3) Nancy Olson's less-formal survey of more than 1,500 academic audiovisual librarians about how their materials were cataloged and classified.[8] Of Ladd's findings, the author says: "As for academic libraries, nonprint collections were measured in *volume equivalents* and were located primarily in universities, not in two or four year colleges. Overall collection needs for academic libraries were reported totalling 158 million volumes, but how much of this was nonprint was not defined."[9] [Emphasis added.] Perhaps the nonprint holdings were microform copies of books and periodicals, which, though audiovisual, are treated bibliographically as if they were printed items-enabling librarians to report these holdings in volume equivalents rather than as a number of individually held audiovisual items.

Olson and Dale asked about cataloging and classification. Olson received replies from 599 librarians. Nearly all her respondents (94%) said they cataloged their collections, although only about half used standard cataloging rules. Nearly all indexed their materials using *Library of Congress Subject Headings* (LCSH), but fewer classified them with a standard classification (74%), evenly divided between the Dewey Decimal and Library of Congress classifications.[10] Dale received replies from fewer than half her sample population (48%), finding that more than half of those who did respond used accession number classifications. Of those who used a standard classification, Dewey was preferred. On the other hand, most respondents (71%) used standard cataloging rules for description and nearly all (96%) used LCSH for subject headings.[11]

The state-of-the-art in 1980 could be summed up very simply: To meet then-current standards, academic libraries needed more of everything-more holdings and more standard cataloging for what they held-as well as to rethink the way they counted materials in order to reflect more clearly what those holdings were.

MORE RECENT TRENDS

As stated above, the author originally planned to compare changes in nonprint media holdings by format in selected academic libraries from each of the fifty states of the United States as reported in the *American Library Directory* to document recent collecting trends. However, the 2000 edition (current at this writing) no longer lists these data; it gives only the number of books and journal subscriptions held.[12] She turned to the 1997-98 *American Library Directory,* which still listed library holdings by format for a selection of media, for statistics on the relative size of print vs. nonprint media holdings at that time.

Libraries serving campuses of state universities from fifteen U.S. states were selected for this sample, a subset of a larger sample of one campus library from each of the fifty states.[13] If nonprint media holdings in these libraries seem small, they would be even smaller for the group of fifty. [Note: The author has tried to be cautious in interpreting the statistics for microforms, which are counted in different ways by reporting libraries. Many include microform versions of volumes of print journals and printed government documents, which, otherwise, have been omitted from this survey, whether bound or unbound.] A few of the numbers jump out, for example, the disparities in CD-ROM holdings among this subset of libraries. (One library reported three kinds of computer-based collections and a second reported two kinds, which were folded into the statistic for CD-ROM.) One could not assume they varied directly with the size of the institution (although Table 1 shows that large libraries were not unlikely to have large numbers of CD-ROMs), for example, the universities in the neighboring states of New Hampshire and Vermont, with enrollments of approximately 12,500 and 10,900, respectively, had widely varying CD-ROM holdings, 11 and 416, respectively, with the larger holdings in the library serving fewer students. The range of CD-ROM collections of those reporting some holdings of this type went from 11 to 1,993. The likely explanation is that some libraries had only started collecting and/or reporting holdings of CD-ROMs in 1997.

The number of visual images in the form of slides, art reproductions, photographs, etc., held in these university libraries varied unpredictably

TABLE 1. Holdings by Format for Selected Libraries

LIBRARY	BOOKS	MICRO	SOUND	MOTION	MAPS	VISUALS	CD-ROM
AZ State U.	2,931,990	5,972,742	253,342		187,147		1,993
U. of AK	1,479,989	1,776,999	15,393		131,047		
U. of CO	2,672,243	5,569,400	85,129	9,696	108,092	347,060	1,900
U. of HI	2,888,498	5,657,508	19,269	12,610	241,559		815
U. of IL	8,096,040	2,837,082	130,069	337,725	609,510	288,832	
IA State U.	2,043,344	2,592,790	14,246	35,046	101,073	233,315	478
U. of KS	481,317	1,094,152	5,615	1,585		6,409	411
U. of MD	2,537,110	5,072,411	123,250	4,513	213,989	9,445	1,936
U. of NV	929,950	3,075,672	40,460	8,156	137,814		148
U. of NH	1,075,851	1,690,520	7,633		127,547	97	11
U. of SC	2,438,230	4,536,484	28,979	8,305	225,174		60
U. of UT	2,160,941	2,859,299	35,587	13,122	190,828	104,251	
U. of VT	728,499	212,898	7,709	3,971	205,899	213,250	416
U. of WI	4,460,132	3,884,292	141,414	8,376	6,914	10,099	1,873
U. of WY	1,134,211	2,720,746		3,414	162,475	69,633	

as well. Five reported none; five reported having more than 100,000 items each; while the rest ranged from 97 items to more than 69,000, with no clear relationship to other size indicators.

A dramatic statistic is the large number of libraries having more than one million books.[14] Only three of the fifteen have book collections smaller than one million. One also sees relatively large numbers of map holdings nearly everywhere, with all but two of the fifteen selected libraries each holding more than 100,000 maps. The author was surprised at the small numbers of motion materials held (that is, films and videos), with six in the above group having fewer than 10,000 items and only one library holding more than 100,000. Variation was wide in sound recording holdings, also, although only one library reported having none. Six libraries reported small collections (fewer than 25,000) of sound materials and four reported large ones (more than 100,000). Some of the universities may have separate music libraries with collections of recorded music not counted as part of the campus's main library.

The numbers of microform holdings, which appear to be the largest of all formats, including books, are dramatically high, but probably consist in part if not totally of rolls of film containing back issues of journals, not volumes of books, dissertations, and/or other monographic items. Since the nonprint materials on which this study focused are primarily monographs and serial title counts generally were avoided, these statistics should be taken with a proverbial grain of salt. Nevertheless, it demonstrates the universality of extremely large microform collections in academic libraries and the need for library viewing facilities. Librarians can assume that users will take sound and videorecordings out to run on their own or classroom equipment, but usually microforms must be used solely within the library. Home and classroom microprojectors are rare. How ironic that microforms, which require projectors for use, putting them clearly into the audiovisual camp, tend to be perceived as if they were printed texts and not as nonprint media.

Table 2 shows the proportions of collections held as books, microforms, and all nonprint formats taken together, for the fifteen libraries. There seems to be little doubt from the results that balance is lacking among the three types of media, with books and microform versions of texts dividing the lion's share of items held between them. Only in two of the fifteen libraries do nonprint materials taken together amount to more than seven percent of the holdings, and the average proportion is less than seven percent.

What would a reasonable balance be? This is not a rhetorical question, but one that academic media librarians have tried to answer over the years. If one believes a reasonable proportion is what each library's users claim to need is purchased by the library, then, clearly, they need very little. On the other hand, if the proportion of nonprint media in OCLC's WorldCat-probably the largest networked bibliographic database used by academic libraries-is used as an average for comparison, all but one of the fifteen libraries in this sample have exceeded the average, which was recently reported in a press release as approximately two percent. Harkening back to the discussion above about the work of the academy, one should ask how much nonprint material is cited in published research. If nonprint items are not the stuff of which research (and, thus, one's scholarly reputation) is made, the compelling drive to collect it widely is absent. In this author's experience, academic media collections intended as classroom teaching aids involve purchasing individual titles solely when a faculty member requests them for specific courses. Nonprint media librarianship in these places is largely a matter of acquiring the titles selected by faculty, storing and preserving them, scheduling and showing them upon faculty request, and purchasing, housing, and maintaining the associated hardware. If a large and active faculty use many nonprint materials in teaching, the media collection may grow, both in the numbers of formats collected and numbers of ti-

TABLE 2. Proportion of Holdings by Media Groups

LIBRARY	TOTAL #	% BOOKS	% MICRO	% NONPRINT
AZ State U.	9,347,214	31%	64%	5%
U. of AK	3,403,428	43%	52%	5%
U. of CO	8,793,520	30%	63%	7%
U. of HI	8,820,259	33%	64%	3%
U. of IL	12,299,258	66%	23%	11%
IA State U.	5,020,292	41%	52%	7%
U. of KS	1,589,489	30%	69%	1%
U. of MD	7,962,654	32%	64%	3%
U. of NV	4,192,200	22%	73%	5%
U. of NH	2,901,659	37%	58%	5%
U. of SC	7,237,232	34%	63%	3%
U. of UT	5,364,028	40%	53%	7%
U. of VT	1,372,642	53%	16%	31%
U. of WI	8,513,100	52%	46%	2%
U. of WY	4,090,479	28%	67%	5%

tles within each format; but it is unlikely to develop at the same rate as if it were being collected to support research and scholarship, which, for subject areas of interest within the institution, tends to be as exhaustive as an institution's finances and space limitations permit.

REPORT FROM OLAC: HOLDINGS IN THE YEAR 2000

Since fresh data on academic library nonprint holdings were not available from the reference source used for the previous section, the author gathered newer information from nonprint catalogers attending the Online Audiovisual Catalogers conference in Seattle. Seventeen librarians responded to a simple questionnaire, asking for estimates of nonprint holdings by format and checkoffs that indicated whether they were represented in the library catalog. Demographic data about the institution (public/private, state/province, urban/suburban/rural setting), advanced degrees offered, and comments also were requested. They were not asked for book holdings. Table 3 displays the results.

Like the previous group, these respondents reported wide disparities in holdings in several formats, including computer-based materials. Two librarians who reported having more than 10,000 electronic resources commented they counted Internet resources and/or electronic

TABLE 3. Current Nonprint Holdings in Selected Libraries

LIBRARY*	MOTION	SOUND	COMPUTER	VISUAL	OTHER
Pvt/MA/r**/m***	6,000	8,500	100	n/a	n/a
Pvt/CA/s/d	700	1,350	200	n/a	n/a
Pvt/IA/r	2,000	19,500	50	n/a	n/a
Pvt/WA/u	4,500	200	n/a	n/a	n/a
Pvt/WA/u	600	1,025	5	n/a	n/a
Pvt/NY/s	2,535	5,000	325	n/a	n/a
Pvt/TX/u/d	1,500	6,000	430	n/a	n/a
Pvt/WA/u	310	723	145	1,185	211†
Pub/BC/u	4,050	1,500	60	n/a	n/a
Pub/CA/u/m	3,000	44,500	30	n/a	n/a
Pub/NC/u/d	1,500	800	450+	n/a	n/a
Pub/IN/u/d	16,900	31,200	2,400	35,000	3,975††
Pub/MO/u/d	3,600	296,750	600	2,265	9,200†††
Pub/SC/m	2,000	1,800	530+	55	n/a
Pub/VA/u/d	18,560	54,156	14,256	422,669	5,200,000‡
Pub/WA/r	1,450	1,567	20	n/a	n/a
Pub&Pvt/NY/r/d	18,555	90,015	13,695	40,370	n/a

* Responses were anonymous and only the state/province, type of locale, and advanced degrees offered were given; thus these are the only identifications.
** r = rural locale; s = suburban locale; u = urban locale
*** m = Master's degrees given; d = Ph.D.s given
† kits †† kits & realia ††† maps & microforms ‡ microforms

journal titles as well as direct access materials like CD-ROMs and floppy disks. It is interesting that, having been asked to report only on nonprint formats, only two respondents added microforms as a category for types not specified in the survey form. Another person wrote "Books" in this category, but gave no statistic for the number of books held.

Several respondents noted in the margins that their collections of films and older types of sound recordings were decreasing. Two specified converting the films to video; others did not say if they were converting the contents of older media to newer forms or simply disposing of them. Several respondents noted having small numbers of videotape reels, long-play sound discs, filmstrips, film loops, and other less-frequently-held formats.

Nearly all respondents reported including all their nonprint media materials in the library catalog. One wrote, "All media [are] fully represented and fully cataloged in local catalog and OCLC"; another commented, "We have always considered nonprint materials and electronic resources to have the same importance to our users as do print materials thus they are cataloged and classed in the same manner as print materials"; a third wrote, simply, "All nonprint media are in our catalog." Only three respondents reported having holdings that weren't included in the catalog, two for tiny numbers of CD-ROMs and one for filmstrips and film loops. This finding is less surprising than one might think since one of the activities at the conference attended by the respondents was workshops teaching standard cataloging for various nonprint formats. Separate workshops covered cataloging for Internet resources and direct access computer files.

On the whole, numbers of nonprint holdings in these libraries, with the exception of a few private institutions much smaller in size than any of the universities described in the *American Library Directory* sample (one conference respondent wrote her library "serves student population of about 650 FTE"), were not much different than the earlier group. For each format, a few large collections stood out; the rest were quite small. Many respondents did not report any visual materials or maps. Generally, comments did not suggest anything out of the ordinary, but two noteworthy exceptions were a respondent who wrote, "Supporting conservatory of music [and] health sciences which use much nonprint material for study, very high priority," and one who said, " . . . we tend to be between 2-5 years ahead of the average library in providing for distance education, access to a variety of electronic materials and variety of multimedia used and represented in the catalog."

THE IMPACT OF ELECTRONIC PUBLISHING

This article has assumed that academic libraries consider electronic resources another form of nonprint media and that media librarians and catalogers are expected to handle them. This is not the case everywhere, although it is not an unusual model.[15] Regarding the collecting process, no one model for assigning responsibility for electronic resources is clear. Sometimes an institutional computer center is responsible. Sometimes a library computer department is created for it or an existing one takes responsibility. In other instances, where the library is responsible but does not designate a separate unit to handle them, its "regular" reference librarians, bibliographers, selectors, and acquisitions staff all play roles in acquiring the resources, functioning in the usual manner.

Interestingly, the contents of electronic resources-particularly electronic journals-mirror the traditional printed formats through which scholarship has long been disseminated, with numerous added advantages.[16] Like microforms, which reproduce printed periodicals and monographs, electronic resources tend to offer access to texts, mainly journals and cumulating databases at the moment, but with growing numbers of online monographic works as well.

Regarding the cataloging, in some academic libraries only the nonprint cataloging librarians-who still had to create original catalog records for most of the media titles purchased-remained at work in catalog departments when they were deprofessionalized and populated with paraprofessional computer inputters in the 1980s.[17] In places where both print and nonprint materials catalogers were employed, any new medium that appeared tended to go to the nonprint catalogers, for whom familiarity with the peculiarities of "hardware" and "software" was assumed. Thus, in a good many libraries, nonprint catalogers were the vanguard of librarians handling electronic resources.

As mentioned above, in connection with a study of how the Internet had affected library collecting, the author interviewed six academic library directors. One of the questions they were asked was to estimate the balance in their libraries between traditional materials they purchased, owned, and shelved, and electronic resources to which they provided access through leases or other licensing arrangements. All responded that the majority of their collections still consisted of owned materials, mainly but not exclusively in printed form, such as books, journals, and microfilm, and some physical nonprint formats such as videos. In one library the materials budget was divided about 12-15% for electronic resources, the rest for traditional materials in all formats, but the share given to the former was rising. In a second, the director saw an accelerating shift from older formats to electronic resources, putting the current division at 70% older formats, 30% electronic resources. She forecast a slow increase that might progress to 60% older formats, 40% electronic resources in two or three years. A third director said her library now held approximately 90% older formats, 10% electronic resources; but she expected it to shift soon to somewhere on the order of a 70%-30% division.

Factors playing a role in the shift to electronic collections included the reliability of distributors in delivering electronic products; the reliability of the products themselves, not only for current documents but for continuing access to older ones; and fair pricing practices. Several directors said the pricing of electronic products was chaotic and arbitrary, making it difficult for libraries to buy them even when they wanted to. One said reliable archiving of electronic resources was a key problem to be resolved before libraries could accept electronic resources completely.

More than one director said different disciplines were moving to online resources at differing rates of speed, but the majority of materials needed by the library were still being published in printed form. One director said that, while her library was spending more money every year on electronic products, orders for hard copy titles also had increased.

These directors believed an evolution, not a revolution, is occurring but none saw a major change in the immediate future. All aimed to employ electronic resources and distribution channels fully to serve their patrons more flexibly, releasing them from having to come to the library in person to be served. They also spoke of serving a widening circle of outsiders in the future-adults living in nearby communities, unaffiliated scholars, elementary and secondary school students, etc.-who now must come to the library to use its resources while meeting the terms of site licenses and contracts for access.

CONCLUSIONS

It would be exaggerating to conclude that the older nonprint media, excluding electronic resources, have not and will not achieve recognition for their scholarly worth in academe. First, this is not true for materials associated with selected fields of study. Libraries serving faculties of art, music, geography, and anthropology, for example, have always valued the nonprint materials associated with their fields and may be counted upon to continue to value and use them in teaching and scholarly studies. And these four fields are not the only ones. Second, some of the older types of recording media are considered valuable not only because of their contents, which may be unavailable in newer formats, but because they have become "collectibles." For example, although the contents have been digitized and enhanced for clearer, more satisfying listening, the fragile, one-sided discs of Enrico Caruso's singing are highly prized in their original form. These factors aside, however, the statistics reviewed in this article seem to lead to the conclusion that, except for microforms, the traditional nonprint media-sound recordings, films, videorecordings, maps, and visual images-considered as a unified body of materials, have competed unsuccessfully with printed materials for a share of collection space in academic libraries-at least, in the sample selected for this study. Some libraries (among them the author's own institution) do not buy or house nonprint media at all, preferring to segregate them in separate units, or spin them off to administrative units outside the library.[18] Nonprint materials seem more used as enrichments or aids to teaching than as raw materials essential for scholarly inquiry. Only microforms appear to rival books in numbers of holdings, and they are treated as if they were printed texts.

One effect of the lack of greater scholarly recognition for traditional forms of nonprint materials is the dearth of bibliographical tools for work with media similar to those on which librarians depend for work with books and journals. There is no broad-based coverage of titles for sale in a *Media in Print* a la *Books in Print.* As mentioned, in 2000, after more than 30 years of OCLC shared cataloging, the proportion of nonprint media records in WorldCat is so small as to be barely noticeable. Nonprint media librarians have had to use whatever tools were available, generally limited to one or a few media, or one or a few producers, to acquire and catalog their collections. The fact that some of these collections are extremely impressive in size and scope is evidence of the enormous efforts made by librarians to identify and gather them title by title. Yet, one fails to hear about large numbers of scholars in all parts of the country clamoring for bigger, better, more complete nonprint collections.

Electronic media, on the other hand, appear to be winning the battle handily for the hearts and minds of scholars everywhere, gaining increasing shares of budgets with each passing year. Even though, for the most part, electronic resources are not owned, shelved, archived, or controlled by the institutions that acquire them, they-bibliographic databases and services, full-text databases and services, nontextual databases, and multimedia resources-play crucial roles now in scholarship and teaching, and may be expected to continue to expand that role in the years to come.

The fact that electronic resources, as a body, lack bibliographical control seems to disturb librarians far more than it does scholars. The concern over lack of bibliographical control on the part of librarians is prompting them to shift their attention to resolve the problem. The exact nature of the resolution and the shape it might take still is unclear, but several initiatives are being pursued and may succeed in bringing order in part, if not entirely, to the chaos of the Internet. For instance, in a limited period of shared cataloging still measurable, at this writing, in months, rather than years, more than 300,000 electronic resource titles have been entered into OCLC's Cooperative Online Resource Catalog (CORC) and many of these titles are not just entered, but also have been organized into subject-oriented lists known as pathfinders. And, just as every book and magazine published is not of interest to academic libraries, neither is everything on the Web.[19]

These developments with electronic resources are good if one defines good as facilitating the work of the institution and conferring a positive value on the hardworking librarians doing the job. Unless and until computer scientists can automate bibliographical control and intellectual access to electronic resources in the way that librarians have taken for granted with printed titles for the last century, the contributions of nonprint media librarians and catalogers seem assured. Attention to materials in older forms of nonprint media continues to shrink as some become obsolete (for example, filmslips and film loops) and others are digitized, crossing over to electronic resources. This is happening with visual images, maps, videorecordings and sound recordings as well as microforms. If the trend to digitize media continues, it should have a generally positive effect on the accessibility and, therefore, the potential use of those resources by scholars and teachers alike.

When the author composed the title for this article, she thought of scholars as the "oil" and media as either "vinegar" or "water," depending on whether the scholars did or did not "mix" with them (pun intended). But, if one changes the image and thinks of older media as the "oil" and electronic resources as the "vinegar," we may hope they will merge into a tasty sauce in the future, replacing the unblendable mess previously formed by books (this time, the "water") and media (again, the "oil").

NOTES

1. This conference was held October 12-15, 2000, in Seattle, Washington, attended by several hundred participants most of whom were responsible for cataloging nonprint materials collected by their libraries, including, in many places, electronic resources.

2. At this writing, the results of the study, titled "Impact of the Internet on Collection Development: Where Are We Now? Where Are We Headed? An Information Study," are to be published in the forthcoming *Library Collections, Acquisitions, & Technical Services* 25, no. 1 (2001).

3. James Gleick, *Genius: The Life and Science of Richard Feynman* (New York: Pantheon Books, 1992), p. 84-85.

4. Saul Bellow, *Ravelstein* (New York: Viking, 2000), p. 10.

5. *Genius*, p. 82.

6. Boyd Ladd, *National Inventory of Library Needs, 1975; Resources Needed for Public and Academic Libraries and Public School Library/Media Centers* (Washington, D.C.: National Commission on Libraries and Information Services, 1977).

7. Doris Cruger Dale, "Cataloging and Classification Practices in Community College Libraries," *College & Research Libraries* 42 (July 1981): 333-340.

8. Nancy B. Olson, "Survey of Audiovisual Materials Collections in Academic Libraries," in *Cataloging of Audiovisual Materials: A Manual Based on AACR2* (Mankato, Minn.: Minnesota Scholarly Press, 1981): p. 1-3.

9. Sheila S. Intner, *Access to Media: A Guide to Integrating and Computerizing Catalogs* (New York: Neal-Schuman Publishers, 1984), p. 99-100.

10. Ibid., p. 96-97.

11. Ibid., p. 97.

12. R. R. Bowker, *American Library Directory 2000-2001* (New Providence, NJ: R. R. Bowker, 2000).

13. First, one public university from each state was selected and holdings data for the main library on one of its campuses was recorded. It soon became obvious, however, that not all libraries report their nonprint holdings in the same way, or, if they have separate units for some or all of the formats, they do not report all of the statistics. Some of the largest institutions reported holdings only of books and printed journals even though one can be certain they hold other types of materials as well. Other libraries gave only the total number of nonprint items held, but did not break them down by format. Thus, the author made a further selection from the fifty state university libraries of a subset of fifteen libraries that reported relatively large and varied nonprint media holdings in most formats, and broke them down by format.

14. Given a choice between number of titles and number of volumes, the author recorded the number of titles.

15. Places where nonprint media and electronic resources are not part of library collections and resources, for all intents and purposes, are not part of the population of academic libraries covered in this article; but, in those places where traditional nonprint media *or* electronic resources, but not both, are part of the library, only the relevant sections of the article would apply.

16. Among these advantages are the rapid distribution via networks to geographically dispersed readers, the ability to search the body of literature using sophisticated techniques, and, most of all, the ability to combine the indexing and abstracting databases with the texts of the articles themselves in one supertool for scholarship.

17. When bibliographic networks like OCLC grew large enough to provide catalog records speedily for the bulk of trade and university press titles, original cataloging did not have to be done for most of the books acquired by academic libraries, and MLS-holding book catalogers were reassigned to other departments or their positions lost by attrition. The process is well described in Ruth Hafter, *Academic Librarians and Cataloging Networks: Visibility, Quality Control, and Professional Status* (Westport, Conn.: Greenwood Press, 1986).

18. Once housed in a library unit known as the Beatley Library Media Center, Simmons College's nonprint materials recently were transferred to a different administrative unit known as Academic Support Services.

19. In a press release dated October 16, 2000, OCLC researchers reported there were 7.1 million unique sites on the Web, of which 41% or 2.9 million sites were freely available to the public, and that the spectacular rate of growth of new websites was beginning to slow.

User-Friendly Audiovisual Material Cataloging at Westchester County Public Library System

Heeja Hahn Chung

SUMMARY. This article describes Westchester Library System's (WLS) efforts to create a user-friendly online catalog for audiovisual materials for the patrons of Westchester County's public libraries by applying local cataloging practices when necessary while adhering to national standards as much as possible. *[Article copies available for a fee from The Haworth Document Delivery Service: 1-800-342-9678. E-mail address: <getinfo@haworthpressinc.com> Website: <http://www.HaworthPress.com> © 2001 by The Haworth Press, Inc. All rights reserved.]*

KEYWORDS. Public library, local cataloging practices, Westchester Library System, audiovisual material cataloging, general material designations (GMD), container title, call numbers, subject headings, video cataloging, online catalog, OPAC

Heeja Hahn Chung is Head of Cataloging and Interlibrary Loan Services, Westchester Library System, Ardsley, NY. She holds a BA in Library Science from Ewha Women's University, Seoul, Korea, and an MA in Humanities from Manhattanville College, Purchase, NY.

The author wishes to thank Beverly Harris, Patricia Luthin, and colleagues at the Westchester Library System, especially Dr. Maurice Freedman and Steven Pisani, for their encouragement, helpful comments, and suggestions for this article.

[Haworth co-indexing entry note]: "User-Friendly Audiovisual Material Cataloging at Westchester County Public Library System." Chung, Heeja Hahn. Co-published simultaneously in *Cataloging & Classification Quarterly* (The Haworth Information Press, an imprint of The Haworth Press, Inc.) Vol. 31, No. 3/4, 2001, pp. 313-325; and: *The Audiovisual Cataloging Current* (ed: Sandra K. Roe) The Haworth Information Press, an imprint of The Haworth Press, Inc., 2001, pp. 313-325. Single or multiple copies of this article are available for a fee from The Haworth Document Delivery Service [1-800-342-9678, 9:00 a.m. - 5:00 p.m. (EST). E-mail address: getinfo@haworthpressinc.com].

© 2001 by The Haworth Press, Inc. All rights reserved.

INTRODUCTION

WLS is a state-chartered, cooperative public library system serving more than 800,000 county residents and all 38 Westchester County public libraries in 42 locations. WLS has been offering centralized cataloging services to its member libraries since the 1960s. Until 1989, these cataloging services were limited to book cataloging only. The cataloging of non-book materials was left to the individual libraries.[1]

In 1988, WLS implemented a turnkey system from UTLAS, Inc. (based in Toronto)[2] and all member libraries began using the system with a bibliographic database that contained only book titles. The need for converting the card records for member libraries' non-book materials into machine-readable records became urgent. In 1989, an outside vendor was engaged to begin retrospective conversion of the four largest music collections in the county. After converting the majority of these collections (32,000 titles comprised of LPs, cassettes, and CDs), the Public Library Directors Association of Westchester County decided to engage an audiovisual (AV) cataloger to catalog non-book materials at WLS. When the AV cataloger was hired, two important steps had to be taken. One was to conduct a countywide survey to determine the size of the collections, types of materials held, status of the shelf lists, and the local AV budgets. The second was to establish a WLS cataloging code for AV materials.

An AV Committee representing the member libraries, the WLS AV consultant, and the WLS Technical Services staff studied the survey results. The Committee decided that the AV cataloger's time would best be spent cataloging the current material first, followed by retrospective video cataloging. At the time, videos and music CDs were relatively new media types but were becoming very popular. Videos were chosen to be the first priority because the size of the collection was manageable and videos were being circulated more heavily than other AV materials. The following years were spent systematically converting all card records for AV materials to MARC records. Since then the popularity of the media collections has grown enormously. Accordingly, WLS allocated more staff hours for AV cataloging in order to handle the cataloging of new material and the retrospective conversion simultaneously. At the present time WLS has over 100,000 AV material titles in its database and a growth rate of over 10,000 titles per year.

The cataloging code for AV material was established primarily by following the book cataloging code. In general, WLS cataloging policies reflect national standards that are flexibly applied to meet local requirements. WLS uses the *Dewey Decimal Classification* schedule,

Library of Congress Subject Headings, and the *Anglo-American Cataloguing Rules 2nd ed., 1998 rev. (AACR2)*. WLS has access to OCLC and Professional Media Services Corporation (PMSC) for AV catalog records, reducing the need for original cataloging. Catalog records for over 80% of WLS's AV materials are found in these utilities, so any local practice that departs from national standards has a significant impact on productivity. Accordingly, WLS has kept local practices to a minimum. The following pages describe WLS local practices that either enhance the cataloging records found in the bibliographic utilities or that depart from national standards to better serve the public.

CALL NUMBERS

When the member libraries started their AV collections, each library had its own home-grown local classification scheme. For music and video collections especially, many libraries continue to use the local classification numbers instead of the DDC numbers assigned by the WLS catalogers. For new media types such as CD-ROM, all libraries use DDC.

AV material call numbers have prefixes to identify the media type. The staff and the patrons absolutely need the prefixes for shelving and locating the items. Many libraries that do not use DDC are also using the same prefixes. WLS uses:

CA for audiocassette
CD for compact disc
CDR for CD-ROM
CF for computer file
DVD for DVD
DVC for descriptive videocassette
KIT for kit
VC for videocassette
WEB for web site cataloging

SUBJECT HEADINGS

WLS consistently adds format terms to all AV materials and genre terms to video recordings.

- Format terms used:

Audiobooks
Audiobooks on CD*

Audiocassettes
Children's audiobooks
Children's audiobooks on CD*
Compact discs
CD-ROMs
DVD videodiscs
Games
Toys
Video recordings
Web sites

A local subject heading (*) is assigned when a Library of Congress Subject Heading (LCSH) is not available to describe the format. This process is always done in consultation with reference staff of the member libraries. When a new LCSH is assigned for the format, WLS usually makes a global change to replace the local term with the new LCSH term. For instance, WLS used the local subject heading "Digital video discs" for DVDs until "DVD videodiscs" became an established LCSH term.

- Genre terms for video recordings:

Adventure films
Animal films
Bible films
Biographical films
Children's films
Comedy films
Documentary films
Fantasy films
Feature films
Foreign films **
Gangster films
Historical films
Horror films
Musicals
Mystery and detective films
Religious films
Samurai films
Science fiction films
Short films

Sports films
Spy films
Vampire films
Video recordings for hearing impaired
War films
Western films

Foreign films (**) are subdivided by nationality, i.e., "Foreign films $z Italy."

CHIEF SOURCES OF INFORMATION AND THE 245 FIELD FOR VIDEO CATALOGING

For videocassettes, the main entry is usually the title. According *to AACR2 Rev.* 7.0B1 Chief source of information, the title from the title frame should be used in the 245 field. However, WLS prefers to use the container title in the 245 field and the title from the title frame in the 246 field when the container title is different from the title frame. It is easier for the patrons and the staff to locate an item by the container title, and in more cases than not an item is known by the container title. In the case of dubbed videos, the container title is often in the dubbed language, thus, WLS uses that as the title in the 245 field.

SAME CONTENTS ISSUED BY DIFFERENT MANUFACTURERS

If the item is reissued by a different manufacturer without any changes in either the content or the format, WLS adds the new issue to the existing cataloging record by adding manufacturers'/music publishers' numbers (028 field), ISBN numbers, and necessary notes instead of creating a new cataloging record. This is a recent change in WLS AV cataloging practice, which takes into account that most public library patrons are not concerned which company manufactured the item as long as the contents are the same. In fact, separate bibliographic records create a problem as evidenced by many cases where patrons place *holds* on the first bibliographic record displayed when the items linked to the second bibliographic record are available. Here the creation of another bibliographic record to crowd the catalog is undesirable.

BRIEF GENERIC MARC RECORDS FOR TOYS AND GAMES

Several WLS member libraries circulate toys and games. To facilitate the circulation of these materials, WLS created several brief generic MARC records that are used instead of full bibliographic records for each individual toy and game. The libraries create item records with short descriptions and/or accession numbers and then attach these item records to the appropriate generic MARC record. WLS created the following twelve generic records that cover three categories of toys and games:

- Toys

  Figures
  Puppets
  Soft toys
  Musical instruments

- Games

  Board games
  Learning games

- Puppets

  Cardboard puzzles
  Foam puzzles
  Wooden puzzles

<Example> A generic MARC record for wooden puzzles

+LD nrm 7u

001 wls00274737

005 19991221161158

008 991221n19uu   nyua j 0 eng d

090 1 $a J PUZZLE

245 00 $a Wooden puzzles $h [game].

655    $a Toys.

655    $a Puzzles.

655    $a Games.

IMPORTANT NOTES IN 5XX FIELDS

The following notes are added consistently when applicable:

- For Videocassettes and DVDs:

  Wide screen version
  Closed-captioned
  In Russian with English subtitles, etc.
  Dubbed in Spanish, etc.

- For Audiobooks:

  Abridged
  Unabridged

- For popular music (Rock, Rap, etc.):

  Parental advisory: explicit lyrics
  Non-explicit version

For the popular music note, WLS opted to use "Non-explicit version" to avoid the judgmental nature of the phrase "Clean version," even though the latter seems to be the dominant industry language, used by a majority of vendors and the Schwann-Spectrum.

505 FIELD SUBFIELD "T"

When subfield "t" in the 505 field was introduced for title indexing, WLS began to add subfield "t" in the 505 field as much as possible when the derived records from OCLC and PMSC databases lacked the subfield code. This process is labor intensive, but is a worthwhile investment for patron access as when, for instance, it enables the patrons to retrieve individual popular songs in a collection. Without the subfield "t," the 505 field is indexed only by keyword and short titles such as "Weight" or "Wave" are impossible to locate. Keyword contents searching may prove to be the most expedient strategy, however, as AV cataloging workloads increase and newer indexing options become available for the OPAC. A separate "Contents" search of the 505 field is being explored to reduce the number of hits in a keyword search. Of course, it would be ideal if all bib-records from the vendors include the subfield "t."

IS THIS A SOUND RECORDING OR A KIT?

Deciding whether a cassette or CD with accompanying text should be cataloged as a book with accompanying material, sound recording with accompanying text, or a kit can be tricky. WLS policy has been:

1. A language cassette or CD accompanied by text is cataloged as a sound recording with accompanying material. Since the sound recording part is intrinsic to learning the language, a majority of the records from the OCLC and PMSC databases treat such items as sound recordings.
2. A book with a CD inserted inside the cover is cataloged as a book with accompanying CD.
3. A children's read-along book that comes in a container with a cassette is cataloged as a kit by changing the GMD to [kit] and Type of Record to "o," even though the records found in PMSC or OCLC treat them as sound recordings. WLS member libraries prefer to have these materials cataloged as kits since they do not shelve well with the rest of the sound recordings due to size and shape variations.

PHONO RECORD ALBUM (LP)

When WLS began the AV cataloging project back in 1989, long-playing records (LPs) were still being actively circulated. All LP titles in the WLS database were converted to the MARC format by outside vendors in the 1980s. Except for those in a few large libraries, most LP collections have been discarded. To distinguish a CD from an LP in the physical description field (300), WLS has been using "sound *compact* disc" for CD instead of "sound disc."

THE ROLE OF GENERAL MATERIAL DESIGNATIONS (GMD)

WLS began to catalog DVD titles in May 1999 using the GMD [videorecording] as prescribed in AACR2. In late 1999, WLS changed its OPAC system to DYNIX. DYNIX has the capability of displaying the GMD in a separate column on the first hit list screen and also allows the patrons to place *holds* from home. Some incidences were reported where patrons placed *holds* on videorecordings from home only to find that they had reserved DVDs instead of the videocassettes they expected. The need to differentiate videocassettes from DVDs was real. In February 2000, WLS began using [DVD] as a GMD, deviating from AACR2. The DVD collection was small enough at the time to change retrospectively.

Once this rule was bent, the floodgate was opened, and it was necessary to review all other media GMDs. WLS catalogs local web sites and introduces them into the OPAC. WLS uses [web site] as a GMD instead of [computer file]. WLS believes this is the most sensible policy for a public library. It uses language the user ordinarily will use and uniquely identifies the format. The GMD [computer file] applies to more than one format and forces the catalog user to do another, and otherwise unnecessary, search.

The GMD [sound recording] is especially problematic, as it does not distinguish CDs from cassettes or from LPs. By way of comparison, a search of other public libraries' catalogs revealed that many libraries employ some creative use of GMDs to differentiate among AV formats. The following are some of the GMDs that were found in other library catalogs:

1. Variation of [sound recording]:

   [abridged sound recording]
   [audiocassette]
   [audiobook]
   [Cassette]
   [Compact disc]
   [Phono record]
   [sound recording (abridged audiobook)]
   [sound recording (unabridged audiobook)];
   [sound recording (compact disc)]
   [sound recording (CD)]
   [talking book]
   [unabridged sound recording]

2. Variation of [videorecording]:

   [DVD]
   [DVD (videorecording)]
   [DVD videorecording]
   [described videorecording]
   [VIDEO]

[Video cassette]
[videorecording (DVD)]

Most the libraries surveyed are members of OCLC, which means they follow *AACR2 1.1C1* List 2 when entering new records in to OCLC but alter the GMD for their local databases. With the explosion of AV material in the marketplace and in libraries, identical titles can be found in many different formats. The OPAC display should assist patrons to identify the format of the material on the first screen. The way MARC is constructed, the GMD could accomplish this easily, but only if it becomes less general and more specific (a Specific Material Designation?) and if AACR2 could be revised more quickly to include GMDs for new formats.

The inadequate ability of the authorized GMD to distinguish among formats has caused WLS to consider other display options. The first option was to change inadequate authorized GMDs to more specific local GMDs. The second option was to create a local field (910 field) for format terms that can then be mapped to display on the first results screen. This second option is already being used by another DYNIX public library system, so even though this would require re-mapping of the WLS database, it would not require entirely new programming by DYNIX. This second option would allow WLS to continue to use the authorized standard GMD, while achieving a more user-friendly OPAC display. However, the drawback of option two is that every AV bibliographic record would need to have a 910 field added to it. Under the first option, only the local GMD would have to be changed. WLS has chosen to replace inadequate prescribed GMDs with more specific local ones. Though this might appear more drastic, it is less labor intensive, does not add to record length, and, as mentioned earlier, in the MARC structure, is the most effectively positioned to display as it follows immediately after the title. WLS plans to make a separate index of its local GMD terms to enhance audiovisual material searching. When this index has been completed, catalogers will no longer need to add the format terms to subject headings.

Consistent cataloging practices, specifically correct tagging of the fixed fields and the addition of format terms for each AV item, has paid off. The retrospective global change of local GMDs was possible at little extra cost when the entire WLS database underwent an authority control process by LTI (Library Technologies, Inc.).

Following is a List of WLS Local GMD versus AACR2 GMD:

WLS GMD	*AACR2 GMD*
<For books>	
[large print]	[text (large print)]
[score]	[music]
<For AV>	
[audiocassette]	[sound recording]
[audiobook]	[sound recording]
[audiobook, abridged]	[sound recording]
[CD]	[sound recording]
[CD audiobook]	[sound recording]
[CD audiobook, Abridged	[sound recording]
[CD-ROM]	[computer file], [interactive multimedia]
[DVD]	[videorecording]
[Described Video]	[videorecording]
[game]	[game]
[kit]	[kit]
[software]	[computer file]
[toy]	[toy]
[video]	[videorecording]
[web site]	[computer file]

Example of the display before and after the GMD change:

Before:

TITLE/AUTHOR	GMD	DATE
1. Hanging up/ Ephron, Delia.		1995
2. Hanging up/ Ephron, Delia.		1996

3. Hanging up Ephron, Delia.	sound recording	2000
4. Hanging up	videorecording	2000
5. Hanging up	videorecording	2000
6. Hanging up Ephron, Delia.	sound recording	2000

After:

TITLE/AUTHOR	GMD	DATE
1. Hanging up/ Ephron, Delia.		1995
2. Hanging up/ Ephron, Delia.	Large print	1996
3. Hanging up Ephron, Delia.	Audiobook	2000
4. Hanging up	DVD	2000
5. Hanging up	Video	2000
6. Hanging up Ephron, Delia.	CD Audiobook	2000

EXPLOSION OF MEDIA TYPES IMPACTS BOOK CATALOGING

The following two cases demonstrate that the explosion of many different media type collections in public libraries have made an impact on book cataloging as well:

1. Public libraries have begun to use [large print] or [text (large print)] as the GMD for large type books.
2. Fiction titles in print format often have the subtitle "a novel" which alphabetically separates the book from the same title in other formats. Patrons thereby often miss the fiction title in the catalog title

search. To avoid this outcome, WLS catalogers began deleting the subtitle, "a novel" from the 245 field. Apparently, this practice is not uncommon among public libraries in recent years.

CONCLUDING REMARKS

In general, AV material takes much longer to catalog than books not only because of its inherent complexity but also because there are no authoritative cataloging records equivalent to the LC cataloging records for books. Even though WLS finds 80% of matching titles from the OCLC database, these records have to be examined carefully as they vary in completeness.

The potential for outsourcing the cataloging function continues to lurk behind the catalogers' increasingly hectic work environment. Most of the AV vendors, such as Baker & Taylor, Follett Audiovisual Resources, Recorded Books, etc., make MARC records available with the purchase of the items. User-friendly local practices such as those described in this article, based on the needs of local catalog users, the extent of local collections, and the functionality of local systems, may be lost if standard MARC records from the vendors are used. Until there is a centralized cataloging source that is sensitive to the needs of public library users, cost savings through outsourcing or replacing professional staff with non-professional staff will inevitably reduce the quality of service.

NOTES

1. Before 1989, individual library non-book cataloging records were not entered into the WLS generated COM catalog (monthly microfiche catalog). Records that were created by an individual library for non-book materials only appeared in that library's local card catalog.

2. CARL bought the UTLAS system in 1991, and subsequently became the WLS vendor. In 1999, WLS converted from CARL to the DYNIX system, an epixtech product.

Cataloging AV in School Libraries

Scott Piepenburg

SUMMARY. School libraries face many unique needs for the cataloging of audiovisual materials (AV). Searchers are relatively inexperienced, some being exposed to an online system for the first time. Librarians who create the records for these users frequently wear many hats, including bibliographic instruction, acquisitions, and management leader. Cataloging is often only one piece of their responsibilities. The users grown in school libraries will depend on the skills imparted to them by a librarian as they progress through the socio-educational system and go on to use public libraries, academic and research facilities, and corporate libraries. The skills they obtain here-knowledge of how an automated system works and how information can be mined from it-serve as a foundation for life-long learning. *[Article copies available for a fee from The Haworth Document Delivery Service: 1-800-342-9678. E-mail address: <getinfo@haworthpressinc.com> Website: <http://www.HaworthPress.com> © 2001 by The Haworth Press, Inc. All rights reserved.]*

Scott Piepenburg is Cataloging Supervisor at AIC, Inc., a library-outsourcing firm located in Canton, MI. He received a Master of Library and Information Science and a Master of Arts in History, from the University of Wisconsin-Milwaukee. At Follett Software Company, he organized and expanded the full-MARC retrospective conversion department and helped to create and populate their Alliance+ and AV Access products. He served for six years as District Cataloger/System Administrator for the Dallas Public School system in Dallas, TX. His publication history includes *Easy Marc and MARC Authority Records Made Easy*. He has presented workshops on cataloging and authority control and conducts one-day training sessions on cataloging and the MARC bibliographic format. He is a member of ALA and OLAC.

[Haworth co-indexing entry note]: "Cataloging AV in School Libraries." Piepenburg, Scott. Co-published simultaneously in *Cataloging & Classification Quarterly* (The Haworth Information Press, an imprint of The Haworth Press, Inc.) Vol. 31, No. 3/4, 2001, pp. 327-340; and: *The Audiovisual Cataloging Current* (ed: Sandra K. Roe) The Haworth Information Press, an imprint of The Haworth Press, Inc., 2001, pp. 327-340. Single or multiple copies of this article are available for a fee from The Haworth Document Delivery Service [1-800-342-9678, 9:00 a.m. - 5:00 p.m. (EST). E-mail address: getinfo@haworthpressinc.com].

© 2001 by The Haworth Press, Inc. All rights reserved.

KEYWORDS. School libraries, audiovisual cataloging, school library automation, online catalogs

INTRODUCTION

School libraries serve a variety of distinct users. Students depend on the library to have sources for their research papers, recreational reading, and exploratory research. The faculty depends on the library to support the research needs of their particular curriculum. This curriculum is often designed in accordance with local, state, or professional guidelines. It may attempt to assist students performing below grade level and also offer advanced students the opportunity to earn college credits. Administrators depend on the school library to maintain a collection that is relevant to the curriculum and within district or state funding agency guidelines, and to serve as a "control point" for some of the more expensive items found in a school.

School librarians have multiple roles. They serve the research needs of students of all grades and ability levels; the needs of teachers for items for classroom use as well as professional growth and development; and administrators who are seeking to show boards and parents that the library isn't just books anymore but also computer software, video recordings, manipulatives, Internet sites, sound recordings, and other items. All these items must be easily and consistently accessible regardless of their form or genre. Users cannot be presumed to "know" what they are looking for.

Into this environment, the school librarian is called upon to educate students about the library-how it is organized, how to find what they need, how to analyze information, and how to think critically. Somebody somewhere has to explain what those funny numbers and letters on a book mean and why some items can be taken home but not others. School librarians are charged with this mission. Students may have familiarity with encyclopedias and dictionaries, but these sources quickly become inadequate for their research. Instructors demand more detail, more sources, and more TYPES of sources.

SCHOOL LIBRARY AUTOMATION

From a simple program called Turtle to rudimentary word processing, computers were seen as the opportunity to organize information. The early systems were able to contain a barcode, a call number, an ISBN number, and 24 characters of title. The Sider, one of the first hard drives at a whopping 5MB helped alleviate this problem; two of them could be changed for the unheard of capacity of 10MB. Later, the DOS-based PC ushered in a new age of automation and 40MB hard drives were followed by those with 80MB.

Fast on the heels of these hardware innovations came honest-to-goodness library automation packages-packages designed from the ground up for libraries with features and specifications driven by users. School libraries, in their role as educators, were called upon to prepare students for research on the university and large public mainframe systems.

With the advent of computers, those vendors that had significant market share in the school library market sought to preserve and convert the data in their databases to an electronic form that could be sold to schools. Programmers, working with catalogers, endeavored to develop automated programs that could convert the existing data records into something at least vaguely resembling a MARC record.

In an effort to maximize data storage, some automation systems passed the incoming records through an algorithm that determined which tags were "unnecessary." Quite often these tags were ones now considered to be particularly valuable for keyword searching-the 5XX, 6XX, and 7XX fields. While we may cringe at the thought of that today, we need to remember that this is when PCs were still in their infancy; storage space was expensive and at a premium; and programmers were being pressed to offer more functionality, taking up more and more valuable disk space.

Libraries all over the country were having their records converted. But automation's most significant rule was often violated-never throw away data; you don't know when you will need it in the future. Authority control was (and sometimes still is) unheard of.

SCHOOL LIBRARY OPACS TODAY

Let's look at where we are today. We now have 20GB hard drives selling for under $200, cataloging available on the net, union catalogs set up in many states (some of which serve their specific users rather than national databases), and, the savior of us all, Z39.50, which allows us to access records all over the world and bring them home to our local system. We are saved. We have cataloging. We don't need the cataloger. We have records. No longer will we be at the whim of big and powerful libraries and vendors. We can get MARC records from the Library of Congress, we can get full MARC records from anywhere, and we have new powerful keyword search strategies. Not only do online catalogs allow keyword searching but their search features have been expanded to encompass more of the tags (more of the MARC record) and include adjacency and wild card search functionality. A search can be formulated to find exactly what we want, given enough time and computer power.

Remember the old adage, "If it's too good to be true, it probably is." It applies to cataloging also. One of the strengths of *AACR2* is that it contains options and provisions for local decisions. Subject schemes are replete with a variety of measures to provide for "customization" of entries, and libraries have been inconsistent in applying cataloging decisions, even within the same district. Even the definition of a "full MARC" record is open to some interpretation. Legacy records populate many systems and shared databases. In all too many school districts, there is not a trained, full-time professional cataloger to create records. The same person who does story time, orders the books, prints overdue notices, grades papers, pushes the chairs in, shelves books, and serves as homeroom teacher also has to create MARC records. Some districts that had a professional cataloger and centralized processing are closing those areas to provide for more "classroom" staff. The cost of another "non-teacher" is too much to bear politically. The expediencies of "more teachers, fewer administrators" is too hard to ignore. Just when school librarians need cataloging help the most, they are receiving it the least.

Fortunately, some districts are solidly committed to good cataloging. They recognize that the most valuable part of library automation is not the computers sitting on the tables-it is not the file server-it is not the interface or application software. The most valuable part of an automation project is the data. Good data results in a high level of flexibility, both in searching and software design. Good records in a district-wide union catalog enable students trained in library skills at one campus to be able to function at another. System responses to queries are predictable and understandable, users know how to search for what they want, and librarians are able to get on with the task of teaching.

WHAT MAKES A SUCCESSFUL SCHOOL AUTOMATION DATABASE?

Detailed cataloging is very important, but accuracy is equally important. Detailed records that represent a poor interpretation of the information are just as damaging as no information. Information entered inconsistently is confusing to students and faculty alike. Faculty, often the forgotten users of the database, depend on the catalog to locate materials that can be used for group instruction. Information from the items being cataloged must be entered accurately, timely, and in a consistent, correct manner. Let's step back and take a longer look at each one of these issues.

Accuracy is very important in a school environment. Users are beginning to develop their language skills and are often confused by similar sounding words, or words that look the same but sound different. They may not understand the concept of title or author. Correctly spelling a word can be a major achievement. In other types of libraries, users are more often able to anticipate these errors and re-formulate their query accordingly; not so with school students. Accuracy is critical. This, coupled with a very low patience factor, can quickly lead to frustrated users and dead-end searches. What is even more important is that these users will be called upon to use other systems in the future-at other school libraries, at the public libraries, and at academic institutions.

Timeliness is another factor in school libraries. Many factors in the acquisition process are outside of the librarian's control, such as principals signing off on purchase orders, purchasing actually placing the order, the vendor shipping it, and delays sometimes caused by a central receiving facility. Realistically, a school semester runs five months, only four of which may be actually devoted to instruction. If a librarian were to order an item on the first day of the semester, the window of time for it to be useful to a student is very short indeed. By the time the item arrives, is "received," and processed, the semester may well be over, or the time for which the item can be most useful has long since passed. States will frequently change curriculum focuses from one year to the next, necessitating new lesson plans, new methods of teaching, new competencies, and new materials to support those competencies. A video or software package that was the "hot" item last year may very well now collect dust on the shelf to be superseded by this year's "little darling" of choice. Given this high rate of obsolescence, the school librarian/cataloger cannot afford to allow items to languish in a processing area for weeks, or even days, at a time.

Thirdly, consistency and correctness may be less obvious to end users than the other two but can just as easily cause failed searches. In a centralized cataloging environment, with the processing center receiving and cataloging items for over two hundred schools in larger districts, consistency becomes a problem. Five or six different catalogers may be working on items from the same series at the same time, each oblivious to what the other is doing. Procedures can help to forestall some of these problems, but even a live authority file may not be dynamic enough. Inconsistencies can occur in the form of an author's name, the use of standard subject headings from one item to another, and whether two titles on a given tape are entered in a 245 ab$c format (or if the series title is used as the 245 $a value and the individual episodes recorded in a 505 but not in 740 tags). In these circumstances, it is not as important to determine which cataloger was "correct" and which was "wrong" as it is to attempt to formulate policies that help to head off these problems. Because of this, a "lead cataloger" or "data quality specialist" is critical to keep all staff working together and to serve as "referee" for problematic records.

At the Dallas Public School District, we employed a staff of approximately 20 paraprofessionals. Each person went through 40 clock hours of classroom training, then 40 hours of supervised on-the-job training. After that, they entered a period of revision that could last from 6 to 12 months, depending on the person. During this time they were assigned to a more experienced person who served as their mentor. The staff worked from a policy guide that was a combined training manual, example book, and style guide. A professional cataloger reviewed each person's original and updated cataloging, made changes as necessary, and coached the staff on improved methodologies.

School districts must be very aggressive in their cataloging policies and rules. Student populations are very fluid. On any given day, the Dallas Public School District had between 1,200 and 1,500 students changing campuses, grades, or facilities. Some students were assigned to special campuses on a temporary basis to meet special needs. These students were still considered to be students of their "home" campus but were temporarily relocated on account of in-district suspension, remedial assistance, pregnancy, or short-term advanced study programs. It is very important for students to be able to carry those skills learned in other grades and campuses to the new facility. The use of a dynamic district database (updated regularly during the day rather than by "batch mode" at night) facilitated this. As students progressed from elementary to middle to high schools, or to a special school or school for the gifted, they knew they were going to see consistency in the library interface and in the cataloging.

For those districts that are unable to provide real-time access to a district union catalog, it is even more important that all cataloging be done at a central facility. When a district is unable to staff a centralized facility, it is even more critical to develop a policy manual. Select a cross-section of the district's librarians and have them develop a policy manual that all will adhere to. In making up this committee, select librarians from all types and levels of schools, from all cataloging skill levels, and from all experience levels. This will prevent the policies from becoming slanted in any one direction.

Once a district has determined a method for creating consistent cataloging records, the district then needs to move on to determining exactly what a good MARC record is. School librarians are all too prone to the siren song of vendors bearing MARC records. Sales representatives for vendors know that they have "MARC records" but sometimes don't know where those records come from, what they do (aside from working in the automation system), or how they even get into the system. The wise school district will ask vendors for a sample disk in order to evaluate the records prior to loading. Unfortunately, many school librarians don't have the skills to recognize a good record. For an example, take a look at the two illustrations of cataloging records (see Record 1 and Record 2). While both are valid, Record 1 has more access points and more ways of getting to the information. The short amount of time invested in creating the longer record is money well invested.

Since many school libraries or districts cannot afford a full-time cataloger, they form consortiums, or cross-district union catalogs. These often occur at the state level, although there are some regional consortia. This has happened in such states as Texas, Oklahoma, Kansas, and Pennsylvania. The state database projects are often funded by state dollars and maintained by a state coordinator. This allows the project to be "tuned" to the needs of that state.

These state organizations face many of the same problems that OCLC faces. Many agencies are more concerned with "getting their records into the database" than with the quality of the database. Coordinating committees face constant struggles trying to balance the goal of high-quality data with that of high inclusion. If the standards are set so high that the records are of outstanding quality, the result would be few participants and the whole goal of record sharing would be unattainable. If the standards are set low enough that just about anybody can qualify, the database becomes filled with duplicate records; records without subject headings, 010 or 020 fields; and video recordings entered as books, thus making it worthless to users. While many of these union projects have a "filter" to catch inadequate records, these filters are often set for the least common denominator, with no effort made to screen out records that are valid MARC records but have no detailed cataloging information. If you set the bar low, people will often work only to

RECORD 1. Sample Cataloging Record-Sound Recording-Fully Cataloged Item. Note the extensive use of contents and summary notes, as well as the multiple **700** information.

```
LDR01199cjm  2200000 a 4500
00519940715210521.0
007sdufsngnnmmneu
008910625s1991    caujzn   a                 d
0241 $a8977891052
02820$aBC 9105$bBrain Child
040  $aTxCatMMA$cTxCatMMA
043  $anwaq---
1102 $aKilauea (Musical group)
24510$aAntigua blue$h[sound recording] /$cKilauea.
260  $aLake Arrowhead, Calif. :$bBrainchild Records,$cp1991.
300  $a1 sound disc (45 min., 26 sec.) :$bdigital, stereo. ;$c4 3/4
in.
500  $aAll pieces except On the edge of reality composed by Russ
Freeman.
538  $aCompact disc.
504  $aIncludes discography.
5050 $aAdventure highway (5:28) -- Antigua blue (4:39) -- The love
goddess (5:28) -- Isle of Lucy (3:42) -- One romantic evening (4:09) -
- Barbados (4:50) -- Pirate's cove (5:32) -- On the edge of reality /
Russ Freeman & Christopher Ho (6:12) -- Sunrise in La Jolla (4:52)
5110 _aBrandon Fields, Clair Marlo, Pat coil, Steve Reid, Russ
Freeman, Christopher Ho, Tony Morales, Daniel Ho.
650 0$aNew Age music.
651 0$aAntigua.
7001 $aFreeman, Russ.
7001 $aFields, Brandon.
7001 $aMarlo, Clair.
7001 $aCoil, Pat.
7001 $aReid, Steve.
7001 $aMorales, Tony.
7001$aHo, Daniel.
```

RECORD 2. Sample Cataloging Record-Sound Recording-Less than Thorough Cataloging. Although it meets standards to be considered a "MARC" record, notice how much less information it contains.

```
LDR01199cjm  2200000 a 4500
008910625s1991    caujzn   a                 d
0241 $a8977891052
040  $aTxCatMMA$cTxCatMMA
1102 $aKilauea (Musical group)
24510$aAntigua blue$h[sound recording] /$cKilauea.
260  $aLake Arrowhead, Calif. :$bBrainchild Records,$cp1991.
300  $a1 sound disc :$bdigital, stereo. ;$c4 3/4 in.
500  $aCompact disc.
5110 _aBrandon Fields, Clair Marlo, Pat coil, Steve Reid, Russ
Freeman, Christopher Ho, Tony Morales, Daniel Ho.
650 0$aNew Age music.
651 0$aAntigua.
7001 $aFreeman, Russ.
7001$aHo, Daniel.
```

that bar. Set the bar higher, in increments, and there is a desire to bring everybody up together and improve quality.

In addition to the difficulty of locating good records to download, school libraries purchase a diverse range of items-books, puppets, video recordings, computer software, boxes of mineral samples, microscopes, skeletons-just about anything that's used in a classroom. Because libraries are relatively secure and users have to "sign out" items, they are often also called upon to be the storage venue for the most expensive pieces of AV equipment. Many districts depend on the library to have a current and consistent inventory of who has which piece of equipment, down to the serial number on a given piece of equipment. One way to accomplish this is for the librarian to create a detailed MARC record for each piece. Other items used in classrooms can also be quite expensive. In a high school environment, four or five science labs may need to share an expensive lab kit. Again, these lab kits are cataloged and stored at the library. Teachers can often reserve these items in advance using a media-booking module. Boxes of rocks used to demonstrate hardness are fairly common, as are collections of minerals, plants, microscope slides, and chemicals. Again, all have to be cataloged in detail; all need to be accessible in the OPAC.

CRITICAL ACCESS POINTS FOR AUDIOVISUAL MATERIALS

One of the most useful cataloging tools for all of these diverse items is the 710 tag. In this field, the librarian can code the manufacturer of the equipment or item. By being able to access this information, it is possible to quickly locate particular makes and models for inventory purposes. In addition to the 710 tag, the 250 field is very useful for recording model numbers in equipment records. Depending on the system, these can be searchable. If not, they still serve as very useful inventory tools. The date an item was added to the collection, as well as the cost, is useful for determining the age of equipment, how much needs to be budgeted for repair costs each year, and when the item should be scheduled for replacement. Depending on the automation system, the holdings record can also serve as a place to store other information like when a bulb was last replaced, what type of bulb it takes, and when it was last serviced, although this is a less typical use for an automation system.

School libraries purchase materials for students and faculty to use. Videotapes, in particular, can differ significantly from those sold to the mass market. Given the relatively small market that school libraries constitute, it is not cost effective to place a single 30 or 60-minute episode on one video. Some vendors will put two or three episodes of a television program on a single videotape, even though the episodes may not have similar content matter. These items need to be available by each title and by all the subjects covered on the tape. This requires the use of 505 and 740 tags to describe the multiple titles and multiple subject headings to accurately provide access to each episode. Again, the use of the 710 is critical to bring items from the same publisher or creator together. Due to the repackaging of many items for marketing purposes, titles on boxes or sleeves may bear little resemblance to the original item. New titles, particularly series, are often created. The librarian needs to determine if these are actually series, series-like entries, or uniform titles. If the library purchases multiple similarly packaged items from the same vendor, but weeks or months apart, decisions made one day may not be the same as those made another day, resulting in inconsistent access in the database. The librarian also needs to ascertain who actually is the producer and distributor of a given item; again, factors which affect retrievability.

At the high school level, students depend on the library to be "relevant" to their daily lives. With the advent of the Internet, libraries are pressed to collect not only items that directly support the curriculum but also to collect items for non-classroom use. In some districts, high school libraries will collect modern re-makes of classic movies, as well as movies based on classic works. Movies based on classic pieces of literature, like *Romeo Must Die* and *West Side Story* touch students' personal lives. These items need to be accessible, both in their own right as well as through their parent work, in this case, Shakespeare's *Romeo and Juliet*. If the video recording is cataloged correctly, the record will contain a 700 subfield t with the title of the original work-*Romeo and Juliet*. In a Windows online catalog environment, a student performing a search on the original work will also be led to movies, sound recordings, and other iterations of the original work. More than one student has picked up an original work because they are curious about where the story came from. This access has always been possible but seldom exercised. Schools must make use of this accessibility to the collection.

Of the faculty who make extensive use of the library, there are those who actively suggest items for purchase and search the collection for those items that can be used in classroom settings. Then there are others who use the same items year in and year out, never checking to see if there are new items. The savvy librarian will look to see what these people are using and, if the topic has a valid place in the curriculum, will attempt to acquire newer, updated material. This material must be cataloged in a way that the non-motivated searcher will find it when looking up their old standbys. Smart subject cataloging, along with good solid cross-references, will make items fly off the shelf.

The 520 tag, which summarizes an item's content, is critical. It is not possible to emphasize too strongly the necessity of good content and summary notes, particularly for AV materials. The 520 tag can be "loaded" with words that, when combined with Boolean operators during a keyword search, will work in concert with the subject headings to guide the user to what they want.

As automation hardware becomes more powerful at a lower price, many search functionalities are being added. One of the most powerful is use of the fixed field area (008 tag) for information screening. In fact, all of the 0XX tags represent powerful access points. The most notable ones are the Leader, the 007, and the 008/006. These allow a searcher, in a properly designed system with properly encoded records, to limit searches by running time, language, year of publication, format, sound characteristics, and accompanying material. Too many librarians have short-changed these areas since "they are not searchable." The irony is that a programmer finds these areas useful because they contain highly coded, standardized, consistently located information. Many systems, when performing a date-qualified search, do not go to the 260 subfield c, but rather depend on the Dates area of the 008. The 007 can be used to differentiate a laserdisc from a DVD or a video from a film. School librarians, in particular, need to code this information accurately since it is of high searchable potential. Failing this access, it is even more critical that a library correctly enter the proper GMD in the 245$h. For students, they may have to specifically have a non-print item for a report; for faculty, they may be looking for something to be used in classroom instruction. Some Windows-based systems no longer display GMDs, but rather utilize an icon that displays based on information in the Leader Type of Record code.

The nature of research in a school library, both by faculty and students, demands more than simple title access. Indexing the names of producers, directors, and music composers is critical for students doing biographical research papers. The entry of actors in 700 tags is also highly recommended. Students will often be called upon to view the works of a particular actor or director, or to see how a composer's works in a movie differ from his or her works for "straight" commercial sale. School libraries need to provide access points consistently, since once students see records created in a particular way, they will expect all records to provide that same level of access. All too often, librarians will fall into the trap of entering only those names which are "significant" or "important"-not significant or important in the movie, but rather those that are significant or important in popular culture. Too many librarians have ignored the insignificant producer of a bizarre movie entitled *THX-1138*. This film, while not receiving critical acclaim, was the first major motion picture by then-novice George Lucas. If properly cataloged, the item is accessible to researchers doing historical background work on George Lucas. If not, his film is lost to the researcher.

For AV records, liberal use should be made of the 7XX tags. As seen above, the 700 tag is very useful, both for finding those involved in a production and for the history of the production. The same can be said of the 710 tag. While students will not generally conduct searches using this information, faculty members use it extensively. They conduct a search for those companies, such as Encyclopedia Britannica and PBS Home Video, that have produced useful items in the past. These searches allow faculty to find items that have a demonstrated track record in the classroom. Make no mistake about it, publisher reputation DOES count. While publisher information may be accessible in a 260 tag, it is in an uncontrolled format in this field. Recording it in a 710 tag places it under authority control, permitting the use of cross-references to link together those publishers that have gone through a variety of name changes, mergers, acquisitions, etc. Instructors frequently will sit down with a vendor's catalog and see what the library owns.

The cataloger needs to assign as many subject headings as is necessary to elucidate the content, as well as the format, of the material. The "rule of three" is of less significance here than fully describing the content of the carrier. Please note the phrase "content of the carrier." This phrase is used since a given carrier (videocassette, laserdisc, CD-ROM, etc.) may have multiple episodes or segments of information on it. On some of the formats, like laserdiscs and DVDs, these titles can be accessed directly, not linearly as on a videotape. As noted earlier, if an item has multiple non-related episodes, it becomes incumbent on the cataloger to make certain that each episode has adequate subject access. If one applies the "rule of three" to each episode, then a video with three episodes on it could have nine subject headings to describe the content.

In addition to these "content" or topical subject headings, there are form and genre subject headings. These are used to indicate special information about the item. These headings can take the shape of "video recordings for the hearing impaired," "computer software," and "short films." In the hands of a trained and skilled searcher, these headings help narrow down the list of items that an instructor would want to use in a classroom environment. It is very important that the terms used here be consistent to facilitate Boolean searches.

The 730 tag, used for uniform titles, is a critical search option for faculty and, to a lesser extent, for students. This tag helps pull together all the particular episodes of a television series or program with a single search. This means that a searcher can find all the library's holdings of the PBS series *Nova* under a single title search. While the list of titles for a program may be extensive, a searcher can use aboutness to scan the titles for the particular episode they are looking for. They can also combine the uniform title with relevant subject descriptors in a Boolean search to find a particular episode they saw or vaguely remember. Again, the effort devoted to good keyword descriptors pays great dividends.

Even though individual episode titles have been entered in the 505 tag, it may be necessary to repeat those episode titles in 740 tags depending on the indexing of your local system. While the 505 is usually indexed for searching by keyword, it frequently is not indexed for title searching, even if it has been subfielded with t and r. For those physical carriers that contain multiple episodes or titles, the 740 permits direct searching of them without having to resort to keyword searches. This benefits a searcher looking for a particular title that has been published by different organizations at different times. A title search will retrieve them all.

Moving back to the top of the MARC record, we find the 008/006 tags, which, for our purposes, will be referenced by the single term "008." School librarians frequently ignore the 008 tag (fixed fields). This is unfortunate since it contains a wealth of information that, while entered elsewhere in the MARC record, is coded in a structured format, facilitating the ability to more efficiently and inexpensively design software to read these codes and data. The proper entry of this information, coupled with the use of a well-designed search interface, permit the librarian, students, and faculty to specify a range of materials, format, running times, target audiences, and country of publication. Each one of these, while not significant on its own, takes on a far larger role when combined with other search parameters.

The 024 and 028 tags have become very valuable search points, especially since one of them is very easy to enter. The Universal Product Code (UPC), found on many items, can be recorded in the 024 field. This is the same barcode that is used by retail merchants for pricing at the checkout line. When entered into an online system and indexed, it can be used to quickly search for items in the database. It is very easy to enter since the user only needs to scan the code using a standard circulation scanner. This then allows the receiving area to quickly scan incoming items to see if they are in the database. If they are, holdings can immediately be added and the item shipped back out, or a routing slip with the bibliographic record can be printed and attached to the item to save time for the catalogers. Note that this is not designed to be a replacement for item barcodes; the UPC will be the same for all copies of a given title.

The 028 field contains the publisher item number. For video recordings, this is frequently found on the spine of the box or the label of the item. For sound recordings, it is on the disc label, and for kits it may be anywhere on the item. These numbers are usually recorded on the item itself, as well as in a publisher's catalog. With these numbers, a searcher can find which items in a vendor's catalog that the library owns. This helps the faculty member to determine which items, if any, are available and which should be suggested to the library for ordering so that a complete set of the subject matter can be retained for consistent educational purposes.

CONCLUSION

The cataloging of items for school libraries needs to satisfy different user groups-students looking for items for their research papers, faculty for items to use in classroom presentations and to foster growth, and administrators to make certain that particular library holdings are consistent with stated curriculum guidelines. Each user brings different wants and needs to the catalog, as well as different searching strategies. The MARC record needs to be entered and coded with multiple levels of redundancy to accommodate these different users and their methodologies. In this age of uncontrolled vocabularies and Internet searching, a library database with consistent, defined terminology and predictable, definable results is the most significant thing we as catalogers can provide to our users.

Non-Print Media at the National Library of Medicine

Diane L. Boehr
Meredith L. Horan

SUMMARY. The National Library of Medicine has maintained a leadership role in the promotion of audiovisual formats for many years. An overview of the development of producing, collecting, and cataloging non-print material at NLM is provided, along with an examination of NLM current cataloging practices. *[Article copies available for a fee from The Haworth Document Delivery Service: 1-800-342-9678. E-mail address: <getinfo@haworthpressinc.com> Website: <http://www.HaworthPress.com> © 2001 by The Haworth Press, Inc. All rights reserved.]*

KEYWORDS. Cataloging practices, audiovisuals, collection development, AVLINE®, media, historical films, national libraries

---

Diane L. Boehr, BS, MLS, is Head, Cataloging Unit II, Cataloging Section, National Library of Medicine, Bethesda, MD; Adjunct Faculty, College of Information Studies, University of Maryland, College Park; and Chair, Media Resources Committee, ALCTS, ALA (E-mail: boehrd@mail.nlm.nih.gov). Meredith L. Horan, BA, MLS, MEd, is AV Cataloger, Cataloging Section; Auxiliary Reference Staff, Public Services Division, National Library of Medicine, Bethesda, MD; and Chair, Cataloging Policy Committee, Online Audiovisual Catalogers, Inc. (E-mail: horanm@mail.nlm.nih.gov).

[Haworth co-indexing entry note]: "Non-Print Media at the National Library of Medicine." Boehr, Diane L., and Meredith L. Horan. Co-published simultaneously in *Cataloging & Classification Quarterly* (The Haworth Information Press, an imprint of The Haworth Press, Inc.) Vol. 31, No. 3/4, 2001, pp. 341-354; and: *The Audiovisual Cataloging Current* (ed: Sandra K. Roe) The Haworth Information Press, an imprint of The Haworth Press, Inc., 2001, pp. 341-354. Single or multiple copies of this article are available for a fee from The Haworth Document Delivery Service [1-800-342-9678, 9:00 a.m. - 5:00 p.m. (EST). E-mail address: getinfo@haworthpressinc.com].

© 2001 by The Haworth Press, Inc. All rights reserved.

INTRODUCTION

The National Library of Medicine (NLM), established in 1836 as the Library of the Army Surgeon General's Office, has emphasized the importance of acquiring health information in print and non-print formats. John Shaw Billings, NLM's first director, and later directors, especially Frank Rogers, recognized the importance of collecting AV materials. Today, the audiovisual collection consists of more than 35,000 titles and has been a part of the library collection for well over a hundred years.

Most of the earliest non-print materials acquired by the Library are now part of NLM's historical collection. While much of this historical collection consists of still pictures, it also contains many historical films, as well as some realia. As early as the 1870s, the Library's first director, John Shaw Billings, acquired a mannequin and skulls for the Library's museum.[1] Billings was intent on including "visual records of the history of medicine"[2] within the collection. Director Frank Rogers established a collection strategy for medical movies as early as the mid-1950s.[3] By 1961, this original non-print collection contained more than 600 items.[4] The current Historical Audiovisuals Collection had its origin in the "Medical Motion Picture Collection," established in 1953 in the Armed Forces Medical Library in Washington, D.C. It moved to the National Medical Audiovisual Facility (NMAF) in Atlanta in 1962[5] under the management of the Communicable Disease Center and later became the National Medical Audiovisual Center (NMAC). The film collection returned to the National Library of Medicine, in Bethesda, Maryland, and eventually, after being part of NLM's Public Services Division for a short time, organizationally became part of the History of Medicine Division. More than 2,500 historical films and videorecordings are now part of this archival collection.

Since the mid-1950s, NLM has recognized the importance of biomedical AV resources and has played a leadership role in integrating these materials into the library functions associated with selection, bibliographic control, and education. This recognition produced AVLINE (AudioVisuals on-LINE). In January 1976, the NLM made AVLINE,[6] a database of audiovisuals, publicly available to its ELHILL® database subscribers. USMARC formatted AVLINE records became available on a subscription basis in July 1985. In December 1994, OCLC loaded the entire backfile of AVLINE, at that time a total of 27,354 records, making the NLM media collection available to OCLC users.

Today, all cataloging records, including books, audiovisuals, journals, computer files, and other materials in the Library's collections are integrated on the Web in LOCATORplus (*http://www.nlm.nih.gov/locatorplus/locatorplus.html*), NLM's online public access catalog. LOCATORplus replaces the catalog databases CATLINE®, SERLINE®, and AVLINE, formerly available through ELHILL. Catalog records should not be confused with citations to individual articles within journals, which are found online in PubMed® (formerly MEDLINE®), or in the print tool *Index Medicus*®.[7]

NLM's PRODUCTION AND EDUCATIONAL TECHNOLOGY COMPONENTS

The National Medical Audiovisual Center, located in Atlanta, became part of NLM in 1967. NMAC's mission was to improve the quality and facilitate distribution of biomedical AVs in medical schools and throughout the biomedical community. NMAC became a central repository for medical films, compiled catalogs of AV cataloging data, and operated a large medical motion picture studio. NMAC staff helped schools design learning resource centers and develop, test, and evaluate instructional media materials. NMAC staff, along with a bounty of films, including those from the original NMAF collection, transferred to Bethesda and its emphasis shifted to acquisition and distribution, rather than production.

Another example of NLM's dedication to the promotion of educational technology in the health sciences began in 1984 with the establishment of the Learning Center for Interactive Technology (TLC), a component of the Lister Hill National Center for Biomedical Communications, which at that time absorbed certain NMAC functions. This center, along with those at the Department of Education and the Smithsonian Institution, became a national demonstration lab devoted to learning and developing microcomputer and videodisc technology. NLM TLC staff offered on and offsite workshops and tutorials using experimental and commercially available products such as PathMac, Electric Cadaver, and Microanatomy Video Library. NLM TLC staff also conducted their own research and development of interactive technology applications. They produced a series of monographs[8] and reports, developed videodisc and computer-based instructional materials, and created courseware and authoring system databases related to biomedical education. The Learning Center's mission has evolved with changes in technology and is now known as The Learning Collaboratory for High Performance Computing and Communication. Although the acronym TLC remains, the Center's focus is on collaborative research and development of next generation computing technologies related to high performance computing projects that NLM is funding.

NLM AND THE MEDIA QUALITY ISSUE

As far back as the 1970s, NLM provided a leadership role in evaluating medical AV resources. NMAC, at that time NLM's audiovisual production arm, conducted team review sessions cooperatively, beginning in 1973, with the Association of American Medical Colleges (AAMC) and the American Association of Dental Schools (AADS) and later in 1975 also in cooperation with the American Nurses' Association (ANA) and the National League for Nursing (NLN). The review process was intended to encourage media sharing in schools and health care institutions and to sensitize audiovisual producers about quality standards. Teams, consisting of outside consultants, included specialists in content, instructional design, and production techniques. The team review process was replaced by individual critical reviews until NLM discontinued the formal review mechanism. "Attributes of Quality in Audiovisual Materials" developed in 1980 by representatives from the National Medical Audiovisual Center, the Health Sciences Communications Association, the American Association of Dental Schools, the American Veterinary Medical Association, the Association of American Medical Colleges, the Association of Biomedical Communications Directors, and the Veterans Administration served as a guide to reviewers.[9]

For the years 1975 to 1981, AVLINE records served as the collection point for this review information, as well as acquisitions and cataloging data. The review data included the ratings of "Highly Recommended," "Recommended," and "Not Recommended" as well as guidance on educational levels and specialty audiences. Critical summaries were also included. Initially, NLM chose to withhold records rated "Not Recommended" from the database after generally notifying the producer about the item's shortcomings. By 1976, the number of "Not Recommended" items had risen to 18.7 percent of the total items reviewed.[10] The exclusion of "Not Recommended" items from the database did, however, fail as a concept. Searchers were unclear whether an item not found in the database was not reviewed or not recommended. Eventually, NLM included all rated audiovisuals in the database, so it was clearer when a particular title had been reviewed, but not highly rated in the review process. NLM, concurrently, was developing and implementing an acquisitions plan to collect high-quality AVs for health professionals, which were current-produced in the past three years-and available nationally, a plan which, in the early 1980s, would supersede the peer review process.

The Library, in collaboration with Health Sciences Communications Association, launched an experimental AV cataloging-in-publication (CIP) program in 1978 to improve bibliographic control of non-print media. A two-day introductory CIP workshop for 11 participating producers was held at NLM. In 1979, the program became part of NLM's regular workflow and was expanded to include additional producers whose instructional materials fell within AVLINE's scope.[11] Brochures were created to foster meaningful and consistent bibliographic information throughout the credit frames and accompanying material. Producers regularly received feedback and their items received top priority in the peer review process. NLM's AV CIP program terminated in 1994. The Library witnessed dwindling interest from the production community and redirected its resources to new receipts.

NLM AND AUDIOVISUALS TODAY

Physically, NLM's current AV collection is housed in several locations. Current non-print material is shelved in the Learning Resource Center, an open stack, publicly accessible collection. Older material is kept in closed stacks, and some rare or historical items are in cold storage at NLM and offsite in Pennsylvania. Eighty-five percent of the AV collection consists of visual materials (videos, motion pictures, or slides), six percent are computer files, and nine percent are sound recordings. The Library's most unique computer file is the Visible Human Project®,[12] consisting of two-dimensional digital images of a male and a female cadaver. The over 55 gigabyte data contain more than 15,000 images in the form of color cryosections, computed tomography (CT) scans, and magnetic resonance image (MRI) scans which are widely shared and reconfigured in a variety of projects.

The Library also has a collection of over 60,000 images dating from the 15th century to the present in the Prints and Photos Collection of the

History of Medicine Division (HMD). It is available to the public through the Images from the History of Medicine (IHM) database available on the Web at *http://wwwihm.nlm.nih.gov*. Other unusual objects like stethoscopes, medicine containers, aboriginal woodcarvings, and prepared slides also reside in HMD, but the bulk of medical objects and specimens, formerly part of the NLM collection, is now housed at the National Museum of Health and Medicine in Washington, D.C.

MEDIA COLLECTION DEVELOPMENT POLICY AT NLM

At NLM, media are selectively acquired according to principles outlined in the *Collection Development Manual of the National Library of Medicine,* 3rd ed. (1993).[13] The Library's intent is to collect substantive English-language non-print titles " . . . produced for use by health professionals or those that are of potential interest to historians."[14] Following these guidelines, NLM targets its collecting efforts on audiovisuals important for current research and education that are likely to be of future historical value. The collection focuses on works that document biomedical innovations, trends in the delivery of health care and professional health care education, important biomedical issues and controversies, public health outreach efforts, and the life and work of notable individuals in biomedicine. Collection emphasis is on authoritative works produced by professional societies and federal health agencies, in standard U.S. formats. Audiovisuals in foreign languages, including those produced in the U.S., and audiovisuals produced elsewhere, even those in English, are collected only when they contain " . . . unique information or are of special historical importance."[15]

GENERAL CATALOGING POLICIES

NLM maintains a single cataloging manual for the entire Cataloging Section. Although certain segments are material specific, the general principle is to have overall cataloging policies that can be applied to all types of material. Cataloging levels, authority procedures, and subject analysis and classification policies are consistent among different materials and formats.

In accordance with AACR2, NLM has always viewed AV material being cataloged. A variety of video machines, movie projectors, slide projectors, and cassette players are available to the AV catalogers.

However, for direct access electronic resources, NLM is cataloging from the items and labels, rather than mounting the pieces, because of the physical and licensing difficulties that can be encountered in trying to run various types of software on a cataloger's desktop machine.

NLM was an early supporter of the streamlining advantages offered by the core cataloging standards developed under the auspices of the Program for Cooperative Cataloging (PCC). In fact, once the PCC core level standard for books[16] was approved, NLM implemented its own core level standard for videorecordings and other visual material, which was used until the formal adoption of the PCC *Core Bibliographic Record for Graphic Materials*[17] and the PCC *Core Bibliographic Record for Moving Image Materials*.[18] In March 1999, NLM adopted the PCC *Core Bibliographic Record for Monographic Computer Files*.[19] NLM catalogs current AV material at the core level if no full cataloging copy is available.

Films that are part of NLM's Historical Audiovisuals Collection are cataloged according to archival cataloging rules from the *Archival Moving Image Materials* (AMIM).[20] The collection includes instructional films, public health documentaries, commercial films with medical themes, public service announcements, histories of medicine on film, recordings of public lectures and ceremonies, and documentary footage of biomedical research. Bibliographic records contain extensive descriptive abstracts.

COPY CATALOGING

Only recently, with the implementation of the Voyager system in 1998, has NLM begun to make use of OCLC copy for AV material. However, because NLM almost always has to add medical subjects and classification to existing records, the copy cataloging procedures are unlike those of most other libraries. All copy cataloging at NLM is assigned to professional librarians. Approximately 80 percent of NLM's AV cataloging remains original cataloging.

The point of copy cataloging is to process materials expeditiously; therefore, NLM attempts to keep editing of copy records to a minimum. In general, choice of main entry is not changed. Omissions of required data elements in the body of a copy cataloging record are supplied and typographical errors are corrected. Using copy means less keyboarding needs to be done by Selection and Acquisition staff who are responsible for providing the skeletal bibliographic record prior to ordering, or upon receipt of material, but continues to require a significant time expenditure on the part of catalogers who still assign a complete complement of subjects and a classification number, as well as verify the bibliographic description and verify that all access points are properly established in the national authority file.

ACCESS POINTS-NAMES

Because of NLM's traditional focus on the medical professional, AV policies for access points have always been slightly different than those of an academic or public library, regardless of whether the cataloging is being done at full or core level.

For original cataloging, NLM emphasizes corporate responsibility in the production of an audiovisual, unless a personal author is clearly named. Generally, only health sciences professionals contributing to a program are included in the bibliographic record. Whether these persons are listed in the statement of responsibility area or listed in a credits note is a matter of cataloger judgment, dependent upon the wording, prominence, and layout of the item.

Prior to 1995, NLM did provide access points for all persons and corporate bodies mentioned in the statement of responsibility and/or the credits note. Beginning with the implementation of the NLM core cataloging policy, for original cataloging, access points are now limited to the first person or body appearing in the statement of responsibility, plus the first person named in the credits note. Text word access is available to retrieve any other names that appear in the body of a record.

NLM applies these guidelines in a similar manner when considering access points in copy cataloging records. Since NLM normally provides access only to principal individuals or entities associated with a title, any other headings are removed from the bibliographic record, although existing 508 (Credits) or 511 (Cast) notes are retained for text word access. As a PCC participant, NLM creates authority records for the national authority file for all access points used on a full or core level bibliographic record in its files. By removing these access points, NLM does not need to search the national authority file or establish new NACO headings for minor contributors on audiovisual copy records. Exceptions are made when these names appear as main or subject added entries, or are retained as access points for any other reasons.

ACCESS POINTS-SUBJECT HEADINGS

The principles of subject heading assignment at NLM are similar to those at any library. Using NLM's Medical Subject Headings

(MeSH®), NLM assigns a complement of terms that accurately and completely describe the contents of the item as specifically as possible without redundancy. Subject access is always considered to be of primary importance, so that even for material receiving core level cataloging, complete subject access is provided, rather than the "at least 1-2 headings" prescribed by the core standard.[21]

MeSH is a systematic thesaurus of medical and related concepts, that is available online at *http://www.nlm.nih.gov/mesh/MBrowser.html*. It is also published in print in three different arrangements: alphabetically (*Medical Subject Headings, Annotated Alphabetic List*),[22] hierarchically in "trees" (*Medical Subject Headings, Tree Structures*),[23] and in a keyword format (*Permuted Medical Subject Headings*).[24]

MeSH allows for the combination of main headings and topical subheadings to fully convey concepts. If more than three subheadings apply to a particular subject, the term is used alone, without any subheadings. Similarly, if more than three specific subjects in the same tree would be appropriate, a more general subject is assigned.

In late 1998, NLM made some major changes in the way subjects are constructed within its own catalog. Rather than using a pre-coordinated approach, with subject strings consisting of topic--subtopic--geographic--language--form, NLM uses only topical and subtopical headings in the 650 field. The geographic subject terms are stored in the 651 field. Publication Types--Genre terms (formerly referred to as form subdivisions), that indicate what items are, either intellectually or physically, are stored in the 655 field in NLM's cataloging system. Only intellectual genre terms, such as Atlases, Examination Questions, or Nurses' Instruction are used in the 655. Physical formats, such as Motion Picture, Slide, or Videocassette were eliminated from the subject strings entirely because the online catalog allows limiting of searches by format, based on the 006 or 007 coding. Since the format is also carried in the general material designation (GMD) (245 $h) and the physical description (300), the added redundancy of also carrying the format in the subject string was felt to be unnecessary. Since Voyager also allows limiting by Language, which is stored in 008 and in 041, language has also been eliminated from the subject string.

These changes were instituted to bring Cataloging Section subject practices into closer conformance with MEDLINE indexing practices, since NLM planned to implement a "gateway" approach to its resources to allow seamless searching across multiple databases. (The initial version of the NLM Gateway is available at *http://gateway.nlm.nih.*

gov/gw/Cmd.) Having consistent policies in subject assignment across databases will ensure more consistent retrieval for users.

The above description reflects records that are seen or accessed directly from NLM's online catalog, LOCATORplus. Records which are distributed to the utilities or to other subscribers have the subject headings in the traditional subject string 650 $a $x $z $v. Behind the scenes programming (combined with some internal coding by catalogers) restructures the subject headings on distributed records, so that terms for language and genre appear attached to the appropriate subject headings with the correct subfielding. Certain subject headings, chiefly age groups, are found as 650s in the ILS, but distributed as topical subheadings. See Figure 1 for examples of a subject display in LOCATORplus vs. the distributed display. For a more complete discussion of NLM subject assignments, see *Application of MeSH for Medical Catalogers,* a document on the NLM Cataloging Section Web page at *http://www.nlm.nih.gov/tsd/cataloging/catmesh.html*.

NLM recognizes that the changes in subject structure have had a particular impact on medical AV catalogers outside the library. If other libraries wish to continue to use physical format subdivisions on subject headings, they may choose to add them to the subject string; however, they are no longer in accord with NLM practice. While NLM was able to do a global conversion which removed all the former physical format subheadings from the records within its own catalog, other libraries have large numbers of records in their files with these older headings. When libraries search pre-1998 records in sources outside the NLM catalog, such as in OCLC and other utilities, confusion may arise because the older records encountered in those sources and in individual library catalogs still have the old subject strings. Despite these difficulties, the internal restructuring of subject headings at NLM holds great promise for enhanced subject retrieval across NLM records of all types.

CLASSIFICATION

NLM provides a classification number for all audiovisual materials, based on the *National Library of Medicine Classification*.[25] The classification number assigned corresponds to the primary subject focus of the material. NLM does not cutter its audiovisuals; instead they are assigned accession numbers which are preceded by letter codes representing the physical format of the material (e.g., VC for videocassette, SL for slide, MP16 for 16 mm motion pictures, etc.), followed by the date

FIGURE 1

Subject strings in NLM ILS and on distributed records:

In VOYAGERplus:	650 12	$a Skin Diseases $x diagnosis
	650 22	$a Skin Diseases $x therapy
	655 7	$a Atlases $2 mesh
Distributed as:	650 12	$a Skin Diseases $x diagnosis $v Atlases.
	650 22	$a Skin Diseases $x therapy $v Atlases.
In VOYAGERplus:	650 12	$a HIV Infections $x prevention & control $9a
	650 22	$a Adolescent Health Services $x organization & administration
	650 22	$a Adolescence
	651 2	$a France
Distributed as:	650 12	$a HIV Infections $x prevention & control $x Adolescence $z France.
	650 22	$a Adolescent Health Services $z France.

of publication of the item. For example, the first video received on substance abuse would be assigned the classification number: WM 270 $b VC no.1 1987, the next video received on that topic would be classed as: WM 270 $b VC no. 2 1991, and so on. Use of accession numbers simplifies shelving, keeping similar formats together on the shelves, and requires minimal rearrangement of material as new items are received. Since the majority of audiovisuals are entered under title, the need for a cutter number to collocate works by the same author is not felt to be very significant.

ENHANCEMENTS TO AV RECORDS

In accordance with the core guidelines, NLM supplies an abstract or summary field when one is readily available from the producer or distributor. The text of the 520 (Summary, etc.) field is preceded with the word "(Producer)," acknowledging that the producer is the source of the text. While catalogers are not expected to develop their own abstracts, they are expected to edit a producer's abstract to remove any judgmental words in order to provide a neutral summary.

Another note that NLM always provides, if applicable, is information about continuing education credit that may be available for viewing an item. While this note is not part of the core standard, or even a note specified in AACR2, knowing that a program is approved for continuing education by a particular group is of great importance to NLM's users. The note also follows NLM's long-term practice of focusing on the educational use of its collection.

As described earlier, older AV records contained reviews of the quality of the material provided through the review process coordinated with the Association of American Medical Colleges. These review data were incorporated into the general note fields of the bibliographic record. Such data still exist on older non-print records in NLM's LOCATORplus.

Older AV records also contained a special NLM-defined field for Procurement Source. In NLM's internal file, authority records had locally designed fields to store addresses and phone numbers for these organizations. As more material was acquired from commercial sources, rather than from universities or hospital faculties, procurement name and address information became less critical for acquisition purposes. Since the workload of maintaining current address information was great, with the implementation of Voyager, the local NLM Procurement Source field was eliminated from the bibliographic record, and distributor information is carried in the 260, if it differs from the publisher. Addresses and phone numbers are no longer carried in NLM authority records.

CONCLUSION

Although the specific details of the AV bibliographic records created by NLM over the years may vary to reflect changing standards and priorities, NLM's commitment to providing quality bibliographic control to this material has remained steadfast. NLM tries to carefully balance the need for timely access to current material with sufficient authority controlled headings for discovery and retrieval. NLM has utilized strategies to increase productivity, such as the implementation of the core record and the use of copy cataloging. NLM is continuing to take a proactive stance on issues related to non-print bibliographic control, and is committed to broadening the expertise of its catalogers as they tackle cataloging of electronic resources. NLM will continue to contribute to the evolving standards needed as the variety of non-print formats continually changes and grows.

NLM is also committed to offering its users the ability to search all of its bibliographic resources with a single search. AV resources are a rich and valuable source of information. When all types of material are integrated into a single catalog, users have a better opportunity to discover the information they really need, regardless of the format. Connecting users with information is ultimately what librarianship and cataloging is all about.

NOTES

1. Wyndham D. Miles, *A History of the National Library of Medicine: The Nation's Treasury of Medical Knowledge* (Bethesda, Md.: National Institutes of Health, National Library of Medicine, 1982), 73.
2. National Library of Medicine, *Collection Development Manual of the National Library of Medicine*. 3rd ed. (Bethesda, Md.: National Institutes of Health, National Library of Medicine, 1993), 8.
3. Miles, 433.
4. Ibid., 434.
5. Ibid.
6. E. Suter and W. H. Waddell, "AVLINE: A Database and Critical Review System of Audiovisual Materials for the Education of Health Professionals." *Journal of Medical Education* 57 (February 1982): 146.
7. National Library of Medicine, *Index Medicus* (Bethesda, Md.: National Library of Medicine, 1960-).
8. Michael Weisberg, *Ergonomic Guidelines for Designing Effective and Healthy Learning Environments for Interactive Technologies* (Bethesda, Md.: National Library of Medicine, 1993). Also available online at URL: *http://tlc.nlm.nih.gov/resources/publications/ergo/ergonomics.html*. Eldon J. Ullmer, *Optical Disc Technology* (Bethesda, Md.: National Library of Medicine, 1990). Craig Locatis, *An Interactive Multimedia Technology Primer* (Bethesda, Md.: National Library of Medicine, 1998). Also available online at URL: *http://tlc.nlm.nih.gov/resources/publications/primer/coverpage.html*. Victor Carr, C. Locatis, J. C. Reid, and E. Ullmer, *An Online Education Sourcebook* (Bethesda, Md.: National Library of Medicine, 1999). Also available online at URL: *http://tlc.nlm.nih.gov/resources/publications/sourcebook/onlinesource bookcoverpage.html*.
9. E. Suter and W. H. Waddell, "Attributes of Quality in Audiovisual Materials for Health Professionals," *Journal of Biocommunication* 8 (July 1981): 6-9.
10. E. Suter and W. H. Waddell, "AVLINE: A Database and Critical Review System of Audiovisual Materials for the Education of Health Professionals," *Journal of Medical Education* 57 (February 1982): 150.

11. "HeSCA/NLM CIP Project Update." *National Library of Medicine News* 33 (December 1978): 2.

12. M. J. Ackerman, "The Visible Human Project: A Resource for Education," *Academic Medicine* 74 (June 1999): 667-70.

13. National Library of Medicine, *Collection Development Manual.*

14. Ibid., 47.

15. Ibid., 48.

16. Program for Cooperative Cataloging, *Core Bibliographic Record for Books,* 1996 <*http://lcweb.loc.gov/catdir/pcc/corebook.html*>.

17. Program for Cooperative Cataloging, *Core Bibliographic Record for Graphic Materials,* 1997 <*http://lcweb.loc.gov/catdir/pcc/coregm.html*>.

18. Program for Cooperative Cataloging, *Core Bibliographic Record for Moving Image Materials,* 1997 <*http://lcweb.loc.gov/catdir/pcc/coremim.html*>.

19. Program for Cooperative Cataloging, *Core Bibliographic Record for Monographic Computer Files,* 1999 <*http://lcweb.loc.gov/catdir/pcc/cfcore.html*>.

20. Library of Congress. AMIM Revision Committee, *Archival Moving Image Materials: A Cataloging Manual* 2nd ed. (Washington, D.C.: Motion Picture, Broadcasting, and Recorded Sound Division, Library of Congress, 2000).

21. Program for Cooperative Cataloging, *Core Bibliographic Record for Moving Image Materials.*

22. National Library of Medicine, *Medical Subject Headings. Annotated Alphabetic List* (Bethesda, Md.: National Library of Medicine, 1975-).

23. National Library of Medicine, *Medical Subject Headings. Tree Structures* (Bethesda, Md.: National Library of Medicine, 1969-).

24. National Library of Medicine, *Permuted Medical Subject Headings* (Bethesda, Md.: National Library of Medicine, 1976-).

25. National Library of Medicine, *National Library of Medicine Classification: A Scheme for the Shelf Arrangement of Library Materials in the Field of Medicine and Its Related Sciences.* 5th ed., rev. (Bethesda, Md.: National Library of Medicine, 1999).

Index

© 2001 by The Haworth Press, Inc. All rights reserved.

AN EXCELLENT RESOURCE BOOK!

A comprehensive overview of the world of e-serials—in one compact volume!

E-SERIALS

NEW EDITION!

Publishers, Libraries, Users, and Standards, Second Edition

Edited by
Wayne Jones, BA, MA, MLS
Head of the Serials Cataloging Section at the Massachussetts Institute of Technology, Sommerville, Massachusetts

This new edition of the seminal 1998 volume gives you a comprehensive overview of the world of e-serials in one compact volume! With contributions from authorities in their respective fields, this book covers publishing, pricing, copyright, acquisitions and collection development, cataloging and metadata, preservation and archiving, projects and innovations, indexing, uniform resources identifiers, and citation.

Contents

Publishing • D-Lib Magazine: Incremental Evolution of an Electronic Magazine • ScienceDirect™ • Pricing • Electronic Serials Costs: Sales and Acquisitions Practices in Transition • Acquisitions and Collection Development • An Eclipse of the Sun: Acquisitions in the Digital Era • Perspectives on the Library as E-Journal Customer, Intermediary, and Negotiator in a Time of Chaos • Collection Development for Online Serials Redux: Now Who Needs to Do What, and Why, and When • Coordination and Collaboration: A Model for Electronic Resources Management • Cataloging and Metadata • A Square Peg in a Round Hole: Applying AACR2 to Electronic Journal • Electronic Serials: Searching for a Chief Source of Information • A Meditation on Metadata • Preservation and Archiving • Digital Preservation and Long-Term Access to the Content of Electronic Serials • Projects and Innovations • Interactive Peer Review in the Journal of Interactive Media in Education: Processes, Tools, and Techniques for Managing Persistent Discourse • Science's Knowledge Environments: Integrated Online Resources for Researchers, Educators, and Students • Serials Solutions: A Method for Tracking Full-Text Electronic Journals in Aggregated Databases • Building DSpace to Enhance Scholarly Communication • Indexing • Indexing Electronic Journals, 2000 • Uniform Resource Identifiers • Uniform Resource Identifiers and Online Serials • Citation • Citing Serials: Online Serial Publications and Citation Systems • Index • Reference Notes Included

$59.95 hard. ISBN: 0-7890-1229-4.
$39.95 soft. ISBN: 0-7890-1230-8.
Available Winter 2002/2003.
Approx. 350 pp. with Index.

AMEX, DINERS CLUB, DISCOVER, EUROCARD, JCB, MASTERCARD & VISA WELCOME!

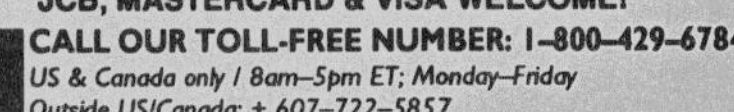

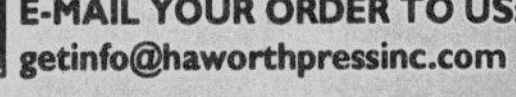

VISIT OUR WEB SITE AT:
http://www.HaworthPress.com

FACULTY: ORDER YOUR NO-RISK EXAM COPY TODAY!
Send us your examination copy order on your stationery; indicate course title, enrollment, and course start date.
You can also complete the examination order form at:
http://www.haworthpress.com/books/textexamform.asp
We will ship and bill on a 60-day examination basis, and cancel your invoice if you decide to adopt! We will always bill at the lowest available price, such as our special "5+ text price." Please remember to order softcover where available. (We cannot provide examination copies of books not published by The Haworth Press, Inc., or its imprints.)
(Outside US/Canada, a proforma invoice will be sent upon receipt of your request and must be paid in advance of shipping. A full refund will be issued with proof of adoption.)

The Haworth Information Press®
An imprint of The Haworth Press, Inc.
10 Alice Street, Binghamton, New York 13904-1580 USA

BIC01

TO ORDER: CALL: 1-800-429-6784 / FAX: 1-800-895-0582 (Outside US/Canada: + 607-771-0012) / **E-MAIL: getinfo@haworthpressinc.com**

❑ YES, please send me **E-Serials**

___ in hard at $59.95 ISBN: 0-7890-1229-4.

___ in soft at $39.95 ISBN: 0-7890-1230-8.

- Individual orders outside US, Canada, and Mexico must be prepaid by check or credit card.
- Discounts are not available on 5+ text prices and not available in conjunction with any other discount. • Discount not applicable on books priced under $15.00.
- 5+ text prices are not available for jobbers and wholesalers.
- Postage & handling: In US: $4.00 for first book; $1.50 for each additional book. Outside US: $5.00 for first book; $2.00 for each additional book.
- NY, MN, and OH residents: please add appropriate sales tax after postage & handling.
- Canadian residents: please add 7% GST after postage & handling. Canadian residents of Newfoundland, Nova Scotia, and New Brunswick, also add 8% for province tax. • Payment in UNESCO coupons welcome.
- If paying in Canadian dollars, use current exchange rate to convert to US dollars.
- Please allow 3–4 weeks for delivery after publication.
- Prices and discounts subject to change without notice.

❑ **BILL ME LATER**($5 service charge will be added).
(Not available for individuals outside US/Canada/Mexico. Service charge is waived for/jobbers/wholesalers/booksellers.)

❑ Check here if billing address is different from shipping address and attach purchase order and billing address information.

Signature ______________________

❑ **PAYMENT ENCLOSED $**______________________
(Payment must be in US or Canadian dollars by check or money order drawn on a US or Canadian bank.)

❑ **PLEASE BILL MY CREDIT CARD:**

❑ AmEx ❑ Diners Club ❑ Discover ❑ Eurocard ❑ JCB ❑ Master Card ❑ Visa

Account Number ______________________

Expiration Date ______________________

Signature ______________________

May we open a confidential credit card account for you for possible future purchases? ( ) Yes ( ) No

Please complete the information below or tape your business card in this area.

NAME ______________________

INSTITUTION ______________________

ADDRESS ______________________

CITY ______________________

STATE ______________________ ZIP ______________________

COUNTRY ______________________

COUNTY (NY residents only) ______________________

[type or print clearly!]

E-MAIL ______________________

May we use your e-mail address for confirmations and other types of information?
( ) **Yes** ( ) **No** We appreciate receiving your e-mail address and fax number. Haworth would like to e-mail or fax special discount offers to you, as a preferred customer. We will never **share, rent, or exchange** your e-mail address or fax number. We regard such actions as an invasion of your privacy.

❑ **YES**, please send me **E-Serials (ISBN: 0-7890-1230-8)** to consider on a 60–day **no risk** examination basis. I understand that I will receive an invoice payable within 60 days, or that **if I decide to adopt the book, my invoice will be cancelled.** I understand that I will be billed at the lowest price. (60-day offer available only to teaching faculty in US, Canada, and Mexico / Outside US/Canada, a proforma invoice will be sent upon receipt of your request and must be paid in advance of shipping. A full refund will be issued with proof of adoption.)

This information is needed to process your examination copy order.

Signature ______________________

Course Title(s) ______________________

Current Text(s) ______________________

Enrollment ______________________

Semester ______________________ Decision Date ______________________

Office Tel ______________________ Hours ______________________

FAX

FAX

THE HAWORTH PRESS, INC., 10 Alice Street, Binghamton, NY 13904–1580 USA

(10) 11/01 BIC01